SPORT, MEDIA AND MEGA-EVENTS

Bringing together many of the most influential scholars in sport and media studies, this book examines the diverse ways that media influences our understanding of the world's most important sport events, dubbed sports mega-events. It sheds new light on how these events have been changed by the media, and have, in turn, adapted to media to further their brand's cultural influence.

Focusing on the central concept of "mediatization" – the permeation of media into all spheres of contemporary life – the book presents original case studies of major events including the Olympics, FIFA, rugby and cricket World Cups, Tour de France, Super Bowl, World Series, Monaco Grand Prix, Wimbledon, and many more. Written from a truly international perspective, this is a seminal work in sport and media studies that reveals the growing political, economic and cultural influences of sport mega-events in contemporary society.

Sport, Media and Mega-Events is an essential text for any course on the sociology of sport, event management, sport marketing, or featuring a cultural, communication or media studies approach to sport.

Lawrence A. Wenner is Von der Ahe Professor of Communication and Ethics in the College of Communication and Fine Arts and the School of Film and Television at Loyola Marymount University, USA. His critical research on mediated sport focuses on gender, race, and commodification. He is editor of the research journal *Communication and Sport*, author of over 130 scholarly articles and chapters, and has published nine books, including *Fallen Sports Heroes, Media and Celebrity Culture*.

Andrew C. Billings is the Ronald Reagan Chair of Broadcasting and Director of the Alabama Program in Sports Communication at the University of Alabama, USA. His research frequently focuses on media renderings of sports mega-events, particularly as they relate to issues of gender, ethnicity, and nationality. He is the author and/or editor of 13 books, including *Olympic Media: Inside the Biggest Show on Television* and over 130 journal articles and book chapters.

SPORT, MEDIA AND MEGA-EVENTS

*Edited by Lawrence A. Wenner
and Andrew C. Billings*

Routledge
Taylor & Francis Group

LONDON AND NEW YORK

First published 2017
by Routledge
2 Park Square, Milton Park, Abingdon, Oxon OX14 4RN

and by Routledge
711 Third Avenue, New York, NY 10017

Routledge is an imprint of the Taylor and Francis Group, an informa business

British Library Cataloguing in Publication Data
A catalogue record for this book is available from the British Library

Library of Congress Cataloging in Publication Data
A catalogue record for this book has been requested

ISBN: 978-1-138-93038-4 (hbk)
ISBN: 978-1-138-93039-1 (pbk)
ISBN: 978-1-315-68052-1 (ebk)

Typeset in Bembo
by Fish Books Ltd.

CONTENTS

ILLUSTRATIONS

Tables

Figure

CONTRIBUTORS

Andrew C. Billings is the Ronald Reagan Chair of Broadcasting and Director of the Alabama Program in Sports Communication at the University of Alabama, USA. His research frequently focuses on media renderings of sports mega-events, particularly as they relate to issues of gender, ethnicity, and nationality.

Raymond Boyle is Professor of Communications at the Centre for Cultural Policy Research at the University of Glasgow, Scotland. He has written widely on media sport and media issues more generally. His most recent book was *The Rise and Fall of the UK Film Council* (with Doyle *et al.*; Edinburgh University Press, 2015).

Toni Bruce is Professor in the Faculty of Education and Social Work at the University of Auckland, New Zealand. Her research interrogates mainstream and online media representations of sport, with particular emphasis on gender, national identity, race/ethnicity and disability. Her latest work is *Terra Ludus*, a novel about media, gender and sport (Sense Publishers).

Michael L. Butterworth is Director and Associate Professor in the School of Communication Studies at Ohio University, USA. His research investigates the relationships between rhetoric, democracy, and sport, with particular interests in national identity, militarism, and public memory.

James Compton is Associate Professor in the Faculty of Information and Media Studies at the University of Western Ontario in London, Ontario, Canada. His research interests lie in the areas of the political economy of communications, journalism, spectacle, and popular cultures.

Bryan E. Denham is Department Chair and Campbell Professor of Sports Communication at Clemson University, USA. His research examines the agenda-setting and agenda-building functions of mass media, with recent work focusing on intermedia agenda-setting processes.

Thomas Fletcher is a Senior Lecturer at Leeds Beckett University, UK. His research focuses on the politics of race/ethnicity and whiteness in sport and leisure. He is editor of *Cricket, Migration and Diasporic Communities* and co-editor of *Sport, Leisure and Social Justice, Diversity, Equity and Inclusion in Sport and Leisure* and *Sports Events, Society and Culture* (all with Routledge).

Kirsten Frandsen is Associate Professor of Media Studies in the School of Communication and Culture at Aarhus University, Denmark. Her research examines the relationship between sport and media, with a focus on historical developments in sports journalism, television, digital media and audiences.

Richard Gruneau is Professor of Communication at Simon Fraser University, Vancouver, British Columbia, Canada. His research interests include social theory, the political economy of communication, media studies, sport, and popular cultures.

Richard Haynes is Professor of Media Sport in the Division Communications Media and Culture in the Faculty of Arts and Humanities, University of Stirling, Scotland. His current research focuses on the historical relationships between sport and the media. He is author of *BBC Sport in Black and White* (Palgrave Macmillan, 2017).

Laura Hills is a Senior Lecturer in Youth Sport in the division of Sport, Health and Exercise Sciences at Brunel University, UK. Her research investigates issues pertaining to sport and social justice with particular interest in gender, social class, qualitative methods, and representation.

John Horne is Professor of Sport and Sociology at the University of Central Lancashire, Preston, UK. He is the author, co-author, editor and co-editor of many publications including most recently *Understanding the Olympics* (with Garry Whannel; 2nd ed., 2016) and *Mega-Events and Globalization* (edited with Richard Gruneau; 2016), both published by Routledge.

Alistair John is a Lecturer in Sports Development in the College of Health and Life Sciences at Brunel University London, UK. His research investigates the neoliberal urban entrepreneurial strategy of funding elite sports events/infrastructure in the "sport city", and he has a further interest in corporate nationalism through sport advertising.

Eileen Kennedy is a researcher at UCL Knowledge Lab, Department of Culture Communication and Media, UCL Institute of Education, UK. Eileen has written extensively about sport, media and gender, including *Sport, Media and Society* with Laura Hills. Her current research is focused on digital education and online learning.

Dominic Malcolm is Reader in the Sociology of Sport at Loughborough University, UK. He has published widely in the sociology of sport, focusing particularly on the social development of cricket and the interdependence of sport and medicine. Recent books include *Globalizing Cricket: Englishness, Empire and Identity* (2013), and *Sport, Medicine and Health: The Medicalization of Sport?* (2016).

Pirkko Markula is Professor of Socio-cultural Studies of Physical Activity in the Faculty of Physical Education and Recreation at the University of Alberta, Canada. Her poststructuralist research focuses on the potential of the moving body to create social change.

Brad Millington is Lecturer in the Department for Health at the University of Bath, UK. His research examines physical cultures, with a specific focus on sport and the environment and on health and fitness technologies.

Michael R. Real is Professor Emeritus in the School of Communications and Culture at Royal Roads University in Victoria, BC, Canada. His research examines the intersection of media and culture, particularly in the way that sports influence human values in America and globally.

David Rowe is Professor of Cultural Research in the Institute for Culture and Society at Western Sydney University, Australia. His principal research interest lies in the sociology of media and popular culture, especially the relationships between sport, culture and media, and the role of news and entertainment media in the formation of informed citizenship.

Damion Sturm is Senior Lecturer in the School of Events, Tourism and Hospitality at Leeds Beckett University, UK. His research interests are in global media cultures (sport, celebrity, fan and material cultures), including explorations of Formula One, cricket and rugby as mediated sporting events.

Holly Thorpe is Associate Professor at the University of Waikato, New Zealand. Her research on action sports, youth culture, media and new technologies, gender, and critical sport for development includes over 60 journal articles and book chapters. Her books include *Transnational Mobilities in Action Sport Cultures*, *Snowboarding Bodies in Theory and Practice*, and the co-edited *Routledge Handbook of Physical Cultural Studies* and *Women in Action Sport Cultures*.

Alan Tomlinson is Professor of Leisure Studies at the University of Brighton, UK. His work focusing on the social history and sociology of sport, leisure and popular culture includes over 30 authored/edited books and over 100 scholarly articles/chapters. His recent books include *FIFA: The Men, the Myths and the Money* (2014), *Football, Corruption and Lies: Re-visiting 'Badfellas', the Book FIFA Tried to Ban* (2016, with John Sugden), and *Understanding International Sport Organisations: Principles, Power and Possibilities* (2017, with Lincoln Allison).

Lawrence A. Wenner is Von der Ahe Professor of Communication and Ethics in the College of Communication and Fine Arts and the School of Film and Television at Loyola Marymount University, USA. His research on communication and sport focuses on critical and ethical assessments of sport spectacle, commodification, and the intersection of gender and race.

Belinda Wheaton is Associate Professor at the University of Waikato, teaching in the sport and leisure studies area. She is best known for her research on the politics of identity in lifestyle sport. Her publications include *The Cultural Politics of Lifestyle Sports* (2013) and the edited collections *Understanding Lifestyle Sport* (2004) and *The Consumption and Representation of Lifestyle Sports* (2012).

Brian Wilson is Professor in the School of Kinesiology at the University of British Columbia, Canada. His authored books include *Sport and Peace: A Sociological Perspective* (2012) and *The Greening of Golf: Sport, Globalization and the Environment* (2016, with Brad Millington), and he has published articles on sport, social inequality, environmental issues, media, social movements, and youth culture.

PREFACE

When we envisioned the contents of this book, we sought the widest scope imaginable to understand sporting mega-events and their mediation. From a cricket pitch in Melbourne to the streets of Monaco to the greens of Augusta National, the aim was to simultaneously uncover the commonality of sports mega-events while exploring distinctions that make each a unique experience and a highly valued media product. That was the easy part.

The more difficult part was identifying and enticing a cast of internationally recognized scholars who would bring diverse understandings of sporting mega-events, sport in socio-cultural and political-economic contexts, and the functioning of media in an era of ubiquitous commodification. We sought leading scholars who brought special expertise that would allow them to interrogate the dynamics particular to a given event and consider how the forces of mediatization were mobilized in specific contexts. We took some time to brainstorm our "dream team" of exemplary scholars and hoped they would embrace our project, as the broad international coverage we desired required their participation in order to facilitate a scholarly showcase that considers a goodly range of diverse contemporary sporting mega-events. Here we were blessed.

The A-list of scholars we sought to author case studies about events for which they held special expertise continually said yes, making time amidst other commitments to participate in this project. The result is *Sport, Media and Mega-Events*, a volume we have been honored to shepherd into existence. In each instance in this volume, from consideration of the Olympics to World Cups of soccer, rugby and cricket, to key "majors" of tennis and golf, to pinnacle events of both bicycle and automobile, to the "super" and "world" branding of American sport championships, to the media manufacture of the "edgy" imagination of the X Games, readers will encounter analyses of sporting mega-events by scholars who bring special understandings about the marriage of big-time sport with big-time media, a marriage that has birthed what we know today as the contemporary sporting mega-event. We think their efforts make this work more than the sum of its parts and are thankful to each of the 25 scholars who have contributed to this volume.

As editors of this volume, each of us has benefitted from the support of our family, friends, and institutions. As with many projects that have come before this one, Larry wishes to foremost thank his wife and companion in all things sporting and recreational, Susan Rice, for her support and advice on this endeavor, which from time to time impinged on our shared time and planned activities. Larry's participation in this project has been made far easier by the support he receives at Loyola Marymount University in his role as the Von der Ahe Chair in Communication and Ethics in the College of Communication and Fine Arts and the School of Film and Television. Thanks goes not only to the Deans of those units, but most particularly to Rachel Van Houten, Larry's executive assistant, for helping to keep many of moving parts of this project in working order.

Regarding Andrew's appreciation, he must start with his wife, Angela, and sons, Nathan and Noah, who are always a healthy dose of support, warmth and laughter. He thanks his colleagues and supervisors within the College of Communication and Information Sciences at the University of Alabama. Moreover, he is thankful for the continued support provided by the Ronald Reagan Endowed Chair in Broadcasting, which provides him with the time and resources that were necessary to complete this edited book in the manner required.

We have very much enjoyed working together as editors on this project and are extremely pleased with the work that has resulted from a group of colleagues who we hold dear. The work that has resulted provides heretofore unseen consideration of a broad range of sporting mega-events. We are optimistic that the collective work here will be of unique and lasting value. We hope that you agree. Given the seminal role that sports mega-events play within the culture of virtually every nation state, we are thankful for the opportunity that Routledge – and specifically series editor Simon Whitmore – have provided to help advance dialogue about a key aspect of sport that is quite intentionally writ large.

Lawrence A. Wenner, Port Townsend, Washington, USA
Andrew C. Billings, Tuscaloosa, Alabama, USA

PART I

Framing sport, media and mega-events

1

THE CURIOUS CASE OF THE MEGASPORTING EVENT

Media, mediatization and seminal sports events

Andrew C. Billings and Lawrence A. Wenner

Media coverage of sports is, by its very nature, ephemeral (Billings, Qiao, Conlin, and Nie, 2015). The temporary loss of the here and now is embraced when we consume mediated sports coverage as a welcome respite from the press of everyday demands (Morse, 1990). Yet, many sports fans recognize that contests that once seemed both urgent and critical often melt into the background in a week's time and are summarily forgotten. The ubiquity of sports contests and the blur of discussions about them across the contemporary mediascape contribute to this liquidity; a new "big game" is seemingly always around the corner and newly-fueled anticipation routinely supersedes reflection about results that have quickly faded in our memories and become trivial in the annals of sporting record.

However, rising above ubiquitous sporting competitions that quickly fade as cultural amnesia are those holding promise to become seminal moments in lived experience and common culture. These are the events and championships that define a sport, solidifying one's fanship, and serving as historical markers that bring order, meaning, and significance to the sports landscape. Very likely it is the relative discontinuity of such moments, when compared to those experienced with all other sports offerings, that makes them special (Roberts, 2004). Some sports offer singular championship contests to define such moments (such as the National Football League's Super Bowl in the US) while others are compartmentalized through a series of annual events, such as the "majors" that mark excellence through achievement in the most important tournaments that mark the year's calendar of competition in international golf or tennis.

With their ability to garner media attention and captivate the public in ways that everyday sport cannot, major sporting events have grown in cultural importance. Increasingly, they define significant moments inscribed in the collective cultural memory, resonating not only with rabid fans, but also for many less passionate about sport. Their appeal resides in transcending the ordinary and being recognized as extraordinary. While the memories of many avid fans of rugby or baseball may blur in recollecting everyday competition, they remain razor sharp in recalling significant moments in a pivotal Rugby World Cup play or what led to a Major League Baseball World Series victory. With constant retelling aiding firm etching into the cultural consciousness, such moments can become influential, undergirding understandings that casual spectators and fans alike bring to sport and the nature and meaning of competition.

It should not be surprising that the experiencing and interpretation of such moments, infused as they are with the potentialities of significance, can interact in compelling ways with one's self-identity and values. Indeed, the uniqueness of this kind of experience may, in some part, explain why so many people have made rituals of consuming megasporting events. As these megasporting events and their audiences have grown, the idea that these larger, grander forms of sport indeed hold much broader cultural significance than everyday and more localized sporting competitions has become societally reified.

Situated thusly, the study of sport-based mega-events offers important opportunities to understand how sport interacts with the collective psyche of contemporary societies and cultures. Horne and Manzenreiter (2006, p. 17) make a strong case that "sports mega-events provide novel ways in which research into national and cultural identity, mobility, and individualization can be approached." It has been made clear that such study can reveal diverse dynamics, from the conveyance of national power (Butterworth and Moskal, 2009; Chen, Colapinto, and Luo, 2012) to drama (Farrell, 1989) to shifts of mood (Knoll, Schramm, and Schallhorn, 2014) to the documentation of history (Roessner, 2014). Building on such inquiry, this book features an international group of distinguished scholars who interrogate key sporting mega-events in a world that is increasingly experienced through media.

Approaching media and sports mega-events

Media, in a very basic sense, makes things larger than life. This is true in the case of the sports mega-event as well. Much supported in the work of Debord (1967/1995), the commodified spectacle that the sports mega-event has become would not be possible without media. So wedded are the two that Horne and Manzenreiter (2006, p. 2) have observed that "an unmediated mega-event would be a contradiction in terms." Thus, we begin our approach to the sports mega-event by drawing on two relevant concepts from media studies, the intertwined and complementary notions of the "media event" and "super media."

Stimulated by the work of sociologists, such as Shils (1962), who were interested in how key cultural events served as rituals to affirm the social fabric through widely shared celebrations, the notion of the media event was conceptualized by Katz (1980; Katz and Dayan, 1985) and advanced in the book *Media Events: The Live Broadcasting of History* (Dayan and Katz, 1992). Dayan and Katz note the rising significance of media in framing and experiencing important cultural events – from a Royal wedding to a Queen's coronation to the funeral of American President Kennedy to the first lunar landing to the Olympic Games – and make a case that these cultural events have been transformed into "media events" that serve as "high holy days of communication" (ibid., p. 1). To participate, people depart from their routines to join in a collective media experience of special occasions. Dayan and Katz (1992) posit that the constituent qualities of media events serve to facilitate social integration by celebrating shared values and validating public rituals of affirmation, noting that these "great ceremonial events celebrate order and restoration" (ibid., p. 9). While the occurrence of two variants of media events characterized by Dayan and Katz – coronations and conquests – do not typically adhere to predictable calendars, the third variant – contests – are distinguished by being calendared media events. One of the most visible variants of the contest media event is, of course, the sporting mega-event. Archetypal of this genre are the Olympic Games, which are manufactured to celebrate "universal" values, from "'globality' or 'one world awareness'" (Roche, 2006, p. 32) to pride of nation to good sportsmanship to appreciation of excellence.

With special attention on recurring aspects of media that *writ large* on the cultural fabric, Real (1989), broke important new ground in showing how the diverse multidisciplinary lenses of cultural studies had special relevance to interrogating the dynamics of the rising influence of what he called "super media." Arguing that issues of personal identity and consciousness, of conflict and bias, of politics and policy, are more effectively articulated and understood through a cultural studies approach to the largest and most celebrated media artifacts, Real's analyses focused not only on super media events, such as the regularized media spectacles of the Olympic Games or the Academy Awards, but also considered how super-sized media influence could be seen in the naturalized rituals and themes associated with those media products – blockbuster movies and television ratings hits – that most captivated public attention and the cultural *zeitgeist*. Real's focus on super media continued a line of work that began with an influential earlier critical assessment of the cultural rituals and functioning of the Super Bowl (Real, 1975). Collectively, Real's work on the intersection of super media with mass cultural events showed that sports were at the center of an increasing amount of mass events in the age of media. With their unique combination of predictable scheduling, unknown outcomes, and predilection for narrative hyperbole, Real recognized that sports mega-events were increasingly dominating the media event space, fueling interest in how sports mega-events edge aside other media events as sites for the creation and contestation of core cultural meanings – about identity, democracy, and the naturalized logics that undergird hegemony and the wielding of cultural power.

In key ways, Real's (1989) book makes a case for a cultural studies approach to super media being a unique opportunity for "synthesis scholarship" (see O'Sullivan, 1999) that inherently bridges different epistemological perspectives that undergird a range of disciplines and fields of inquiry, a disposition that is embraced in the varied approaches seen in this volume. Real's arguments also importantly countered a common truism about sports – that sports are a microcosm of society – by posing that the inverse was true as well – that society was a microcosm of sport – and that this would be most particularly evident in its grandest forms.

Cognizant of this, Eastman, Newton, and Pack (1996) argued that the manifestations of "media events" and "super media" within the sporting realm were of such recurring importance that they deserved more specific attention. They termed these "megasports," which have archetypically been defined as sporting events for which consumers set an appointment on their sporting calendars. As it is quite evident that most sport spectators do not attend sport mega-events in person, megasport calendars tend to mirror media calendars. Holding a place on calendars, fans of golf set aside the second weekend in April for the Masters and tennis buffs set aside late June and early July for Wimbledon's fortnight of competition.

In tandem with this work anchored in media studies, the production and functioning of sport spectacles increasingly garnered attention from a diverse group of scholars concerned with the socio-cultural and political-economic impacts of sport (see most recently Gruneau and Horne, 2016). Much of this work grows from foundational work by Roche (2000). In situating the cultural significance of sport spectacles, Roche characterized "megaevents," a broader term encompassing and dominated by "megasports," as "large-scale cultural (including commercial and sporting events), which have dramatic character, mass popular appeal, and international significance" (ibid., p. 1).

Roche posed that inquiry about the sporting mega-event was important from a variety of perspectives. Such research could be driven by interest in:

1 the personal (megasport as rite of passage);
2 national historical (megasport as venue for national storytelling/"truth" telling);
3 cultural historical (megasport as advancement of high culture); and
4 sociological (megasport as rendering of cultural values/priorities).

In this, Roche (2000) makes a strong case for broadening study of the sporting mega-event to include inquiry that looks well beyond sporting competition to the political and economic structures and forces that embrace and enable them. He notes that:

> Mega-events can be seen as having at least a two-dimensional character as tourist events (in the realm of global tourist culture and the global tourist industry/cultural economy) and also as media events (in the realm of global media culture and the global media industry/cultural economy). From each of these perspectives, megaevents represent temporal and spatial "localisations" of potentially globally relevant global cultural activity and flows (of people, information, and images).
>
> *(Roche, 2000, p. 27)*

Roche's (2000) work stimulated considerable debate about the priorities and characterization of work focused on the sporting mega-event. For example, Real (2013) notes distinct offsets of perspective embraced by those who approach high-profile sporting events in variant ways, including "mythic ritual," "spectacle," "mega-event," "behavioral reaction" or "game" (ibid., p. 34). Others, such as Roberts (2004) argue for the necessity of focusing on the role of media as central to an event's "super-sizing," noting that a mega-event must inherently involve a mass conveyance of discontinuity with other events, transmitted to an audience of billions rather than millions, something possible only with the demand and command media attention.

Studies throughout a recent edited volume by Gruneau and Horne (2016) also recognize the centrality of media to understanding the sport mega-event. In focusing on how the effects of globalization play out in everyday lived experience with sporting mega-events, much evidence shows how integral new media strategies that engage social communication have become to consuming and interpreting these events. In this environment, Gruneau and Horne argue that sporting mega-events "have become normalized as seemingly natural features of the rhythms of modern life, an unfolding horizon of festivals of modernity, anticipated like the changes of the seasons" (ibid., p. 1).

Yet, as media-aided social communication transacts in communities of diverse character, from localized groupings of family and friends to interest-based communities that feature members with shared dispositions from across the globe, their role in sense-making about sporting mega-events can be complex and far-ranging. Recognizing this, Gruneau and Horne (ibid.) argue for systematic case study of such events to better understand how sporting logics can cross national boundaries in ways that transcend the partitions created by "imagined political communities" (Anderson, 1983, p. 6). For Gruneau and Horne, essential issues are at stake.

> The critique of sporting mega-events has become an important aspect of globalization because it provides a transnational social and political space for public discussion that exceeds the boundaries of nation-states. This lends itself to greater opportunities to evaluate mega-events from multiple standpoints of global justice, postcolonial aspirations, and other important ethical, social, political, and ecological issues of our time.
>
> *(Gruneau and Horne, 2016, p. 6)*

To our minds, their bold assessment seems not only justifiable, but also obvious in light of the rising magnitude and significance of sporting mega-events. Their work points to the integral role of media in both making the magic and raising the stakes of sporting mega-events. In doing so, it creates a warrant for the work in this volume that seeks to answer key questions about the role of media in a diverse set of sporting mega-events that take place across the globe.

Yet, in approaching the sports mega-event, it is important to recognize that not one size fits all. Although Muller (2015) notes that a mega-event must achieve four size-related status markers – visitor attractiveness, mediated reach, cost, and transformative impact – he argues for an index to help interpret these according to an event's scale. He makes a case for raising the Summer Olympic Games to a new echelon: a "giga-event" (ibid., p. 636), while characterizing other events, such as the Rugby World Cup or Super Bowl, as "major events" at levels below mega-event status. Still, such distinctions are often blurry lines. As the case studies in this volume approach events, roughly arranged from the "giga" to "mega" to the "major," the focus remains on how media plays a role in attempting to elevate each event to a higher status. After all, following the Olympic motto, each event's overarching goal remains: *citius, altius, fortius.*

When sports are not merely sports

In their striving for elevated cultural importance and marketplace dominance, megasports events are mediated in a manner contradistinctive to expectations associated with virtually all other sporting events. Indeed, any non-megasporting event resulting in a memorable moment is deemed remarkable in its uniqueness, while any megasporting event that does not yield a memorable event is likely viewed as an underwhelming disappointment. As producers know that sports media audiences often consume live sporting events to bear witness, megasports are packaged in a manner that is perpetually pregnant, with noteworthy moments as an omnipresent expectation, rather than something seen as unlikely but desired (Billings, 2008). With sporting mega-events, the probability of significance becomes a question of "when" not "if."

Still, our interest in megasports in this book is driven by larger issues than such events being able bring seminal moments for sports fans to witness. We are most interested in the transformative processes stemming from the production and consumption of mega-sporting events as media spectacle. In this light, Wenner's (2006) heuristic of the dynamic tensions often at play in understanding sports-based spectacles, as revealed in an examination of the 2004 Super Bowl controversy surrounding Janet Jackson and Justin Timberlake's halftime performance (culminating in exposing Jackson's breast), suggests regularly occurring super themes that often drive and come to characterize seminal moments that are remembered in experiencing megasporting events. As expressed in dyadic pairings, these included:

1 pop and hip-hop;
2 sex and gender;
3 race and ethnicity;
4 young and old;
5 celebrity and hero;
6 mass and fragments;
7 technology and activity;
8 national and global;
9 super and ordinary;
10 frame and game;
11 selling and distraction;

12 control and denial; and
13 deviance and distaste.

(Wenner, 2006, pp. 52–55)

A key issue tacitly implied within such a characterization of super themes is that narratives fashioned in driving interest in megasporting events often focus on the significance and magnitude of the contest, with conjecture about outcomes often secondary to engaging controversy and signing cultural significance. It is worth noting that not featured in this characterization of super themes is "wins and losses," because the sporting mega-event is about much more than that. In telling ways, seminal moments in sport are often marked by when sport, and the usual frames used to interpret it, intersect with or are superseded by one of these macro-level super themes. As Billings notes:

> Ironically, millions of people claim to be sports fans precisely because they wait in eager anticipation for the moments in which sports are no longer about sports. When a 59-year-old Tom Watson stands in the 18th fairway trying to win his sixth British Open Championship, the event is no longer about golf; it is about testing the boundaries of time and age to determine whether there is a point in which the legendary athlete must walk into the sunset. When Kerri Strug lands a one-legged vault in the 1996 Olympic team gymnastics competition, the event is no longer about gold medals; it is about whether a person can desire something badly enough to defy gravity if only for a few seconds.
>
> *(Billings, 2011, p. 188)*

In recognizing that the pull of such themes underlies much attraction to sporting competitions at their highest levels, contributing authors in this book use a set of diverse theoretical lenses to understand the "grander" dynamics at play in media strategies in framing and transacting with specific sports mega-events. In considering their interrogations of a wide range of media events that are built around sport, we hope readers will better understand how sport informs society by prioritizing the lenses of byzantine and interlocking media systems and recognize that these are systems driven by strategic objectives, not only in the marketplace but of the body politic. To advance these goals, one must first be aware of some unique qualities of the megasporting event as a media and cultural product.

Characteristics of megasporting events

A key takeaway from the characterizations offered by Eastman, Newton, and Pack (1996), Roche (2000), and Muller (2015) is that while sports mega-events encompass a wide range of sports, nations, and interests, they nonetheless share some key characteristics. Horne and Manzenreiter (2006) note that, with the advent of the 1984 Los Angeles Summer Olympics as a true financial game-changer, "the main axis of concern about sports mega-events, however, has swung from their political use to their economic use" (ibid., p. 18). Nevertheless, such a binary distinction between the political versus the economic is unnecessarily limiting as both aspects cast long shadows. The influences of the political and the economic are not only considerable, but their intermix and interactivity are essential to contemporary understandings of the megasporting event. Beyond the concerns such as these advanced in the aforementioned works, at least four other characteristics of the megasporting event product deserve mention:

1   pre-eminent competition;
2   predictable occurrence;
3   opportunities for historical comparison; and
4   transcendence of traditional meanings of sport.

We consider each briefly below.

Pre-eminent competition

A megasporting event can often include "amateurs," but rarely do the events include anything not under the umbrella of premier forms of competition. From the over 10,000 athletes competing in a Summer Olympic Games to a pair of teams pitted against one another in a Cricket World Cup final, a megasporting event is noteworthy in that a fair share of the winnowing has already taken place. Far more athletes and teams have vied unsuccessfully to be able to compete in megasporting events. And while some events such as golf's men's and women's British Open Championship are technically open to all, the ultimate competition is preceded by weeks, months, and sometimes years of preliminary qualifying contests. In light of this focus on the best of the best, sports fans expect to witness competition at its highest level, meaning that one is bearing witness to the pinnacle of a sporting competition in the same manner that Americans watch the Oscars to assess and celebrate the best in a given year of film, or that British fans tune into the Olivier Awards to witness who and what is dubbed best of show in London stage plays and musicals. The dynamic spectacle inherently present in most any sporting event is encompassed by and overtaken by the elitism that defines and colors a megasporting competition (Kassing *et al.*, 2004).

Predictable occurrence

With non-megasporting events, one can never quite predict when a key competition will occur. Sometimes one early glance at a seasonal schedule highlights a possible contest of epic proportions, many of which frequently fail to materialize. Other times key matchups reveal themselves only after earlier competitions make a particular – largely random – date and time more important than any other date on the sports calendar. Megasports operate separately from these organic structures, with many events scheduled nearly a decade in advance. Olympic sites are awarded 7 years before an event. Football and rugby World Cups typically follow a similar model, with some having been awarded as much as 12 years before an event. Other megasporting events are seemingly scheduled in perpetuity. While picking a winner can involve high odds, it likely is a good bet that the first Saturday in May 2040 will also feature the Kentucky Derby horse race at Churchill Downs.

Opportunities for historical comparison

Most megasporting events offer enough consistency for comparisons to be made not merely year-to-year, but generation to generation. Experiencing a mega-sporting event in the present contextualizes sporting and cultural achievements of the past. Media narratives do more than remind of us of facts such as that both Jesse Owens and Usain Bolt won the 100- and 200-meter sprinting gold medals seven decades apart. Media narratives not only inspire awe but, more importantly, link discrete events by framing meaning historically in cultural imaginaries that invite comparison. Thus, a story of Jesse Owens and Usain Bolt is necessarily more than one about two athletes from different times. Because of this, the mediation of sporting mega-events provides regularized occasions for the blurry meshing of sport history with cultural history. The consistency of megasporting achievements over time enables ready comparison, but media narratives frame where things stand today in a current assessment of history that is celebrated and reified. In consuming mediated accounts of the modern megasporting event, we are offered many opportunities for historical comparison. But, as with any telling of history, the tale is influenced by the sensibilities and priorities of the teller.

Transcendence of traditional meanings of sport

Obviously, winning a megasporting event remains prominent in the minds of all involved, from competitors to spectators. An athlete's career apex is defined by whether one secures victories in such key moments. Lionel Messi and Cristiano Ronaldo will likely be viewed (at least by some) as falling short of legendary status if each is unable to secure a World Cup victory (which has not happened at the time of this writing). Basketball's LeBron James will inevitably be compared to Michael Jordan in terms of NBA championships won. However, for athletes participating in the megasporting event – and for the fans and other stakeholders able to be present to bear witness – simply being able to participate in some form is considered an achievement in and of itself. Sometimes this is defined in areas beyond winning a competition entirely. For example, when British sprinter Derek Redmond tore a hamstring in his 400-meter semi-final race at the 1992 Olympic Games, nations bonded over watching his father run to the track and help his son to the finish line. In provoking such reactions, megasports reach beyond everyday sporting events. They have become, as renowned sports journalist Mike Lupica (2006) noted about the Olympic Games, the "world's most spectacular reality series."

Megasports, media and mediatization

Our introduction thus far has made a case for the importance of studying the marriage of media and sport in understanding megasports events. In the long history of the socio-cultural study of media, the focus of individual studies has most often been centered on one of three areas of concern:

1   media institutions and production;
2   media content and texts; and
3   media audiences and reception.

These distinctions, of course, embrace the component parts of a basic sender-message-receiver model of communication. Scholars, most particularly those approaching media from a cultural studies perspective, argue that all three areas need to be part of media studies inquiries (Real, 1989). From this perspective, to not consider all of these components, as well as their interrelationships and inter-activity, results in isolated and incomplete understandings. Most at risk here is gaining sufficient context to understand larger political-economic forces overlain on and at play in the communication process. Towards that end, we have asked each of the contributing authors in this volume to feature consideration of at least two of the three of the communication process triumvirate in their inquiries and assessment of megasporting events.

In addition, we have asked each author to consider evidence about "media effects" on the sports mega-event from the perspective of mediatization, a vantage point that has gained support in recent years for its promise in revealing often overlooked but important media effects on societal structures and the experiencing of everyday life (Hepp, 2013; Hjarvard, 2013; Lundby, 2009). Advocates of the mediatization perspective make a case for the necessity of broadening how media effects are conceptualized. Recognizing how pervasive the "logic" of media has been in being strategically integrated into diverse institutional and organizational practices, the mediatization lens seeks to reveal how media effects may be seen well "beyond media" in virtually every crevice of the cultural fabric. As Hjarvard has put it, mediatization focuses on "how social institutions and cultural processes have changed character, function, and structure in response to the omnipresence of media" (Hjarvard, 2013, p. 2).

The basic notion that media leaks integrally into other aspects of life is by no means a new realization. Indeed, the honing of mediatization as a theoretical frame to understand the contemporary cultural condition may be found in important earlier work by Altheide and Snow (1979) about "media logic" that took notice of the increasing tendency for actors and institutions to be media sensitive or "friendly" to strategically garner political and economic advantage. Thus, it may be little surprise that interest in the mediatization concept has risen in tandem with concern over the commodification of culture. In a very basic sense, Livingstone's (2009, p. 1) claim that there is now a "mediatization of everything" synergizes with

Debord's (1967/1995, p. 29) observations about our present society of the spectacle residing in a "world of commodity."

Indeed, it is this connection – to spectacle, and most particularly commodified spectacle – that drives our interest in how mediatization plays out in the context of sports mega-events, events that are perhaps the most common manifestation of spectacle in contemporary times. Our directive to contributing authors to consider how mediatization may be revealed in individual sporting mega-events builds on foundational work by Frandsen (2014, p. 525) who makes a strong case that the media–sport relationship provides "*an example sine qua non*" of mediatization. With a focus on television at the historical center of a larger media–sport production complex, she notes that mediatization in sport is necessarily "highly influenced by both the cultural fields in question and the social and cultural contexts" and argues that "[p]rofound reflections on the specificities of the field of sport, on television, and on differences and historical changes in terms of media systemic and sports systemic contexts are thus informative musts if we want to understand the role of media in relation to sports in more general terms" (ibid., p. 530). We believe that her claim that the "mediatization of sport is a matter of specificity where inter-relatedness, globalization, and commercialization have come to play a significant role" (ibid., p. 525) because of the communication powers of both sport and media is particularly applicable to the study of the sporting mega-event where the political and economic stakes are higher and where the powers to influence are heightened. Thus, in the chapters ahead, examination of the role of media in sporting mega-events is necessarily informed by considering the broader forces of mediatization.

Considering sport, media and mega-events

We are fortunate in this volume to feature a distinguished group of scholars from across the globe who use diverse lenses to consider sport, media and mega-events. The two chapters that follow this one feature complementary but contrasting vantage points to evaluate the sporting mega-event as a social, cultural, political and economic phenomenon. Leading the way is John Horne in Chapter 2, a foundational scholar in the study of mega-events, who examines the possibilities and scope for contesting and resisting dominant media messages about sports mega-events. In interrogating the terms and conditions of how symbolic contestation is played out, Horne draws upon the work of Stuart Hall and Stan Cohen to explore the range and limits of alternative readings of media content and the meanings associated with sports mega-events. Chapter 3 features the thinking of a premier social theorist of the political economy of sport, Richard Gruneau, and a media sociologist, James Compton, whose work has been influential on understanding the cultural performance of media spectacle. Noting that scholarly writing on the relations between media and mega-events have moved in a critical direction, Gruneau and Compton acknowledge that the Durheimian legacy has provided insight into ritual meanings, symbolization and modes of collective identification. Posing that such concerns have limited analyzing social relations of power, they argue for a Marxist approach to move the study of the sports mega-event beyond a media-centric approach in order to understand broader practices influencing contemporary life.

Following these paired overarching framing chapters, the core chapters of this book (Part II) are composed of a grand set of "megamediasport event studies." These case studies, authored by leading researchers in sport and media studies, showcase a rich variety of approaches to studying the sporting mega-event. The case studies are arranged roughly by the scale of events. While the order of these chapters is influenced by Muller's (2015) characterization of "giga," "mega," and "major" events, we argue that such distinctions are inherently blurry, and have thus resisted clustering chapters into discrete categories.

Still, the first two case study chapters consider complementary articulations of the most "giga" of sporting events, the Summer and Winter Olympic Games. In Chapter 4, one of the foremost scholars of institutional power in sport, most particularly its wielding within non-governmental organizations, Alan Tomlinson, considers the broad swath of "28 Olympic Summers" in providing an analysis seated in historical and methodological reflection about understanding the Olympic mega-event. Chronicling the march of globalization, commodification, and mediatization, Tomlinson's analysis chronicles three phases of development in the Summer Olympic Games:

- Phase 1 (1886–1928): socio-political project of modest economic scale;
- Phase 2 (1932–1980): political intensification interrelated with international political dynamics and increasingly sophisticated media technologies; and
- Phase 3 (1984–2016): commodification of the Olympic brand and media product through the global reach of capital.

In Chapter 5, noted cultural studies scholar Pirkko Markula focuses on the evolution of television production techniques that "made" the Winter Olympics into a global event and how these techniques have evolved in an era of digital and social media. In considering trends of representing the Winter Games hosts and athletes in broadcast production, Markula's analysis reveals the intertwined impacts from social processes of commercialization, globalization, urbanization, and mediatization.

The next series of chapters explores the varied terrain of World Cups as mega-sporting events. In considering the most clearly "mega" of these from a mediated standpoint, the FIFA World Cup, two key researchers known for studies of football and sport journalism, Richard Haynes and Raymond Boyle, discuss recent debates on mediatization processes and sport to explain why media and football have evolved into a global event that has such a socially and culturally powerful presence in many people's lives (Chapter 6). By tracing the historical development of media technologies in covering the FIFA World Cup, they reveal how the terms and conditions for control of the media spectacle have evolved, changing amidst the uncertainties of convergent and divergent media where the forces of mediatization raise questions about media hegemony and the dominance of national and tele-visual framing of the mega-event. Next, a key cultural studies scholar of media and sport, Toni Bruce, interrogates the Rugby World Cup experience from the vantage points of fans and non-fans alike, demonstrating the full range of passions – both positive and negative – generated by sports mega-events (Chapter 7). Exploring media representation in relation to patriotism, mediation, commercialization, and politicization, her analysis reveals the national and emotional intensities and tensions between the media logic of the Rugby World Cup and how individuals variantly experience the event. Following this, two premier scholars of cricket culture, Dominic Malcolm and Thomas Fletcher, consider the functioning of the International Cricket Council's Cricket World Cup to illustrate how media–sport relationships are structured by a sport's contextual specificities (Chapter 8). They trace cricket's structural and cultural norms and the evolution of the game's commercialization and mediatization. Their analysis of the 2015 World Cup concludes that the organization and media presentation of that event, by adherence to the game's conventions, may conspire in a way that paradoxically consigns it to second class status.

The next four chapters focus on key events in sports that, in contrast to World Cup events, may be thought of more as individual than team events and with more appeal, in distinct ways, to more particularized groupings of fans. Chapter 9, authored by a trio of notable media and sport scholars, Eileen Kennedy, Laura Hills and Alistair John, considers Wimbledon as the most elite and prestigious of the "major" tournaments in tennis. Reliant on observations of spectators and officials in the town of Wimbledon, the queue, grounds and courtside, they deconstruct the apparent "purity" of Wimbledon traditions, showing their reliance on forces of mediatization manifest through television, the official website, social media, advert-ising and promotional artefacts. Chapter 10, by two scholars concerned about the environmental impacts of sport, Brad Millington and Brian Wilson, examines how diverse forces of mediatization conspire in producing in the Masters Golf Tourna-ment and an Augusta National syndrome. They argue that this syndrome, in which media-appropriate golf courses enlist broad tools and technologies to keep golf courses green in color only, is very much anchored in this event's wedding to television for its success. Following this, a key mediatization and sport scholar, Kirsten Frandsen, considers how integrally related the Tour de France bicycle race is to the framing of geography and ethos of commodified tourism (Chapter 11). She argues this framing of the event's meaning in its televisual rendering has contributed to the event's success as the meaning of sport is anchored to the meaning of places. In Chapter 12, focusing on the Monaco Grand Prix and Indianapolis 500 automobile races, key automobile racing scholar Damion Sturm shows how these two events are built upon mediatized projections of European glamour and global Americana, respectively. The study provides intriguing contrasts between the Monaco projection of wealth, privilege, and elitism from its locale and Indy's pageantry and ceremonial rituals anchored in idealized American values and patriotism.

The next set of chapters considers a group of events that, while outsized and certainly "major," may not qualify as formally qualify as "mega," at least according to Muller's (2015) guidelines, as they aspire to reach beyond regional and national boundaries to find truly global audiences and influence. More pertinently, they are typically framed by media as mega-events within their regional and national boundaries, making their perceived import perhaps higher than Muller's metrics would dictate. Here we find studies of the AFC Asian Cup and the US-based football Super Bowl, baseball World Series, and the NCAA college basketball championships. In Chapter 13, foundational media and sport scholar David Rowe examines the AFC Asian Cup, an event that he argues is simultaneously national, regional and global. In examining the dynamics of producing ways of seeing sport events, Rowe shows how the processes of mediatization are integral to redrawing symbolic existential boundaries for events aspiring to be global. Next, two influential media and sport scholars, Michael Real and Lawrence Wenner, both known for their critiques of increasingly commodified sport, revisit the spectacle of the Super Bowl, an American football championship game that has long topped national television ratings (Chapter 14). Comparing the Super Bowl 50th anniversary event in 2016 to the state of affairs chronicled in a foundational study (Real, 1975) of 1974's Super Bowl, this study uses the lens of "super media" to show how, even as many of the mythic rituals and structural dimensions associated with the event remain, mediatization and commodification have "super-sized" the event through their strategic employ of technology, history, and nation. In Chapter 15, another US-centered mega-major event, Major League Baseball's ethnocentrically named World Series, is considered in light of American exceptionalism and the media rituals associated with it by a leading rhetorical critic, Michael Butterworth. His analysis explores how the forces of contemporary mediatization play out in historicizing and experiencing of an event rooted in five foundational myths that underlie American exceptionalism and shows how, increasingly, online media have influenced the ritual production of baseball mythology in an era of both neoliberalism and transitional changes to American identity. The final chapter in this grouping, by key communication and sport scholar Bryan Denham, provides a comparative analysis of the tenor of and changes in the US men's and women's national collegiate basketball championship tournaments – events that are marketed as and collectively define "March Madness." Denham's analysis in Chapter 16 shows how these tournaments have contributed to the global expansion of basketball, which has in turn impacted the rosters of teams that compete, and by extension, the nature of the event's television coverage.

The final chapter in this volume (Chapter 17) considers the X Games, an event which has no natural comparator among the other featured case studies. However, as it is perhaps the first media-initiated sporting event that is both global in scale and aspires to the legitimacy and reach of other sporting mega-events, it is particularly worthy of our attention. As noted by chapter authors Holly Thorpe and Belinda Wheaton, two scholars who have led understanding of lifestyle sports, the X Games is about re-imagining youth and sport, albeit in a highly commodified media package. Their analysis chronicles the development of the X Games as part of ESPN's strategy to reach new younger audiences and how reaction from this action sport audience shifted from initial resistance to acceptance and celebration. Their analysis highlights how the forces of mediatization in the X Games, as a media-manufactured event, differ from more traditional sports mega-events.

In this volume, a diverse set of scholars helps us offer an extended range of case studies and distinct vantage points on the sporting mega-event as a political, economic, and cultural phenomenon. In collectively shining light on the central role of media in shaping and growing these events and further, by considering the broader effects of mediatization on their development, the chapters in this volume share in advancing an essential understanding: that sport-centered media spectacles are about much more than sport.

References

Altheide, D.L. and Snow, R.P. (1979). *Media logic*. Beverly Hills, CA: Sage.

Anderson, B. (1983). *Imagined communities* (2nd ed.). New York: Verso.

Billings, A.C. (2008). *Olympic media: Inside the biggest show on television*. London: Routledge.

Billings, A.C. (2011). Reaction time: Assessing the record and advancing a future of sports media scholarship. In A.C. Billings (ed.), *Sports media: Transformation, integration, consumption* (pp. 181–190). New York: Routledge.

Billings, A.C., Qiao, F., Conlin, L.T. and Nie, T. (2015). Permanently desiring the temporary? Snapchat, social media, and the shifting motivations of sports fans. *Communication and Sport*, online first, doi: 10.1177/2167479515588760

Butterworth, M.L. and Moskal, S.D. (2009). American football, flags, and "fun;" The Bell Helicopter Armed Forces Bowl and the rhetorical production of militarism. *Communication, Culture and Critique*, 2(4), 411–433.

Chen, C.C., Colapinto, C. and Luo, Q. (2012). The 2008 Beijing Olympics opening ceremony: Visual insights into China's soft power. *Visual Studies*, 27(2), 188–195.

Dayan, D. and Katz, E. (1992). *Media events: The live broadcasting of history*. Cambridge, MA: Harvard University Press.

Deacon, D. and Stanyer, J. (2014). Mediatization: Key concept or conceptual bandwagon? *Media, Culture and Society*, 36(7), 1032–1044.

Debord, G. (1967/1995) *The society of the spectacle* (trans. D. Nicholson-Smith). New York: Zone Books.

Eastman, S.T., Newton, G.D. and Pack, L. (1996). Promoting prime-time programs in megasporting events. *Journal of Broadcasting and Electronic Media*, 40, 366–388.

Farrell, T. (1989). Media rhetoric as social drama: The Winter Olympics of 1984. *Critical Studies in Mass Communication*, 6(2), 158–182.

Frandsen, K. (2014). Mediatization of sports. In K. Lundby (ed.), *Mediatization of communication* (pp. 525–543). Berlin: Mouton de Gruyton.

Gruneau, R. and Horne, J. (eds) (2016). *Mega-events and globalization: Capital and spectacle in a changing world order*. London: Routledge.

Hepp, A. (2013). *Cultures of mediatization*. Cambridge: Polity.

Hjarvard, S. (2013). *The mediatization of culture and society*. London: Routledge.

Horne, J. and Manzenreiter, W. (2006). An introduction to the sociology of sports mega-events. *Sociological Review*, 54 (suppl. s2), 1–24.

Kassing, J.W., Billings, A.C., Brown, R.S., Halone, K.K., Harrison, K., Krizek, B., Meân, L.

and Turman, P.D. (2004). Communication in the community of sport: The process of enacting, (re)producing, consuming, and organizing sport. *Communication Yearbook, 28,* 373–410.

Katz, E. (1980). Media events: The sense of occasion. *Studies in Visual Anthropology, 6,* 84–89.

Katz, E. and Dayan, D. (1985). Media events: On the experience of not being there. *Religion, 15,* 305–314.

Knoll, J., Schramm, H. and Schallhorn, C. (2014). Mood effects of televised sports events: The impact of FIFA World Cups on viewers' mood and judgments. *Communication and Sport, 2*(3), 242–260.

Livingston, S. (2009). On the mediation of everything. *Journal of Communication, 59,* 1–18.

Lundby, K. (ed.) (2009). *Mediatization: Concept, changes, consequences.* New York: Peter Lang.

Lupica, M. (2006). Parting shots. Television broadcast. *ESPN's SportsReporters,* February 12.

Morse, M. (1990). An ontology of everyday distraction: The freeway, the mall, and television. In P. Mellancamp (ed.), *The logics of television* (pp. 193–221). Bloomington, IN: Indiana University Press.

Muller, M. (2015). What makes an event a mega-event? Definitions and sizes. *Leisure Studies, 34*(6), 627–642.

O'Sullivan, P.B. (1999). Bridging mass and interpersonal communication: Synthesis scholarship in HCR. *Human Communication Research, 25,* 569–588.

Real, M.R. (1975). Super Bowl: Mythic spectacle. *Journal of Communication, 75,* 31–43.

Real, M.R. (1989). *Super media: A cultural studies approach.* Thousand Oaks, CA: Sage.

Real, M. (2013). Reflections on communication and sport: On spectacle and mega-events. *Communication and Sport, 1*(1–2), 30–42.

Roberts, K. (2004). *The leisure industries.* London: Palgrave.

Roche, M. (2000). *Megaevents and modernity: Olympics and expos in the growth of global culture.* London: Routledge.

Roche, M. (2006). Mega-events and modernity revisited: Globalization and the case of the Olympics. *The Sociological Review, 54*(s2), 25–40.

Roessner, L.A. (2014). Sixteen days of glory: A critical-cultural analysis of Bud Greenspan's official Olympic documentaries. *Communication, Culture and Critique, 7*(3), 338–355.

Shils, E. (1962). The theory of mass society. *Diogenes, 39,* 45–66.

Wenner, L.A. (2006). Sports and media through the super glass mirror: Placing blame, breast-beating, and a gaze to the future. In A. Raney and J. Bryant (eds), *Handbook of Sport and Media* (pp. 45–62). Mahwah, NJ: Lawrence Erlbaum Associates.

2

SPORTS MEGA-EVENTS

Mass media and symbolic contestation

John Horne

New developments in the technologies of mass communication, especially the development of satellite television, have created the basis for global audiences for sports mega-events. The expansion of mega-events has been facilitated by the formation of a sport–media–business alliance that transformed professional sport generally in the late twentieth century. Through the idea of packaging (via the tripartite model of sponsorship rights, exclusive broadcasting rights and merchandising, sponsors of the Olympics and the two biggest international football events – the FIFA Men's Football World Cup and the UEFA Men's Football Championship, or Euro) have been attracted by the vast global audience exposure that sporting mega-events achieve. Interest in hosting sports mega-events has proliferated because they have become seen as valuable promotional opportunities for nations, cities and regions – the aim being to generate increased tourism, stimulate inward investment and promote both the host venues and the nation of which they are a part to the wider world as well as internally. Much research has since documented and theorized the transformation of sports' most important tournaments from physical contests and local festivals into global mediated spectacles (for example see Gruneau and Horne, 2016; Horne and Manzenreiter, 2006; Horne and Whannel, 2012; Roche, 2000; Rojek, 2013).

In this context, it is valuable to ask: What are the possibilities and scope for contestation and resistance to dominant media messages about sports mega-events? How is symbolic contestation played out? What different media are used? What alternative readings ("decodings") of media content are possible? It is beyond the scope of this chapter to answer these questions in detail, but it is possible to indicate why such questions are important and some of the ways in which they might be explored. The chapter will suggest that the work of Stan Cohen and Stuart Hall, two of the most influential British postwar social scientists, have contributed different ways of understanding the role of the media in constructing social reality. They provide insights into the media's role in both over-reacting to as well as exaggerating (amplifying) social concerns or social issues and also, at times, under-reacting and downplaying (denying) others (Cohen, 2001, 2002; Critcher, 2003; Hall *et al.*, 1978).

This chapter will first examine the nature of contestation and specifically symbolic contestation with respect to sports mega-events. Second, it will look at the mediated social construction of sports mega-events. Third, it will consider what a decoding of sports mega-events might entail, utilizing the ideas of Stuart Hall and Stan Cohen. Fourth and finally, it will examine some examples of symbolic contestation at recent sports mega-events and indicate where further research and study of symbolic contestation could develop our understanding of the mediatization of sports mega-events.

Disenchantment with and contestation of sports mega-events

It has long been recognized that the Super Bowl is "a spectacle of American ideology collectively celebrated" (Real, 1975, p. 42; see also Chapter 14, this volume). A subsequent study, *Contesting the Super Bowl* (Schwartz, 1998), examined the work of a team of ethnographers and documentary photographers who sought to critically examine the XXVI Super Bowl between the Washington Redskins and the Buffalo Bills held in Minnesota/Minneapolis-St Paul in 1992. Author Dona Schwartz (1998) stated that her intentions were thus: "Aware of the intense boosterism surrounding the Super Bowl, we hoped to take a more penetrating look at the unfolding spectacle and produce an independent interpretation of the events we witnessed" (ibid., p. 7). She concluded however that that there was "no essential Super Bowl to be laid bare, hidden beneath the layers of hype and fabrication" (ibid., p. 8). Rather, Schwartz and her co-researchers were confronted by a mediation process in which there was a "struggle over the production of meaning" (ibid.). While in the build-up to the event the American Indian Movement (AIM) was offered a platform for protest (about the use of Indian mascot names by sports teams, among other things) by the presence of the media "the riotous jumble of sights and sounds overpowered their voices, and the celebration absorbed dissent" (ibid., p. 114). Schwartz concluded that the Super Bowl offered a "gaudy, deformed tapestry of extravagance and want, hegemony and resistance that expands while threatening to unravel" (ibid., p. 136).

The Super Bowl continues to be one of the biggest globally mediated sports events but, arguably, that description of a "deformed tapestry of extravagance and want, hegemony and resistance" finds echoes in a general disenchantment with the hosting of other sports mega-events that has been spreading in recent years – at least in democratic nations. In the past 5 years, the Winter Olympic Games, the Commonwealth Games, and the Summer Olympic Games have all seen either a low uptake of opportunities to host them, or results from plebiscites or referenda in places as diverse as Munich, Oslo, Edmonton, Vienna and Boston, have indicated that politicians and the citizens of certain cities are no longer interested in hosting them. This does not mean that there are no locations interested in hosting these mega-events, but it is interesting to consider why this disinclination to host has happened. Possibly the reluctance to be involved with sports mega-events is connected to a recognition of the systemic crisis in the governance of international sport – in addition to the corruption allegations surrounding FIFA, the IAAF and the IOC in recent years, there are ongoing concerns about the integrity of the governing bodies of volleyball (FIVB), weightlifting (IWF), handball (IHF), swimming (FINA), boxing (AIBA) and tennis (ATP). Alternatively, it may be a response to the spread of austerity as a central ideological feature of neoliberalizing governing regimes that has led to sharp reductions in public expenditure on welfare and other social support mechanisms. It may be, therefore, that citizens recognize the "new right two step" identified by Giulianotti *et al.* (2015, p. 103) and ushered in by hosting sports mega-events, that also involves state-led privatization (Raco, 2014). Perhaps the disenchantment toward the hosting of sports mega-events has spread because of increasingly effective symbolic contestation of the promises and rhetoric of mega-event boosters?

Giulianotti *et al.* (2015) provided a valuable examination of different types of public opposition surrounding the London 2012 Olympic and Paralympic Games. They did not, however, focus on the forms that this contestation and opposition took in the mass media, and therefore did not analyze symbolic contestation itself. While symbolic contestation can sometimes be treated as less "real" or serious, it can take different forms and may have different degrees of impact. Two broad categories are humorous and evidence-based forms of symbolic contestation. Humorous contestation can take different forms in different media: lampoon, comedy, satire, parody, and mimicry via images, prose, song, and cartoons. Hence the adoption of names such as "Fatso," the alternative mascot, and "Pissoff" (People Ingeniously Subverting the Sydney Olympic Farce), one of the opposition groups, during the Sydney 2000 Olympic and Paralympic Games (Cashman, 2006; Lenskyj, 2002) can be seen as poking fun at the serious symbolism of the Olympic mega-event. Prior to the Beijing Olympics in 2008 the "curse of the fuwa" became an Internet meme amidst condemnations of human rights abuses and other conditions in China, again suggesting that the choice of five mascots (fuwa) ahead of the 2008 Games had not been propitious (Eimer, 2008). A year before London 2012, the disturbances in cities across the UK lead to the creation of widely circulated images mocking the security and stability of the London event. Polluted water in Rio de Janeiro and the possibility of pollution from the nuclear disaster area in Fukushima in Japan have also given rise to depictions of mutated animal life related to the 2016 and 2020 Summer Olympic and Paralympic Games via the Internet.

Factual, evidence-based contestation occurs in several different ways as well. The production of dossiers identifying human rights and other abuses, for example through the Popular Committees in Brazil since 2013, reports by charities and combined campaigns such as Playfair, websites such as RioOnWatch, blogs by academics and journalists such as Hunting White Elephants and Rio Gringa, as well as academics operating as "public sociologists" involving their scientific work with public activism, are all examples of the forms that factual symbolic contestation can take (for an example of the factual dossier produced by the Popular Committee in

Brazil see RioOnWatch, undated; for discussion of some of these websites and blogs see Millington and Darnell, 2014). Occasionally this work feeds into the mainstream media. Investigative journalism, such as that of Andrew Jennings (2015), is another example of this. Occasionally such reporting appears in unexpected places in the mainstream media – for example, the normally right-wing and conservative British newspaper *The Daily Mail*. During an event itself, however, media of all political persuasions tend to support the games, as we will see shortly.

The media circuit and the social construction of news about sports mega-events

On Friday, July 27, 2012, thousands of people attended the Opening Ceremony of the London 2012 Olympic Games; at its peak, *The Independent* newspaper reported that an audience of 27 million watched the ceremony live on TV in the UK, and an estimated 900 million people watched it worldwide (Independent, 2012). At the same time, an incident was taking place near to the London Olympic Stadium involving over a hundred people on bicycles taking part in a regular "Critical Mass" event (Lezard, 2012, pp. 24–25; O'Hagan, 2012). According to Shiv Malik (2012, p. 16) writing in *The Guardian*: "A man who cycled 9,320 miles from India to join Olympic celebrations in London was held by police as part of a mass arrest of cycling campaigners during last week's Opening Ceremony." Malik continued:

> Aedewan Adnan from Malaysia, who had joined his father in Kolkata in November to raise money for charity and support the Malaysian Olympic team, was held by police with 181 others including a 13-year-old boy after participating in last Friday's Critical Mass – a monthly event which seeks to promote safe road cycling by riding in numbers – after getting too close to the Olympic stadium.
>
> *(Malik, 2012, p. 16)*

Aside from coverage in *The Guardian* and *The New Statesman*, however, there was little attention paid in the media to the impact heightened security concerns during the hosting of London 2012 had upon the Critical Mass ride. The fact that coverage of the opening of the mega-event took precedence over a regular event is not surprising, but it does indicate the difficulties posed for any symbolic contestation or alternative media narrative to find space, especially during the mega-event itself.

Analysis of the media circuit in general has asked who says what, how, to whom, through which media, and with what effect. Media analysis has focused theoretically on production, messages, and reception, while empirically it has engaged with institutions, content, and audiences respectively (Rowe, 2004). This has led to the recognition of the mediated social construction of sports mega-events. News and reporting about sports mega-events is framed such that primary and secondary definers of a situation are differently valorized and positioned with respect to the events. Following the work of Stuart Hall and others it has become a sociological axiom that the mass media coverage of any large news story involves a process of struggle between competing groups: essentially between the primary and secondary definers (Hall *et al.*, 1978). The site of the struggle is to define social reality and this struggle involves uneven power relations – of resources, timing and legitimacy.

Those propagating different discourses about mega-events include what I will here call legitimizers, de-legitimizers, revisers, and transformers (see Table 2.1). The "hierarchy of credibility" (Becker, 1967) favors the organizers and legitimizers of sports mega-events. In the past 15 years or so professional sport has witnessed a dramatic increase in the use of public relations expertise (Boyle, 2006). This expertise has been widely deployed by the organizations responsible for the staging and encouragement to stage sports mega-events – including the International Olympic Committee (IOC) and the Federation Internationale de Football (FIFA) – and especially since the early 1990s and two decades of investigative journalism that offered to *de*-legitimize and reveal the "dark side" of sports mega-events (e.g. Simson and Jennings, 1992; Jennings, 1996, 2006; Jennings with Sambrook, 2000).

Mega-event discourses – spoken by planners, architects, engineers, policy makers, journalists and academic social scientists – tend to be technocratic or critical, top-down or bottom-up. In the case of sports mega-events "boosters" and "supporters" (legitimizers and revisers) tend to have greater resources and influence over media coverage, such as the Organizing Committee for the Olympic Games (OCOG), the IOC, politicians and athletes, but they still need to manage public opinion and potential threats to reputation from "skeptics" and "activists" (de-legitimizers and transformers) and thus try to manage reputational risk (Jennings, 2012). All Olympic Games organizers "begin in the bright sunshine of publicity when the bid is won and then for the next six years have to face a blizzard of critical coverage" (Horne and Whannel, 2012, p. 18). Skeptics and activists may try to use the "platform" of a mega-event to promote causes by "hijacking" or "piggybacking" the event (Price, 2008). While the old principle that "bad news" makes bigger headlines applies to sports mega-events, the skeptics' arguments can in turn be incorporated, defused or dismissed as those of "naysayers" or "party poopers" by those considered primary definers, that is, the organizers of the games.

When it comes to coverage in the media, sport and sports mega-events especially blur the usual journalistic categories of news, education and entertainment (Billings, 2008). Treating news as a "social product" means recognizing the various institutional, organizational, commercial, contractual and situational influences on reporting, coverage and presentation. Hence selection, representation and meaning are all aspects of the mediated form of sports mega-events. There is a tendency for

TABLE 2.1 The field of mega-event discourse

Technocratic – boosters and supporters	*Critical – skeptics and activists*
Legitimizers (e.g. instrumental; deliver)	De-legitimizers (e.g. resist; uncover)
Revisers (e.g. modify; reform)	Transformers (e.g. alter; democratize)

broadcasting to be more celebratory, with print media more critical (Moragas *et al.*, 1996). Having paid large sums for the rights to cover a mega-event, it is hardly surprising that some TV channels will not allow anything other than a positive image to suffuse their coverage. The print media have fewer constraints, but specialist journalists rarely leap to criticize those they depend on. Non-sport journalists often lead the reporting on major critical issues and scandals. Internet journalism, although offering an alternative, can be equally for or against mega-events.

The Olympic cycle has become an ever-present media story. In any one year the Summer or Winter Olympic Games is being hosted – or decisions are being made about hosting one or the other. The Olympic story, like a lot of sport itself, remains the ideal news story – featuring as it does an unpredictable event occurring within a predictable time frame. Different newsworthy issues emerge at several different stages: before a decision is made to bid to host an event, the bid process itself, what happens at decision time, the build-up to the event, "Games-time," in the immediate period after an event, and the longer term "legacy."

In the long build-up to any Olympic Games or other sports mega-event, the media coverage is often focused on two central questions: "will it go over budget?" and "will the facilities be ready in time?" The answer to both questions is usually "yes" (Horne and Whannel, 2010, p. 766). After the Games commence, however, "there is a massive turning inward of the media to events in the arena and the stadia" (ibid.). As Whannel (1984, p. 30) stated 30 years ago, the Olympics is the "ultimate media festival." Additionally, sports journalist Rob Steen perceptively commented before London 2012:

> The tone within the UK press ... will depend on the medal count and the impact of the Coalition Government's spending cuts ... The expense of an Olympic Games must be justified by glory and, at the very least, organizational competence. Broadcasters ... are inclined to exaggerate the good.
> *(Steen, 2012, p. 225)*

Issues raised in the media in the twelve month build-up prior to London 2012, for example, included concerns over legacy promises, a potential crisis of legitimacy because chemical company Dow was a sponsor of both the IOC and the London Games, civilian surveillance by drones and rocket launchers on the roofs, the potential for transport congestion, and ticket scandals. During the Games, initial concern at the lack of a Team GB gold medal after four days of competition lead to the publication of a "Keep calm and carry on ... We've still got Wiggo" poster in *The Guardian*, referring to cyclist Bradley Wiggins, who had become the first British rider to win the Tour de France the weekend before London 2012 began (Guardian, 2012).

Undoubtedly after the Games began the British media began to act as flag-waving fomenters of the "feel-good factor" rather than dispassionate critics. Despite the fact that the BBC sport budget had been cut by 20 per cent as the license fee was frozen by the Coalition government, the BBC produced 2,500 hours of live Olympic TV, and used 765 reporters during the Olympics alone (compared with 550 Team GB athletes). There was blanket coverage from 6 am to 1 am daily across multiple digital TV and radio channels. It was estimated that 90 per cent of the population watched at least 15 minutes of coverage (Thomas, 2012).[1] The British print media devoted an average of 46 pages daily to Olympic coverage, with Olympic stories appearing on front, news, and feature pages, as well as sport pages (Edgar, 2012). Newspapers that were generally wary and skeptical of the Games – such as *The Guardian* – also came out to support them – "Leave go your cynicism and let the Games commence" (Kettle, 2012, p. 1). As Steen (2012, p. 215) noted, "the atmosphere created on the ground by the crowd and the sense of occasion may lead to the suspension, or outright surrender, of one's critical faculties."[2]

The outcome also confirmed Steen's statement that "In any nation hosting a major [international event] ... the media's default position is patriotic, even blindly nationalistic" (Steen, 2012, p. 225). This appears to have become far more marked – in the UK at least – than it used to be. Furthermore the British media continued to set the agenda for future mega-events – including the Football World Cup Finals in Brazil in 2014 and Summer Olympic and Paralympic Games in Rio de Janeiro in 2016 – by focusing on security, environmental, and health concerns rather than the impact of evictions and the denial of housing rights in places designated to host the events in Brazil (see Zirin, 2014; Horne and Whannel, 2016).

Decoding sports mega-events

To make theoretical sense of these empirical developments it is helpful to recall the work of two leading sociologists of mass communication, Stuart Hall and Stan Cohen. Stuart Hall's (1973) essay, "Encoding and decoding in the television discourse," drew upon the political sociology of Frank Parkin (1972), who argued that the normative order of a society could be conceived as composed of three "meaning-systems." These offered different moral interpretations of class inequality and, in turn, acted as key social sources of stability in society. He identified the dominant value system, the subordinate value system and the radical value system. Each influenced the "social and political perceptions of the subordinate class" and variations in the attitudes of individuals and groups within this class were "dependent on differences in access to these meaning-systems" (ibid., pp. 81–82). Adopting these insights, Hall argued that the mass media encoded meanings according to these different systems, suggesting three broad "interpretive" or "reading" positions. Following Hall, regarding sports mega-events, we can identify three possible readings of sports mega-events:

1   People who believe they (and the local community and, indeed, the nation) benefit from the events, economically and socially – the "dominant" position.
2   People who have an ambivalent or "negotiated" position about mega events, believing them to be good in some ways but not necessarily so in others, with benefits that are mixed or are unevenly distributed; this means that you can

enjoy some aspects of the spectacle, while disliking others, yet feel the whole issue is really beyond the actions/powers of individuals.

3   People who believe that mega events benefit the upper classes but this is hidden behind a veil of ideological rhetoric suggesting the events benefit everyone. For this reason public expenditures on them should be opposed. Similarly, the themes emphasized in media accounts of the events act as powerful modes of legitimation for a host of ideological standpoints associated with class, gender, race and, most importantly, a blind commitment to meritocracy within the ideological confines of neoliberalism. The use of public expenditures for such events is therefore a travesty – the "oppositional" position.

These positions are caricatures, and, of course, even the most superficial research would reveal them to multiply into a number of other complex variations; this was Parkin's argument as well (Parkin, 1972, p. 82). Hall (1973, p. 13) introduced a Marxist interpretation to this complexity. His point was that the whole system of meaning is "structured in dominance," and, therefore, that negotiated and oppositional positions tend to be marginalized or articulated in ways that never threatened the dominant or hegemonic position. The role of social science, however, is to investigate how these different readings operate in specific circumstances.

In two of his most celebrated books, Stan Cohen explored the way the media over-report and under-report certain social issues and circumstances. In *States of Denial* (Cohen, 2001) and the foreword to the thirtieth-anniversary (3rd) edition of *Folk Devils and Moral Panics* (Cohen, 2002), he explored the way that the concept of "folk devil" focused on the symbolic contestation over marginal and deviant subcultures, while "moral panics" suggested the exaggerated coverage given to specific episodes and issues involving them – that is media *over-reaction.* "Moral panic" suggests that something not fully deserving of important and lengthy treatment is acknowledged as critical. "Denial," on the other hand, is about cover-up, evasion, and giving too little importance to some issue or concern – that is media *under-reaction.*

For Cohen (2001, p. 51) denial "refers to the maintenance of social worlds in which an undesirable situation (event, condition, phenomenon) is unrecognized, ignored or made to seem normal." Cohen (2010) argues that previously denied realities should be brought to public attention, realities exposed, and consciousnesses raised about the different elements that go into a social problem. Sociologists have no privileged status in pointing this out and suggesting remedial policies – they are just another claims maker – but they can expose "under-reaction (apathy, denial and indifference)" and "over-reaction (exaggeration, hysteria, prejudice and panic" (Cohen, 2002, p. xxxiv). Cohen (ibid., p. xxxiii) remarked that: "my own cultural politics entails … encouraging something like moral panics about mass atrocities and political suffering – and trying to expose the strategies of denial deployed to prevent the acknowledgement of these realities." Moral panics can become a "critical tool to expose dominant interests and ideologies" (ibid., p. xxxiii). Cohen thus identifies the basis for a cultural politics of moral panics and suggests that *anti-denial movements* may seek to develop their own moral panics about injustices. The next paragraphs briefly sketch these processes with reference to London 2012 in the UK and the build up to the 2014 World Cup in Brazil and the Rio 2016 Summer Olympics and Paralympics.

Contesting sports mega-events

Changes in resistance and media contestation reflect different phases of the build-up to an Olympic Games or other sports mega-event, as well as the different media forms and technologies that have existed. The opportunities for media-based contestation before TV, since TV, and since the Internet have obviously been different. At the same time, global corporate, commercial and media-oriented "Prolympism" (Donnelly, 1996) has only been in existence since the 1980s. Since the adjustment to the Summer and Winter editions of the Olympics in the 1990s, when the Winter Olympics was held in 1992 and 1994 to introduce a new 4-year cycle, the Olympics has become a perpetual media story.

Differences exist between media coverage during the build-up to a sports mega-event (which can take 7 years or more) and during Games time; and also whether the mega-event is at taking place at home or abroad. This influenced the tone for reporting London 2012 in July and August 2012, as it was dependent on the outcomes of the competitions. In the UK the social construction of the Olympics in the print media and broadcasting shifted after the commencement (especially between August 1 and 8, 2012), from when Team GB had won no gold medals, to the "super Saturday" when several track and field gold medals were secured, along with success for cyclist Bradley Wiggins and tennis player Andy Murray. After that the tone of media coverage became more nationalistic and celebratory.

Local and national print and broadcast media covered few of the negative issues associated with London 2012 – the removal of the Manor Gardens Allotment Society (MGS) from the Olympic site in east London was one exception that made it onto mainstream BBC TV – for further discussion see Hayes and Horne (2011) and Porter *et al.* (2009). But the largest amount of coverage given to the negative aspects appeared on networking counter media and especially the website Games Monitor (Cheyne, 2014). Very little coverage was given to the role of the anti-sweat-shop campaign "Playfair 2012" (Timms, 2012).

Sports mega-events in the "global North" in the past 15 years – Sydney 2000, Vancouver 2010, and London 2012 – have tended to develop brownfield sites, attempt to minimize ecological impact, and have a strong legacy emphasis. Those staged in the "global South" – Beijing 2008, Sochi 2014, and Rio 2016 – have not been so overtly concerned about their ecological impact, despite claims to the contrary, and instead have had a strong developmental and "coming out party" emphasis. Events in the global North have had a relatively low level of displacement and infrastructural impact compared with those in the global South.

Hence prior to the Rio Olympics in 2016 (and the FIFA Men's World Cup in 2014) there have been a series of land grabs and the removal of thousands of people in marginalized communities (e.g. "favela" such as Vila Autódromo, and Morro da

Providência) as part of a broader, accelerated, urban regeneration policy. This has been covered in some mainstream media outside Brazil, but the main focus has been on security, the completion of stadiums, demonstrations in 2013 and shortly before the 2014 World Cup itself, rather than removals from favelas per se. Again networking counter media – especially the blog Hunting White Elephants and RioOnWatch (Rio Olympic Neighbourhood Watch) – have been regular conduits for information about these developments (see Millington and Darnell, 2014 for a discussion of this; see also www.geostadia.com and http://rioonwatch.org).

Occasionally videos and films about these developments have been made available on YouTube, but the reach and audience for these is considerably smaller than the mainstream media (see, for example, Articulação Nacional da Copa Ancop, 2013). Alternative development plans for threatened communities, the *Mega-events and Violations of Human Rights in Rio de Janeiro* dossier prepared by the Comite Popular da Copa e Olimpiadas do Rio de Janeiro in 2013 (Popular Committee for the World Cup and Olympics, RJCPCO) and the Brazilian National Association of Graduate Studies and Research in Urban and Regional Planning (ANPUR) declaration on mega-events, are hardly mentioned at all outside the networked counter media.

Conclusions and future research

Michael Burawoy and Karl von Holdt (2012, p. 198) noted that towards the end of his life sociologist Pierre Bourdieu began to investigate "the conditions under which the weight of social order may be destabilised or challenged." In *Pascalian Meditations* for example, Bourdieu (2000) argued that the symbolic order constitutes a space of relative autonomy that allows for "struggles over the sense of the social world" (Burawoy and von Holdt, 2012, p. 198). His suggestion was that symbolic contestation becomes a necessary part of engagement with the world for academics that are interested in changing, rather than just interpreting it, and not just the domain of journalists and other media workers.

It was noted earlier how the "struggle over the production of meaning" (Schwartz, 1998, p. 8) has continued with respect to sports mega-events other than the Super Bowl.[3] The shift of the two biggest sports events organizers, FIFA and the IOC, toward holding mega-events in the global South, or developing market economies, in the past decade connects with recent attempts to link sport and social development. But mega-events in the global South are compromised by the weaker position of the host countries to bear the burden of hosting and the opportunity costs being relatively much higher than in the advanced economies. The media presentation of the capacities of the hosts in the global South also becomes an essential part of the outcome.[4]

This chapter has attempted to introduce and set the stage for some of the more specific analyses of sports mega-events to be found in the rest of the book. It has suggested that there needs to be more investigation of the uneven power relations involved – to access to the media, to have media legitimacy, and to define situations through narrative accounts. While there has been recognition that contemporary media audiences are active and have some power, especially via social media, it is also argued that "astro turfing," the production of fake "grassroots" movements or synthetic positive audience responses, is an ever-present possibility (Glaser, 2011, pp. 46–51). Astro turfing is no less likely to be used to generate excitement about sports mega-events, as in other commercial or political campaigns.

Protests about sports mega-events have mainly been couched in terms of their costs and legacies, human rights and their environmental impacts. The following features of the *symbolic contestation* of sports mega-events needs further examination in the future: media agenda setting, (e.g., the focus on security rather than evictions and housing rights that occurred in both London and Rio); the different forms of media used by sports mega-event "boosters" and "skeptics"; the use of media by social movements – as "oppositional" or "event coalitions" involved in resistance against mega-events in different societies; the imbalance of power and "hierarchy of credibility" associated with different media; the involvement of marginalized people in resistance to sports mega-events; and alternative "readings" and decodings of media output.

Acknowledgements

This chapter draws on material presented in a plenary session on "Megaeventos, mídia e lutas simbólicas" at the II Conferência Internacional Megaeventos e Cidades in Rio de Janeiro in April 2014, and a talk presented at the Sport, Leisure and Social Justice symposium in Eastbourne (University of Brighton) in September 2013. I would like to thank Rick Gruneau and Garry Whannel for providing comments on sections of an earlier version of this chapter. Any deficiencies in the argument remain my responsibility.

Notes

1 Television channel C4 were exclusive rights holders for the 2012 Paralympic Games and ran a series of advertisements featuring the strapline "Thanks for the warm up" towards the end of the Olympic Games. Using the song "Harder than you think" by American rap group Public Enemy as the theme tune C4 produced almost an equal amount of saturation coverage of the Paralympics in 2012.

2 By mid-July *The Guardian* was asking "Ten days to go – what could go wrong?" (*The Guardian*, July 17, 2012), but on the eve of the Games it featured a front cover headline: "Time to find out who we are" (Jonathan Freedland, *The Guardian*, July 27, 2012). For the next two weeks the British press as a whole featured increasing amounts of front-page color photographs, souvenir posters, free booklets and other Olympic giveaways.

3 The most recent Super Bowl, in San Francisco in February 2016, attracted protests about the nearly $5 million public spending on infrastructure, especially a "Super Bowl City" street fair, with protesters using the hash tag #tacklehomelessness on Twitter as an organizing tool to challenge the priorities of San Francisco city authorities (Wong, 2016; Zirin, 2016).

4   For example, in May 2014, less than three weeks before the men's football World Cup began, British newspapers reported problems with the quality and safety of the food available at the five star hotel being used by the England football team (Philipson *et al.*, 2014).

References

Articulação Nacional da Copa Ancop (2013). Copa 2014: Quem ganha com esse jogo? Retrieved from www.youtube.com/watch?v=aAX0zSfrJK4 (accessed 24 November 2016).

Becker, H.S. (1967). Whose side are we on? *Social Problems, 14*(3), 239–247.

Billings, A.C. (2008). *Olympic media: Inside the biggest show on television*. London: Routledge.

Bourdieu, P. (2000). *Pascalian meditations*. Cambridge: Polity.

Boyle, R. (2006). *Sports journalism*. London: Sage.

Burawoy, M. and von Holdt, K. (2012). *Conversations with Bourdieu: The Johannesburg moment.* Johannesburg: University of Witwatersrand Press.

Cashman, R. (2006). *The bitter-sweet awakening: The Legacy of the Sydney 2000 Olympic Games.* Sydney: Walla Walla Press.

Cheyne, J. (2014) Tessa Jowell – Joan of Arc of the Allotments? *Games Monitor*, March 27. Retrieved from www.gamesmonitor.org.uk/node/2178 (accessed 24 November 2016).

Cohen, S. (2001) *States of denial: Knowing about atrocities and suffering*. Cambridge: Polity Press.

Cohen, S. (2002). The cultural politics of moral panics. In his *Folk devils and moral panics* (3rd ed.) (pp. vii–xxxvii). London: Routledge.

Cohen, S. (2010). The political agenda of moral panic theory: Constructing a sociology of importance. Moral Panics in the Contemporary World Conference, Brunel University. Retrieved from www.youtube.com/watch?v=xV5-HFqY0PY (accessed 24 November 2016).

Critcher, C. (2003). *Moral panics and the media*. Buckingham: Open University Press.

Donnelly, P. (1996). Prolympism: Sport monoculture as crisis and opportunity. *Quest, 48*(1), 25–42.

Edgar, A. (2012). The future of reporting at the Olympic Games. Unpublished presentation presented at the Olympic Games: Meeting New Challenges Conference, Oxford University Club, Oxford.

Eimer, D. (2008). Beijing Olympic Fuwa mascots "have cursed" China in unlucky 2008. *The Daily Telegraph*, June 21. Retrieved from www.telegraph.co.uk/news/worldnews/asia/china/2168554/Beijing-Olympic-Fuwamascots-have-cursed-China-in-unlucky-2008.html (accessed 24 November 2016).

Giulianotti, R., Armstrong, G., Hales, G. and Hobbs, D. (2015). Sport mega-events and public opposition: A sociological study of the London 2012 Olympics. *Journal of Sport and Social Issues, 39*(2), 99–119.

Glaser, E. (2011). *Get real: How to tell it like it is in a world of illusions*. London: Fourth Estate.

Gruneau, R. and Horne, J. (eds) (2016). *Mega-events and globalization: Capital and spectacle in a changing world order.* London: Routledge.

Guardian (2012). Team GB poster. *The Guardian*, July 31. Retrieved from www.guardian.co.uk/sport/interactive/2012/jul/31/team-gb-poster-keep-calm-and-carry-on (accessed 24 November 2016).

Hall, S. (1973). Encoding and decoding in the television discourse. Stencilled Paper 7. Birmingham: Centre for Contemporary Cultural Studies, University of Birmingham.

Hall, S., Critcher, C., Jefferson, T., Clarke, J. and Roberts, B. (1978). *Policing the crisis: Mugging, the state and law and order*. London: Macmillan.

Hayes, G. and Horne, J. (2011). Sustainable development, shock and awe? London 2012 and civil society. *Sociology, 45*(5), 749–764.

Horne, J. and Manzenreiter, W. (eds) (2006). *Sports mega-events: Social scientific analyses of a global phenomenon*. Oxford: Blackwell.

Horne, J. and Whannel, G. (2010). The "caged torch procession": Celebrities, protesters and the 2008 Olympic torch relay in London, Paris and San Francisco. *Sport in Society, 13*(5), 760–770.

Horne, J. and Whannel, G. (2012). *Understanding the Olympics*. London: Routledge.

Horne, J. and Whannel, G. (2016). *Understanding the Olympics* (2nd ed.). London: Routledge.

Independent (2012). London 2012 opening ceremony audience hit 900 million predicts IOC. *The Independent*, August 7. Retrieved from www.independent.co.uk/sport/olympics/news/london-2012-opening-ceremony-audience-hit-900-million-predicts-ioc-8015361.html (accessed 24 November 2016).

Jennings, A. (1996). *The new lords of the rings: Olympic corruption and how to buy gold medals*. London: Pocket Books.

Jennings, A. (2006). *Foul! The secret world of FIFA: Bribes, vote rigging and ticket scandals*. London: Harper Sport.

Jennings, W. (2012). *Olympic risks*. Basingstoke: Palgrave Macmillan.

Jennings, A. (2015). FIFA, Sepp Blatter and me. *Panorama*, December 7. BBC TV. Retrieved from www.bbc.co.uk/iplayer/episode/b06tkl9d/panorama-fifa-sepp-blatter-and-me (accessed 24 November 2016).

Jennings, A. with Sambrook, C. (2000). *The great Olympic swindle: When the world wanted its games back*. London: Simon & Schuster.

Kettle, M. (2012) London 2012: leave go your cynicism and let the Games commence. *The Guardian*, July 25, p.1. Retrieved from www.theguardian.com/commentisfree/2012/jul/25/london-2012-cynicism-games-commence (accessed 26 October 2016).

Lenskyj, H. (2002). *The best Olympics ever? Social impacts of Sydney 2000*. Albany, NY: SUNY Press.

Lezard, N. (2012). *The Nolympics: One man's struggle against sporting hysteria*. London: Penguin.

Malik, S. (2012). Olympic tourist caught up in cycling protest arrests. *The Guardian*, August 3, p. 16.

Millington, B. and Darnell, S. (2014). Constructing and contesting the Olympics online: The Internet, Rio 2016 and the politics of Brazilian development. *International Review for the Sociology of Sport, 49*(2), 190–210.

Moragas, M. de, Rivenburgh, N.K. and Larson, J.F. (eds) (1996). *Television in the Olympics*. London: John Libbey.

O'Hagan, E.M. (2012). The Olympic spirit? *New Statesman*. Retrieved from www.newstatesman.com/blogs/voices/2012/07/olympic-spirit (accessed 24 November 2016).

Parkin, F. (1972). *Class inequality and political order*. St Albans: Paladin.

Philipson, A., Carter, C. and Harkness, T. (2014). World Cup preparations in chaos as unsafe food found and "state of emergency" declared in host city. *The Daily Telegraph*, 27 May. Retrieved from www.telegraph.co.uk/sport/football/teams/england/10858440/World-Cup-preparations-in-chaos-as-unsafe-food-found-and-state-of-emergency-declared-in-host-city.html (accessed 24 November 2016).

Porter, L., Jaconelli, M., Cheyne, J., Eby, D. and Wagenaar, H. (2009). Planning displacement: The real legacy of major sporting events. *Planning Theory and Practice, 10*(3), 395–418.

Price, M. (2008). On seizing the Olympic Platform. In M. Price and D. Dayan (eds), *Owning the Olympics* (pp. 86–114). Ann Arbor, MI: Digital Culture Books/University of Michigan.

Raco, M. (2014). Delivering flagship projects in an era of regulatory capitalism: State-led privatization and the London Olympics 2012. *International Journal of Urban and Regional Research, 38*(1), 176–197.

Real, M. (1975). Super Bowl: Mythic spectacle. *Journal of Communication, 25*(1), 31–43.

RioOnWatch (undated). Popular committee launches final human rights violations dossier ahead of Rio 2016 "exclusion games." Retrieved from www.rioonwatch.org/?p=25747 (accessed 24 November 2016).

Roche, M. (2000). *Mega-events and modernity*. London: Routledge.

Rojek, C. (2013). *Event power: How global events manage and manipulate*. London: Sage.

Rowe, D. (2004). *Sport, culture and the media: The unruly trinity* (2nd ed.). Maidenhead: Open University Press.

Schwartz, D. (1998). *Contesting the Super Bowl*. London: Routledge.

Simson, V. and Jennings, A. (1992). *The lords of the rings: Power, money and drugs in the modern Olympics*. London: Simon & Schuster.

Steen, R. (2012). The view from the press box: Rose-tinted spectacles? In J. Sugden and A. Tomlinson (eds), *Watching the Olympics: Politics, power and representation* (pp. 213–227). London: Routledge.

Thomas, L. (2012). Bigger than the royal wedding, 90% of Britons saw Games on TV. *The Daily Mail*, August 13. Retrieved from www.dailymail.co.uk/news/article-2187868/ London-2012-Bigger-Royal-Wedding-90-Britons-saw-Games-TV-26m-tuned-closing-ceremony.html (accessed 24 November 2016).

Timms, J. (2012). The Olympics as a platform for protest: A case study of the London 2012 "ethical" Games and the Play Fair campaign for workers' rights. *Leisure Studies, 31*(3), 355–372.

Whannel, G. (1984). The television spectacular. In A. Tomlinson and G. Whannel (eds), *Five ring circus: Money, power and politics at the Olympic Games* (pp. 30–43). London: Pluto.

Wong, J.C. (2016). Dispatch San Francisco. Protesters cry foul on Super Bowl City. *The Guardian*, February 5, p. 22.

Zirin, D. (2014). *Brazil's dance with the devil: The World Cup, the Olympics and the fight for democracy*. Chicago, IL: Haymarket.

Zirin, D. (2016). The streets of San Francisco: "Super Bowl City" meets tent city. *The Nation*, February 4. Retrieved from www.thenation.com/article/the-streets-of-san-francisco-super-bowl-city-meets-tent-city (accessed 24 November 2016).

3

MEDIA EVENTS, MEGA-EVENTS AND SOCIAL THEORY

From Durkheim to Marx

Richard Gruneau and James Compton

Sporting mega-events are often singled out for the opportunities they provide to understand the complex and sometimes contradictory dynamics of globalization. According to Roche (2006) the Olympic Games, in particular, invite researchers to consider the hyper-mediated character of international spectacle and its links to broader processes of globalization. In Roche's view, the Olympics "create a unique cultural space and provide unrivalled opportunities to dissolve spatial and temporal distance, to participate in a national global community and to promote individual and collective experiences of 'globality' or 'one world' awareness" (ibid., p. 32). Indeed, the "predictably recurrent" global broadcast of the Olympics, along with their often "positive and celebratory" reproduction of so-called universal values of sportsmanship and togetherness is cited by Roche as empirical evidence that mega-events constitute specific examples of "media events" – what Dayan and Katz (1992, p. 1) have called "high holidays of communication."

The "media event" thesis, as presented by Dayan and Katz, has been enormously influential in the study of cultural and political phenomena ranging from the Olympics to British Royal weddings and the funeral of John F. Kennedy – events that are global in reach and impact. Their perspective draws heavily on many of Emile Durkheim's ideas about the nature and roles of public rituals, "collective consciousness," "collective effervescence," and social integration. In this chapter we provide a review of Durkheimian influences in studies of media and large-scale public events, with specific reference to Dayan and Katz's analysis of media events and to recent assessments of the strengths and weaknesses of their work. Social theorists acknowledge that the Durkheimian legacy has provided insight into ritual meanings, symbolization and modes of collective identification (Lukes, 1977), but there is growing recognition that this has occurred at the *expense* of analyzing logics, inequities and conflicts associated with capitalist accumulation and neoliberal globalization. To accommodate such concerns we argue that there has been a trend in recent years to reconsider ideas found in the work of Karl Marx.

Postwar neo-Durkheimian perspectives on media and mega-events

In *The Elementary Forms of Religious Life* (1915), Durkheim argued that certain situations and events produce modes of "collective effervescence" that express and maintain religious feelings and beliefs. These work to renew "collective represen-tations" associated with sacred beliefs in society. Durkheim is interested in two aspects of this process. On the one hand, he undertakes an interpretive analysis of the meanings of religious beliefs and practices, seeing them as cognitive means through which individuals understand the world and represent to themselves the society of which they are members. On the other hand, he considers the most "elementary forms" of these meanings as functional prerequisites of societies. Durkheim was convinced that public rituals play a vital role in maintaining func-tionally necessary modes of social solidarity, including collective sentiments, ideas and identities. He worried that an apparent breakdown of social bonds between individuals and their communities and the emergence of *anomie* – a modern form of egoistic estrangement and social dislocation – were partially explainable by declining numbers of public rituals (Durkheim, 1915, pp. 427–428; Lukes, 1977, pp. 55–57).

Durkheim viewed the spread of *anomie* as a result of rapid changes of values associated with secularization, urbanization, self-centered individualism and an increasingly complex division of labor. These ideas were consistent with similar concerns raised by other early twentieth century intellectuals about urban anonymity, ennui, and normlessness as conditions of modernity (e.g., Simmel, 1900/1978, p. 484). The growth of new mass media were widely seen to accelerate these problems, suggesting that modern Western societies were increasingly "mass societies" in which much of the face-to-face contact and social intimacy of earlier times had been lost (Brantlinger, 1983; Swingewood, 1977). It was in this context that the apparent declines of "primary group" social connections and of meaningful community rituals could be viewed as indices of social pathology.

After the Second World War, a wave of neo-Durkheimian thinking in Europe and North America sought to make a counter argument: that public rituals in Western societies were more present than ever in social life and that they were increasingly connected to modern media systems in a positive rather than a negative way. Large-scale public media events in particular were seen to be amen-able to a neo-Durkheimian analysis, revealing them to be vital mechanisms of social integration in diverse and plural modern Western societies. The work of Edward Shills, Elihu Katz, and Paul Lazersfeld played significant roles in the popularity and influence of this postwar version of neo-Durkheimianism. For example, Katz and Lazersfeld's influential early postwar study, *Personal Influence* (1955), claimed to rediscover a vital and significant primary group influence in behavioral media effects. Against the view of a so-called "European" tradition that posited anonymous and isolated masses as a condition of modern life, Katz and Lazersfeld proposed that US postwar society was a dense network of meaningful customs and small group ties (Pooley, 2006, pp. 4–8).

Shils supplied the narrative frame for this interpretation in a broader critical discussion of the limits of mass society theories (Shils, 1962; Pooley, 2006). The combination of apparent social scientific evidence of the resiliency of community in the US and the growth of postwar affluence across the global North, accompanied a growing confidence in the quality of life in Western democracies in general and in the role of media as vital organs that disseminated information and contributed to social order. Shils's early sociological work was focused on analyzing the underpinnings and conditions of this modern social order, leading him to undertake (with co-author Michael Young) one of the earliest studies of a postwar mega-event: the coronation of Queen Elizabeth in England (Shils and Young, 1953). According to Shils and Young, the coronation was a "series of ritual affirmations of the moral values necessary to a well governed and good society" (cited in Lukes, 1977, p. 57). Celebratory festivities, along with radio, television and press coverage of the event, created a nationwide "communion" through which people became more aware of their mutual dependence, connections to their society at large and to the Queen. The promotion of order through social integration was the key function of this highly mediated celebratory event.

A number of ideas from work in the 1950s by Katz and Lazersfeld, along with that of Shils and Young, and a host of other similar analysts of public rituals and events (cf. Lukes, 1977), were refined and repackaged through the 1980s (Katz, 1980; Katz and Dayan, 1985) culminating in Dayan and Katz's book *Media Events: The Live Broadcasting of History* (1992). Dayan and Katz argue that media events (e.g., the 1969 moon landing; the funeral of US President Kennedy, the Olympics) make their claim to "high holiday" status by breaking life's everyday routine to create a sense of special occasion. Media events are highly dramatized "narrative genres" in which citizens take time out of their regular schedules to join together as part of a collective televisual audience. As with other scholars working in the neo-Durkheimian tradition, Dayan and Katz emphasize how these "great ceremonial events celebrate order and its restoration" (1992, p. 9).

Three narrative "scripts" for media events are identified: *contests conquests* and *coronations*. Each script is a representational form corresponding to one of Max Weber's typology of types of authority: legal/rational, charisma and tradition (Weber, 1958). Contests include sporting events, such as the Olympics, but also extend to televised senate hearings, which Dayan and Katz (1992, p. 26) refer to as "rule-governed battles of champions." Conquests involve special occasions in which a leader or hero figure asserts his/her charismatic authority to break new ground for the future. Finally, echoing the work of Shils and Young, coronations are noted for their ceremonial character, usually involving funerals and parades (ibid.). In the Anglo-Western world, one can arguably place English Royal weddings beside Olympic opening and closing ceremonies. Despite their differences, say

Dayan and Katz, each of these scripts, or types of media events, celebrates *modes of reconciliation* – with the rule of law, one's opponent or universal experience.

Dayan and Katz divide the "high holiday of communication" metaphor into three linguistic categories which prove to be important to their "highly circumscribed" definition of a media event: syntactic, semantic and pragmatic. At the *syntactic* level media events are "interruptions" of routine. Regular programming is cancelled or suspended to make way for the live broadcast of the media event that takes place at predetermined remote locations. *Semantically*, these events are said to be ripe with meaning, speaking with reverence to the greatness of the event. At the *pragmatic* level, media events enthrall worldwide audiences for whom the occasion is treated as festive (see Dayan and Katz, 1992, pp. 10–13).

To further develop their analysis of collective effervescence and the interpretive meaning of rituals, Dayan and Katz turn to the cultural anthropology of Victor Turner (1974, 1984), who argues that the syntactic, semantic and pragmatic aspects of media events combine to foster so-called "liminal" states, which are the "in-between" stage of ritual, when the structure of society is temporarily suspended. Liminal states are moments when rules may be bent or broken and social reality is not understood as taken for granted, but instead is open to possibilities of "what could or should be" (Turner, 1984, p. 22). According to Dayan and Katz:

> during the liminal moments, totality and simultaneity are unbound; organizers and broadcasters resonate together; competing channels merge into one; viewers present themselves at the same time and in every place. All eyes are fixed on the ceremonial center, through which each nuclear cell is connected to all the rest. Social integration of the highest order is thus achieved via mass communication.
>
> *(Dayan and Katz, 1992, p. 15)*

For Dayan and Katz, media events are a distinctive *genre* of communicative act that promote liminal moments of cultural reflexivity, utopian introspection and longing.

Eric Rothenbuhler provides a notable early examination of Dayan and Katz's ideas in the analysis of a sporting media/mega-event. Following a survey of television audiences for the 1984 Summer Olympic Games, Rothenbuhler argued that evidence supports the "media events" thesis. For example, in respect to the "conquest" trope, he argued:

> the modern Olympics are also a regularly recurring celebration of a coherent set of values, beliefs, and symbols. They are predominantly understood to celebrate the performance of individuals, the ideal that competition produces the good, an idealization of participation as its own reward, friendship between competitors, the value of hard work, international understanding, and other related values.
>
> *(Rothenbuhler, 1988, p. 64)*

More recently, Xi Cui (2013) reported similar findings in his analysis of the Beijing 2008 Opening Ceremony. He outlined the syntactic, semantic and pragmatic components of the Olympics and concluded: "the ceremonial television genre of media events is still alive" (ibid., p. 1231).

Rothenbuhler (1993) later underlined the neo-Durkheimian roots of the media events thesis, arguing both for a Durkheimian approach to communication research more generally and for the study of ritual and communication as an antidote to "cynics" on the political right and the left who are suspicious of the *manipulation* of "ceremony, media productions, and appearances, common to the humanities and the social sciences" (Rothenbuhler, 2010, p. 63). In contrast to such cynicism—and in a manner roughly similar to arguments made about Olympic rituals by the US anthropologist John MacAloon (1984) – Rothenbuhler argues that ritual produces effects through the *willing* participation of audiences. This invites a more "nuanced" approach to the analysis of media spectacles than arguments about "bread and circuses" or audience passivity. Drawing on ideas about "media logic" developed initially by Altheide and Snow (1979), and citing Niklas Luhmann's (2000) concept of "autopoiesis," Rothenbuhler proposes a view of media events as "messy" *self-organizing* systems:

> My hypothesis is that the model and the conditions of its success developed simultaneously as broadcasters and audiences trained each other, so to speak, and organized in a new form of relation around a new form of communication.
>
> *(Rothenbuhler, 2010, p. 67)*

Issues of power, ideology, inequality and conflict

Rothenbuhler has admitted that the "Olympic tradition is not without controversy" and that none of the Olympics going back to 1896 have been "a pure expression" of Olympic idealism (Rothenbuhler, 1988). This is an important caveat, although, it fails to acknowledge that "Olympic idealism" itself is a historically and spatially specific cultural construction, with residues of Western colonial ideology and social class exclusivity (cf. Brownell, 2008; Gruneau, 2006; Hoberman, 1986; Young, 1984). Furthermore, Rothenbuhler's analysis of media events provides virtually no standpoint from which to analyze the workings of power, ideology or conflict. This is a problem faced by neo-Durkheimian analyses of public rituals and media events more generally (Compton, 2004; Lukes, 1977). The point is underlined by Nick Couldry (2003, pp. 37–39) who advocates for a "post-Durkheimian" approach to media rituals that can account for the "unequal distribution of symbolic power" at play in the construction of what he calls the "myth of the mediated center." Shared societal values do not exist a priori; they are *constructed*, in part, through the exercise of mediated symbolic power which "naturalises" the appearance of a social and cultural center, an imagined "core truth" regarding "'our way of life', 'our' values" (ibid., p. 45).

Couldry's sympathetic attempt to extend the media event thesis to account for social relations of power acknowledges arguments made by a host of Marxists and critical theorists in the 1970s and 1980s – and even those of comparatively mainstream social theorists such as Steven Lukes (1977) and Charles Tilly (1981) – who strenuously criticized a number of key Durkheimian ideas. Among other things, these critics attacked the paradigmatic status given to the "problem of order" in Durkheimian analysis, the difficulties of identifying cohesion and consensus on core values in modern Western societies, and the suggestion that such a consensus is achievable or even desirable. Many critics argued instead that it was more important to analyze the capacity of *some* groups over others to define or shape the contours of this imagined consensus. Lukes (1977, p. 73) referred to this as the "mobilization of bias" and others, more closely aligned with Marxism, linked it to the production of ideology or to the struggle for cultural or political hegemony. Neo-Durkheimian perspectives in the analysis of public or media rituals in sport were criticized along similar lines during the 1970s and 1980s by writers who found inspiration in the writings of Antonio Gramsci and/or in the critical cultural studies perspective developed by Stuart Hall (e.g., Hargreaves, 1982; Jhally, 1989).

Couldry seems unaware of the voluminous writing in sport studies on relations between media, ideology and symbolic power, much of which has been influenced by issues and debates associated with various forms of neo-Marxist analysis. When he discusses critical perspectives on media rituals more broadly he paints all Marxian-inspired perspectives with a functionalist brush, suggesting that they simply reproduce similar problems to those found in Durkheim. In Couldry's view, the Marxist attempt to reveal ideological "processes that mystify an underlying level of domination" (2003, p. 44), and thereby promote capitalist stability, is reminiscent of the way symbolic systems in Durkheimian analysis ostensibly serve the interests of social solidarity. The only difference is one form of solidarity is seen as inherently mystifying and negative, while the other is seen as inherently enriching and positive. According to Couldry (ibid., pp. 45–46), both perspectives reproduce "the myth" of an existing "natural centre."

We have some sympathy with this argument but, at best, it is a partial characterization. Couldry ignores several decades of Marxian political and cultural analysis focused on class conflict surrounding the "making" of culture (Thompson, 1968), class struggles over language and symbolic forms in the production of ideology (Hall, 1982), and the suturing of various class and non-class discourses into a hegemonic discursive formation (Hall *et al.*, 1979). The rejection of functionalism in economically reductionist Marxist accounts of ideology was a pivotal moment in the development of all of these analyses. In contrast, Couldry's "post-Durkheimian" mode of analysis is sensitive to the "field of conflict" in social life and to inequalities in symbolic resources and power (Couldry, 2003, p. 137), but he is extremely vague about how media events or *symbolic* power connect to, or constitute, other forms of power, such as economic and political power, or how the exercise of symbolic power might be implicated in producing or reproducing various relations of domination.

Through the 1980s and 1990s, neo-Durkheimian accounts of media rituals, and of the sacred or ceremonial meanings of media events, were refreshed through the work of Jeffrey Alexander and his colleagues, who sought to emphasize the importance of affect and shared meanings in plural civil societies in the West against decades of functionalist and economically reductive social criticism (cf. Dayan and Katz, 1988). As part of this project, Alexander and his colleagues sought to differentiate what they saw as "a strong" research program for cultural studies, heavily focused on depth interpretation, against the supposedly "weak" quasi-Marxian undertones that ran strongly through much of the writing of that era (Alexander and Smith, 2001). While the theoretical inflections sometimes varied, new writing on "globalization" in the late 1980s and 1990s promoted a similar emphasis on the complexity of shared cultural meanings in mediated rituals, especially in conjunction with global media and mega-events.

Roland Robertson's influential theoretical work on globalization (Robertson, 1990) is notable here, as is Maurice Roche's early work on mega-events and modernity (Roche, 2000). Both Robertson and Roche position their projects as an attempt to go beyond what they believe are the limitations of reductive Marxian political economy perspectives on globalization, global culture and global events. In Robertson's words (1990, p. 28), it was necessary to leave behind the "economistic" focus of Marxian World Systems theories, or theories of media or cultural imperialism, to emphasize "culture and the agency aspect of the making of the global system." Roche (2000) argued similarly for a more "complex" analysis of how mega-events can be associated with globalization, and especially with the formation of "global culture." In making this argument, he argued for the continued applicability of Dayan and Katz's (2002) analysis of "media events" and noted how the sense of community and shared identity evident in earlier mega-events must now be understood as part of a global circuit of cultural exchanges – a "transnational and universal dimension of human society that can be experienced in dramatic and memorable ways both by performers and by media spectators" (ibid., p. 2).

This sense of cultural globalism is highlighted more recently by Couldry and his colleague Andreas Hepp (2010), who follow Rothenbuhler's earlier lead in labeling critics who warn of the negative implications of media events as overly cynical (Hepp and Couldry, 2010). Like Roche, they argue for a more plural reading that situates national media events within globalization and new forms of "deterritorialized" social connectivity made available through the expansion of the Internet and other new media technologies (ibid., p. 10). As media have increasingly become complex transcultural phenomena, Hepp and Couldry argue there are "thickenings of media communication, produced not only by the mass media (television, radio) but also by the Internet and other digital media, covering different forms of 'mediated quasi-interaction'" (ibid., pp. 10–11). In reformulating the media events thesis for the digital age, Hepp and Couldry propose a pluralistic "global-transcultural frame." Focus is placed on *multiple* "constructions of a common 'we,' and of many varied national, ethnic, religious, subcultural and other voicings of that 'we.' The key to critical analysis, in their view, lies with a layered contextual understanding of how these cultural thickenings 'are constructed as centering' through the operation of symbolic power" (ibid., p. 12).

At first sight, this seems reminiscent of a Marxian view of ideology, except that the "centering" discussed by Hepp and Couldry is not actively connected to the critique of domination or inequality as lived material experience. We certainly agree that dramatic storytelling is constitutive of mega-events and that multiple and variegated social actors are hard at work trying to assert their version of common sense, in an environment of "cultural thickenings." Hepp and Couldry's analysis is bolstered in this regard by their recognition that media events are not always socially harmonizing and often promote conflict. Here, they play the neo-Durkheimian game in reverse, where the media event appears to promote multiple forms of identification and social solidarity that sometimes come into conflict with one another.

However, Durkheimian analysis lacks theoretical sensitivity to the existence of significant contradictions and inequities in society between these forms of identification and solidarity. By contrast, a focus on contradiction, inequality and conflict is a core idea in Marxian analysis where social classes, for example, can become aware of their interests in various ways, inevitably involving means of communication, and fight it out with other classes, ideologically, politically and economically (cf. Marx, 1850/1964). At the same time, Marxian analysis attempts to draw attention to situations where class interests are able to represent themselves relatively successfully as if they were in the general interest. This latter anti-Durkheimian argument is evident in early critical work undertaken on the Calgary Stampede and Grey Cup football festival in Canada by Ossenberg and Listiak. In their view, a neo-Durkheimian focus on social integration has an underlying ideological character because it misrepresents middle class "binges" of identification and solidarity as if they were in the interest of *everyone* who lives in the city (Listiak, 1974; Ossenberg, 1969).

Acknowledging conflicts, disruptions, and differences in media rituals and events, as Hepp and Couldry do, adds a vital degree of fluidity to the neo-Durkheimian or post-Durkheimian analysis. In a similar sense, James Carey has drawn attention to rituals of excommunication, shame and status degradation, and how they can define "the permissible range of social discourse," and the possible "consequences for transgressing this range" (1998, p. 55). After surveying the recent history of media events and mega-events, both Dayan and Katz concede a similar point (Dayan, 2010; Katz and Liebes, 2007), citing the increased frequency and scale of the live broadcasting of terror and war (Katz and Liebes, 2007), and how the ubiquity and mobility of "new media has reintroduced individualized reception." In Dayan's memorable phrase, "Agon is back" (2010, p. 27):

> Media events produce cynical behaviors. They foster rather than suspend disbelief. Spectators and publics act like Clausewitzian strategists. While they do so, they are themselves being negotiated, acquired, or stolen. Media events

still mobilize huge audiences, but they have lost a large part of their enchant-ment. Bureaucratically managed, they are an exploited resource within a political economy of collective attention. Their magic is dissipating. They have become strategic venues.

(ibid., p. 28)

This recognition of media events as "strategic," and as an "exploited resource with a political economy of collective attention," is insightful, although the point is not developed further. More importantly, Dayan's point is arguably cynical in its own right because it implies that audiences are expressing narrow, self-interested, motives for protesting, rather than legitimate grievances. There are echoes here of Durkheim's concerns, made a century earlier, about the anomic character of modern life. Yet, what Dayan sees as the dissipation "of magic" can be interpreted from a more critical perspective as the unraveling of ideology. Having conceded that there is now no guarantee that media events will assist with benign social inte-gration, Dayan and Katz fail to offer a satisfying solution to a range of other questions. If there is a visible struggle over social values, and if this plays out, in part, within large-scale mega-events, how does this occur? What resources are available to social actors in such struggles and are they equally available? How are these competing narratives produced? Through what circuits are they relayed and how do the instrumental efforts of state and corporate actors intervene? Do some narratives count more than others? If so, why, and whose interests do they serve? Is there a greater market in opinion, or a greater economic market, for some narra-tives more than others?

Göran Bolin (2010) attempts to answer some of these questions by trying to move beyond suggestions that media events have been "hijacked" by state, media or other social actors. He argues instead for a dialectical approach in which "inter-national events are orchestrated with the media in mind" (ibid., p. 128). The modern Olympics, he points out, "did not exist before mass press towards the end of the 1800s" (ibid.). Bolin rightly criticizes Couldry in addition to Dayan and Katz for taking a media–centric focus. Media play a principal role in helping to shape the social order, but they do so in intimate relations with the market, the state, and corporate actors. These relations are mutually constitutive. For example, Armand Mattelart has shown how the "modern" Olympic Games developed their distin-ctive cultural form in close association with the emergence of nineteenth century industrial exhibitions as new "spaces of spectacle" (Mattelart, 1996, pp. 112–132). How can one distinguish the power of the media to produce reality from other powers that cooperate in the production?

Horne and Manzenreiter (2006) argue that the emergence of sporting mega-events as global economic and cultural behemoths in the late twentieth century occurred through a dense matrix of intersecting tendencies and powers. They cite (1) improvements in communication technologies (and especially digital tech-nologies) that allowed for the production and valorization of global audiences of unprecedented size, (2) the growth and integration of a global promotional (and, we would add, digitally networked) "sport–media–business alliance," and (3) broad changes in economic and political global networks that allowed mega-events to become "valuable promotional opportunities for cities and regions" in competition with each other for global investment capital, international status, and the opportunity to brand themselves as world class tourist destinations. We would add that these changes occurred in the context of an accompanying set of transitions associated with the spread of neoliberal ideology on a global scale in the late twentieth century, including (a) widespread market deregulation and the opening of borders to increasingly mobile capital, (b) a strengthening of transnational corporate power, and (c) a near global assault on labor and the welfare state; and new international geopolitical struggles and alignments (cf. Gruneau and Horne, 2016, pp. 8–18).

Couldry (2003) acknowledges that media today are so embedded in society that they can *only* be separated from it analytically. The key point, in his view, is to acknowledge the depth and significance of symbolic power. However, it seems more accurate to analyze media and sporting mega-events as part of a fluid *ensemble* of institutions and practices involving mutually constitutive relations of both symbolic *and* material powers. Acknowledging this complexity may well lead us to abandon the concept of distinctive and exceptional "media events" altogether. No large-scale sporting event today is *planned* without the media in mind, and no sporting mega-event is *staged* without the presence and influence of networked global media in a variety of digital, audio and visual platforms and formats. Similarly, there are few circumstances in contemporary life other than sporting mega-events that provide such diverse and lucrative opportunities for synergies between media and marketing interests on a global scale and for valorizing global audiences.

Global competition between cities and regions for sporting mega-events – and between corporate media and marketing interests for media rights to such events – has led to a considerable cluttering of global event schedules, making the idea of distinctive "high holidays" of communication more difficult to sustain than in the past. There continues to be a special atmosphere associated with obvious top tier mega-events such as the Olympics, men's soccer World Cup, and the US football Super Bowl, with mainstream media coverage reproducing this aura. However, a host of lower tier sporting "mega-events" have also become important strategically, economically and symbolically at regional and international levels and draw intense media attention. Examples include the European Championship (Euro), COPA America, and African Nations Championship in soccer, the Pan American, Asian, and Commonwealth Games, and World Cups in rugby and cricket. Moreover, digital media today have an omnipresent character, offering an endless stream of observations and commentaries to all these events. In a global capitalist world where many commodities are increasingly ephemeral, the production of such highly mediated events in many parts of the world has come to rival the more traditional making of things. As this has occurred, the lines between economy and culture, and between mediation and experience, have become almost impossible to disentangle.

Sporting mega-events have also become sites for intense and highly politicized contestation, with media playing a paradoxical role. On the one hand, they allow global visibility for oppositional groups who attempt to "seize the platform" of the event (Price, 2008); on the other hand, media also valorize the audiences that observe, comment on, and react to these protest groups and their actions (Compton, 2016). In that sense, conflict narratives in the lead up to the event, about such things as LGBT activism, prior to the 2014 Winter Olympics in Sochi, or human rights abuses, as in Qatar's World Cup preparations, or political turmoil in Brazil prior to the 2014 men's football World Cup inevitably become vital parts of an overall political economy of collective attention. But, these conflict narratives and sources of social unrest also appear to have an irrepressible character. Sporting mega-events have become much more than sites for expressions of aggravated individual cynicism; rather, they are now among the world's most prominent forums to protest and debate the irrationalities of neoliberal capitalist globalization with its accompanying modes of exclusion and marginalization.

Conclusion

Over the last decade, critical writing on relations between media and mega-events has moved in a decidedly critical direction. In this transition, the neo-Durkheimian underpinning of the "media events" tradition has been increasingly challenged as a standpoint for social analysis. More broadly, the line of social analysis running from Katz's and Shils's early work in the 1950s and 1960s, to Katz and Dayan's work in the 1980s and 1990s, and to contemporary proponents of the media events perspective, has not offered an effective standpoint for analyzing some of the most pressing global issues associated with contemporary media and mega-events, including those that are built around sport. When criticism does occur from this perspective it tends to express a rather antiquated concern for the "de-ritualized" character of modern life with accompanying concerns over an amorphous and broad breakdown in values.

Notwithstanding the work of writers such as Couldry, Hepp and Rothenbuhler, the critical turn today appears to be moving toward a recovery and reconsideration of ideas more closely associated with a Marxian tradition of social criticism. Commenting on their perception of a new critical mood evident in academic research after the global financial crisis of 2008, Fuchs and Mosco (2012) claim boldly: "Marx is back." But, to say that "Marx is back," or that he *should* be back, immediately raises the question of which Marx we are talking about. We want to conclude by arguing that the social theory of media and mega-events today needs a dynamic neo-Marxian political economy that leaves nineteenth century Hegelian teleology and Marxist functionalism behind and is open to the analysis of multiple sources of identification and domination (cf. Anderson, 2010). But, at the same time, we believe Marxism's insistence on situating every practice in the ensemble of social relations that make up the production and reproduction of social life is absolutely fundamental in order to move beyond the media-centric character of earlier analyses.

An important part of this project requires ongoing assessment of the role played by relations between media and mega-events in the promotion of capitalist exchange on a global scale, thereby expanding or contracting possibilities and opportunities available for various groups, classes, and nations (cf. Gruneau and Horne, 2016). To cite just a few issues, many of which are covered elsewhere in this book, this would include the analysis of:

1   how audiences for mega-events are *both* objects *and* subjects of the production of sporting spectacle, for example, through the commodification of audience agency (e.g., on Facebook or Twitter) and the networked integration of social media;
2   the acceleration of capitalist accumulation through the growing emphasis on the production of events as opposed to material goods;
3   media discourses associated with mega-events as opportunities both to frame public rituals in the direction of neoliberal values and to resist such framing;
4   the financialization of mega-events and the short-term horizon of interests at play in the absorption and circulation of capital;
5   mega-events as "states of exception" which set in motion often savage initiatives of neoliberal urban development, such as the forced "pacification" of favelas prior to the 2014 World Cup in Rio de Janeiro;
6   mega-events as "globalizing" sites of labor exploitation, as was documented by the large number of work-related deaths connected to the building of stadiums for the upcoming men's soccer World Cup in Qatar;
7   mega-events as constitutive features of global power shifts and reactions to them; and
8   mega-events as opportunities to promote clientalism and corruption – such as FIFA's longstanding pay-to-play scandals.

In summary, if Agon associated with media and mega-events is indeed "back," we need a renewed critical political economy perspective to examine and explain it.

Acknowledgements

The authors would like to thank Enda Brophy and Scott Timcke for their comments on an earlier draft of this chapter.

References

Alexander, J.C. and Smith, P. (2001). The strong program in cultural sociology. In J. Turner (ed.), *The handbook of sociological theory* (135–150). New York: Kluwer.
Altheide, D. and Snow. R. (1979). *Media logic.* Beverly Hills, CA: Sage.
Anderson, K.B. (2010). *Marx at the margins: On nationalism, ethnicity, and non-Western societies.* Chicago, IL: University of Chicago Press.

Bolin, G. (2010). Media events, Eurovision and societal centers. In N. Couldry, A. Hepp and F. Krotz (eds), *Media events in a global age* (pp. 124–138). New York: Routledge.

Brantlinger, P. (1983). *Bread and circuses: Theories of mass culture as social decay*. Ithaca, NY: Cornell University Press.

Brownell, S. (2008). *The 1904 Anthropology Days and Olympic Games: Sport, race and American imperialism*. Lincoln, NB: University of Nebraska Press.

Carey, J. (1998). Political ritual on television: Episodes in the history of shame, degradation and excommunication. In T. Liebes and J. Curran (eds), *Media, ritual and identity* (pp. 42–70). New York: Routledge.

Compton, J. (2004). *The integrated news spectacle: A political economy of cultural performance*. New York: Peter Lang.

Compton, J. (2016). Mega-events, media and the integrated world of global spectacle. In R. Gruneau and J. Horne (eds), *Mega-events and globalization: Capital and spectacle in a changing world order* (pp. 48–64). New York: Routledge.

Couldry, N. (2003). *Media rituals: A critical introduction*. London: Routledge.

Cui, X. (2013). Media events are still alive: The opening ceremony of the Beijing Olympics as media ritual. *International Journal of Communication*, 7, 1220–1235.

Dayan, D. (2010). Beyond media events: Disenchantment, derailment, disruption. In N. Couldry, A. Hepp and F. Krotz (eds), *Media events in a global age* (pp. 23–31). New York: Routledge.

Dayan, D. and Katz, E. (1988). Articulating consensus: The ritual and rhetoric of media events. In J. Alexander (ed.), *Durkheimian sociology: Cultural studies* (pp. 161–186). Cambridge: Cambridge University Press.

Dayan, D. and Katz, E. (1992). *Media events: The live broadcasting of history*. Cambridge, MA: Harvard University Press.

Durkheim, E. (1915). *The elementary forms of religious life* (trans. J. Swain). London: Allen & Unwin.

Fuchs, C. and Mosco, V. (2012). Introduction—Marx is back: The importance of Marxist theory and research for critical communications study today. *Triple C* (special issue), *10*(2), 127–148.

Gruneau, R. (2006). Amateurism as a sociological problem: Some reflections inspired by Eric Dunning. *Sport in Society: Cultures, Commerce, Media, Politics*, *9*(4), 559–582.

Gruneau, R. and Horne, J. (2016). (eds), *Mega-events and globalization: Capital and spectacle in a changing world order*. London: Routledge.

Hall, S. (1982). The rediscovery of ideology: Return of the repressed in media studies. In M. Gurevitch and J. Woolacott (eds), *Culture, society and the media* (pp. 52–86). London: Methuen.

Hall, S., Critcher, C., Jefferson, T., Clarke, J. and Roberts, B. (1979). *Policing the crisis: Mugging, the state and law and order*. London: Macmillan.

Hargreaves, J. (1982) Sport and hegemony: Some theoretical problems. In H. Cantelon and R. Gruneau (eds), *Sport, culture and the modern state* (pp. 103–140). Toronto: University of Toronto Press.

Hepp, A. and Couldry, N. (2010). Introduction: Media events in globalized media cultures. In N. Couldry, A. Hepp and F. Krotz (eds), *Media events in a global age* (pp. 1–20). New York: Routledge.

Hoberman, J. (1986). *The Olympic crisis: Sport, politics, and the moral order*. New Rochelle, NY: Aristide O. Caratzas.

Horne, J. and Manzenreiter, W. (2006). An introduction to the sociology of sports mega-events. *The Sociological Review*, s2, 1–24.

Jhally, S. (1989). Cultural studies and the sports media complex. In L. Wenner (ed.) *Media, sports and society* (pp. 70–93). Newbury Park, CA: Sage.

Katz, E. (1980). Media events: The sense of occasion. *Studies in Visual Anthropology, 6,* 84–89.

Katz, E. and Dayan, D. (1985). Media events: On the experience of not being there. *Religion, 15,* 305–314.

Katz, E. and Lazersfeld, P.F. (1955). *Personal influence: The part played by people in the flow of mass communications.* Glencoe, IL: Free Press.

Katz, E. and Liebes, T. (2007). No more peace! How disaster, terror and war have upstaged media events. *International Journal of Communication, 1,* 157–166.

Listiak, A. (1974). Legitimate "deviance" and social class: Bar behavior during Grey Cup week. *Sociological Focus, 7*(3), 13–44.

Luhmann, N. (2000). *The reality of the mass media* (trans. K. Cross). Stanford, CA: Stanford University Press.

Lukes, S. (1977). *Essays in social theory.* London: Macmillan Press.

MacAloon, J. (1984). Olympic Games and the theory of spectacle in modern societies. In J. MacAloon (ed.), *Rite, drama, festival, spectacle: Rehearsals toward a theory of cultural performance* (pp. 241–280). Philadelphia, PA: Institute for the Study of Human Issues.

Marx, K. (1850/1964). *The class struggles in France.* New York: International Publishers (orig. published 1850).

Mattelart, A. (1996). *The invention of communication* (trans. S. Emanuel). Minneapolis, MN: University of Minnesota Press.

Ossenberg, R. (1969). Social class and bar behavior during the Calgary Stampede. *Human Organization, 28*(1), 29–34.

Pooley, J. (2006). Fifteen pages that shook the field: *Personal Influence,* Edward Shils and the remembered history of mass communication research. *Annals of the American Academy of Political and Social Science, 608* (November), 1–27.

Price, M. (2008). On seizing the Olympic platform. In M. Price and D. Dayan (eds), *Owning the Olympics: Narratives of the new China* (pp. 86–114). Ann Arbor, MI: University of Michigan Press.

Robertson, R. (1990). Mapping the global condition: Globalization as the central concept. *Theory, Culture and Society, 7*(2/3), 15–30.

Roche, M. (2000). *Mega-events and modernity: Olympics and expos in the growth of global culture.* London: Routledge.

Roche, M. (2006). Mega-events and modernity revisited: Globalization and the case of the Olympics. *The Sociological Review, 54*(s2), 25–40.

Rothenbuhler, E.W. (1988). The living room celebration of the Olympic Games." *Journal of Communication, 38*(4), 61–81.

Rothenbuhler, E.W. (1993). Argument for a Durkheimian theory of the communicative." *Journal of Communication, 43*(3), 158–163.

Rothenbuhler, E.W. (2010). From media events to ritual to communicative form. In N. Couldry, A. Hepp and F. Krotz (eds), *Media events in a global age* (pp. 61–75). New York: Routledge.

Shils, E. (1962). The theory of mass society. *Diogenes, 39,* 45–66.

Shils, E. and Young, M. (1953). The meaning of the coronation. *Sociological Review, 1,* 63–81.

Simmel, G. (1900/1978). *The philosophy of money* (trans. T. Bottomore and D. Frisby). London: Routledge & Kegan Paul.

Swingewood, A. (1977). *The myth of mass culture.* London: Macmillan, 1977.

Thompson, E.P. (1968). *The making of the English working class.* Harmondsworth: Pelican Books.

Tilly, C. (1981). *As sociology meets history*. New York: Academic Press.

Turner, V. (1974). *Dramas, fields, and metaphors: Symbolic action in human society*. Ithaca, NY: Cornell University Press.

Turner, V. (1984). Liminality and the performative genres. In J. MacAloon (ed.), *Rite, drama, festival, spectacle: Rehearsals toward a theory of cultural performance* (pp. 19–41). Philadelphia, PA: Institute for the Study of Human Issues.

Weber, M. (1958). The three types of legitimate rule (English translation). *Berkeley Publications in Society and Institutions*, 4(1): 1–11.

Young, D.C. (1984). *The Olympic myth of Greek amateur athletics*. Chicago, IL: Ares Publishers.

PART II

Megamediasport event studies

4

TWENTY-EIGHT OLYMPIC SUMMERS

Historical and methodological reflections on understanding the Olympic mega-event

Alan Tomlinson

A core idea in theoretical and definitional debate concerning the role and significance of media in the modern world is that the media are vital – not merely
optional – to the institutional processes and practices constituting a particular
sphere of culture and society. Stig Hjarvard (2013, p. 44) calls "mediatization" a
new theoretical perspective which acknowledges the central "*transformative
influence of the media*" in particular spheres such as politics, religion, play and
habitus. The concept of mediation, with its emphasis on a relatively clear and
direct – though never simply linear – transmitting process, gives way to this
newer conceptual approach as a recognition of the media's generative role
"whereby culture and society to an increasing degree become dependent on the
media and their logic" (ibid., p. 17). High-profile and large-scale events in the
global cultural calendar – and the case we are concerned with here is that of the
Summer Olympic Games from 1896 to 2016 – are, in this sense, no longer
merely mediated by a ragtag band of marginal journalists reporting to a small and
indifferent national public such as was the case in Athens in the inaugural
modern Olympic Games; rather, they are a phenomenon in themselves, attracting
armies of correspondents, broadcasters, communicators and commentators
making sense of not only the outcome of sporting encounters but also of
competing agendas, ambitions and aspirations of nations, and representing
increasingly powerful media institutions and conglomerates with a global reach.
Contrast the presence of 5,800 accredited press journalists and many thousands
more broadcasters, new media reporters and citizen journalists at Rio de Janeiro
in 2016 with the 11 journalists in attendance at the inaugural 1896 Games in
Athens. Sports mega-events are, in this sense, mediatized in a "process characterized by a *duality*, in that the media have become integrated into the operations
of other social institutions and cultural spheres, while also acquiring the status of
social institutions *in their own right*" (ibid., p. 17).

The fact that the Olympics, and equally high-profile events such as the men's football World Cup, command the biggest global audiences across an expanding range of platforms – in turn attracting some of the highest levels of investment in event-sponsorship in history – is illustrative of the influence and the hold of the mediatization process on the sports mega-event in the global media landscape of the early twenty-first century. Of course, particular modes of consumption can alter the balance between the formal elements in any such equation, and the explosion of digital media into the consumer–media landscape is a development with such equilibrium-disturbing potential; the smartphone of 2016 is a very long way indeed from the traditional television screen (Frandsen, 2014). In the first four of the eight selected cases considered in the empirical section of this chapter, the Summer Olympic Games 1924–1936, there were no television screens to speak of, though elements of a mediatized sporting sphere were beginning to take shape. Prior to consideration of these cases, and of the Games of 1984, 1992, 2008 and 2012, I consider questions of background, scale and historical periodization.

History and method

The Olympic Games have been held – apart from the disruption of two World Wars – in an uninterrupted cycle of summers that straddles three centuries. Just one year – 1916 – was lost to the first of these conflicts, and two – 1940 and 1944 – to the second. This is hardly a novel observation but it is an important fact, allowing the IOC to construct a solipsistic celebration of a distinctive institutional and cultural history. That the Games could draw upon a classical cultural source for inspiration allowed its founder Pierre de Coubertin to employ a trans-temporal and trans-historical rhetoric in his campaigning for support for the initiative, drawing on the heroic qualities of a past epoch and the purported relevance of those idealized qualities for the future of a conflicted and troubled world. Generations of invaluable Olympic scholarship and research have contributed to our understanding of this astonishing and resilient historical narrative, and to the contribution of societies of all kinds to the sustaining of the de Coubertinesque vision. It is not the intention here to review or evaluate such work, were that even possible, but to see in the ruptures and continuities of the Olympic narrative how the blend of economic, political, cultural, and social interests and institutions has been regularly remade as the Olympic phenomenon has ground its way to the centre of the contemporary media landscape, to its unprecedentedly prominent place in the mediatization of sport. To grasp such ruptures and continuities, the concept of "chronotope" may prove helpful.

The term "chronotope", as used by the Russian literary critic Mikail Bakhtin (1981), refers to a socio-cultural formation that comprises what historian Peter Burke (2006, p. 231) nicely labels, with reference to the entity "Europe", "a space-time package". Bakhtin's book-length essay on the chronotope was written in 1937–1938, its "concluding remarks" of more than 15 pages written in 1973, just a couple of years before Bakhtin's death. His focus was upon literary works, arguing that chronotopes "are the organizing centers for the fundamental narrative events of the novel ... the place where the knots of narrative are tied and untied" (Bakhtin, 1981, p. 250). He contrasts the works of novelist Dostoevsky with those of fellow Russian Tolstoy, for whom "the fundamental chronotope is biographical time, which flows smoothly in the spaces – the interior spaces – of townhouses and estates of the nobility" (ibid.). For Dostoevsky, "time is essentially instantaneous ... as if it has no duration" (ibid., p. 248), whereas "Tolstoy loves duration, the stretching-out of time" (ibid., p. 249). Bakhtin points to biographical time and space as the primary chronotope in Tolstoy's work, followed by the chronotopes of nature, and idylls of the family and labour/peasant work (ibid., p. 250). The chronotope is, in a broad and simple sense, the framing – major or minor – theme of the writer's narrative.

More than just some free-floating literary theme, the chronotope is a specific temporal–spatial construction that gives meaning to the socio-cultural formation. For Bakhtin, temporal–spatial expression in the "form of a sign" (ibid., p. 258) is critical to the generation of meaning, and for meanings to enter our social experience. Paramount in Bakhtin's thinking is the recognition of the active role of listeners and readers in the generation of dialogical interactions: such dialogue "enters the world of the author, of the performer, and the world of the listeners and readers. And all these worlds are chronotopic as well" (ibid., p. 252). How, then, does this concept illuminate Olympic history?

What must be held in mind here, as we consider the equilibrium sought – and often achieved or established – by the IOC and Olympic movement, is how time and space are constantly reconfigured in an Olympiad and the staging of the Olympic event: history must be rendered relevant, time stands still via tradition and ritual while simultaneously chiming with the contemporary and the progressive; records are sought in a moral conundrum espousing the primacy of participation while rewarding the dominance of the champion or victor. The Olympics comes into the media arena of its time with chronotopic baggage, ready to be remodelled and, in part, restructured, to suit the participants and onlookers of the particular time and place. As I have shown in studies of the Olympic spectacle, every Olympic ceremony is a "necessary arrogation" (Tomlinson, 1999), a reinterpretation for a time and place of a phenomenon that in its variously mediated or mediatized retelling and remaking, asserts a resilient chronotopic set of ideals alongside the values – new, novel or technologically innovative – that modern sport and nation-states contributing to the Olympic story so frequently seek to convey. It is necessary to recognize this interpretive premise for any adequate understanding of the series of 28 Olympic summers that have, to date, sustained the momentum of the Olympic phenomenon.

History, scale and more method

In its glossy booklet celebrating the completion of the centennial Olympics in Atlanta, Georgia, USA, in 1996, the International Olympic Committee (IOC) acknowledged its responsibility to cultivate a strong and reliable relationship with the media:

> Over almost one hundred years of history, from the eleven journalists who attended the first modern Olympic Games in Athens in 1896 to the 13,275 accredited for the Games in Atlanta in 1996, the IOC has been called upon to structure itself so as to be able to meet the professional needs of a group that is as large in numerical terms as that of the athletes and officials together.
>
> *(IOC, 1997, p. 75)*

There is an almost begrudging tone here, as if the media requests are a kind of intrusion in a private party – which, of course, is how the exclusive club of the great and the good initially saw things early on in modern Olympic history. The statement goes on to confirm that media relations had become for the century-old body a commitment as well as a chore and the "IOC has therefore provided itself with specialized commissions, whose role is to provide it with advice and to give organizing committees the benefit of the most appropriate opinions on how to meet the expectations of all forms of media" (ibid., p. 75). Commissions for the press, and for radio/television, had therefore become well-established aspects of the Olympic administrative apparatus, and they carried the responsibility "to provide media representatives during the conduct of the Games with appropriate centres and subcentres for their professional work, with the backup of proven technology, affordable and convenient accommodation and functionally reliable transportation" (ibid., p. 75).

The language of this commitment is plain, but ambitious in conception and implementation: "to reach all parts of the planet instantaneously" (ibid., p. 77) in the form of emotions, texts, images and sounds, in live or recorded/retrospective form. Eleven print journalists back in Athens in 1896 were penning idiosyncratic and marginal items for indifferent editors (unless these were Greek); in Atlanta, usurper of Athenian ambitions to stage the centennial event 100 years on from its inaugural contribution, the 13,000 plus media personnel were fuelling a global media machine in which the Games themselves had become an equal partner with the media in staging the international spectacle. It is in this sense that the biggest of national and international sporting mega-events have become mediatized, contributing alongside media institutions to the escalation of the transnational, global sporting calendar.

The sheer growth of the Olympics – in events, participants, partners (such as sponsors), media/broadcasting professionals, potential global audiences – has led to concern on the part of the IOC and other interests that things have grown too big: what the IOC itself began to call "gigantism". Long-term commentators on and statisticians of the Olympics, Wallechinsky and Loucky (2008), commented in their edition of *The Complete Book of the Olympics*, timed to coincide with the Beijing Summer Games: "Frankly, the issue of gigantism is somewhat over-stated" (ibid., p. 36). Some sports or events could be cut from the programme, they suggested; and pressure on the Olympic Village could be relieved by reducing the number of team officials and non-athletes: "Athletes need coaches, but the roster of Olympic participants is bloated with bureaucrats and hangers-on" (ibid.). There are initiatives in the Games that could be seen to address some of these issues; for instance the introduction at Rio 2016 of Rugby Sevens, rather than the dominant 15-per-side form, is an interesting and largely successful smaller-scale innovation. But the very fact of the escalating scale and profile of the Games – and its concomitant global viewing market – makes such obvious and simple downscaling next to impossible: the sheer size and claimed reach of the Games is what fuels the economy of the event, attracting with consistency the huge sums from the broadcasters and the sponsors. The event is not just there any longer as an object reported, transmitted and beamed to the world by a selective media; rather, all media must aspire to if not actually be there at the event, at a time when the Olympics themselves are mediatized and, as such, integrated with media institutions in a partnership of cultural production and reportage.

Things were not always thus, as we know from the tiny media presence at the first Olympic Games. The 28 Summer Olympic Games might, therefore, be sub-divided into three categories. As with any act of historical periodization, temporal borders might be blurred and there is no definitive moment, date or year when one category simply transformed into another. But there are dimensions of scale, profile and characteristics that permit a useful classification, and this lends itself to a form of tabulation of three phases.

Overall, we see in this categorization a shifting balance between the cultural, the economic, and the political. This is not to say that the Games existed in some sort of pre-lapsarian idyll of innocence until Californian razzmatazz appeared on the scene; that there was no political rivalry at the early Games (witness the Anglo-

TABLE 4.1 Three main phases in the growth and expansion of the Summer Olympic Games

Olympic Games phases	Olympic Games within phases
Phase 1, 1896–1928: Socio-political project on modest economic scale (8 host cities)	1896 Athens; 1900 Paris; 1904 St. Louis; 1908 London; 1912 Stockholm; 1920 Antwerp; 1924 Paris; 1928 Amsterdam
Phase 2, 1932–1980: Political intensification interrelated with international political dynamics and increasingly sophisticated media technologies (11 host cities)	1932 Los Angeles; 1936 Berlin; 1948 London; 1952 Helsinki; 1956 Melbourne; 1960 Rome; 1964 Tokyo; 1968 Mexico; 1972 Munich; 1976 Montreal; 1980 Moscow
Phase 3, 1984–2016: Commodification of the Olympic brand and media product through the global reach of capital (9 host cities)	1984 Los Angeles; 1988 Seoul; 1992 Barcelona; 1996 Atlanta; 2000 Sydney; 2004 Athens; 2008 Beijing; 2012 London; 2016 Rio de Janeiro

Source: This table is a modified version of the untabulated discussion in Tomlinson (2005, pp. 51–56, 60).

American rivalries at the London 1908 Games); or that the 1936 Berlin Olympics were not a watershed in the media technology applied to the mass sporting spectacle (by film-maker Leni Riefenstahl, via her patron Josef Goebbels, the Nazi Party's master of propaganda). Trends are tendencies, not unambiguous trajectories. But this sort of periodization enables us to identify turning points, shifting balances of interest and influence. And it is not at all coincidental that the two pivotal Games were in the USA, on the edge of the New World where the City of Angels was developing the world's biggest dream factory. Los Angeles modernized and politicized the Games in 1932; with the continuity of the Games in serious jeopardy after the human rights crisis of Mexico, the terrorist crisis of Munich, the fiscal and boycott crisis of Montreal, and the Cold War boycott of Moscow, the entrepreneurs of California could rip apart the Olympic rulebook and remake the hosting model.

In this sense, a periodizing take on the history of the modern Olympics needs to be informed at not just the level of the individual event, but in the context of the process of what France's Annales School called the *longue durée* (long duration).[1] In the context of fierce intellectual debates concerning the challenge of the new social sciences to the established discipline of history, Ferdinand Braudel (1969, pp. 79–80) wrote: "A sociology of events ... does not record the direction, the speed or slowness, the ascent or descent of the movement which carries along any social phenomenon".[2] Social scientists, he believed, should engage with "the long time span" (ibid.). The historian – and, certainly, the historically informed sociologist – should explore the "dialectic of duration" that is crucial for grasping "the crux of social reality ... this living, intimate, infinitely repeated opposition between the instant of time and that time which flows only slowly" (ibid., p. 26). Braudel championed a history of the *longue durée*, extended century-plus time spans beyond the traditional historical focus on the single event. The latter generated too often a "headlong, dramatic, breathless rush" (ibid., p. 27) of a narrative. He also identified a third kind of historical narrative, that of the conjuncture, often a cycle, from a decade up to half-century. But any such new history of conjunctures, he observed, must make up a whole orchestra of the different rhythms of a society and its culture. The move between the *longue durée* and the event, the recognition of a conjunctural narrative, allows us to characterize phases and periods; for instance, the development of European sport in the first third of the twentieth century can be seen as an intertwining rhythm of processes: "internationalism/incipient global-ization; intensifying mediatization; emergent individualism; the rise of celebrity and consumption" (Tomlinson and Young, 2011, p. 423). Such a characterization provides the possibility of identifying, within the historical dynamics of change and continuity, processes of transition between and across, for instance, the phases identified in Table 4.1.

For Braudel (1975), the history of the *longue durée* is the opposite of the history of events: "Social science has almost what amounts to a horror of the event. And not without some justification, for the short time span is the most capricious and the most delusive of all" (ibid., p. 28). But the historian, Braudel believed, must be aware of the validity and interrelatedness of all three of these time dimensions. He consistently argued for a balanced analytical approach to the understanding of the long-term structure of societies and a focus upon the shorter-term realities of the conjuncture. A focus upon the individual event could be exciting but also dangerous and misleading; as he put it in the first volume of *The Mediterranean*, we "must learn to distrust this history with its still burning passions" (ibid., p. 21).[3] The challenge remains, though, of integrating the close-reading of the event into the analysis of the conjuncture. Alongside a theoretical-cum-pragmatic recognition of the centrality of the chronotype in socio-cultural and political-economic formations and constructions, this provides a fruitful conceptual and analytical toolbox for an understanding of the long-term continuities and the temporal transformations in the historical articulations and manifestations of the phenomenon of the Olympics.

An overview of the history of the modern Olympics is best understood, following such analytical lines of thinking, through a periodization of its 120-year long history from Athens to Rio de Janeiro: 28 Olympic summers but understandable – in terms of identifiable cycles of determination and values such as those indicated in Table 4.1 above – cycles of 32, 53 and 35 years respectively (for the second and third phases, the 3 years following the end of the previous phase have been calculated into the sum of the emerging phase or new cycle). Such periodization connects the event with the process, the particular with the overarching. It is not watertight, nor are such analytical constructions intended to be. For instance, a version of Phase 3 is to be found in Jules Boykoff's (2014) synthesizing concept and definition of "celebration capitalism", the component parts of which are: "lopsided public–private partnerships; festive commercialism; the security industry windfall; feel-good sustainability rhetoric; and a media-fostered political-economic spectacle" (ibid., p. 23). Boykoff states explicitly that this model of the Olympics "did not materialize overnight" but "developed incrementally as the Olympic Games evolved and as the International Olympic Committee's power expanded" (ibid.). He notes that the Los Angeles Games of 1932, in its innovations, was important in "charting out some of the key tenets of celebration capitalism" (ibid., p. 26), though the periodization offered in this chapter marks Los Angeles's second Olympic summer as the pivotal transformative moment/event that marked the emergence of a distinct conjunctural cycle, resonating with Boykoff's model of celebration capitalism.

The historical and methodological points discussed above inform consideration of the Games covered in the following section: from Phase 1, the Paris 1924 and, in lesser detail, the Amsterdam 1928 Games; from Phase 2, the Los Angeles 1932, and, in a general commentary, the Berlin 1936 Games; and from Phase 3, Los Angeles 1984, Barcelona 1992, and, summatively, Beijing 2008 and London 2012. Each Olympic Games has its own chronotopic characteristics, as a necessary arrogation of the Olympic project and rhetoric in the particular historical moment and geo-political space. Yet the continuities have meanings, connections of generative influence, spawning a genealogical legacy of inherited meanings, values, claims, and ideologies. Engaging with the selected Games, their media profiles and values underlying particular events, from these analytical perspectives and interpretive debates, provides illuminating material for consideration of the ways in which the development and expansion of the Summer Olympics has been shaped, re-shaped and remade, becoming intensifyingly mediatized, and passing through transitional processes along the way.

Transition 1: From Phase 1 to Phase 2

Phase 1

Paris 1924

The Paris 1924 Olympics Press Commission accredited 724 journalists, around 675 of whom actively reported on the events (Official Olympic Report – Paris, 1924, pp. 806–813). These were – for the most part, after the USA presence of 45 press personnel – dominated by the European written press, best represented by, after the host nation France (182), Great Britain (40) and then Spain (36); and, from the east of Europe, Hungary and Czechoslovakia (the USSR of course rejected the Olympian concept at that time). The representation of the media also shows the unsurprisingly heightened interest of the journalists from across the Olympic city's own country. However complex, sophisticated, and technologically advanced Olympic media coverage has become, however global the participatory and spectator bases, a host city will still generate disproportionate coverage and stories that pitch the spectacle to the host audience more than to the heterogeneous worldwide audience. The Paris media profile was essentially parochial, even though the event had 3,000 plus athlete-participants, a figure not exceeded until Berlin 1936. National pride and the boosting of the home population's sense of identity with the Games were the chronotopic elements of Paris 1924.

Amsterdam 1928

Very similar in scale to the Paris Games, Amsterdam's 1928 Games provided for 600 journalists in the stadium's Press Stand, though at events elsewhere the smaller press stands had limited capacity: 261 at fencing, 138 at wrestling and weight-lifting, and 196 at swimming (Tomlinson, 2005, pp. 52–53). Typewriters, writing spaces and some telephone booths were also provided (Official Olympic Report – Amsterdam, 1928, p. 247).

Visiting journalists were seen as a source of "propaganda made for the Games" (ibid., p. 255), the event offering a vehicle for "occasional propagative articles on Holland in general and Amsterdam in particular" (ibid., p. 253). However modestly, a communicative modernity, plus a self-serving form of image-management, defined the chronotope of Amsterdam 1928.

Phase 2

Los Angeles 1932

Although Los Angeles (LA) was, in statistical terms, a smaller event than its five predecessors as host cities, it was significant in its conceptualization of the Games and its explicitly political rationale, in marking the event's importance in the immediate years following the Great Crash of 1929 (Tomlinson, 2006). The Organizing Committee saw the press as pivotal to the staging of the event, and the Press Department was the first organized department, set up in December 1929: "to serve as a bureau of information to Olympic groups as well as a news disseminating agency for the World Press" (Official Olympic Report – Los Angeles, 1932, p. 45). This was a concept of reciprocal news-making from the start, what the report immodestly but wholly accurately hailed as "the first systematic news service during the preparatory period of an Olympiad" (ibid., p. 45).

The stadium was adapted for the anticipated press presence by eliminating 2,000 regular seats below the original press box and installing 706 "special places for press correspondents" (ibid., p. 67) with "adequate seating room and generous counter space for each representative, and with sufficient aisle space to permit easy access to the various parts of the press stand, including the Press Telegraph department immediately at the rear of the Press section" (ibid., pp. 67–68); accredited press numbered 875 (ibid., p. 123).

LA '32 provided a technologically sophisticated communication system to maximize the local and international speed and reach of information, concentrating upon as swift a dissemination of results as possible, through the "graphic communication of records and information" (ibid., p. 162) to audiences in the main stadium and other sites, and via the press to the rest of the world. Teletypewriter machines were used for this, and by means of this system "the official results of all events wherever held were available at the Olympic Stadium almost at the instant they were completed, the spelling and all other information correct, ready for immediate dissemination" (ibid., pp. 163–164).

To ensure correct and complete communication of information "to the hundreds of Press representatives was more difficult" (ibid., p. 165). Print or mimeograph was too slow to produce, and could not reach a scattered, diverse constituency across all sites of Olympic-related activity. The answer was to be found in the Stock Exchange, and several hundred electrically operated writing machines were installed, allowing "a single newspaper representative to cover the Games without leaving his seat at the stadium" (ibid., p. 165). Information reached all the journalists in long rolls of paper, fragments of which could be immediately relayed to distant destinations via telegraph companies. Speed and reach of communication in a politically sensitive and dramatically connecting world was the major chronotope of LA '32.

Berlin 1936

Berlin learnt much from LA's progressivism and allied that knowledge to its political and technological strengths. Chief organizer Carl Diem aimed to provide a "common festival" with no reference to "national or economic considerations" (Official Olympic Report – Berlin, 1936, p. 251). Nazi propaganda master Joseph Goebbels could thus state that the Olympics gave the German nation the chance to "cooperate in large international projects designed to further international peace" (ibid., p. 300). Studies (Mandell, 1972; Hart-Davis, 1986; Guttmann, 2002) confirm the communicative sophistication of the Berlin operation, and the national enthusiasm for the event, but few of the 2,800 journalists said by the Official Report to have covered some aspect of the "festival" commented on the "veiled evil" (Miller, 2008, p. 109) that staged the 1936 event. As a chronotope, Berlin 1936 combined a technological progressivism with a ruthless political project, ideologically driven and justified in disingenuous declarations of commitment to universal peace and tolerance.

Transition 2: From Phase 2 to Phase 3

To track the changes in the scale of the Olympic spectacle across Phases 2 and 3 – what we are calling Transition 2 – we take four Summer Games from the third phase and comment on the escalation of the media profile of the events, and the intensifying alignment of interests of the sporting and the media/communications spheres. These are Los Angeles 1984, Barcelona 1992, and in a more summative format Beijing 2008 and London 2012.

Los Angeles 1984

To reiterate, Los Angeles '84 allowed the entrepreneurial hosts to rewrite the rules of the game. Tehran, capital of Iran, had dropped out of the running and LA alone remained in negotiation with a desperate IOC, securing in effect a rewrite of the terms of the hosting role. In his memoir of his Olympic years, IOC president Lord Killanin (Killanin, 1983) entitled his chapter on LA '84 "On slippery slopes to Los Angeles"; the LA bid, pitched in Athens in 1978, comprised "a document … uncompromising in its demands", dictating terms as the only bidder in the game: "In effect, they said that the Games would be run their way and there was to be little account taken of the rules of the IOC or its traditions and protocol" (ibid., p. 97). Killanin added that if the Olympic Movement had not been at such a low ebb at that time, the LA bid would have been rejected outright. But the IOC had no choice, and LA's explicit proposal that "they were going to run the Games as a commercial company" (ibid., p. 98), with the city "making no financial contribution whatsoever" (ibid.) was the only offer on the table. In a face-saving compromise LA's original application was rejected by the IOC, but the Games were provisionally awarded to the city subject to confirmation of a contract respecting Olympic rules. Ten months of wrangling ensued and an intervention at White House level helped resolve the decision, just as numerous IOC members were calling for new bids. The LA bid also had within it the main television contract and the IOC had little if any scope for negotiation. Essentially, the LA '84 team had a free rein in commercializing the Games as never before, and achieved this through its "corporate relations program" (Perelman, 1985, pp. 94–107): 35 sponsors each contributed a minimum of $4 million in cash and/or in-kind services and products, and were granted immediate use of all LA '84 symbols, top hotel rooms and block purchase of 585,700 tickets; 64 supplier companies provided needed cash, products or services, and were granted use of just the "Star in Motion" symbol and only 14,300 tickets; and 65 licensee companies, eight of which were sub-licensees of Adidas, were authorized to make and sell souvenirs, passing on 10 per cent of their takings to the Organizing Committee.

And of course, following the boycotted Moscow Olympics, in this gift to Cold War ideologists and ideologues, there was the broadcasting bonanza that covered this celebration of capitalism and consumerism. The "festive federalism", as the event designers labelled the "urban confetti" (also referred to as an "invasion of butterflies") that shaped the look of the event, interwove the event's emblems and Olympic pictograms with "a color palette that replaced the traditional red, white and blue with a more festive and international scheme composed predominantly of magenta, vermillion, chrome yellow and aqua" (Perelman, 1985, pp. 107–108). This, purportedly, brought the residents "a heightened sense of excitement, emotion and history" (ibid.). In the Reagan years, with a Cold War agenda fuelling the opening and closing ceremonies, LA '84 worked with the media to construct an uninhibited celebration of US values and entrepreneurial capitalism.

This cultural, political and economic mix attracting the broadcasters was gold-dust to the organizers. The initial projection for revenue from the sale of TV rights was $105 million, but "the organizers exceeded all expectations with over $287 million in receipts" (ibid., p. 288), 225 million of which (78.4 per cent) came from ABC Sports, the overall figure constituting a 900 per cent increase on what the same company paid for the rights to the 1976 Montreal Games; the previous Summer Games, in Moscow, had gone to NBC for $85 million. The Los Angeles entrepreneurial initiative established rights-holding deals with 156 nations, bringing the Games organizers and eventually the IOC itself into more developed collaborations with the broadcasters. Television rights for Seoul went for $403 million, for Barcelona $635 million, rising beyond $930 million for the centennial event in Atlanta 1996. They rose to almost $2 billion for Beijing 2008 (Pound, 2004, p. 168). The London 2012 rights cycle raised $4,087,600,000; and for the Rio de Janeiro 2016 Games cycle, rights showed a 7.1 per cent increase from the London figure, at $4.1 billion (IOC, 2016, p. 128).[4]

The primary chronotopic themes of LA '84 were ideological and economic, producing an encomium to the democratic values of the "free world", and a proto-type for a more commercialized, privatized and commodified model of the sporting spectacle. And 8,700 news media were accredited, outnumbering the 7,078 athletes (Sanders, 2013).

Barcelona 1992

A celebratory transparency shaped the words of the chief executive of the Barcelona organizing committee, COOB '92. Josep Miquel Abad, hailing the Barcelona report as the first Official Report of a Games ever to go on sale to the public, said that it would go beyond a "select group of people" and the abbreviated versions previously available to the press: "We wanted to round off the job with a piece of work which will be thorough, free of secrets and within the reach of everyone" (Official Olympic Report – Barcelona, 1992, p. 27),[5] the media providing the capacity "to broadcast our message loud and clear … to the four corners of the earth". His pre-games hyperbole – this first volume of the report was completed before the Games actually began – scaled Olympian heights: "we scatter to the four winds the enthu-siasm of our people, which has been decisive, since the outset, in the will to offer the best and most universal Olympic Games in history" (ibid.). Abad could combine this communicative universalism with the Olympic moral high ground geared to bringing together the youth of the world in "a great festival of peace and youth" confirming faith in the human condition: "The energy and the enormous human potential that spring from the Olympic Games serve … to prove that people are still anxious to live moments of joy" (ibid., p. 24).

Barcelona '92 became the model Games claiming to succeed on multiple levels of impact:

* urban transformation of the city and its neglected infrastructure;
* profiling of the city's wider regional cultural politics in the emphasis on the relative cultural autonomy of Catalonia;
* unsurpassable visuals with the mountains and seascapes of the Mediterranean dominating broadcasters' decision-making;
* a carnival atmosphere in the city integrating the local population, visitors and fans, and even the athletes who could simply walk the short distance from the Olympic Village to the centre of the city and Las Ramblas;
* a turning point away from the Cold War Games, with the former Soviet Union competing as the "Unified Team", topping the final medal table above the USA, Germany and China (the host country Spain an honourable sixth);
* the return of South Africa from its apartheid-based expulsion since 1960; and
* a small team of "Independent Olympic Participants" for stateless individuals or refugee athletes from the Balkan fallouts and the Yugoslavia conflict.

Compulsory drug testing had been introduced after the Seoul Summer Olympics of 1988, and Barcelona seemed to project a new, open and inclusive future for the Games. Of course the embedded contradictions of the Olympic project were not resolved or superseded in Barcelona: the IOC president Juan Antonio Samaranch was himself from the city, though as the Games approached he was being exposed as a Fascist underling of the Franco regime in his previous, diplomatic career; to make way for the athletes' village, some of the local people lost their jobs and/or their livelihoods; and the prices, as so often for the sporting spectacle, were beyond the budgets of the majority. Barcelona had been awarded the event in October 1986, but had faced criticism in the planning and implementation process, as a sceptical world media expressed doubts as to the competence of the city to take on such a mega-event.

But the media world descending on Barcelona for the event itself sensed a new mood. The Organizing Committee had prioritized good media relations from the start, dealing with 7,449 reporters in the 5 years leading up to the event (Official Olympic Report – Barcelona, 1992, p. 33). The total number of accredited media was 12,831 (4,880 print press, 7,951 audiovisual), though some counts including non-accredited media put the "total media personnel estimate" at closer to 19,000 (de Moragas Spa *et al.*, 1995, p. 40). The main press centre's square metreage was 248 per cent that of LA '84 and 64 per cent that of Seoul '88 (ibid., p. 38). The media presence was increasingly recognized as pivotal to the event, in a collaborative approach to the staging of the Games. Barcelona was a genuine spectacle, also showing that a local politics of Catalan identity could chime with the national aspirations and interests of the Spanish state: "the predominance of dual rather than polarized national identities, and inclusive rather than exclusive nationalism, proved to be stabilizing factors contributing to national integration" (Hargreaves, 2000, p. 165). The Barcelona Games signalled, chronotopically, an openness and optimism in a post–Cold War world, an inclusivity that through the Olympic ethos could be said to transcend cultural and political divisions.

Beijing 2008 and London 2012

Beijing 2008 generated a global audience of 4.7 billion viewers, according to Nielsen, an increase from 3.6 billion watching the Olympic action at Sydney 2000, and 3.9 billion following Athens 2004. The 2008 figure approximates to 70 per cent of the world's population, and China claimed that 94 per cent of Chinese viewers watched Olympic TV coverage (Nielsen, 2008). London 2012 surpassed this, "with 4.8 billion unique viewers at least sampling some portion of the Games" (Billings and Kim, 2014, p. 184). The variation in such counts, or estimates, is insignificant as there is no disagreement on the sheer scale of the reach of the Summer Olympics as a mediatized cultural product in a globalized world. London 2012 prepared to welcome up to 28,000 members of the media. US broadcaster NBC alone sent 2,700 people, who would work in a vast broadcast centre. The main press centre in London was the size of the Tate Modern gallery (Booth, 2012).

The politics of identity framing the national self-representation of Beijing and London in their respective opening and closing ceremonies were different; a nationalist mainstream narrative characterized the Beijing Opening Ceremony, while London presented a cultural history of the UK with an ironic, playful and left-of-centre twist and flavour, "a vision of British history and the making of an increasingly multi-cultural British nationalism" (Tomlinson, 2013, p. 51):

> Its brilliant conceit was the green hillock up which the common people, the industrialists and the politicians could all climb, in times of turbulence and dramatic social and cultural change; the mound acted as a people's platform, accessible to all at the different points of British history.
>
> *(Tomlinson, 2013, p. 51)*

At Beijing 2008 the framing narrative was much more mainstream, the ceremonies constituting "a grand statement not only of cultural capital accumulated over centuries and of communist unity, but also a message of a nation strong and ready to assert its 'rightful' global economic place" (Miles, 2014, p. 160). The discursive and ideological elements of the sport mega-event are of course multi-faceted, and Monroe Price has noted that rather than any single "strong unified message, the Beijing Olympics had already become", before the event itself, "polyphonic, multivoiced, many themed" (Price, 2008, p. 2). But in formulaic terms, Beijing and London were deeply comparable events, confirming a model of the sport mega-event at the heart of the mediatized global culture of our times. The extravagant budgets of Beijing and London, on facilities and the ceremonial spectacles – these latter pitched at the local, national and global audiences and constituencies – confirmed the Olympic event as an exemplar of Boykoff's celebration capitalism, a joint product of the alliance of global interests across the sporting and media industries/spheres. Chronotopically, Beijing and London were thematically different in their stated historical and political narratives, but both exhibited the ultra-commodification of the sporting mega-event. The place of Rio de Janeiro in this trajectory across 28 Olympic summers is speculated upon in the concluding comments.

Concluding comments

LA '32 and Berlin '36 were identified by Roche (2000) as pioneering media-technological events, laying foundations for a media-driven commodification of the Olympics. These, and the other later examples considered here, show an intensification of scale of media activity, locating the Olympic event as more than just a sideshow on the global stage, rather an emergent cultural product prominent within the global political economy. Media technologies, global markets and the professionalization of sport would accelerate this trend. Miller *et al.* (2001) identified "five simultaneous, uneven, interconnected processes" characterizing sport at the turn of the century: "Globalization, Governmentalization, American-ization, Televisualization, and Commodification", which are "in turn governed by a New International Division of Cultural Labour" (ibid., p. 4). The Olympic mega-event is the embodiment of such processes, mediatized and marketized as the phenomenon has escalated in scale and global profile. The nature and nuances of such changes and transitions can be incremental and elusive, but a concern with the interconnectedness of separate events, the chronotopic specificities of such events and the recognition of shared conjunctural characteristics of some events offers a useful integrated framework for understanding the genesis, significance and resilience of the Olympics within the calendar of mega-events in the contemporary world, and the moments and phases of transition that have been driven by the mediatization process.

Rio 2016 will prove an interesting case. Awarded the Games in 2009, as the global economic crisis was burgeoning, it successfully staged the event despite political and economic turmoil within Brazil, the dissolution of the optimistic projections of the BRIC (Brazil, Russia, India and China) bloc, and widespread domestic as well as international scepticism about the capacity of the city to meet the demands of the hosting role. But the plans came in on time: the broadcasters had their stories along with the stunning mediascapes of Rio; the event made new superstars such as the US's 19-year-old Simone Biles, and all but canonized the great Jamaican sprinter Usain Bolt; and Brazil improved its performance in the medal table. If "winning the 2016 bid when the other candidate cities were from more established global powers was a way to position oneself for a domestic and international audience, in symbolic and discursive spheres, among the international leaders" (Schausteck de Almeida *et al.*, 2014, p. 280), then, in relation to one core objective for Rio and Brazil, the Games could be considered a relative success. Internal disquiet at the opaque costs of the Games, eloquently expressed in the rows of empty seats at many Olympic venues, and local indifference to the Paralympic Games, would not erase the accomplishment of an element of the soft-power and reputational aspirations in staging South America's first-ever Games. And what Cohen (2016, p. 56) has labelled the "Olympic compact" remains intact, sustaining a model of the sporting spectacle based on an "economy of worth … provided by the worlds of economy, industry and the marketplace". In a BBC World Service discussion at the end of the Rio Olympics I proposed that the lack of a local audience took away some of the Olympic sheen, and a consultant to Tokyo 2020 retorted that way over 90 per cent of those watching the Olympics do so on television – which of course is what suits the IOC's key partners from the broadcasting and marketing giants.

Rio showed some pragmatism, forced by financial cuts to stage an opening ceremony costing a mere tenth of London's £27 million (US$41.5 million) opener; Beijing splashed out $100 million for its four-hour welcome to the global audience (Panja, 2015). This more modestly scaled carnivalesque spectacle may establish a trend for Tokyo 2020, which has already scrapped the late Zaha Hadid's winning design for the Olympic stadium, replacing it with a much-reduced and modest project. Yet estimates put the overall cost of the Games, including Olympic-related infrastructural projects, at $12 billion, $4.6 billion of which was for sport-related costs (Tomkiw, 2016). The transition to the Phase 3 Olympic model appears complete, the Olympic product a revolving circus of consumption and a triumph of capitalist spectacle as well as human athletic and performative endeavour.

Billings (2008, p. 13) calls Olympic telecasts an "incredible juggernaut of mass media power and influence". Continuing scrutiny of the characteristics of the 28

Olympic summers will show how a mediatized sport culture emerged through the impact of distinctive events in evolving conjunctural phases that have, in the *longue durée*, created and sustained the juggernaut of the Olympic media spectacle.

Notes

1   This section draws upon Tomlinson and Young (2011).
2   Succeeding quotations are from Braudel's "History and the Social Sciences: The Longue Durée" (Braudel, 1969, pp. 25–54; originally published in 1958).
3   Braudel's major works include ongoing reflections on his historical method in a series of prefaces and some conclusions (see Braudel, 1975, pp. 16–21; Braudel, 1973, pp. 15, 442–444).
4   These figures refer to the IOC's revenue for Olympiad cycles, which includes rights to the Winter Games as well as the Summer Games. To give a more dispersed profile to its "partners", the IOC separated the winter and the summer events from each other after the 1992 events in Albertville (France) and Barcelona.
5   The Abad claim is not strictly true, as the report on LA '84 was published as a paper-back book (Perelman, 1985).

References

Bakhtin, M.M. (1981). Forms of time and of the chronotope in the novel. In M. Holquist (ed.), *The dialogic imagination: Four essays by M.M. Bakhtin* (pp. 84–258). Austin, TX: University of Texas Press.

Billings, A.C. (2008). *Olympic media: Inside the biggest show on television.* Abingdon: Routledge.

Billings, A.C. and Kim, Y. (2014). Shaping viewer experiences: The biggest spectacle on television's grandest stage. In V. Girginov (ed.), *Handbook of the London 2012 Olympic and Paralympic Games, Volume Two: Celebrating the Games,* (pp. 184–194). New York: Routledge.

Booth, R. (2012). London 2102: Olympic venues prepare for world's media. *The Guardian,* June 26. Retrieved from www.theguardian.com/sport/2012/jun/26/london-2012-olympic-venues-media (accessed 24 November 2016).

Boykoff, J. (2014). *Celebration capitalism and the Olympic Games.* New York: Routledge.

Braudel, F. (1969). *On history* (trans. S. Matthews). Chicago, IL: University of Chicago Press.

Braudel, F. (1973). *Capitalism and material life 1400–1800* (trans. M. Kochan). New York: Harper & Row.

Braudel, F. (1975). *The Mediterranean and the Mediterranean world in the age of Philip II,* vols 1 and 2 (trans. S. Reynolds). Harmondsworth: Penguin.

Burke, P. (2006). How to write a history of Europe: Europe, Europes, Eurasis. *European Review, 14*(2), 233–239.

Cohen, P. (2016). The Olympic compact: Legacies of gift, debt and unequal exchange. In G. Poynter, V. Viehoff and Y. Li (eds), *The London Olympics and urban development: The mega-event city* (pp. 48–69). New York: Routledge.

De Moragas Spa, M., Rivenburgh N.K. and Larson, J.F. (1995). *Television in the Olympics.* London: Libbey.

Frandsen, K. (2014). Mediatization of sports. In K. Lundby (ed.), *Mediatization of communication* (pp. 525–543). Berlin: Mouton de Gruyter.

Guttmann, A. (2002). *The Olympics: A history of the modern Games* (2nd ed.). Urbana, IL: University of Illinois Press.

Hargreaves, J. (2000). *Freedom for Catalonia? Catalan nationalism, Spanish identity and the Barcelona Olympic Games.* Cambridge: Cambridge University Press.

Hart-Davis, D. (1986). *Hitler's Games: The 1936 Olympics.* New York: Harper & Row.

Hjarvard, S. (2013). *The mediatization of culture and society.* New York: Routledge.

IOC (1997). *The Olympic movement.* Lausanne: International Olympic Committee.

IOC (2016). *IOC Annual report 2015: Credibility, sustainability and youth.* Lausanne: International Olympic Committee. Retrieved from https://stillmed.olympic.org/media/Document%20Library/OlympicOrg/Documents/IOC-Annual-Report/IOC-Annual%20Report-2015.pdf#_ga=1.213810259.635893392.1412523930 (accessed 24 November 2016).

Killanin, L. (1983). *My Olympic years.* New York: William Morrow.

Mandell, R.D. (1972). *The Nazi Olympics.* London: Souvenir Press.

Miles, S. (2014). The Beijing Olympics: Complicit consumerism and the re-invention of citizenship. *Contemporary Social Science, 9*(2), 159–172.

Miller, D. (2008). *The official history of the Olympic Games and the IOC: Athens to Beijing, 1894–2008.* Edinburgh: Mainstream Publishing.

Miller, T., Lawrence, G., McKay, J. and Rowe, D. (2001). *Globalization and sport: Playing the world.* London: Sage.

Nielsen (2008). Beijing Olympics draw largest-ever global TV audience. September 5. Retrieved from www.nielsen.com/us/en/insights/news/2008/beijing-olympics-draw-largest-ever-global-tv-audience.html (accessed 24 November 2016).

Official Olympic Report – Amsterdam (1928). *The Ninth Olympiad, being the Official Report of the Olympic Games celebrated at Amsterdam, issued by the Netherlands Olympic Committee (Committee 1928)* (ed. G. Van Rossem, trans. S.W. Fleming). Amsterdam: J.H. De Bussy.

Official Olympic Report – Barcelona (1992). *Official Report of the Games of the XXV Olympiad Barcelona 1992, Volume 1: The challenge – From the idea to the nomination.* Barcelona: COOB '92.

Official Olympic Report – Berlin (1936). *The XIth Olympic Games Berlin, 1936: Official report* (ed. C. Diem). Berlin: Wilhelm Limpert.

Official Olympic Report – Los Angeles (1932). *The Games of the Xth Olympiad: Los Angeles 1932 Official Report.* Los Angeles, CA: Xth Olympiade Committee of the Games of Los Angeles.

Official Olympic Report – Paris (1924). *Les Jeux de la VIIIme Olympiade, Paris 1924: Rapport officiel,* vol. 4. Paris: Comité Olympique Français.

Panja, T. (2015). Rio Olympics ceremony to cost 10% of London's lavish event open. *Bloomberg News,* September 22. Retrieved from www.bloomberg.com/news/articles/2015-09-22/rio-olympics-ceremony-to-cost-10-of-london-s-lavish-event-open (accessed 24 November 2016).

Perelman, R.B. (ed.) (1985). *Olympic retrospective: The Games of Los Angeles.* Los Angeles, CA: Los Angeles Organizing Committee.

Pound, R.W. (2004). *Inside the Olympics: A behind-the-scenes look at the politics, the scandals, and the glory of the Games.* Toronto: John Wiley & Sons.

Price, M.E. (2008). Introduction. In M.E. Price and D. Dayan (eds), *Owning the Olympics: Narratives of the new China* (pp. 1–13). Ann Arbor, MI: University of Michigan Press.

Roche, M. (2000). *Mega-events and modernity: Olympics and expos in the growth of global culture.* New York: Routledge.

Sanders, B.A. (2013). *The Los Angeles 1984 Olympic Games.* Charleston, SC: Arcadia Publishing.

Schausteck de Almeida, B., Júnior W.M. and Pike, E. (2014). The 2016 Olympic and Paralympic Games and Brazil's soft power. *Contemporary Social Science, 9*(2), 271–283.

Tomkiw, L. (2016). How much have the Rio Olympics cost Brazil? Budget of the Games explained. *International Business Times,* August 5. Retrieved from www.lbtimes.com/how-much-have-rio-olympics-cost-brazil-budget-games-explained-2397764 (accessed 24 November 2016).

Tomlinson, A. (1999). *The game's up: Essays in the cultural analysis of sport, leisure and popular culture.* Aldershot: Ashgate.

Tomlinson, A. (2005). Olympic survivals: The Olympic Games as a global phenomenon. In L. Allison (ed.), *The global politics of sport: The role of global institutions in sport* (pp. 46–62). New York: Routledge.

Tomlinson, A. (2006). Los Angeles 1984 and 1932: Commercializing the American dream. In A. Tomlinson and C. Young (eds), *National identity and global sports events: Culture, politics, and spectacle in the Olympics and the Football World Cup* (pp. 163–176). Albany, NY: SUNY Press.

Tomlinson, A. (2013). The best Olympics never. In M. Perryman (ed.), *London 2012: How was it for us?* (pp. 47–61). London: Lawrence & Wishart.

Tomlinson, A. and Young, C. (2011). Sport in modern European history: Trajectories, constellations, conjunctures. *Journal of Historical Sociology, 24*(4), 409–427.

Wallechinsky, D. and Loucky, J. (2008). *The complete book of the Olympics.* London: Aurum Press.

5

TWENTY-TWO OLYMPIC WINTERS

The media and the (non-)making of the Games

Pirkko Markula

> For bid and organising committees, sponsors, television networks and developers, the summer games represent global sport's gold medal, and the winter games a mere silver.
>
> *(Lenskyj, 2012, p. 88)*

Compared to the Summer Olympics, the Winter Olympics are the second cousin of the Olympic family.[1] Although only about one-third of the size of their much larger counterpart, the Winter Olympics, nevertheless, attract significant media attention. For example, the 2010 Vancouver Winter Olympics gained 1.8 billion television viewers and, in addition, were credited as the first "social media Games" (Miah and Jones, 2012). The most recent Winter Olympics in Sochi 2014 were watched by 2.1 billion viewers and were present in such social media platforms as Facebook, Twitter, Instagram, and diverse Internet webpages (IOC, 2014).[2] While social media has increased the accessibility of the Winter Olympics, television remains the major medium for broadcasting the Games and thus, a major funding source through the sale of televising rights. Television, thus, plays an important role in the making of the Winter Olympics.

In this chapter, I focus on the mediatization processes of the Winter Olympics by considering first, the historical development in "making" the Games through the integration and evolution of television production techniques and second, by following the trends of representing the Winter Olympics in broadcast productions. Through these major themes, I map the intertwined impact of the social processes of commercialization, globalization, urbanization, and mediatization on the Games.

Mediatization and the making of the Winter Olympics

> [M]ediatisation refers to a more long-term process, whereby social and cultural institutions and modes of interaction are changed as a consequence of the growth of the media's influence.
>
> *(Hjarvard, 2011, p. 124)*

After 30 years of the first modern Summer Olympic Games in 1894, the first Winter Olympics Games were held in Chamonix, France in 1924. Originally, five sports – bobsleigh, curling, ice hockey, Nordic skiing, and skating – constituted the Games. While only two sports, biathlon and luge, have been added to the original sports, the number of disciplines and events under each of the main sports has increased significantly. The most recently added disciplines are freestyle skiing (1992), short track speed skating (1992), and snowboarding (1998) that now collectively hold about one-third of all events in the Winter Games (32 events of the 98 total events) (see Table 5.1).

While "a financial disaster," the week of winter sports in 1924 was a "sporting and political success" that popularized skiing and other winter sports in France (Chappelet, 2010, p. 3). The sport disciplines that take place either on ice or snow thus joined the Olympic family and continue to dictate the locations and, particularly, the participating nations of the Winter Games. This context also determines the role the media play in the making of the Winter Olympics.

The framework of mediatization illustrates how the media have become intertwined with and influence social institutions such as sport (Hjarvard, 2011). Continually evolving through contradictory circumstances, incidents, and needs, mediatization intertwines the history of television broadcasting and the development of the Winter Olympic Games. In this long-term process, mediatization aligns with the processes of globalization, urbanization, and commercialization (Frandsen, 2014; Hjarvard, 2011).

The development of mediatization: television and the Winter Olympics

> It is as a spectacular television event that the Olympic Games must be understood. As such it has been shaped by the forces of commodification, globalisation, digitalisation.
>
> *(Whannel, 2012, p. 263)*

Schulz (2004) has suggested that mediatization is characterized by extended communication beyond immediate time and space. Television is the medium that has transmitted the Winter Olympics to the spectators not attending the events. Because mediatization actualizes over time, I, following other scholars (Slater, 1998;

TABLE 5.1 Winter Olympics 1924–2014

Year	Location	Nations	Athletes Men	Athletes Women	Sports	Disciplines	Events	World TV revenue (US$m)	The US TV rights (US$m)	Spectators
1924	Chamonix, France	16	247	11	6	9	16			
1928	St. Moritz, Switzerland	25	438	26	4	8	14			
1932	Lake Placid, United States	17	231	21	4	7	14			
1936	Garmisch–Partenkirchen, Germany	28	566	80	4	8	17			
1948	St Moritz, Switzerland	28	592	77	4	9	22			
1952	Oslo, Norway	30	585	109	4	8	22			
1956	Cortina, D'Ampezzo, Italy	32	687	134	4	8	24	1st televised		
1960	Squaw Valley, United States	30	521	144	4	8	27	0.05	0.05 CBS	
1964	Innsbruck, Austria	36	892	199	6	10	34	0.937	0.59 NBC	
1968	Grenoble, France	37	947	211	6	10	35	2.6	2.5 ABC	600 000
1972	Sapporo, Japan	35	801	205	6	10	35	8.5	6,4 ABC	
1976	Innsbruck, Austria	37	892	231	6	10	37	11.6	10 ABC	
1980	Lake Placid, United States	37	840	232	6	10	38	20.7	15.5 NBC	
1984	Sarajevo, Yugoslavia	49	998	274	6	10	39	102.7	91.5 ABC	
1988	Calgary, Canada	57	1122	301	6	10	46	325	309 NBC	
1992	Albertville, France	64	1313	488	6	12	57	292	243 CBS	8 million
1994	Lillehammer, Norway	67	1215	522	6	12	61	353	295 CBS	10.7 million
1998	Nagano, Japan	72	1389	787	7	14	68	513.5	375 NBC	10.7 million
2002	Salt Lake City, United States	78	1513	886	7	15	78	738	443 NBC	2.1 billion
2006	Torino, Italy	80	1548	960	7	15	84	833.5	617 NBC	3.1 billion
2010	Vancouver, Canada	82	1522	1044	7	15	86	1279.5		1.8 billion
2014	Sochi, Russia	88	1714	1159	7	15	98	1290		2.1 billion

Source: IOC Olympic Marketing Fact File, 2013 edition (www.olympic.org); IOC Factsheet Women in The Olympic Movement, 2014 (www.olympic.org); Individual Olympic Games IOC's Marketing Reports (www.olympic.org); Winter Olympic Games (en.wikipedia.org/wiki/Winter_Olympic_Games).

Whannel, 2012), examine the reciprocal relationship between television and the Games through four distinctive eras: pre-television (before 1936), emergence of television without satellites (1936–1967), globalization of television with satellites (1968–1987), and the era of digital transformation (1988–present).

The emergence of television

The Winter Olympics in Cortina d'Ampezzio, Italy 1956 Games were the first televised Winter Games. After the Second World War, the televising technology had developed rapidly and was used now as a tool of political propaganda in the midst of the Cold War.[3] As a first attempt to experiment with televising a multi-sport event to international audiences, no television rights revenue was generated (Guttman, 1986).

The organizing committee of the next Winter Olympics in 1960 in Squaw Valley, USA sold the televising rights to the US television network, the Columbia Broadcasting System (CBS), for a bargain price of US$50,000. The Winter Olympics, thus, were the forerunners of revenue generation through televising rights that since have come to dominate the funding structure of the Olympic Games (Whannel, 2012).

Globalization of television

Although CBS had originally bought the televising rights for both the Winter and Summer Olympics, in the 1970s and 1980s, the American Broadcasting Company (ABC) became an important maker of the Winter Olympics that held lucrative advertising potential in the large US market (Whannel, 2012). This commercial prospect resulted in extremely competitive bidding for the Olympic televising rights in the US. The rapidly escalating payments made the US televising rights holder a major funder of the Olympic Games. As Table 5.2 illustrates, almost the entire broadcasting revenue of the Winter Olympics at this time was attributable to the US televising rights.

As the primary funders, the US television networks obtained increasing power over running the Olympics. For example, when ABC paid a record US$309 million of the Calgary 1988 televising rights, the organizers changed the program to accommodate the US viewers with popular American sports, ice hockey and figure skating, scheduled in primetime. In addition, the Games took place over three weekends (16 days instead of usual 12 days) to increase the spectatorship (and, thus, advertising potential) in the States. Similarly, CBS obtained special privileges during the Lillehammer 1994 Olympics. They were allocated special space and facilities but, more importantly, were allowed to produce their own broadcasts parallel to the host broadcaster that provided the international feed – a privilege unavailable to any other Olympic broadcasting partner (Puijk, 2000).

With the 1980s as the golden time for bidding wars, ABC lost money during the 1988 Winter Olympics as it could not retrieve its rights payment in advertising revenue. It also lost the Olympics to CBS, which paid 20 percent less for the rights for the next Games in Albertville in 1992. As a result, the IOC feared losing income from the US networks and, initiated by ABC, instigated a change to the Olympic schedule. The Winter Olympics were to be organized in separate years from the Summer Olympics to protect the American network from having to pay for two sets of televising rights for the same year. The new schedule, thus, was designed to maximize the advertising income during the US Olympic broadcasts (Lenskyj, 2012; Whannel, 2012). As a result, the Lillehammer Games followed the 1992 Albertville Olympics after only 2 years, in 1994. This was one of the major influences of television-induced commercialization on the Winter Olympics, a premier example of mediatization driving the logic of how a sporting event presented itself.

Concomitantly, the IOC was concerned about being dependent on the funds from televising rights, 95 percent of which came from the US television network (Tomlinson, 2012). While the televising rights had proved a viable funding source already under the IOC president Avery Brundage (1952–1970) – actually a staunch opponent of commercialism and professionalism – it was not until the leadership of Juan Antonio Samaranch (1980–2001) that additional funding sources for television rights were realized (Tomlinson, 2012). After establishing a Commission for New Sources of Finance in 1982, Samaranch granted the exclusive marketing rights to Horst Dassler's (the owner of Adidas) sponsorship agency International Sport and Leisure (ISL). The ISL created a global marketing program based on "rights-bundling" of Summer and Winter Olympics as well as all the National Olympic Committees and International Sport Organizations (that collectively form the IOC). The Olympic Programme (TOP) was only open to selected,

TABLE 5.2 Winter Olympic funding from US televising rights

Winter Olympic year	Funding from the US television network (US$ million)	Entire funding from televising rights (US$ million)	Percentage of US television network funding from entire funding
1960	0.05	0.05	100
1964	0.59	0.937	63
1968	2.5	2.6	96
1972	6.4	8.5	75
1976	10	11.6	86
1980	15.5	20.7	78
1984	91.5	102.7	89
1988	309	324.9	95
1992	243	291.9	83
1994	295	352.9	84
1998	375	513.5	73
2002	443	738	60
2006	617	833.5	74

Source: IOC Olympic Marketing Fact File, 2013 edition (www.olympic.org).

invited sponsors without the rights to advertise within the Games. What made the TOP (or the Olympic Partners as the program is currently known) lucrative was the exclusivity of an association with the "clean games" that are "above" advertising (Whannel, 2012). As Whannel (ibid., p. 265) explained: sponsors are "buying into association with the world's most recognized symbol, the five rings, a symbol that connotes world excellence."[4] While the TOP sponsorship has reduced the reliance on TV rights, the Vancouver 2012 Olympics still received 50 percent (US$2.57 billion) of its revenue from television rights and 40 percent from sponsorship including the TOP partners – US$866 million – and local sponsors.

The era of digital transformation

In addition to funding, the IOC has endeavored to obtain greater control over the television feed of the Games. The Olympics were traditionally televised by a host television organization that provided the international feed. This was usually a subdivision of a national television corporation (such as the Norwegian Broadcasting Corporation for the Lillehammer 1994 Olympics; Puijk, 2000) or one of the commercial national TV channels that won the rights to act as the "host broadcaster" (such the Canadian Television Network, CTV, in the 1988 Calgary Olympics; MacNeill, 1996). In 2001, the IOC established the Olympic Broadcasting Services (OBS) to run the televising of the Games centrally. Currently, the OBS exclusively commissions the broadcasters that provide the different aspects of the television coverage (Toohey and Veal, 2007; Whannel, 2012). For example, the Olympic Broadcasting Services Vancouver, as a subsidiary of OBS, provided the entire international feed in 2010 (IOC, 2010). Similarly, OBS produced and transmitted all the coverage from the Sochi Olympic Games (IOC, 2014).

The expansion of digital technologies, particularly the Internet and user-generated social media, have emerged as another challenge for the IOC – how to assume control of these modes to monetize their broadcasting value? How to avoid losing live television audience to the Internet? One strategy agreed between NBC (the current American TV rights holder) and the IOC is to allow buying of the rights for several Olympiads in advance. For example, the NBC spent US$2.2 billion combined for the 2010 Vancouver Winter Olympics and the 2012 London Summer Olympics (Billings, 2008; Whannel, 2012). In 2011, NBC acquired the rights to broadcast the Olympic Games until 2012 and in 2014, further secured "the broadcast rights across all media platforms, including free-to-air television, subscription television, internet and mobile" from 2021 to 2032 with US$7.65 billion (Maylan, 2014). With this strategy, the IOC is able to secure stable funding for several Olympiads at the time.

The era of digitalization is characterized by the invention of social media through which individual users are free to post information on the World Wide Web. This means that any spectator can now post videos, pictures, and narratives about the Winter Olympics on the Internet outside the centrally controlled, official Olympic media outlets. To address this threat to its brand and to its potential revenue, the IOC acted to digitally "geo-block" the illegal, unsanctioned broadcasts (Whannel, 2012). However, while the Internet can pose a threat to Olympic funding, the IOC also has to embrace the large audiences using these media outlets or risk losing its status as an organizer of international mega events (Miah and Jones, 2012). Indeed, the Nagano 1998 Olympics were the first to provide an official web home page (IOC, 1998). The Vancouver Olympic Games in 2010 were available on more than 100 websites worldwide; had their own Facebook pages and Twitter accounts; and encouraged spectators to share their photographs through Flickr (Miah and Jones, 2012). They did not, however, carry live online communication of the event (Pena, Damajo and Arauz, 2014). The Sochi 2014 Games had 230 dedicated digital channels (155 websites and 75 apps) that carried a total of 60,000 hours of digital broadcast coverage compared to 48,000 hours shown on television. In addition, the OBS launched the Olympic Video Player (OVP) app to provide live streaming and on-demand video, which was used in 95 countries and territories to consume over two million hours of video and audio. For the first time, the Internet broadcast exceeded the television coverage hours (IOC, 2014).

Historically, television broadcasting has played a central role in stimulating the mediatization of the Winter Olympics. This process has been aided by the US anti-monopoly regulations that have resulted in fierce competition for the television rights between the main US networks. The networks have been motivated by the lucrative audience ratings and the following advertising potential. Thus, as shown earlier, televising of the Winter Olympics is inextricably intertwined with the commercialization characteristic of the cultural era of high modernity (Hjarvard, 2011). The US network television rights have provided major funding and thus, have dictated, globally, the development of the Games. In the beginning of the mediatization process, the American television rights holders gained relative independence from the control of the IOC, which then had to exercise its institutional power to rebalance the scale. Digital technology has again unstablized these relations by providing platforms for multiple media to replace the dominance of television as the main medium for broadcasting the Winter Olympics. The IOC initially attempted to limit the multimedia access, but has now brought this under its umbrella of OBS services in addition to "bundling" the broadcasting rights across all media platforms in the main media rights contracts. With the continued economic concentration of media industries (like the NBC network), different media now operate together under the same commercial and professional objectives (Deuze, 2007; Frandsen, 2014), also to produce the Olympic broadcasts. The IOC, nevertheless, strictly governs its brand, the Olympic rings – the brand that remains the most valuable commercial asset for the Olympic marketing program (IOC, 2014), which lessens the IOC's dependency on the powerful media and increases its ability to regulate the mediatization process.

The Winter Olympics have continued to thrive in the mediatized context of global sport. No doubt, they have benefitted from their relationship to their much larger cousin, the Summer Olympics. For example, the American network NBC's television rights contract (that still provides about 50 per cent of revenue of the Winter Olympics) includes both the Summer and Winter Olympics. Furthermore, each TOP partner is locked into a 5-year plan that extends to Winter Olympics that, by themselves, might not attract global sponsors of the same caliber as the Summer Olympics. In any case, the monetization of TV broadcasting has enabled the IOC, in Whannel's (2012, p. 269) words, to move from "genteel poverty" of amateurism to "grand luxury" and with it, the Winter Olympics have also emerged from relative obscurity to a global mega event with 3,000 athletes from 88 countries competing for an audience of 2.1 billion.

The images of the Winter Olympics

> Television has been a dissemination tool of athletes' images of effort, success or failure and Olympic values (as well as being the source of funding for the Olympics).
>
> *(Pena, Damajo and Arauz, 2014, p. 154)*

Following Frandsen (2014, p. 535), "television's use of both pictures and sound" and its "unique ability to convey the sporting experience" have further brought the Winter Olympics closer to a wider, global audience. However, the televised images also potentially change the way we view both the Games' hosts and their athletes. If the mediatization has enabled the global expansion of the Games, it has also highlighted some of the problems related to organizing a mega-event.

The image of the Winter Olympics hosts

> Historically, the Olympic Games offer nations and communities "opportunities to showcase their cultures."
>
> *(Dyreson, 2010, p. 55)*

The Winter Olympics are no exception. For example, the 1924 Olympics were to transmit the image of Chamonix as a winter tourism destination, but also to re-instate France as a leading nation of Europe (Terret, 2010). The Chamonix Games also set a precedent for the types of locations imagined suitable for the Winter Games.

Traditionally the Winter Olympics were located in small ski resorts (e.g., St Moritz, Squaw Valley, Garmisch-Partenkirchen, Cortina, Lake Placid) that longed to attract more tourists by providing better transport and lodging procured through the Games. The rapid technical development of the sports and their infrastructure as well as the concern for suitable climate conditions in relatively vulnerable (mountain) environments have put pressure on the organizers to negotiate the increasingly obvious environmental concerns for the steadily expanding Games. For example, some of the sporting structures turn to so-called "white elephants" (e.g., ski jumps, the bobsleigh hill) that are unusable for general audiences after the Games (e.g., Chappelet, 2010; Dansero and Mela, 2012; Terret, 2010). Such environmental concerns have resulted from the expansion supported, partly, by the media revenue.

Protests against building the facilities arose early in the history of the Winter Olympics. Already in 1932, the local activists successfully lodged complaints about felling trees to construct sport sites in Lake Placid, which is located within the Adirondack National Park where the New York State law prohibits any changes in the natural landscape (Chappelet, 2010). As similar opposition rose during the later Lake Placid Games in 1980, with the increased media presence, it was increasingly difficult to find hosts for the much larger Winter Olympics after 1980. For example, the citizens of several small mountain resorts in the Alps voted down the candidacies for hosting the Games (ibid.). The Albertville 1992 Games in France raised further serious environmental concerns (Boykoff, 2013; Chappelet, 2010; Terret, 2010). Although the organizers of these multi-site Games aimed to take the environment into account, building the ski jumps and the bobsleigh hill were, once again, controversial and visibly reported in the press. A protest march organized by an environmental group before the Opening Ceremony was displayed worldwide in the media (Terret, 2010). Prepared to offset the negative image, the first International Conference of Winter Olympics Games Host Cities held in 1991 and the Earth Summit, which popularized the phrase "sustainable developed," in 1992, resulted in an amendment to the Olympic Charter for "a responsible concern for environmental issues" (Boykoff, 2013, p. 48). When the Winter Olympics 1994 were awarded to small, mountainous Lillehammer in Norway, the organizers, aided by funds from the Norwegian government, followed the idea of sustainable development, nicknaming their Olympics the "green games." Puijk (2000) found that even in the generally critical Norwegian press, these Olympics obtained much positive reporting. Due to their continued expansion, however, the Winter Olympics have been relocated to more urban settings.

After Nagano (1998), the IOC has awarded the Winter Olympics to larger cities (Salt Lake City, Turin, Vancouver). These cities seem primarily concerned with building a favorable image for themselves. For example, Dansero and Mela (2012) observed that Turin, an industrial mid-size city in northern Italy, bid for the Olympics to create a distinctive image comparable to Rome, Milan, or Venice. Many of the events took place in the mountain region adjacent to Turin, but the city was the focus of the multi-center "Olympic region" – a concept that now became central to organizing Winter Olympics in urban settings. Continuing "the heavy focus on environment aspects," the Turin hosts composed "the Olympic Green Card": guidelines on how to organize sustainable Olympic Games (ibid., p. 189). Vancouver, the host of the 2010 Olympic Games, followed suit by including environmental stewardship, sustainable practices, and sustainable living as their major goals[5] (Chappelet, 2010; Lenskyj, 2012). Through mediatization processes, the expanded and increasingly commercialized Winter Olympics have now become entangled with another social process of high modernism, urbanization (Hjarvard, 2011).

The mediated image is embedded in the narratives the hosts choose to tell about themselves. Each organizing committee now devotes significant effort to structuring a desirable story line for itself. Dyreson (2010), for example, noted that the organizers of the Salt Lake City 2002 Olympics engaged in "intense efforts to make sure that the IOC and the international media" could relate to the Mormon state of Utah as a familiar, charming, and modern "heartland of the American west, home of awesome pioneers, stunning vistas and the frontiers spirits" (ibid., pp. 56–57). Several researchers note the hyper-real nature of such "meta-narratives:" they create *simulacra* (simulated realities without originals) rather than a realistic representation (Real, 2012, p. 227). Such simulacra are particularly evident in use of images of the native peoples (e.g., Dyreson, 2010; Forsyth and Wamsley, 2005; Hogan, 2010; Lenskyj, 2012) during the bidding process and particularly, in the Opening and Closing Ceremonies of the Games.

The Opening Ceremony reaches some of the largest audiences in the Winter Olympic Games. For example, the Sochi 2014 Opening Ceremony was viewed by three billion people worldwide.[6] These celebrations are especially designed to promote the chosen narrative of the nation, state, and the host city by drawing from select historical and cultural resources. As Hogan (2010, p. 138) noted: "The Olympic opening ceremonies … simplify, amplify, and depoliticize national (invented) traditions and extend the narrative of nation back in time to an age well before the official founding of the nations." For example, the Salt Lake City 2002 Olympics Opening Ceremony celebrated multiculturalism and featured the five Native American nations of Utah wearing their traditional costumes; a representation that, according to Hogan, ignored the continued conflict and discrimination between the white settlers and the Native Americans. This Opening Ceremony was held only a few months after the events in 9/11 and it was further constructed as a unified narrative of the US in an opposition to the Muslims and "middle-eastern looking people" (ibid., p. 147) as an "evocation of the US 'war on terror'" (ibid., p. 147). While the media facilitates the celebration of such dominant narratives, they also provide space – albeit less visible – for alternative voices.

The Winter Olympics have been remarkably free of the boycotts that have affected several Summer Olympics,[7] but have been the targets of multiple scandals, protests, and conflicts. Such issues as the Albertville 1992 environmental problems, the Salt Lake City bidding bribery scandal in 2002, the Vancouver failure of accountability, Aboriginal protests and exclusion of the women's ski jumping in 2012 (see also Vertinsky, Jette and Hofmann, 2009), and the Russian anti-gay legislation in Sochi 2014 have been widely reported around the world. In addition to the hosts, images of the participating athletes fill the national and global media narratives.

The image(s) of the Winter Olympics athletes

> Contemporary sporting practice, including the Olympic sport, is implicated
> in continuing inequalities based on ethnicity and gender.
>
> *(Hogan, 2010, p. 135)*

The Winter Olympics have traditionally drawn athletes from Northern and Central Europe, North America, and Asia which have winter conditions suitable for practicing the snow and ice-based sports included in the Games. As noted earlier, however, the participant base has widened due to a targeted strategic selection of sport disciplines. In addition, the IOC has engaged in a concerted effort to expand the media coverage to such non-traditional Winter Olympics locations as Africa. For example, in cooperation with the Canal France International and the Torino Olympic Broadcasting Organization, the IOC negotiated an agreement to offer television coverage from the 2006 Turin Olympics free to 40 sub-Saharan countries (Toohey and Veal, 2007). The Sochi 2014 Games were broadcast free to Middle East, North and sub-Saharan African nations through television, online, and mobile platforms (IOC, 2014). Despite the increase in the Winter Olympics coverage, critical sport scholars continue to be concerned about its content.

The IOC has consistently increased women's participation from only 11 in 1924 to more than 1,000 athletes (40.4 per cent) in the Sochi 2014 Winter Olympics (Donnelly, Norman and Donnelly, 2015; see also Table 5.1). While strides towards equal participation have been made, the media continue to marginalize and trivialize women athletes (e.g., Lenskyj, 2012). In their analysis of gender in Canadian broadsheet *Globe and Mail* during the Winter Olympic Games 1924–1992, Urquhart and Crossman (1999) discovered that while the coverage increased over time, women athletes were consistently underrepresented compared to male athletes and trivialized through depictions in gender-appropriate sports (e.g., figure skating) that were located in the latter pages of the sport sections. Several researchers point to an emphasis of storytelling designed to maximize the audience numbers (and to include also viewers who do not typically watch sports) on the American TV network broadcasts (e.g., Angelini, MacArthur and Billings, 2012; Puijk, 2000; Whannel, 2012). While the Winter Olympics offer an exceptional platform to showcase women athletes who usually receive scarce TV coverage, these narratives construct a particular type of femininity. For example, Daddario (1994) demonstrated that women athletes' sporting achievements were trivialized through infantilizing comments (e.g., use of nicknames) or depictions as daughters or sisters rather than athletes in the CBS coverage in Albertville, 1992. In a series of studies, Billings (e.g., Billings, 2008; Billings, Brown and Brown-Devlin, 2015; Billings, *et al.*, 2008; Billings and Eastman, 2003) has demonstrated that while women receive more coverage than in other sporting events in the US, "the Winter Olympics routinely feature a larger clocktime gender gap than the Summer Olympics" (Angelini *et al.*, 2012, p. 263): if women athletes generally receive 24 percent of Summer Olympics clocktime, only 2 percent of the Winter Olympics clocktime features women. The rivalry between American figure skaters Nancy Kerrigan and Tonya Harding in the wake of the Lillehammer 1994 Olympics is a rare exception. Their performance is the highest-rated Olympic evening in US history (Angelini *et al.*, 2012; Baughman, 1995; Puijk, 2000).

Conclusion

In this chapter, I have aimed to demonstrate the long term processes of how the media have come to impact the Winter Olympics, which have steadily grown into a global sporting mega-event. Television, particularly, has increased the mediated reach of the seven winter sports, some of which have a rather limited competitor base. This mediatization process has been inexorably intertwined with other transformative social and cultural processes of high modernity (Hjarvard, 2011) as commercialization, globalization, urbanization, and privatization have further transformed the Winter Olympics. The commercialization of the Games can be largely attributed to the opportunities to sell televising rights. The US television networks' "bidding wars," particularly, interweaved commercialization and mediatization resulting in changes favoring American viewership estimated to secure advertising revenue. In this commercial environment, the Winter Olympics have benefitted from their close relationship to their cousin, the Summer Olympics. For example, all the media rights and sponsorship agreements include both Summer and Winter Olympics (and currently also the Youth Olympics) and thus, to capture the lucrative audience and advertising markets of the Summer Games, the prospective US network needs to also support the Winter Games.

The televised Winter Olympics now have broad global reach that has enabled steady growth of events and participating athletes. The expansion of the Winter Olympics has, nevertheless, resulted in hosting them in urban environments that are able to accommodate the required infrastructure and increased media personnel (Miah and Jones, 2012). The social media reach across all continents has further enabled the Winter Olympics to claim a position as a global sporting mega-event.

Through televised broadcasts the Winter Olympics have entered the privacy of the spectators' homes (Frandsen, 2014). In this process, the media takes responsibility for private communication as well as public communication (Hjarvard, 2011). The digital technology has been deeper integrated within everyday lives to further enhance the individualized spectator experience. The digital media has also transformed the politics around the control of the Games.

The Winter Olympics have been forerunners in the inclusion of social media and, as a smaller event, serve as a platform for experimentation to inform the Olympic media practices (Pena, Ramajo and Arauz, 2014). The "new media" create challenges for monetization, but also opportunities to broaden the potential audience necessary for survival in the commercialized sport mega-event industry. Pressed between the need for global reach for commercial gain and control over the value of its product, the IOC continues to wrestle over the control of funding and media coverage in the age of user-generated content. While the new media enable formations of new communities and different ways of experiencing sport, it has both multiplied and accelerated the pace of communication (Frandsen, 2014). Consequently, this made it more difficult for sport organizations such as the IOC to predict and control the mediated content of their events.

While the IOC attempts to manage the increasingly complex mediatization processes, the sale of television rights continues to dominate the funding structures for the Winter Olympics (comprising about 50 per cent of revenues). Therefore, the interests of the television right holders and the IOC continue to intersect: to gain more audience for the Games, the media and the IOC exist in a symbiotic relationship. The consequent expansion of the Winter Olympics has reduced the number of cities willing to host the Games. For example, the 2022 Winter Olympics had only two bidders, Almaty (Kazakhstan) and Beijing (China), with such possible host as Oslo (Norway), Stockholm (Sweden), and Krakow (Poland) pulling out due to governmental and public opposition to the estimated costs of the Games (Abend, 2014; Pramuk, 2015). In this situation, the "necessity" of mediatization continues to be a considerable force shaping the Winter Olympics as an event that is continually affected by larger political, social, and cultural forces such as commercialization, globalization, urbanization, and privatization.

Notes

1   The most recent Summer Olympics in London 2012 had 10768 athletes from 204 nations participating in 302 events in 26 sports (https://en.wikipedia.org/wiki/ 2012_Summer_Olympics). The Sochi 2014 Winter Olympics hosted 2873 athletes from 88 nations participating in 98 sport events in 7 sports and 15 disciplines (IOC, 2014; Donnelly, Norman and Donnelly, 2015).
2   Muller (2015) classified the London 2012 Summer Olympic Games and the 2010 Football World Cup in South Africa as the largest recent sporting mega-events with media reach of three billion viewers. With significantly fewer viewers, the Vancouver 2010 Winter Olympic Games (media reach of 2.1 billion spectators) were the same size as the 2012 European Football Championships but larger than the 2010 Common-wealth Games in Delhi, 2011 Rugby World Cup in New Zealand, or the 2013 Super Bowl in New Orleans, USA.
3   While the Winter Olympics were of interest to only limited geographical areas, they were at the center of the Cold War due to Soviet Union's Olympic debut in Cortina where it won the most medals, with its rival, the USA, placing only seventh in the medal table (Toohey and Veal, 2007).
4   The Calgary Games in 1988 were the first Winter Olympics to benefit from the TOP sponsorship. The Sochi Winter Olympics, 2014 TOP (VII) had ten partners (Coca-Cola, ATOS, DOW, GE, McDonald's, Omega, Panasonic, PandG, Samsung, and VISA) (IOC, 2014).
5   The other goals included Aboriginal participation, accountability, and social inclusion.
6   In the later official report the Games had 2.1 billion viewers total (IOC, 2014).
7   Only Taiwan has boycotted the 1980 Winter Olympics in Lake Placid as a protest against the IOC, which allowed China to participate for the first time since 1956 (Hill, 1992).

References

Abend, L. (2014). Why nobody wants to host the 2022 Winter Olympics. *Time*, October. Retrieved from http://time.com/3462070/olympics-winter-2022 (accessed 24 November 2016).

Angelini, J.R., MacArthur, P.J. and Billings, A.C. (2012). What's the gendered story? Vancouver primetime Olympic glory on NBC. *Journal of Broadcasting and Electronic Media*, *56*, 261–279.

Baughman, C. (1995). *Women on ice: Feminist essays on the Tonya Harding/Nancy Kerrigan spectacle*. New York: Routledge.

Billings, A.C. (2008). Clocking gender differences: Televised Olympic clock time in the 1996–2006 Summer and Winter Olympics. *Television and New Media*, *5*, 429–441.

Billings A.C. and Eastman, S.T. (2003). Framing identities: Gender, ethnic, and national parity in network announcing of the 2002 Winter Olympics. *Journal of Communication*, *53*, 369–386.

Billings, A., Brown, K. and Brown-Devlin, N. (2015). Sports draped in the American flag: Impact of the 2014 Winter Olympic telecast on nationalized attitudes. *Mass Communication and Society*, *18*, 377–398.

Billings, A.C., Brown, L.C., Crout, J.H., McKenna, K.E., Rice, B.A., Timanus, M.E. and Ziegler, J. (2008). The Games through the NBC lens: Gender, ethnic, and national equity in the 2006 Torino Winter Olympics. *Journal of Broadcasting and Electronic Media*, *52*, 215–230.

Boykoff, J. (2013). Celebration capitalism and the Sochi 2014 Winter Olympics. *Olympika*, *22*, 39–70.

Daddario, G. (1994). Chilly scenes of the 1992 Winter Games: The mass media and the marginalization of female athletes. *Sociology of Sport Journal*, *11*, 275–275.

Dansero, E. and Mela, A. (2012). Bringing the mountains into the city: Legacy of Winter Olympics, Turin 2006. In H.J. Lenskyj and S. Wagg (eds), *The Palgrave handbook of Olympic studies* (pp. 178–194). Basingstoke: Palgrave Macmillan.

Deuze, M. (2007). *Media work*. Cambridge: Polity Press.

Donnelly, M.K., Norman, M. and Donnelly, P. (2015). *The Sochi 2014 Olympics: A gender equality audit*. Research Report. Toronto: Centre for Sport Policy Studies, Faculty of Kinesiology and Physical Education, University of Toronto.

Dyreson, M. (2010). Olympic Games and historical imagination. Notes from the fault line of tradition and modernity. In V. Girginov (ed.), *The Olympics: A critical reader* (pp. 50–64). London: Routledge.

Forsyth, J. and Wamsley, K. (2005). Symbols without substance: Aboriginal peoples and the illusion of Olympic ceremonies. In K. Young and K. Wamsley (eds), *Global Olympics: Historical and sociological studies of the modern Games* (pp. 227–248). Amsterdam: Elsevier.

Frandsen, K. (2014). Mediatization of sports. In K. Lundby (ed.), *Mediatization of communication* (pp. 525–543). Berlin; Mouton de Gruyton.

Guttman, A. (1986). *Sports spectators*. New York: Columbia University Press.

Hill, C. (1992). *Olympic politics*. Manchester: Manchester University Press.

Hjarvard, S. (2011). The mediatisation of religion: Theorising religion, media and social change. *Culture and Religion*, *2*, 119–135.

Hogan, J. (2010). Staging the nation: Gendered and ethnicized discourse of national identity in Olympic Opening Ceremonies. In V. Girginov (ed.), *The Olympics: A critical reader* (pp. 135–150). London: Routledge.

IOC (1998). *The XVIII Olympic Winter Games, Nagano 1998: Official report.* Retrieved from https://library.olympic.org/Default/doc/SYRACUSE/66018/the-xviii-olympic-winter-games-official-report-nagano-1998-the-organizing-committee-for-the-xviii-ol?_lg=en-GB#_ga=1.235041032.807505082.1477554293 (accessed 24 November 2016).

IOC (2010). *IOC marketing, Vancouver 2010: Media guide.* Retrieved from www.olympic.org/documents/ioc-marketing-and-broadcasting (accessed 24 November 2016).

IOC (2014). *Marketing report, Sochi, 2014.* Retrieved from www.olympic.org/documents/ioc-marketing-and-broadcasting (accessed 24 November 2016).

Lenskyj, H.J. (2012). The Winter Olympics: Geography is destiny? In H.J. Lenskyj and S. Wagg (eds), *The Palgrave handbook of Olympic studies* (pp. 88–102). Basingstoke: Palgrave Macmillan.

MacNeill, M. (1996). Networks: Producing Olympic ice hockey for a national television audience. *Sociology of Sport Journal, 13*(2), 103–124.

Maylan, A. (2014). Agreement ensures the long-term financial security of the Olympic Movement. Retrieved from www.olympic.org/news/ioc-awards-olympic-games-broadcast-rights-to-nbcuniversal-through-to-2032/230995

Miah, A. and Jones, J. (2012). The Olympics movement's new media revolution: Monetisation, open media and intellectual property. In H.J. Lenskyj and S. Wagg (eds), *The Palgrave handbook of Olympic studies* (pp. 274–288). Basingstoke: Palgrave Macmillan.

Muller, M. (2015). What makes an event a mega-event? Definitions and sizes. *Leisure Studies, 34,* 627–642.

Pena, E.P., Damajo, N. and Arauz, M. (2014). Social media in the Olympic Games. In A.C. Billings and M. Hardin (eds), *Routledge handbook of sport and new media* (pp. 153–164). New York: Routledge.

Pramuk, J. (2015). The Winter Olympics problem: Nobody wants them. August. Retrieved from www.cnbc.com/2015/08/07/the-winter-olympics-problem-nobody-wants-them.html (accessed 24 November 2016).

Puijk, R. (2000). A global media event? Coverage of the 1994 Lillehammer Olympic Games. *International Review for the Sociology of Sport, 35,* 309–330.

Real, M. (2012). Who owns the Olympics? Political economy and critical moments in the modern games. In V. Girginov (ed.), *The Olympics: A critical reader* (pp. 221–238). London: Routledge.

Schulz, W. (2004). Reconstructing mediatization as an analytical concept. *European Journal of Communication, 19,* 87–101.

Slater, J. (1998). Changing partners: The relationship between the mass media and the Olympic Games. In R.K. Barney, K.B. Wamsley, S.G. Martyn and G.H. MacDonald (eds), *Global and cultural critique: Problematizing the Olympic Games* (pp. 49–68). London, ON: University of Western Ontario.

Terret, T. (2010). The Albertville Winter Olympics: Unexpected legacies – failed expectations for regional economic development. In J.A. Mangan and M. Dyreson (eds), *Olympic legacies: Intended and unintended political, cultural, economic and educational* (pp. 20–38). London: Routledge.

Tomlinson, A. (2012). The making – and unmaking? – of the Olympic corporate class. In H.J. Lenskyj and S. Wagg (eds), *The Palgrave handbook of Olympic studies* (pp. 233–247). Basingstoke: Palgrave Macmillan.

Toohey, K. and Veal, A.J. (2007). *The Olympic Games: A social science perspective* (2nd ed.). Wallingford: CABI.

Urquhart, J. and Crossman, J. (1999). The *Globe and Mail* coverage of the Winter Olympic Games: A cold place for women. *Journal of Sport and Social Issues, 23,* 193–202.

Vertinsky, P., Jette, S. and Hofmann, A. (2009). "Skierina" in the Olympics: Gender justice and gender politics at the local, national and international level over the challenge of women's ski jumping. *Olympika, 18,* 25–56.

Whannel, G. (2012). The rings and the box: Television spectacle and the Olympics. In H.J. Lenskyj and S. Wagg (eds), *The Palgrave handbook of Olympic studies* (pp. 261–273). Basingstoke: Palgrave Macmillan.

6

THE FIFA WORLD CUP

Media, football and the evolution of a global event

Richard Haynes and Raymond Boyle

> The Olympics, fragmented into thousands of competitors, hundreds of nations and dozens of sports, cannot attract the interest of so many, nor can it plausibly offer the same simplicity of narrative comprehensible to the world in a mere ninety minutes. ... In an era of unprecedented global economic, ecological and cultural interdependence, in which the community of fate in which we live is nothing less than humanity as a whole, the greatest singular opportunity we possess for looking at ourselves and each other together is a football tournament.
>
> *(David Goldblatt discussing the 2006 football World Cup in Goldblatt, 2007, p. 901)*

> It's live [2014 World Cup in Brazil], it's public and it's controversial so we are set up for this to be possibly the biggest Twitter event in history.
>
> *(Lewis Wiltshire, Head of Global Partnerships, Twitter UK in Benady, 2014, p. 38)*

The FIFA football men's World Cup can be characterized as a global universal sporting mega-event, which is increasingly married with large-scale cultural events for investment in tourism and attracting a broader audience via global media (Roche, 1992). More recently, Muller (2015, p. 638) has suggested a refining of the definition of mega-events, with the FIFA World Cup sitting with an elite group of what he calls "giga-events" above "major" and "mega" events. In other words, the World Cup is so ubiquitous as a major international sporting event that it is almost impossible to avoid across all media outlets and platforms. The circuits of promotion that focus on the event are now so overwhelming that the entire month of the tournament occupies vast areas of media content in a manner consistent with what Whannel (2001) calls a "vortextual" media event: all-consuming and culturally hegemonic.

Since the late-1960s, audiences in developed countries have taken for granted the opportunity to watch major sporting events such as the World Cup on television. This sense of expectation has been socially and culturally shaped by the mega-event's evolving relationship with television, which many would agree dominates the timing, structure and framing of the event. Increasingly concerned with the centrality of media to its global success, the mediatization of the World Cup has, therefore, been historically formed and shaped by a range of social, cultural, economic and technological processes (Frandsen, 2016). These processes are also historically uneven – in both time and communicative spaces (Schlesinger, 2000) – and are contingent on specific interventions by individuals, organizations and advances in technology that have created a complex set of inter-relationships between the global event and the media. Exploring how the particular systemic features of FIFA's premier tournament have evolved, as well as how particular broadcast technologies and operations have sought to bring the event to audiences, can help explain why the World Cup has an extensive global reach and a seemingly universal appeal.

The 4-year cycle of the men's World Cup produces an omnipresent context of global football culture, which includes prolonged qualification prior to the mega-event itself. When allied to the perpetuation of FIFA Rankings, the U20 World Championship, the Women's World Cup Finals and a plethora of other FIFA branded tournaments, activities and products, it is easier to understand how the media and everyday reference to the "World Cup" circulates in what Silverstone (1999, p. 6) once called the "texture of our lives." Through this process – increasingly referred to as mediatization – the World Cup has, alongside the Olympics, become the *sine qua non* sports mega-event (or giga-event) characterized by the merging of sport, culture and communications (Muller, 2015, p. 638) The social influence of this process can be recognized in how we expect major events to be televised; we expect to see the World Cup Finals; we expect to be presented with analysis and commentary; we expect to be entertained – and, in the context of sporting nationalism – we often expect to be uplifted by victory or deflated in defeat. For some, the World Cup is also the antithesis of their social and cultural worlds, but its universality makes it virtually impossible to ignore. The mediatization of the World Cup, therefore, has a socially and culturally powerful presence in our lives whether we want it to or not.

If one traces the development of television technologies alongside a regular tournament like the World Cup in a longitudinal context, what one finds are similarities in the marketing and rhetorical power of such technology as "modern" and symptomatic of the times they were being introduced. However, such claims of "modernity" often failed to recognize either continuities in the production of television, or the differences in the reception of the event by nations, ethnicities, genders and ages. We want, then, to consider two threads of the mediatization of the World Cup in this chapter. The first traces the historiography of the rhetorical use of the televised coverage of the World Cup, which helps us understand how new technologies are accommodated in the institutional structures of global sports organizations and broadcasters to make a sport mega-event "televisual." The second focuses on the nature of the World Cup as a global media event and how it is consumed. Transformations in the socio-technological consumption of football, in the home, in public spaces and via networked-mobile media and the carnivalesque nature and heavily mythologized meanings associated with the World Cup raise important questions for how we understand the concept of mediatization in the context of the World Cup as a unique global media event. The World Cup as a global media event has developed its own dynamics of spectatorship (Rowe, 2000), and these dynamics have been socially and culturally transformed by the rise of what Hutchins and Rowe (2012) have termed "Networked Media Sport."

Of course, in tracing these transformations in the media coverage and reception of the World Cup, we cannot avoid recognition of the contemporary crisis in the governance of the sport. The charges of corruption and money laundering, reaching the highest echelons of FIFA's executive, have sullied the gloss, which the Swiss-based governing body and its tournament may once have enjoyed among its various stakeholders. The public scandal of FBI investigation and dawn raid arrests in Switzerland of senior FIFA executives at the behest of the US Department of Justice in May and December 2015 confirmed long held beliefs by some scholars (Sugden and Tomlinson, 1998) and investigative journalists (Jennings, 2006, 2015) that the World Cup and associated activities of FIFA had become part of a dynastic fiefdom headed by its now defamed former President Sepp Blatter. Ironically, the media's role in the deposing of Blatter and corrupt FIFA executives served to emphasize the divergent and contradictory relationships the media have had with football's world governing body over several decades.

The televisual World Cup

Following Tomlinson's (2014) use of Robertson's (1992) temporal-historicizing of globalization to characterize the evolution of FIFA as an organization from "take off" to the "struggle-for-hegemony" and finally a phase of "uncertainty," we propose a similar historical schemata for assessing the televising of the World Cup. How did the World Cup become *televisual* through organizing itself for television? Loosely drawn, we identify three eras of rhetoric about the technological transformations in the televising of the World Cup. These are:

* *1954–1962:* The initiating phase of international television football.
* *1966–1998:* The hegemonic struggle for control of the media spectacle.
* *2002–present:* The uncertain age of convergent processes and divergent media.

In creating these schematic eras we want to emphasize there are overlaps and continuities across these periods of World Cup television history. Nevertheless, we believe it is important to differentiate between some key eras of technological, operational and cultural transformations in the televising of the tournament as a global sport mega-event.

1954–1962: The initiating phase

The World Cup, like television, began in the 1930s. In the British context, pre-war abstention by its four national associations – England, Scotland, Wales and Ireland (later Northern Ireland from 1953) – certainly influenced the lack of media reporting of the event in Britain and its lack of visibility in public life. None of the 1930s tournaments were televised, although all were filmed and the 1938 World Cup finals appeared in cinema newsreels across the world. The 1938 finals were also extensively covered on radio across mainland Europe and Brazil, via shortwave transmission. Elements of internationalization of communications were, therefore, embedded from the start of the World Cup (Geraghty, Simpson and Whannel, 1986).

In 1950, following suspension of the World Cup during the Second World War, British teams entered the tournament for the first time. This had some effect on the coverage of the event in Britain, and the BBC carried some radio commentaries and eye-witness reports from England's games, including ignominious defeat to a team of amateurs from the United States. Brazilian plans to launch their first television service were delayed by two months, and therefore missed the opportunity to televise the World Cup for the first time (Varela, 2014).

The year 1950 also represented a watershed in the history of British, and indeed European, television with the development of new portable radio links that enabled BBC engineers to transmit a television signal from Calais to the English south coast and on to London. The Anglo-French experiments paved the way for the first televising of the World Cup from Switzerland in 1954 as part of a "Television Continental Exchange" involving eight countries, which formed a new collaborative organization, the European Broadcasting Union (EBU). A series of programmes were transmitted between June and July 1954, and the Swiss contribution from Berne included ten matches from the World Cup, which represented the largest contribution to the exchange by any one country by a significant margin (Fickers, 2012). For the BBC's chief engineer Michael Pilling, the experiment represented an opportunity "to advantage the universality of the picture as a way of overcoming the language barrier" (Pilling, 1954, p. 4).

This rhetoric of "universality" reflected the collaborative tenor of the post-war age. Each participating national broadcaster – many of them less than one year in operation, many borrowing equipment and expertise from the BBC – had their own commentator for the same pictures, situated either at the stadium or in a remote studio. The technique of segregating background sounds or "effects" from commentary had first been used during the coronation of Queen Elizabeth II in 1953, when the BBC's live broadcast had been successfully transmitted across Europe (Fickers, 2012). The "Eurovision" experiment – a phrase coined by British journalist George Campey of the *London Evening Standard* in 1951 – represented the beginning of a now standard global broadcasting format for the delivery of international sporting events with a combination of "unilateral" and "multilateral" feeds, thereby enabling each national broadcaster to appropriate international broadcasts for local audiences. It remains an important device for national cultural and linguistic identification with a global media event (see Haynes, 2014).

The "Eurovision" links once again proved a successful means of relaying live transmissions of the matches across Europe during the World Cup Finals from Sweden in 1958. Symbiotic relationships between broadcasters and World Cup organizers began to emerge, as stadia were adapted to accommodate commentators from European broadcasters and the Swedish Football Association were pressured for the first time (albeit unsuccessfully) to schedule the timing of games to accommodate the needs of television. For instance, FIFA had scheduled many of the games on the same date and the same time, and in an attempt to relax this policy the BBC's Head of Outside Broadcasts, Peter Dimmock, wrote to request that FIFA revise the timetabling of significant fixtures. It was the first time television had attempted to interfere with the organization of the World Cup, but Dimmock's request fell on deaf ears.[1] The World Cup finals in Sweden introduced a new level of partnership and commercial opportunism on the part of FIFA (the EBU paid the Swedish FA 1.5 million kronor in rights), but it also opened up opportunities for television producers to pursue more interventionist strategies with World Cup hosts, such as ensuring stadia accommodated cameras and commentators. The 1958 World Cup consolidated television's transnational role in bridging territorial divides, and cemented the position of football as an emergent point of transnational cultural universality. As Tomlinson (2014) has argued, FIFA's profile exponentially grew as it shifted through the phases of globalization, driven by values of internationalization and harmony in world football. Nevertheless, in spite of exposure to new styles of play and international stars, the coverage of international football remained rooted in a very strong national frame. For example, the handling of British coverage of the 1958 Finals by the BBC centred on the performances of England, Scotland, Wales and Northern Ireland, and a film crew from the BBC's flagship programme *Sportsview* were sent to Sweden to provide additional footage for British audiences (Haynes, 2017). In this way, by blending unilateral feeds from host broadcasters with multilateral coverage of national broadcasters, television evolved to play a compelling role in fostering strong nationalist sentiment and emotion around the World Cup.

In 1962, live television transmissions to Europe from the World Cup in Chile were impossible. European broadcasters therefore turned to some extraordinary measures to get footage of the event to viewers. The BBC coverage aimed to get recorded action of key matches to British viewers approximately forty-eight hours after each match had finished (Radio Times, 1962). The process of transporting and developing the film was meticulously planned and described in the *Radio Times*:

> Each film must be flown from Santiago to Lima, Peru – from Lima to Panama – Panama to Miami – and Miami to New York. That takes approximately fourteen hours. Then the ninety minutes of film must be processed in New York and rushed to Idlewild Airport to be put on the first available transatlantic jet.
>
> *(Radio Times, 1962, p. 4)*

The resources invested by the BBC in their coverage from Chile were symbolic of the emerging perceived importance of the World Cup among broadcasting elites. BBC Audience Research from 1962 indicated the enforced delay and unusual scheduling meant the BBC's coverage of the 1962 finals received a fairly subdued public response. The delayed recordings from Chile in 1962 simply did not carry the same sense of spectacle and suspense as the live coverage from Switzerland and Sweden. However, in this "initiating" phase, broadcasters fostered an appetite for the public adoption of television through its commitment to invest in transcontinental coverage of the World Cup as an emergent mega-event.

1966–1998: The hegemonic struggle for the control of the media spectacle

Television coverage of the 1966 World Cup in England represented both the pinnacle in the pioneering epoch of World Cup coverage, and the starting point for a new, televisual age of international football on television. Again, the introduction of new technologies played a significant role in transforming the visual language of World Cup coverage, and a discursive turn in the cultural, political and economic significance of the World Cup represented by the breadth of television coverage and the increasing focus on stars (Whannel, 2001). From 1962 FIFA took control of the television rights negotiations, and the portent of the inflation of television rights began in 1966, when the EBU signed a deal worth $800,000, whereas it had only offered $75,000 for the tournament in Chile (Chisari, 2006). By the end of this era, in 1998, FIFA's licensing rights to television were worth Sfr. 130 million. With this, the commercial value of television became central to FIFA's finances. Beginning in 1974, following the election of Joao Havelange to supersede Sir Stanley Rous as President, how this income was distributed among the FIFA's national members became increasingly politicized and open to corruption (Tomlinson, 2014).

The increased investment by broadcasters in the World Cup was met by an increased desire by broadcasters to manage the scheduling of the tournament to suit the needs of television (in 1966 kick-off times were staggered wherever possible) and also innovate new methods of coverage. The BBC had introduced video recording technology to its sports programming in 1964, which helped accelerate the editing process and enabled the innovation of action replay technology. Bryan Cowgill, who headed up the BBC's 1966 World Cup coverage, had seen slow-motion technology while visiting tennis commentator Jack Kramer at his home in Los Angeles (Cowgill, 2006), reverse engineered ABC's video replay machine for use on the BBC's airing of England's opening match against Uruguay. Bemused viewers telephoned the BBC to ask if something was wrong with the transmission. In subsequent letters to the *Radio Times*, viewers reported being left "breathless" at seeing the technology for the first time (*Radio Times*, 1966).

The 1966 World Cup proved to be a landmark event in the manipulation of the image and the subsequent conventions of televised football. It was the first World

Cup to be transmitted to South America (Mexico) via satellite, and the level of professionalization in planning the broadcasts was, at that time, unsurpassed. Part of our argument here is that the World Cup had become a premier showcase for the techniques of television and televising sport. The introduction of new technologies, often in synchronicity with sport mega-events, is negotiated and contingent on a variety of factors that can relate to the innovative vision of television engineers and sport producers, market conditions and consumer appropriation. One technology that producers in 1966 wanted to be made available but were denied was colour transmission, which, according to broadcaster Peter Dimmock, was scuppered by the British government who felt the domestic manufacturing industry was not yet ready to compete with American and Japanese rivals.[2]

Throughout this time, the World Cup also became an important site for innovations in the presentation of football, particularly from the studio. Television producers, in varied ways in different nations, constantly innovated new styles of World Cup coverage, including reliance on panels of analysts, pundits and "tel-experts" for each and every match (Tudor, 1975). The then new processes of "scene setting," half-time analysis and full time "post mortem" remain generic conventions across the world in television coverage of the sport (ibid.). The focus on footballers as personalities, which in turn legitimized the television anchors' own claims to "star" status, became a standard strategy in covering the World Cup (Whannel, 1992).

World Cup coverage in the 1980s and 1990s continued in this vein. The use of technology to manipulate the television image, with replays, stop frame and virtual overlay of graphics, such as various tracking devices and so on, became standard tools for analysing and setting the parameters of knowledge and understanding of the game (ibid.). The time given over to these techniques has also increased and one panoptical effect of such intensive scrutiny has been the gradual undermining of the authority of the referee. The moral high ground of governance over football now firmly rests with television whose critical gaze constantly and consistently challenges the credibility of referees (Colwell, 2000), something FIFA tried to remedy with the introduction of goal-line technology in 2014 (FIFA, 2014).

To summarize the transformations in the relationship between television technology and the World Cup during this era, it is important to stress the shift in emphasis in technological rhetoric that occurred from 1966 onward. A preoccupation with the technological efficacy of television reflected in the "initiating phase" of World Cup television, was eclipsed by the need to produce heightened narrative pleasures through the patina of a "star" system, with its associated entertainment values and increased competition for the attention of viewers. Competition between rival networks in any one nation – in the UK, between the BBC and ITV – meant the viewing experience was guided far more by the personalities on the screen and engagement with narratives of entertainment and stardom, rather than narratives that focused on the technological wizardry of television to create a co-presence for viewers as if they were at the live event.

However, the period of relatively small incremental changes in television technologies between the late-1960s and late-1990s would be disrupted by significant transformations in the television sport environment caused by increased competition from pay-TV and the influence of the Internet.

2002–present: The age of convergent processes and divergent media

The final era of televising the World Cup began in earnest in 2002 and in the age of convergent, networked media sport continues to develop in complexity with each new World Cup tournament. A significant indicator of change was the decision by FIFA to sell its television rights for 2002 and 2006 through two intermediaries, the Swiss marketing company ISL and the German media group Kirch in a deal worth £1.45 billion (Tomlinson, 2014). The move broke the decades-long relationship with the EBU in Europe and opened the door for nation-by-nation deals including pay-TV companies. The deals proved apocalyptic to both ISL and Kirch, who could not finance the huge credit required to service the deals, but in Brazil (SportTV, ESPN Brazil, FOX Sports and BandSports), Spain (Gol Television), France (beIN Sports) and Italy (Sky Italia) and a number of other nations, part of the television coverage of the World Cup now resides under subscription television services because of FIFA's changing commercial strategy (Tomlinson, 2014). Major event legislation in Europe that sought to protect public access to the World Cup could not, in some instances, prevent a premium being placed on many of the matches with the exception of the semi-finals and final themselves. The only exception here has been in the UK, where FIFA's challenge against the "listed events" legislation that protects the entire World Cup tournament being on free-to-air television, was overturned by the European General Court (Wilson, 2013).

This turn of events emphasized the important role that football has played around the world in the evolution of new media modes of delivery and consumption. Football has an enthusiastic, ready-made audience, who, in significant numbers, also happen to mutually belong to a demographic of young male "early adopters" of new information and communication technologies – a fact not lost on the sports media industries and advertising companies eager to market new services to affluent, predominantly male, consumers (Sweney, 2010).

Evidence of football's commercial appeal abounds in the way that new digital media products and services, from HD television, 4G mobile "smart" phones and online betting have targeted this group to understand what is at stake. The list of companies that have used football in their promotional strategies reads like a who's who of the global media and telecommunications industries. Sky, Virgin, BT, Vodafone, Orange, T-Mobile (now EE), Nokia, Sony and Apple have all, at some point, invested large sums of money in promotional campaigns, particularly pushing the "second-screen market," including advertising and sponsorship to woo football fans (Johnson, 2014).

As we have seen, the World Cup has frequently provided an umbrella for the innovative introduction of new technologies by broadcasters. Where the 1998 FIFA

World Cup could be equated with the "take-off" phase of domestic Internet use, the 2002 event took place in a progressively mature Internet environment and this convergent and complex viewing experience has continued through 2006, 2010 and 2014. For example, the panoply of communication services for the 2010 and 2014 World Cups from the BBC were impressive: high definition and interactive television, video-on-demand including every game and a selection of highlights from previous World Cups, live online streaming using the BBC's iPlayer technology (available online, through games consoles or Internet enabled televisions), and there were increasingly ubiquitous online commentaries, blogs and Twitter postings. Information-rich sources were produced on mainstream websites, often authored by television studio pundits. But there were also a range of other sources including links to social media, which again came from television football pundits, which became more expansive as they engaged in broader conversations with their network of followers and readers.

The remainder of this chapter focuses on the patterns of media consumption of a World Cup. While recognizing change, we argue that television's dominance is far from being usurped in this age of uncertainty.

One World Cup: many narratives?

Throughout this chapter, we show how the football World Cup has become a well-established mega-media or giga-event. The FIFA World Cup 2014 secured an in-home television audience of 3.2 billion, with the tournament final being watched by an in-home television audience of over 1 billion (Kantar Media, 2015, p. 8). While audiences around the world may watch the same matches, how they are made sense of, framed and discussed takes place often through a national lens, driven by both ideological and commercial imperatives (Boyle and Haynes, 2009). What is striking in an era characterized by the networked media sport economy (Hutchins and Rowe, 2012) is how patterns of continuity in terms of media–audience relationships run parallel to significant changes.

As Joe Moran (2013, p. 371) observes about the relationship between television and the viewing public in the UK, "If the television era was over ... it didn't feel like it." He was commenting on the end of analogue television in the UK in 2012 and its termination as it was replaced by digital transmission, hence digital became the only way to watch television, and the perception that new forms of social media were replacing television as a cultural form. We argue that his sentiments are equally applicable to the public's relationship with television coverage of the football World Cup. While the aggregation of global television audiences must be approached with caution, the research (Kantar Media, 2015) on international and domestic television audiences for the 2014 World Cup held in Brazil are still illuminating for a number of reasons. They identify the residual strength of television as the central platform for watching live sport, but also highlight how people are accessing mediated sport via a variety of screens.

Television is dead?

Television audience data remind us that there is no other event that attracts as consistently high television viewing figures internationally as the World Cup. While global figures were similar to the 2010 World Cup held in South Africa (Asian viewership was down, in part as a result of the significant time difference), all-time record average audiences were generated in countries such as Germany (the final attracting 34.5 million television viewers), and the Netherlands. In the USA, we saw the most-watched football match on American television with 18.2 million watching ESPN's coverage of the USA and Portugal (Kantar Media, 2015), with the figure rising to 25 million when Univision viewers are included (Kissell, 2014). Without becoming fixated with numbers, it remains the case that television remains the crucial conduit for bringing the World Cup to publics around the world, and football remains a compelling form of television to deliver large audiences in an age where mass and simultaneous television viewing is waning.

What the research also highlights is the importance of acknowledging "out-of-home" viewing of football and television (and the difficulty in capturing this data) and the "non-TV consumption" via broadband and mobile of the event, reflecting the growth in the public and collective experience of watching live football, not at the arena, but rather in designated public spaces. This is, of course, not new and the beaming of live matches back to home stadiums has a long tradition in British football culture. However, the rise of both formal and informal "fan zones" has now become an established part of the physical and cultural landscape of cities hosting major sporting events since the first official Fan Fest was held at the FIFA World Cup in Germany in 2006 (Klauser, 2011).

The commercial value for pubs and bars of screening live coverage and the collective experience of watching events with others is a key artefact of events such as the World Cup. Reflecting on how collective public viewing of major football tournaments such as the World Cup has grown in tandem with the rising commonality of HD and big screen television, Moran observes:

> Such public television was, of course how Baird [one of the inventors of television] had once imagined the future of his invention. His former laboratory at 22 Frith Street in Soho was now an expresso bar [...] and much of the back wall was taken up with a huge TV screen, which lit up the room when football matches, especially Italian ones, were shown. When a goal went in the customers celebrated with a fervour that would have astonished the forty scientists from the Royal Institution who once queued up in evening dress along a narrow staircase in order to inspect a quivering image of the head of a ventriloquist's dummy.
>
> *(Moran, 2013, p. 300)*

Indeed, the residual popularity of collective television viewing of football was also vividly captured by Stockdale and Platt's (2014) photographic journey through the crowds at the 2014 World Cup in Brazil. Their photo essays (see www.watching theworldcup.com) document the ubiquity of World Cup media coverage. Stockdale and Platt argue:

> From waiting rooms to bus stations, beauty salons to banks, shops to supermarkets, everyone in Brazil seems to be tuning into the matches. For the entire month – everywhere you go – you can't escape the World Cup.
>
> *(Stockdale and Platt, 2014, p. 7)*

This perception is borne out by the in-home viewing figures that saw, for example, 42.9 million people watch the opening game between Brazil and Croatia on TV Globo (Kantar Media, 2015). This figure does not include the collective viewing, captured dramatically in Stockdale and Platt's (2014) work and also the 600,000 visiting fans who travelled to Brazil to watch live matches in the stadium, but did so also on television.

Kelner (2012) reminds us of how national television coverage of major football tournaments such as the World Cup have become cultural touchstones for audiences, becoming part of shared collective memory. Thus, for England fans (and a wider television audience), the tears shed on the pitch by the England player Paul Gascoigne during their defeat in the semi-final of the 1990 World Cup in Italy was a moment that captured television's ability to transform a player and team's relationship with its audience. Kelner argues:

> Clearly, in a multi-platform, time-shift, niche market world, there will be fewer of those landmark occasions when the nation unites in a common cause, and increasingly the experience will be shared through social networking. But sport will still create unforgettable moments, like Gazza's tears, that live more vividly on TV than at the live event. The tears were not even visible to those in the stadium.
>
> *(Kelner, 2012, p. 267)*

What we have is a more complex—and often layered—media experience around events such as the World Cup, with television coverage (in the home, via a variety of screens, both large and small, both public and private) sitting at the centre of this mediated experience. Hence, the 2014 World Cup in Brazil saw:

> More online coverage than any other previous FIFA World Cup with 188 licensees offering 2014 FIFA World Cup Brazil coverage via websites, media players and apps. Not only was there more coverage but also there were also more people than ever watching via these channels.
>
> *(Kantar Media, 2015, p. 27)*

In the digital and social media age, television remains central to this "new media" ecology (Boyle, 2014). It is also worth noting that television is not operating in isolation from other media. Major sports broadcasters such as the BBC or Sky in the UK will offer their content – often in real time – across a range of platforms, allowing the viewer to watch the television coverage on PC and mobile, as well as seeking to deepen their engagement with viewers through a provision of a range of World Cup related content across all platforms.

The growth of social media platforms allows debate, discussion, comment and information to flow around these touchstone television moments before they occur and, of course, long after the event has finished—in this sense more accurately reflecting the cycle of fan talk, which has always existed well beyond the actual event. This is a tendency that radio recognized many years ago in the creation of the fan phone-in format. Of course, this more complex mediated environment is also well recognized by those interested in events such as the World Cup for corporate commercial reasons, rather than being motivated simply to increase the communication flow between fans.

For example, at Brazil 2014, Adidas, one of the main corporate sponsors, deployed 50 people at its social media "war room" during the World Cup to both manage social media promotion in real time across a range of platforms, as well as rebutting adverse or inaccurate material pertaining to their brand on social media. Again, the notion of corporate brands running "war rooms" as part of event promotion is not new and pre-dates the digital environment. However, the focus on the social media dimension of the brand is a significant shift; brands now seek to influence and shape the online conversation taking place around events such as the World Cup. Social media offers the opportunity for individuals and groups to construct a counter narrative to that being carried by mainstream media, although it is also worth remembering that it often requires more mainstream media to pick up on this counter narrative before it gains traction and wider public attention. It is also important to recognize that social media chatter can also serve to act as a form of echo chamber, with groups simply reinforcing their already well-established opinions (Wenner, 2014).

The challenges faced by journalists and the print media of this more complex World Cup media environment are considerably greater than for their counterparts working for rights holding media organizations. As Hutchins and Rowe note about the role of sports journalists in the networked media sports environment:

> The field of sports journalism has revealed how its "structures and principles" are in flux, the "rules of the game" have become loose and contentious, and the once relatively robust habitus of (especially male print-based) sports journalists has turned fragile and permeable.
>
> *(Hutchins and Rowe, 2012, p. 150)*

Even if one agrees with this analysis, sports journalism remains an important part of the process by which often similar narratives get produced and reproduced around such mega-media events as the World Cup.

For example, Hammett (2011) argues that British media representations of the South African 2010 World Cup relied on remarkably similar discourses about South Africa (the high crime rate in the country, the fear of security at the tournament and potential travel difficulties). The media platforms you were seeking out information about the country from diversified only as the tournament progressed and journalists began reporting on their own experiences in the country rather than relying on conventional wisdom about life in South Africa. Critical work (cf. Tendai and Mhiripiri, 2014) on that World Cup highlight the contested nature of social and national identities, and the differing narratives around the tournament and South African culture and society that domestic and international media generated. The work shows how a more complex media environment, facilitated by a more fluid media space, revealed diverse identities being expressed as the country attempted to use the World Cup to initiate and redefine its own sense of collective identity.

Conclusion

In this chapter, we argue that, if we take a long view on the media's relationship with the World Cup, what becomes evident is the growing layers of complexity that characterize both its mediation and the mediated event's engagement with supporters, fans and viewers. This complexity masks strong elements of continuity, such as the centrality of television, or "television-like" content providing access to the live event, and that "liveness" remains central to the value of football on television.

Furthermore, our analysis provides reminders about the crucial central role that forms of nationalism and expressions and representations of mediated collective identity continue to play in shaping the popularity and compelling appeal of an event such as the football World Cup. We see no reason to think this appeal will not remain despite the ongoing reputational difficulties, that show little signs of abating, that continue to plague the governing body of the world game, FIFA.

Notes

1   The issue of scheduling of matches for the 1958 World Cup was discussed in a memorandum from Jack Oaten to Peter Dimmock, 21 October 1957. BBC Written Archives Centre (WAC) T14/1,869/1
2   Author interview with Peter Dimmock, 20 January 2009.

References

Benady, A. (2014). The 20th World Cup: A social game. *PRWeek*, June, 38–41.
Boyle, R. (2014). Television sport in the age of screens and content. *Television and New Media*, 9, 746–751.
Boyle, R. and Haynes, R. (2009). *Power play: Sport, the media and popular culture* (2nd ed.). Edinburgh: Edinburgh University Press.

Chisari, F. (2006). When football went global: Televising the 1966 World Cup. *Historical Social Research, 31*, 42–54.

Colwell, S. (2000). The "letter" and the "spirit": Football laws and refereeing in the twenty-first century. In J. Garland, D. Malcolm and M. Rowe (eds), *The future of football: Challenges for the twenty-first century* (pp. 201–214). London: Frank Cass.

Cowgill, B. (2006). *Mr. Action Replay.* Kings Lynn: Sports Masters International.

Fickers, A. (2012) The birth of Eurovision: Transnational television as a challenge for Europe and media historiography. In A. Fickers and C. Johnson (eds), *Transnational television history: A comparative approach* (pp. 13–32). London: Routledge.

FIFA (2014). Goal-line technology set up ahead of FIFA World Cup. 1 April. Retrieved from www.fifa.com/worldcup/news/y=2014/m=4/news=goal-line-technology-set-ahead-fifa-world-cup-2311481.html (accessed 24 November 2016).

Frandsen, K. (2016). Sports organisations in a new wave of mediatisation. *Communication and Sport, 4*(4), 385–400.

Geraghty, C., Simpson, P. and Whannel, G. (1986). Tunnel vision: Television's World Cup. In A. Tomlinson and G. Whannel (eds), *Off the ball: The football World Cup* (pp. 20–35). London: Pluto.

Goldblatt, D. (2007). *The ball is round: A global history of football.* London: Penguin.

Hammett, D. (2011). British media representations of South Africa and the 2010 FIFA World Cup. *South African Geographical Journal, 93*(1), 63–74.

Haynes, R. (2014) The maturation of Olympic television: The BBC, Eurovision and Rome 1960. *Stadion: International Journal of Sport History, 38/39*, 163–182.

Haynes, R. (2017). *BBC sport in black and white.* London: Palgrave.

Hutchins, B. and Rowe, D. (2012). *Sport beyond television: The Internet, digital media and the rise of networked media sport.* London: Routledge.

Jennings, A. (2006). *Foul! The secret world of FIFA: Bribes, vote rigging and ticket scandals.* Edinburgh: Harpersport.

Jennings, A. (2015). *The dirty games: Uncovering the scandal at FIFA.* London: Century.

Johnson, L. (2014). FIFA World Cup unveils second-screen digital push. *Adweek*, 30 May. Retrieved from www.adweek.com/news/technology/fifa-world-cup-unveils-second-screen-digital-push-158033 (accessed 24 November 2016).

Kantar Media (2015). *2014 FIFA World Cup Brazil.* London: Kantar Media.

Kelner, M. (2012). *Sit down and cheer: A history of sport on TV.* London: Bloomsbury.

Kissell, R. (2014) Nearly 25 million watch USA v. Portugal match on ESPN, Univision. Retrieved from http://variety.com/2014/tv/news/usa-portugal-match-nets-espns-highest-ever-world-cup-rating-1201242091/ (accessed 6 June 2016).

Klauser, F. (2011) The exemplification of "fan zones": Mediating mechanisms in the reproduction of best practices for security and branding at Euro 2008. *Urban Studies, 48*(15), 3203–3219.

Moran, J. (2013). *Armchair nation: An intimate history of Britain in front of the TV.* London: Profile Books.

Muller, M. (2015) What makes an event a mega-event? Definitions and sizes. *Leisure Studies, 34*(6), 627–642.

Pilling, M. (1954). [No title.] *Radio Times*, 21 May, 21.

Radio Times (1962). Summer grandstand. *Radio Times*, 25 May, 4.

Radio Times (1966). Letters. *Radio Times*, 11 August, 5.

Robertson, R. (1992). *Globalization: Social theory and global culture.* London: Sage.

Roche, M. (1992). Mega-events and micro-modernization. *British Journal of Sociology, 43*, 563–600.

Rowe, D. (2000). Global media events and the positioning of presence. *Media International Australia incorporating Culture and Policy, 97*, 11–21.

Schlesinger, P. (2000). The nation and communicative space. In H. Tumber (ed.), *Media power, professionals and politics* (pp. 99–115). London: Routledge.

Silverstone, R. (1999). *Why study the media?* London: Sage.

Stockdale, J. and Platt, D. (2014). Watching the World Cup: A photographic journey exploring crowds at the World Cup 2014 in Brazil. Retrieved from www.watching theworldcup.com (accessed 24 November 2016).

Sugden, J. and Tomlinson, A. (1998). *FIFA and the contest for World Football.* Cambridge: Polity Press.

Sweney, M. (2010). World Cup 2010: Millions of women will watch – but the ads will aim at men. *The Guardian*, 9 June. Retrieved from www.theguardian.com/media/2010/ jun/09/world-cup-2010-women-ads (accessed 24 November 2016).

Tendai, C. and Mhiripiri, N.A. (eds) (2014). *African football, identity politics and global media narratives: The legacy of the FIFA 2010 World Cup.* London: Palgrave Macmillan.

Tomlinson, A. (2014). *FIFA: The men, the myths and the money.* London: Routledge.

Tudor, A. (1975). The panels. In E. Buscombe (ed.), *Football on television* (pp. 54–65). London: BFI.

Varela, M. (2014). The opening ceremonies of television in Mexico, Brazil, Cuba and Argentina. In S. Anderson and M. Chakers (eds), *Modernization, nation-building and television history* (pp. 19–35). London: Routledge.

Wenner, L. (2014). On the limits of the new and the lasting power of the mediasport inter-pellation. *Television and New Media, 15*(8), 732–740.

Whannel, G. (1992). *Fields in vision: Television sport and cultural transformation.* London: Routledge.

Whannel, G. (2001). *Media sport stars: Masculinities and moralities.* London: Routledge.

Wilson, B. (2013). FIFA loses free-to-air World Cup battle. *BBC News*, July 18. Retrieved from www.bbc.co.uk/news/business-23288211 (accessed 24 November 2016).

7

THE RUGBY WORLD CUP EXPERIENCE

Interrogating the oscillating poles of love and hate

Toni Bruce

Global mega-events like the Rugby World Cup are unique moments, separate from daily life, that can unite people through a sense of being part of something larger than themselves and sharing an experience that matters deeply. Such events can evoke a wide range of emotions including joy, sadness, anger and even hate. It is this range of responses that I bring to life through a cultural studies discursive analysis of media coverage and the words and actions of survey respondents, public posters to news websites, interviewees and those observed during fieldwork at the last three quadrennial World Cups (see also Bruce, 2013, 2014). Drawing upon the concept of mediatization, I explore its effects on a small nation, for which the sport of rugby union and the men's national rugby team, the All Blacks, have long been understood as the nation's "greatest passion" (Quinn, 1993, p. 201).

Most rugby research has conceptually adopted a top-down approach, focusing on the articulation of rugby and nationalism created by power brokers such as politicians, journalists, advertising executives, rugby officials and elite rugby players (e.g. Fougere, 1989; MacLean, 1999; Phillips, 1999; Ryan, 2005; Scherer and Jackson, 2007). In contrast, my focus is the "assumptions, hopes, needs, longings and interests of ordinary people" (Hobsbawm, 1991, p. 10) who are rarely directly involved in creating rugby discourses. The impetus for this longitudinal research was a growing sense of a disconnection between the cultural importance attributed by the media to the performances of the All Blacks and how ordinary New Zealanders actually felt about rugby.

Mediatization

Mediatization can be seen as "a *long-term* process" that "implies *transformation* of practices and institutions" including media, which takes place in the "*interplay* between changes in communication media and the societal, political and cultural context" (Lundby, 2014, p. 19; Frandsen, 2014; Hepp and Krotz, 2014; Livingstone and Lunt, 2014). Taking as a starting point the argument that the relationships between media and sport are "highly influenced" by the cultures and social contexts in which they are experienced (Frandsen, 2014, p. 530), I discuss the findings in relation to tensions emerging from the "co-evolution" of men's rugby union, in which media and sport have each "spurred" changes in the other (Livingstone and Lunt, 2014, p. 708). More specifically, Frandsen (2014, p. 525) explains that "mediatization of sport is a matter of specificity where interrelatedness, globalization, and commercialization have come to play a significant role due to the communicative features of both television and sports".

Mediatization is a theoretically and methodologically open concept that enables research at multiple levels (Zierold, 2012). I locate my research at the level of "the 'everyday' of the lifeworld" (Lundby, 2014, p. 19), investigating in a bottom-up fashion the diversity of reactions *within* a single nation to the mediatization of rugby and the All Blacks. In the face of intensifying globalizing and commercializing pressures, I conceptualize rugby's place in national culture as a specific "problem construction" composed of *moments* (such as the articulation of rugby to nationalism) and media *objects* (such as media coverage, public reports and public discussion) (Kunelius, 2014, p. 82). Lundby (2014, p. 22) further explains that "To be mediatized, these moments have to transform common attitudes and conceptions or to be skewed in one direction or another." He proposes that the extent of media saturation "shapes the individual interaction of the social actors, and influences the problem construction that brings them to act or not to act" (ibid., pp. 22–23). As a result, my research explores multiple observations of objects and moments that show how the sociocultural practice of sporting nationalism in relation to rugby has transformed over time.

The mediatized moments and objects of my research comprise diverse methods employed during three Rugby World Cups, including fieldwork at live matches, public viewing sites, fan trails, parties, bars, workplaces and private homes, analyses of print and online news coverage, live broadcasts and public comments on newspaper websites, and in-depth interviews and self-selecting surveys. Due to space limitations, the audience evidence is based primarily on comments from three non-representative surveys that, despite their varying methodology and sizes, produced substantially similar results: a 2007 convenience sample (131 respondents), online self-selecting surveys in 2011 (267) and 2015 (1,188), and some comments on news sites in 2015. The media evidence draws from analysis of 2011 and 2015 news coverage on the online portals of New Zealand's top online news sites, the *New Zealand Herald* and news aggregator *Stuff*, both of which attract over a million views each month (Riddiford, 2015), as well as hard copy coverage in the highest circulation daily (the *Herald*) and Sunday (the *Sunday Star Times*) newspapers. Research and media coverage pre-dating 2007 are incorporated to identify the "larger sociocultural processes" (Lundby, 2014, p. 9) in which rugby's mediatization is embedded.

Mediatizing rugby

New Zealand hosted and won the inaugural Rugby World Cup in 1987, hosted and won it again in 2011, and became the first men's team to win back-to-back World Cups in 2015, making the All Blacks the most successful men's Rugby World Cup team ever. However, both rugby and New Zealand have changed markedly since the inaugural Rugby World Cup. In New Zealand, top level men's rugby has rapidly transformed from an amateur, club-based game run by volunteers into a professional, commercialized and mediatized global brand – a change that has not always been positively received (Laidlaw, 1999; Phillips, 2000; Romanos, 2002). Such transformations reflect wider social, political, demographic and economic changes in New Zealand, such as increased immigration, ethnic diversity and an ageing population, that have exerted pressures on rugby's place in the national imagination. For example, declines in television ratings, player numbers and attendance at live games, and a range of public surveys, suggest that levels of interest in rugby may be waning (Robson, 2009; UMR, 2011).

The sport's recent development has involved a corporatized and increasingly visibly commoditized relationship between the professional players, New Zealand Rugby, television broadcasters, advertisers and sponsors. It has, in Frandsen's terms (2014, p. 539), become a "strategic partnership based on mutual understanding and the creation of a shared product". The result is numerous structural changes that reflect almost all elements of Frandsen's description of sporting mediatization: including type, frequency and scheduling of elite-level competitions, changes in production values, uniforms, and concerns with how athletes and coaches interact with media. For rugby, media-driven structural changes have included rescheduling of events from spectator- and player-friendly daytime matches to prime-time evening viewing, the introduction of new camera angles and referee microphones, new short-form televised events such as Rugby Sevens (which made its Olympic debut in 2016), the television match official (TMO) who may view television replays to help the referee decide whether points have been scored, and the shift of broadcasts of elite tiers of men's rugby from free-to-air to pay television, leaving more than 50 per cent of New Zealand households without easy access to viewing games. Since 1995, the amateur, three-nation, Super Rugby competition has transmuted into a professional, five-nation, four-conference competition including teams from South Africa, New Zealand, Australia, Argentina and Japan. The extended annual playing schedule has also reduced the involvement of All Blacks players in the national provincial competition (Silk and Jackson, 2000).

In contrast to established histories of professional sport in Europe and North America, rugby has experienced an accelerated transformation into a mediatized product since 1995, which was already underway in the last years of amateurism. For Hutchins and Phillips (1999, p. 154), the 1991 Rugby World Cup "represented a sea change in the presentation, commodification and consumption of international rugby" as rugby "entered an integrated, global, commercial, media market". Laidlaw (1999) argues that ensuing transformations – such as the emergence of professionalism in 1995 and a $100 million deal with global clothing giant Adidas (Philp, 1997) – produced "a growing sense of unease, if not resentment, among supporters of the game that it is somehow being taken away from them" (Laidlaw, 1999, p. 174). He noted that the stadium redevelopments excluded "those who can't afford the price of a seat" while the entry of pay TV into the New Zealand broadcasting market meant "If you want to watch it on television you have to subscribe" (ibid.). Thus, Laidlaw concluded that "the game now responds not to nationalistic fervour of an adoring public but to the television programme schedulers and the corporate sponsors" (ibid.). Researching professionalism's convulsive impact, sports journalist Joseph Romanos (2002, p. 11) described rugby as "a game in crisis", its position as the national sport as under serious threat, and reported "almost nationwide disenchantment with many aspects of the game" (ibid., p. 12). This view was reinforced when New Zealand lost the 2003 Rugby World Cup co-hosting rights, generating significant angst in rugby circles, and resulting in an Independent Inquiry and over 120 articles in the *Herald*, including one that noted "The demands of the professional age have tripped up the rugby union too often for comfort" (Herald, 2002a, ¶3). Coverage also dramatized rugby fans' "public outrage" (Herald, 2002b, ¶4) and a pervasive concern that they felt "that their destiny is out of their hands" (Martin, 2003, p. 8). Only 5 years after the official shift to professionalism, Silk and Jackson (2000, pp. 137–138) argued that rugby's transmutation "perhaps best exemplifies the shifting terrain of sporting culture in a more deregulated, privatised, consumerist and globally interdependent New Zealand".

In New Zealand, the powerful articulation of rugby to nationalism produces "deep attachments" (Anderson, 1991, p. 4) which are evident in Richards's (1999) description of the historic place of men's rugby in national culture (while also identifying the gendered dimensions of its fandom):

> Nothing, it seemed, was bigger than the game. ... just about every male school kid could repeat the names of all visiting players. So could most of their fathers. All Black victories were sweet and expected. Defeats were national disasters. Rugby was godlike. To question that was to question New Zealand. To suggest that a rugby tour should be cancelled or even disrupted was sacrilege and defilement rolled into one.
>
> *(p. 237)*

The remainder of the chapter explores the ways that individuals exert agency in their adaptation to the transformation of "social patterns and cultural horizons" that are triggered by mediatization, including their "reflexive interpretation of the possible room to act in and against the media" (Lundby, 2014, p. 30). I highlight four elements of mediatization – patriotism, mediation, commercialization, and politicization – that trigger intense emotions, which are evident in a representative quote below.

Rugby, since turning professional is not the game it was. The All Blacks are a hyped up, media driven, precious outfit. Witness the "special" meetings with those players who were not included in RWC squad. Pathetic. The "journey" they had to go through, the counselling etc, absolute nonsense. Also the All Blacks of the past were a faceless, silent, mystical outfit, like Soviet Russia, nowadays they have to be personalities and their opinions are always sought. Most of them are brainless and have nothing much to say anyway...

(54, male, police officer, 2015)

Exemplar survey quotes used throughout include demographic information (which differed by year). The vast majority of survey respondents were Pakeha (of white European descent). Public comments made on news sites cite the poster's online name, date of post and news site. Comments appear as originally written.

Patriotism – the All Blacks are *our* team

The dominating cultural and media discourse around Rugby World Cups clearly articulates the All Blacks to nationalism (Bruce, 2013; Jackson and Scherer, 2013), enabling the All Blacks to command the "profound emotional legitimacy" associated with nationalism (Anderson, 1991, p. 4). Rugby World Cup broadcasts attract significant television audiences. In a country of just over 4.5 million, four 2011 All Blacks games are still in the top-ten most-watched television events, with estimated audiences ranging from 1.6 to over 2 million (Jackson and Scherer, 2013). Over 1.4 million watched the All Blacks 2007 quarter-final loss, and over 1.1 million watched the 2015 final (Jackson and Scherer, 2013; Pearson, 2015). Sky Television subscriptions increased during the 2015 Cup but have since dropped dramatically (Pullar-Strecker, 2016). All survey respondents were aware of the articulation – "Rugby culture is impossible to ignore in this country. RUGBY!!!!111!111!!!" (38, male, electrician, 2015) – but their reactions ranged widely.

Some respondents who were uninterested in rugby reported feeling like lepers or outcasts, finding themselves left out of conversations or constructed by others as unpatriotic: "I think we are told that as New Zealanders we ought to like rugby and support the All Blacks ... I think there is a message conveyed in the media that disliking rugby is unpatriotic" (36, male, lecturer, 2015). One explained that he is "called un-New Zealand, a non-New Zealander and a Traitor" when he says he does not like rugby (43, male, construction project manager, 2011). Another wrote, "people almost critique you for not supporting the all blacks ... you are a traitor" (31, male, student, 2015). Another identified being uninterested as "an unpopular stance" and questioned the overall level of interest while simultaneously identifying the power of the articulation of rugby to nationalism to silence people: "those at work talk about loving it but i know that not all do, but they don't speak up for fear of being labelled a 'wet rag'" (53, X, lecturer, 2015). On an active and contested *Stuff* comments section (359 responses), one poster tried several times to explain what not being a fan felt like, concluding with:

Look, all I'm saying is that someone who doesn't like rugby doesn't have a safe place to express that in this country. At best you get sidelong looks and accusations of not being "patriotic". At worst you get your face kicked in. Believe it or not, that does get old.

(Charles Farley, 28 October 2015)

Another on the same comments section described seeing "my own friend get punched by her boyfriend when she said it wouldn't matter 'all that much if the Aussies win on Saturday if it's a good game'" (Tui_ChCh, 28 October 2015). Such reactions demonstrate how the "dissenting voices" of those who do not feel included "are dangerous voices ... subject to active practices of de-legitimation, symbolic violence, marginalisation or exclusion" (Bruce, 2014, p. 39), and may reflect the intensity of fan support for the articulation of rugby and nationalism.

For one fan, "It's how I identify as a kiwi, through the success of the All Blacks" (23, male, student, 2015). Another explained "our country lives for rugby. It's part of our culture and history" (18, female, 2007). Others saw it as obvious why they wanted an All Blacks win: "Because its the All Blacks duhhh ... they are representing our country which makes me sooooo proud to be a kiwi" (52, female, welder, 2015). Another responded, "Stupid question / / They ARE our national team!" (38, male, sales manager, 2015). For these New Zealanders, the mediatization of rugby has not dimmed their commitment and interest. Indeed, terms like national pride, national identity, pride, proud, patriotism and loyal were commonly used to explain why they supported the team. One wrote: "My life would be close to being over if we don't get up. GET UP THE MIGHTY ALL BLACKS!!!" (23, male, account manager, 2015). For another, "The all blacks are part of our national identity" (25, male, student, 2015). The narrow focus on the national men's team in these quotes is supported by the assumption of survey respondents that most New Zealanders are primarily interested in the All Blacks. In 2015, 84 per cent of survey respondents estimated that most New Zealanders were interested or very interested in the All Blacks, 78 per cent in the World Cup and only 57 per cent in rugby.

The multiple dimensions of fandom and nationalism are encapsulated in the comments of a 2015 survey respondent:

A sense of national pride, and the determination to go "back to back"! I believe that rugby is part of the fabric and wallpaper of our society, it brings people together and unites us in a common goal and sense of achievement when it is done! We may not all be All Blacks, or married to them, or related to them, but we can all share in the sense of achievement when we succeed. The All Blacks are such exceptional ambassadors for our country abroad and at home, representing us well in meet and greets with the public, and with VIPs. We should be proud of them, and do our best to support them in their endeavour to achieve success again in 2015.

(28, female, mother)

However, the intertwining of rugby and patriotism may cause pain as well as pleasure for fans, as seen in reactions to the unexpected 2007 quarter-final loss. On this and other issues, emotional intensity was evident the way that respondents' handwritten or typed responses contained excessive or unnecessary capitalization, double and triple underlining, crossing out, and use of exclamation points and swear words: for example, "Fucking horrible. I felt like throwing the TV out of the window" (20, student, 2007). Indeed, in 2007, many of the 131 survey respondents expressed shock and disbelief at what was, by most accounts, a surprising (but not unprecedented) defeat at the hands of the French. There is evidence of people being literally stunned by the loss. Respondents used terms such as "extremely shocked", "totally unexpected", "surprised", and "couldn't believe" to describe their immediate reactions, which were similarly reflected in their physical responses: "sat in shock for around 10 mins" (23, female, student) or "A lot of words were spoken, But the look on everyone's face was as if we [had] all seen a ghost" (21, student). For approximately half this group, shock quickly shifted to disappointment or sadness ("I sobbed"; 22, male, student) and even to anger that led to swearing at the referee or coach, punching or burning objects and tagging. The most profound descriptions of the intensity of reactions were provided by female respondents who observed the reactions of males. An 18-year-old waitress explained "I was at work at the local pub. We opened early especially so the locals could watch the game. I've never seen so many heartbroken men in my life. There was anger during the game but silence after." Others described similar levels of affect: "My flatmates (boys) were gutted <- swearing etc. The people down the road lit a couch on fire" (19, female, student); "My [boyfriend] cried a bit, went 4 a walk … he saw people kicking over fences, setting stuff on fire and tagging stuff about the Ref everywhere" (20, female, student). Male respondents were more likely to express a profound sense of disappointment at the result, often using the terms gutted or devastated. Even among non-rugby fans, there was empathy for the emotions of friends, relatives and wider society. For example, "Main reaction was a sense of self loss, sadness and heartbreak both personally as well as for a society in a whole … People have been acting very solemn, down and not really talking about it a lot. Some have been angry, some depressed" (20, student). Another reported a group of people "drowning in their sorrows with alcohol with a big 'The ref + France suck' written on the gate behind them" (21, student). Generally, the negative affect was relatively fleeting, seemingly without significant impact on daily life, although one respondent reported cancelling a planned brunch because "friends so upset" (21, female, student). Others reported males in their lives going for walks or runs to shift their emotions, and several decided on self-imposed media bans: "A week's silence & mourning seemed in order – I also deliberately avoided all media for a few days, just to avoid the maudlin NZ media" (44, male).

The intensity of these described emotional and physical reactions are a potent reminder of the affective dimensions of individuals' "deep attachments" (Anderson, 1991, p. 4) to the national men's team, which ranged from joy to despair, and from inclusion to exclusion. They reveal how nationalism is simultaneously embodied, affective and relational (Wetherell, 2012).

Mediation – media "hype"

If mediatization is the long-term, transformative change as a result of the inter-action between communication media and broader social and cultural contexts, then mediation is the process by which objects (images and discourses) about specific topics or issues are circulated. In New Zealand, rugby's position as the most visible and mediated sport is indisputable. Although not as dominant as football in Europe, which can claim as much as 50 per cent of newspaper coverage (Jorgensen, 2002), rugby is the dominant sport in New Zealand newspapers, claiming 19 per cent of space in a full-year analysis of the *Herald* in 2008, and 21 per cent in a smaller newspaper (Bruce, Sedon and Dawson, 2009).

During Rugby World Cups, the team's fortunes are considered significant enough to garner frequent front-page newspaper coverage, and appear as the lead item on news broadcasts. During fieldwork in 2011, a radio producer explained to me that her station required a Rugby World Cup story for every news broadcast. The *Herald* renamed itself the *Rugby Herald*, labeled international news about countries competing in the Cup as "News from Home" and devoted its entire front page to the Cup on five of the first nine days of the event. In 2015, all 42 analysed *Herald* print editions featured a front-page promo related to the Cup, and approxi-mately 1,000 stories appeared in the online edition. The *Sunday Star Times* placed rugby stories on the front page in five of the ten editions analysed, and 80 per cent featured rugby promos. The day after the win, the newspaper dedicated its entire front cover to a close-up of the captain's sweat-stained, serious face, with PRIDE written in capital letters down the left hand side and a graphic of the Cup. Online, TVNZ's *One News* produced over 950 videos and/or articles over a two-month period around the Cup, an average of 11 per day.

The extensive mediation of the Cup was highly visible to the 2015 survey part-icipants. For example, one wrote, "the top 15 articles each day across NZHERALD and STUFF are the ABs and the RWC" (35, male, public servant), while Meandog (*Herald*, 1 November 2015) complained, "TV1 News last night was a FULL HOUR of rugby, not a bit of other news was mentioned". In 2011, comments were similar: "Radio announcers seemed to think that there was nothing else happening in the world. TV News was lead by Rugby nearly every night" (43, male, project manager).

The mediation of the Cup and the All Blacks caused tension and resistance along multiple dimensions. First was access to live games on Sky TV (which in 2015 required an approximately $1,000 annual subscription including Sky Sport). For more than 70 respondents, lack of access affected their ability to watch what they wanted. As one put it, "Not free to air, held to ransom by sky, can only watch what is put on prime, which is fuck all" (24, male, catering).[1] For another, "I can't afford SKY. It is very poor that this is not on free-to-air TV" (56, female, teacher advisor). Public responses on *Stuff* reflected similar perspectives: Stuff 4kiwis (28 October 2015) wrote, "we wouldn't mind all this hype, if we were able to see the actual 80 minute game. But we don't get any of it. All we get are the AB inspired commercial ads. Unless of course you have the money to buy Sky TV. Most people don't have that money to spare."

Returning to Lundby's argument that mediatization occurs when "common attitudes and conceptions" are transformed or "skewed in one direction or another" (Lundby, 2014, p. 22), I argue that the tone and content of survey responses identify the discomfort of some respondents with structural transformations in rugby mediation (no longer free to air) and the skewed direction and intensity of representation. For example, in surveys and public comments on news sites, there was widespread agreement that the mainstream media was overdoing the coverage: words such as blanket, overkill, excessive, saturation, overload, massive, too much, and nauseating were commonly used, alongside more colorful phrases such as "shoved down everyone's throats", "sycophantic fawning", "constant blah blah blah about every little thing" and "bombardment of all blacks propaganda". For example, "Saturation level media coverage gives the impression that everyone is obsessed with the RWC and the All Blacks' prospects of winning" (50, male, public servant, 2015). For one *Herald* poster, Merv (1 November 2015), "the thugby world cup has so polluted all NZ 'news' sources for so long, that I had had a guts-full before the first game started".

Those resistant to the media's focus most frequently categorized it as hype, including many of the 45 per cent of 2015 respondents who felt there was more coverage than needed. For example, "Can't wait for it all to be over, had a guts full of all the media hype" (52, female, public relations, 2015). They also critiqued the way that rugby escaped the confines of the sports pages and sports news to dominate all forms of news media, which made it difficult if not impossible to avoid: "I avoid the coverage like the plague but have it forced upon me when watching TV 'news' which consists of Rugby overkill minutae, boring, boring boring" (65, female, retired, 2015). Another retired woman explained: "Coverage coverage coverage … we are swamped by it as it is deemed NEWS" (70, female, 2015). It was particularly retired people who objected to the efflorescence of rugby coverage beyond its normal boundaries, as evident above and in the length of responses, such as below:

> the TV news programmes have gone crazy devoting huge amounts of time to any minor story related to the All Blacks in the UK. They have no sense of proportion. Really important news stories have been ignored or relegated to 15 second newsbites to enable them to devote at least a quarter of the news to a rugby game EVERY NIGHT!
>
> *(66, male, retired, 2015)*

Other respondents critiqued the stretching of stories and the trivial nature of much of the material. For example, "too much (especially on the shirts they would be playing in)" (30, female, 2007) and "way too much. And they focused on stupid details (what the AB's had for breakfast, who's got a sore thumb…) it seems they are covering it even when nothing is happening" (31, female, 2007). In 2015, one poster explained, "There's media overkill, and there's MEDIA OVERKILL – Stuff, One News, 2-bit dj's on EVERY damn station prattling on about it. A cave is looking good" (AlHalco, *Stuff*, 28 October 2015). The following post encapsulates something of Frandsen's (2014) description of mediatization as having potentially diverse and contradictory effects across different domains:

> I love the world cup. What I am sick of is the sycophantic fawning and cheerleading from much of the NZ media and Sky commentators and sadly a lot of NZ seem to buy into the rubbish they speak. The media are selling a product – to me rugby will always be first and foremost a sport. I don't buy into the product but love the game.
>
> *(printer1, Stuff, 28 October 2015)*

Media hype, along with other changes in rugby, has reduced rather than enhanced enjoyment for some former rugby fans, particularly men. For example, "I think the media over does it, I dont [want] to know every detail about what the players do off the field, I did once enjoy watching rugby before the high profile hype and professionalism" (42, male, service technician, 2015) and "Media overkill has actually reduced any enthusiasm for the games" (53, male, librarian, 2015). For some, it has completely turned them off: "Years ago, I used to enjoy watching All Black games, but the years of media overkill on the RWC have made me anti-rugby" (67, male, retired, 2015).

Thus, overall, the sample indicates that media coverage is seen as heavy-handed, exhaustive and, for many respondents, overkill to the point of causing considerable irritation.

Commercialization – All Blacks in my fridge

As a process, mediatization is strongly linked with commercialization which, among other economic elements, is a "particularly significant engine for change" (Frandsen, 2014, p. 528). With New Zealand's late entry into professional sport, some survey respondents were highly critical of what they saw as "hypercommercialisation" of what one called "the grubby narrow commercial world that runs Rugby" (52, female, orchard worker, 2011). The view of another respondent – "Let's not overlook that this is all about MONEY" (51, male, dairy farmer, 2011) – clearly reflects Romanos's (2002, p. 13) argument that "professionalism means one thing – the only god worshipped is money".

In 2015, several participants were particularly upset by a sponsor's decision to create black milk containers, drawing on the association of black with patriotic support for the All Blacks. For example, "I am sick to death of the marketing campaigns nationwide. Why do we need black milk bottles with JERSEY #s on them? It's RIDICULOUS!!! …Stop rebranding my milk bottles for crying out loud!" (24, female, pre-service teacher). Another wrote:

> I hate the way in which all the businesses try and jump on it – black milk bottles and other products that have no connection with sport, Air NZ images of rugby players in their hiphop safety video. That makes the RWC feel more all-encompassing and invasive, getting into your fridge and into the ad breaks of non-rugby TV programmes.
>
> *(62, female, student)*

This process of commercial sponsors associating their brands with nationalism has transformed some respondents' relationship to the team: "All Blacks are a commercial brand posing as a national sports team. I feel a false sense of identity" (46, male, teacher, 2015). For MrT1978, mediatization was a key component in lack of interest: "I was put off rugby … when, I think, the All Blacks turned from being a national team into a brand" (*Stuff*, 28 October 2015).

I conclude this section with a post that reflects the intersecting nature of resistance to mediatization:

> I don't hate rugby, I just find the game mind numbingly boring, and I find the professional game, the All Blacks in particular, to be over commercialised. Not to mention the ABs being way too over exposed, be it silly stories in the press about their favourite songs or what they had for breakfast that morning, to their endorsement of any product imaginable from milk to credit cards and everything else in between that can be painted black.
>
> *(C.J., Stuff, 28 October 2015)*

As with media hype, commercialization has turned away some former fans: "Corporations own the ABs now so we lost all interest in them and the sport itself" (58, female, invalid beneficiary). Factchecker (*Stuff*, 28 October 2015) explained that he used to watch every All Blacks match because "it meant something then" but was no longer interested because the team was "over commercialised", and sighmin (*Stuff*, 28 October 2015) was "being put off after being an avid follower" because of the growing cost, commercialization and politicization of the game and players.

Politicization

A final area of critique of mediatization was seen in the reaction to Prime Minister John Key inserting himself into All Blacks coverage. Respondents used terms such as thoroughly dislike, detest, can't stand, and majorly turned off to describe their feelings about media coverage that featured Key and the players. In 2015, they described the players as "political pawns" and "John Key's play things", and the Prime Minister as "ruining the All Blacks brand", "riding on their coat-tails", "swooning and fawn[ing] all over the team", and "turning the All Blacks into a corporate buddy". As one put it, "RUGBY has been hijacked by john key" (45, male, unemployed). Another wrote, "I don't like the Prime Minister using the RWC for political gain" (51, male, engineer). Some public comments on news stories reflected the survey responses, such as Mary Lamb (*Herald*, 1 November 2015) who wrote, "Shame about AB's becoming the PM's marketing tool."

As with media hype and commercialization, politicization was cited by some posters as a reason to turn away from the sport. Rinchin (*Stuff*, 28 October 2015), who objected to "the blatant use of the AB's as a PR machine for John Key", explained that "it's the political involvement that has turned me from part of the silent majority who couldn't care less into a full blown hater." Politicization even made several hope for an All Blacks loss. For example: "almost hoping that New Zealand lose just to wipe the smirk off the PM's face" (37, female, social researcher), or "I want them to lose so I don't have to hear John Key crowing" (39, male, music/ design). The following quote perhaps best summarizes the ways in which mediatiz- ation has transformed some New Zealanders' relationships with rugby:

> Far too much use of them as political pawns. The corporatization and branding of rugby is tedious – they're everywhere. I used to enjoy watching rugby, but at some point I realized that it is all about overpaid "jocks" … thumping into each other for big corporates and big money. … In the old days rugby players might have also been lawyers, builders, teachers … now they're just jocks and walking billboards.
>
> *(42, male librarian, 2015)*

Conclusions

Frandsen (2014, p. 530) argues that relationships between media and sport are "highly influenced" by the cultures and social contexts in which they are experienced. Thus, it is important to recognize that the "social patterns and cultural horizons" (Lundby, 2014, p. 30) that inform New Zealanders' current relationships with rugby have a long history dating back more than a century. Mediatization's cataclysmic impact on the elite levels of the sport has, therefore, occurred very recently within that extended horizon. Investigating the tensions, public anxieties and "specific and contested discourses that shape our understanding of the problem at hand" (Kunelius, 2014, p. 82) has revealed the diverse and sometimes contra- dictory ways in which individuals exert agency in their adaptation to mediatization, including their "reflexive interpretation of the possible room to act in and against the media" (Lundby, 2014, p. 30).

While evidence such as high television ratings for Rugby World Cup matches, comments on news sites and survey responses suggest that mediatization has had little impact on the articulation of rugby and nationalism for some fans, there is also evidence that mediatization processes have transformed other New Zealanders' relationships with the All Blacks, including intensifying their resistance to rugby as a mediatized product. The analysis of media coverage and public responses to the mediatized object that is the Rugby World Cup points to powerful emotions generated by shifts in the way that rugby is structured and mediated. The trajectory of professional rugby towards an increasingly commercialized, mediated and politicized environment appears to trigger intense reactions. The affective power of media and cultural discourses around rugby appear to work in two directions: one that bolsters feelings of pride, patriotism and national belonging, and one that alienates, angers or frustrates.

Indeed, turning a mediatization lens on the evidence from this longitudinal research reveals shifting patterns of identification and engagement with rugby that strongly suggest a level of resistance to mediatizing processes that, for some, particularly those over 40 who valued the amateur era, has decreased their formerly strong commitment to and emotional investment in the success of the national men's rugby team. Thus, it appears that the mediatized moments of Rugby World Cups may contribute to the transformation of "common attitudes or conceptions" (Lundby, 2014, p. 22) about rugby's place in the national imagination.

If Lundby is correct that the extent of media saturation "shapes" individuals' interactions, including what causes them "to act or not to act" (ibid., pp. 22–23), the evidence here suggests that the trajectory of rugby's mediatization has caused some New Zealanders to turn away from a sport that previously brought them joy and belonging, even to the point of becoming rugby haters. I conclude that the kinds of reactions evident in this research and more broadly in New Zealand culture point to a form of contestation and resistance to mediatization that may reflect a long-term transformation in how New Zealand's sporting nationalism is constructed.

Note

1 Prime TV (Sky's free-to-air subsidiary) offered delayed coverage of every All Blacks pool match, highlights of other games and live coverage of two quarter finals, the All Blacks semi-final, the bronze final and the final (Cunliffe, 2015).

References

Anderson, B. (1991). *Imagined communities: Reflections on the origin and spread of nationalism.* Verso, London.
Bruce. T. (2013). (Not) a stadium of 4 million: Speaking back to dominant discourses of the Rugby World Cup in New Zealand. *Sport in Society, 16*(7), 899–911.
Bruce, T. (2014). A spy in the house of rugby: Living (in) the emotional spaces of nationalism and sport. *Emotion, Space and Society, 12,* 32–40.
Bruce, T., Sedon, C. and Dawson, D. (2009). Media representation of sports in two New Zealand newspapers: Analysis of a full year of coverage. Unpublished manuscript, University of Waikato, Hamilton.
Cunliffe, R. (2015). Prime announces 2015 Rugby World Cup coverage. *Throng,* 1 April. Retrieved from www.throng.co.nz/2015/04/prime-announces-2015-rugby-world-cup-coverage (accessed 24 November 2016).
Fougere, G. (1989). Sport, culture and identity: The case of rugby football. In D. Novitz and B. Willmott (eds), *Culture and identity in New Zealand* (pp. 110–122). Wellington: G.P. Books.

Frandsen, K. (2014). Mediatization of sports. In K. Lundby (ed.), *Mediatization: Concept, changes, consequences* (pp. 525–543). New York: Peter Lang.

Hepp, A. and Krotz, F. (eds) (2014). *Mediatized worlds: Culture and society in a media age.* Basingstoke: Palgrave Macmillan.

Herald (2002a). Editorial: Rugby Union wrong in World Cup fiasco. *New Zealand Herald*, 12 March. Retrieved from www.nzherald.co.nz/nz/news/article.cfm?c_id=1&objectid=1191084 (accessed 24 November 2016).

Herald (2002b). Editorial: Rugby board must go. *New Zealand Herald*, 25 July. Retrieved from www.nzherald.co.nz/nz/news/article.cfm?c_id=1&objectid=2196971 (accessed 5 January 2017).

Hobsbawm, E.J. (1991). *Nations and nationalism since 1789: Programme, myth, reality* (Canto edition). Cambridge: Cambridge University Press.

Hutchins, B. and Phillips, M. (1999). The global union: Globalization and the Rugby World Cup. In T.J.L. Chandler and J. Nauright (eds), *Making the rugby world: Race, gender, commerce* (pp. 149–164). London: Frank Cass.

Jackson, S.J. and Scherer, J. (2013). Rugby World Cup 2011: Sport mega-events and the contested terrain of space, bodies and commodities, *Sport in Society*, *16*(7), 883–898.

Jorgensen, S.S. (2005). Industry or independence? Survey of the Scandinavian sports press. *Mondaymorning*, November, pp. 1–8.

Kunelius, R. (2014). Climate change challenges: An agenda for de-centered mediatization research. In K. Lundby (ed.), *Mediatization of communication* (pp. 63–86). Berlin: Mouton de Gruyter.

Laidlaw, C. (1999). *Rights of passage: Beyond the New Zealand identity crisis.* Auckland: Hodder Moa Beckett.

Livingstone, S. and Lunt, P. (2014). Mediatization: An emerging paradigm for media and communication research? In K. Lundby (ed.), *Mediatization of communication* (pp. 703–723). Berlin: Mouton de Gruyter.

Lundby, K. (ed.) (2014). *Mediatization of communication*. Berlin: Mouton de Gruyter.

MacLean, M. (1999). Of warriors and blokes: The problem of Māori rugby for Pākehā masculinity in New Zealand. In J. Nauright and T. Chandler (eds), *Making the rugby world: Race, gender, commerce* (pp. 1–26). London: Frank Cass.

Martin, G.J. (2003). The game is not the same: A history of professional rugby in New Zealand. Master's thesis, Auckland University of Technology, Auckland.

Pearson, J. (2015). Prime beats Sky as more than one million Kiwis tune in to watch the All Blacks win the Rugby World Cup final. *Stuff*, 2 November. Retrieved from www.stuff.co.nz/sport/rugby/international/73589391/Prime-beats-Sky-as-more-than-one-million-Kiwis-tune-in-to-watch-the-All-Blacks-win-the-Rugby-World-Cup-final (accessed 24 November 2016).

Phillips, J. (1999). The hard man: Rugby and the formation of male identity in New Zealand. In J. Nauright and T. Chandler (eds), *Making men: Rugby and masculine identity* (pp. 70–90). London: Frank Cass.

Phillips, J. (2000). Sport and future Australasian culture. In J.A. Mangan and J. Nauright (eds), *Sport in Australasian society: Past and present* (pp. 323–332). London: Frank Cass.

Philp, M. (1997). Stars and stripes: What does Adidas get for its $100 million deal with the All Blacks? *Listener*, 22 November, pp. 18–21.

Pullar-Strecker, T. (2016). Big drop in Sky TV subscribers after Rugby World Cup, $300m wiped off shares. *Stuff*, 6 May. Retrieved from www.stuff.co.nz/business/industries/79689666/Big-drop-in-Sky-TV-subscribers-after-Rugby-World-Cup-300m-wiped-off-shares (accessed 24 November 2016).

Quinn, K. (1993). *The encyclopedia of world rugby* (rev. ed.). Artamon, NSW, Australia: ABC.

Richards, T. (1999). *Dancing on our bones: New Zealand, South Africa, rugby and racism.* Wellington: Bridget Williams Books.

Riddiford, J. (2015). Stuff and NZ Herald audiences continue to grow in Nielsen's latest online rankings. *Stop Press,* 4 November. Retrieved from http://stoppress.co.nz/news/kiwis-prefer-googling-and-facebooking-stuffs-popularity-growing (accessed 6 April 2016).

Robson, T. (2009). Rugby's interest rates fall sharply. *The Dominion Post,* 6 August. Retrieved from www.stuff.co.nz/sport/rugby/2724314/Rugbys-interest-rates-fall-sharply (accessed 24 November 2016).

Romanos, J. (2002). *The Judas game: The betrayal of New Zealand rugby.* Wellington: Darius Press.

Ryan, G. (ed.). (2005). *Tackling rugby myths: Rugby and New Zealand society 1854–2004.* Dunedin: University of Otago Press.

Scherer, J. and Jackson, S.J. (2007). Sports advertising, cultural production and corporate nationalism at the global–local nexus: Branding the New Zealand All Blacks. *Sport in Society,* 10(2), 268–284.

Silk, M. and Jackson, S. (2000). Globalisation and sport in New Zealand. In C. Collins (ed.), *Sport in New Zealand society* (pp. 99–113). Palmerston North: Dunmore Press.

UMR (2011). *Rugby World Cup anticipation.* August. Thorndon, Wellington: UMR Research.

Wetherell, M. (2012). *Affect and emotion: A new social science understanding.* London: Sage.

Zierold, M. (2012). Mass media, media culture and mediatisation. In B. Neumann.and A. Nunning with M. Horn (eds), *Travelling concepts for the study of culture* (pp. 337–352). Berlin: Mouton de Gruyter.

8

THE INTERNATIONAL CRICKET COUNCIL CRICKET WORLD CUP

A "second class" megamediasport event?

Dominic Malcolm and Thomas Fletcher

2015 was the least eventful men's International Cricket Council (ICC) Cricket World Cup (CWC) of the twenty-first century.[1] Its single "major" controversy came when the ICC president, Bangladesh's Mustafa Kamal, threatened to resign from his non-executive post if an umpiring decision which, he felt, led to his nation's exit from the tournament was not investigated. Subsequently, he was excluded from the trophy presentation ceremony and retaliated by threatening to reveal "mischievous things" taking place in the politics of international cricket (ICC, 2015a).

There is, of course, some irony in the portrayal of this CWC as uneventful for these quadrennial events are frequently marred by controversy. The 2011 CWC was awarded to a joint India–Pakistan–Bangladesh–Sri Lanka bid that was submitted late. After being de-selected as co-hosts due to security concerns, Pakistan initiated legal proceedings against the ICC (Samiuddin, 2009). During the tournament, Bangladesh fans attacked the West Indian team bus and fought police following victory over England (Bandyopadhyay, 2013). Four years before that the CWC, staged in eight different Caribbean states, was dogged by speculation that the Pakistani coach, the former England cricketer, Bob Woolmer, had been murdered (Malcolm *et al.*, 2010). In 2003 England and New Zealand forfeited matches due to security concerns in Zimbabwe and Kenya; in England's case, in diplomatic protest at human rights abuses in Zimbabwe (Holden, 2010). One of the world's leading players, Australia's Shane Warne, also failed a drugs test.

To those unfamiliar with cricket, these events will jar with the ideological conceptions of the game as genteel and civilized (Fletcher, 2015; Malcolm, 2013). However, citing these events also alerts the reader to the importance of context in understanding the CWC as a "megamediasport" event for "mediatisation is ... not at all a uniform socio-cultural change following the same paths across different fields" (Frandsen, 2014, p. 530). Rather, certain elements of cricket are vital to understanding both the game in general and the 2015 ICC CWC in particular. Consequently, this chapter begins with an overview of cricket's structural and cultural context. Following Frandsen (ibid.), it then provides a historical perspective to the commercialization and mediatization of the game, before examining the implications of context and development for the structure and presentation of the event. Specifically, an analysis of the institutions/production and content/text of the 2015 ICC CWC suggests that mediatization reinforces – rather than ruptures – this sport's traditions and conventions. Thus, the chapter argues that the media–sport relationship does not have an essential logic whereby the former comes to overwhelm the latter, but is structured by the contextual specificities of a sport and its personnel.

The structural and cultural context of cricket

Fundamental to an understanding of cricket are three interlinking features: the game's complexity and statistical orientation, the structure of its international competition, and its multiple, co-existing, game forms.

Elaborate rules

The game's rules are notoriously elaborate. Its 42 laws (and five appendices) encompass 116 pages (MCC, 2010). Contributing to this complexity is an extreme form of quantification. The average edition of *Wisden Cricketers' Almanack* – the annually published "bible" of cricket – contains approximately 1,000 pages of numerical data and 50 pages of text. Records embrace the minutiae of the game (e.g. the most runs scored for a particular wicket against a particular team at a particular venue). This statistical complexity bolsters the game's enigmatic, esoteric and essentially English character. Cricket is a "visually distinct manifestation of Englishness, but at the same time that everybody can see it, like a cryptic crossword, only certain people have the 'code' required to make sense of it" (Malcolm, 2013, p. 163).

Exclusionary structures

The structure of international cricket is riven with exclusionary mechanisms. Cricket's 105 member nations are structured into a fairly rigid three-tier hierarchy: Full (10); Associate (38); and Affiliate (57) Members (ICC, undated). In *practice* membership status is closely linked to a nation's relationship with the former British Empire. Full members have greater voting rights on the ICC Executive Committee, greater access to competitions like the CWC and, once attained, "Full" member status has never been revoked. Complicating the organizational structure is the variability of members' constitutions (the West Indies is a multi-state confederation; the side always referred to as "England" formally represents the England and *Wales* Cricket Board), and the fluidity of player "nationality". The England cricket team, in particular, has appropriated the playing talent of other member nations as a consequence of its centrality to Empire. Indeed, England's captain at the 2015 ICC CWC, Eoin Morgan, first played international cricket for an Associate member, Ireland. Many of the emerging nations (e.g. Scotland, Canada, USA) are highly dependent on migrant labour. We would assert that no other sport is so deeply embroiled in post-colonial politics (Malcolm and Waldman, 2017; Fletcher, 2015).

Multiplicity of game forms

International cricket is played over multiple game forms. Initially, international cricket contests consisted of two innings of indefinite length per side but within an overall duration normally restricted to five days. Due to playing inequalities, early games frequently entailed teams with different numbers of participants. Consequently, to distinguish between these and contests between sides with an equal number of players, the terms "Test" and "First Class" match were applied. Below the international level, shorter versions of cricket have always been the norm.

Whilst many sports have variants, the relationships between cricket's multiple game forms – namely "Test" or "First Class" cricket , one-day internationals (ODIs) usually consisting of one 50-over innings per side, and most recently Twenty20 cricket, consisting of one 20-overs innings per side – is distinct. First, equipment is not standardized between the different game forms. Second, the hierarchy of game forms in other sports is much clearer. Whereas the Fédération Internationale de Football Association (FIFA) produce (for each sex) a single table ranking football playing nations, the ICC produce (for each sex) a table for each of the game's three formats. Third, the international cricket programme is highly complex and differentiated. The ICC CWC exists alongside the ICC World Twenty20 (a biennial, 20-overs, 16-team tournament) and the ICC Champions Trophy (quadrennial, 50-overs, eight-teams) as well as the ICC Intercontinental Cup and ICC World Cricket League Championship (competitions for Associate and Affiliate members competing in matches for over five days and one day respectively). A system called the "Future Tours Programme", which obliged all Full members to play home and away Test matches against each other once every 4 years, has recently been abandoned, while proposals for a World Test Championship continue to be debated (Wilson, 2014). It is an anomaly that the premier cricketing competition uses a format which cricket nomenclature implicitly defines as "Second Class".

Commercialization and mediatization of cricket

These three interlinking features need to be understood in light of commercial and media-related developments, for although the trajectory of contemporary cricket is very different from the path pursued for the last 100 years, the conflict between cricket as an ideal and cricket as an industry actually pre-dates most contemporary sports forms. Since codification (mid-1700s), cricket has witnessed numerous incarnations in the name of progress and modernization. However, perhaps not surprisingly, the sport–media complex has been at the heart of cricket's recent (r)evolution. In this most traditional of sports, it would take until the 1960s for the game's administrators to make major concessions to foster a more accessible and entertaining consumer sport (Wright, 1994). Subsequently, the game's longest and most prestigious format, the Test match, has become an endangered species as commercial investors and the public have shown a determined preference for shorter competition formats.

The speed of cultural change is contingent on prevailing definitions of culture and the demands and expectations of multiple parties. It is widely considered that the commercialization of cricket in England experienced a step change in 1963 with the introduction of the first one-day competition, the Gillette Cup (Wright, 1994). The Gillette Cup was a knockout competition for the seventeen "First-Class" English counties (anomalously including Glamorgan of Wales) and consisted of a preliminary eliminator, three rounds of midweek matches, and a Saturday Final at Lord's in London (the "spiritual home" of cricket). These five days of cricket were spread over four months. Over the next 50 years, one-day games would increase in both frequency and concentration. The sale of broadcasting rights to this format, plus the intensive marketing and globalization of the game, enabled cricket to become a "mediasport".

Various iterations of the game's shorter form have come and gone over the last 50 years. Kerry Packer's "World Series Cricket" was the earliest sustained attempt to turn cricket into a mediatized spectacle (Harriss, 1990; Cashman, 2011). This limited-overs competition was contested by players wearing coloured clothes (rather than the traditional whites) and played under floodlights with a white ball. The events, widely denigrated as raucous "circuses" and "pyjama cricket", were heavily resisted by cricket's authorities (Sturm, 2015b). While Packer's stylization subsequently achieved a degree of acceptance, even shorter alternatives have emerged in pursuit of a commercially lucrative formula. In New Zealand, for example, "Action Cricket" was played in 1992–1993. This 20-over format allowed two games to take place on the same day. Subsequently "Cricket Max" (1996–2003), a three-hour format where teams would twice bat for ten overs, was introduced with the unique selling point of the "max zone"; an area at either end of the pitch where, once the ball entered, the score for the shot was doubled. Similarly, in Australia, "Super Eights" (1996–1997) reduced teams from 11 to 8 players. A hybrid "Cricket Super Max Eights" also met with limited success (Sturm, 2015a).

Ironically, given England's perceived role as guardian of the traditions of cricket, it was here that the format that many now see as the game's greatest potential for future growth, Twenty20, was introduced. Such was the immediate commercial success of Twenty20 that a number of domestic-based and internationally resonant Twenty20 competitions have come and gone over the last decade. Current iterations are the "Indian Premier League" (IPL), Australian "Big Bash", "Bangladesh Premier League", "Caribbean Premier League" and "Pakistan Super League" (established 2016). Despite having established the format and witnessed its commercial success elsewhere around the world, the UK's current Twenty20 competition is perceived to lack comparable global appeal, leading to speculation that a UK city-based competition is imminent (Ammon, 2015).

Of all such competitions, the IPL has unquestionably had the greatest commercial and cultural impact. Introduced in 2008, it is based upon a city franchise system and has an annual televised player auction. The current eight squads are each a mix of Indian (minimum 14) and overseas (maximum 10) players. Up to four foreign players are allowed in any starting 11. When the event began in 2008 the original eight franchises were bought for US$724 million and broadcasting rights were sold to Sony for US$1.94 billion over a 10-year period (Gupta, 2010). As of 2014, the IPL is estimated to be worth in excess of US$7 billion. Financially, the IPL dwarfs anything else in cricket, making more money each year than two CWCs combined (Rumford, 2011); evidence of the shifting power relations that underpin the "post-Westernisation" (Rumford, 2007) of cricket. As a consequence, the IPL poses a direct challenge to the status of the CWC as cricket's premier global event.

The IPL, and Twenty20 in general, has become emblematic of the mediatization and commercialization of the game. Twenty20 is an exemplar of cultural change in a sport that has "run the gamut from colonial symbol with arcane and, for many, unteachable rules to a spectacle aimed at lay audiences and markets" (Axford and Huggins, 2010, p. 1328). While it is not uncommon for sports to adapt to suit the needs of television, sponsors and other stakeholders (Frandsen, 2014), the extent to which cricket has changed to suit commercial interests – changing rules, playing at night and fundamentally restructuring competitions – is unprecedented. While Twenty20 incorporates the game's fundamental elements (i.e. the game is still contested between 11 wo/men on a 22-yard strip of grass involving bat and ball), viewers experience a simulacrum of the sport, a "hyper-cricket" (Axford and Huggins, 2011).

Yet, ironically the sport remains deeply conservative. Graeme Wright (a former editor of *Wisden Cricketers' Almanack*) has argued that "modern" formats offend the sensibilities of cricket purists. In pointing to the apparent appetite for "simplicity, an impatience with the long view and, instead, a demand for instant gratification and a disdain for what was subtle" (Wright, 1994, p. 17), he epitomizes the view that the game is betraying its inheritance in order to further short-term commercial goals. Indeed, for many traditionalists, the opportunities made possible by one-day cricket – especially Twenty20 – are accompanied by a series of threats which emanate from the rapid commercialization and mediatization of the game, and the unresolved tensions between different formats (Axford and Huggins, 2011; Rumford and Wagg, 2010). The ECB was the only national governing body to prohibit its national players from competing in the IPL's launch season, despite their protestations over potential financial losses (Mehta *et al.*, 2009), but the IPL continues to generate tensions in particular between the West Indian Cricket Board (WICB) and West Indian players.

Specifically, Rumford and Wagg (2010, p. 7) question whether the commercial imperatives of cricket can be sustained across three different formats. They note that Twenty20, and the IPL in particular, "does not dovetail into other cricketing structures; it competes with (and threatens) them". Consequently, the sustainability of ODIs/50-overs cricket is questionable, especially in a context where India so overwhelmingly dominates the market and so clearly favours Twenty20 cricket over other forms (Mehta, 2009; Rumford, 2011). Consequently, the current and future status of the CWC as the premier cricketing competition is in doubt. The CWC is not only "Second Class" in name, but also in terms of income-generation and audience numbers.

The 2015 ICC CWC stands at the convergence of these developmental trends. It is a form of the game originally and purposefully designed for mediated consumption and the flagship event of the international cricket calendar. Yet, concurrently, it is also firmly locked into the structural logics of the traditions of cricket, remaining enigmatically complex and exhibiting peculiar international dynamics. It stands in constant comparison with both a more prestigious (Test match) and more popular/commercial (Twenty20) variant. In the next two sections, we explore how these things impact on both the structure of the tournament, and the content of its mediated presentation.

The ICC men's Cricket World Cup: a megamediasport event?

In light of the above, it is important to consider the extent to which the CWC is in fact a "megamediasport event". The characteristics of mega-events are well established. Mega-events are "large-scale cultural (including commercial and sporting) events, which have a dramatic character, mass popular appeal and international significance" (Roche, 2000, p. 1). Mega-events are deemed to have significant consequences for the host city, region or nation in which they occur, and attract considerable media coverage (Horne, 2010). For Roche (2008), mega-events are short-term events with significant long-term pre- and post-event impacts on the host nation.

Sports mega-events can further be classified by scale, scope and reach (Roche, 2000). According to Horne (2010) "first-order" events include the Summer Olympic and Paralympic Games and the (men's) FIFA Football World Cup. "Second-order" events include the Winter Olympic and Paralympic Games, the (men's) Union of European Football Association (UEFA) Championships, and the International Association of Athletics Federations (IAAF) World Championships. Finally, "third-order" events include the Asia and Pan American Games, the African Cup of Nations and the America's Cup in sailing.

Where does the CWC sit within such a typology? CWCs are demonstrably large-scale events. The combined television audience for the 2011 version was a reported 2.2 billion people (Sturm, 2015b) and this persuaded ESPN and STAR to purchase the television rights for ICC events (estimated to have cost US$2.2 billion over 8 years), thus integrating the sport with global media giants *Disney* and

News Corporation. The 2015 version was broadcast in seven languages across 220 territories. In all, 1,400 members of the media attended the event (ICC, 2015b). The tournament's finale, contested between the co-host nations, became the most-watched cricket match ever in Australia, with national viewing figures peaking at 4.218 million (Sinclair, 2015). Earlier in the tournament, a match between India and Pakistan became the most watched cricket match in history, with an estimated global television audience of over one billion (Sarkar, 2015).

What Axford and Huggins (2010) call the (tele)mediatization of cricket was evident in the way consumers could interact with and through cricket's "new" media technologies (e.g. via texting, blogging, tweeting, contributing to online proto "communities", online gaming, and in-game betting). The ICC claimed that the tournament website attracted 26.25 million unique visitors, and 227 million page views overall, and that the tournament app became the market leader in a total of 48 countries (ICC, 2015b). Two Twitter-based controversies arose during the tournament. In the first, a fan's call for West Indian batsman Chris Gayle to be dropped was retweeted by the president of the WICB, Whycliffe Cameron (Premachandran, 2015). In the second, Scotland's Majid Haq was sent home after sending a tweet implying that his de-selection was racially motivated (Madeley, 2015).

CWCs can also be considered mega-events in terms of their impact beyond the confines of the tournament itself. Preceded by extended qualifying tournaments which structure the international fixtures of Associate and Affiliate members, the 2015 tournament was also notable for forcing the 2015 IPL to be put back a few weeks later than its traditional timeslot, and for the delayed release of a number of Bollywood films (Shah, 2015). The legacy of the tournament was evident during subsequent cricket contests, as journalists speculated about how the 2015 CWC had instigated a fundamental re-stylization of both ODI and Test match tactics. Most enduringly, the event helped brand New Zealand, which "seemed to be granted especial attention with clichéd and hyperbolic praise as 'perfect hosts', for embodying the spirit of the CWC, and for collectively embracing the event as a nation" (Sturm, 2015b, p. 236). In this respect, therefore, the 2015 CWC was a significant cultural and political event shaping conceptions of cricket in general and New Zealand nationhood in particular.

However, despite the CEO of the ICC describing it as "the most sought after prize in cricket and one of the greatest tournaments in world sport" (cited in Horne, 2010, p. 1556), the CWC is outside the first order of mega-events. A fundamental reason for this is the geo-political position of cricket, which, in turn, derives from the game's English and Imperial traditions. Seven of the ICC's ten Full members, and five of the 11 CWCs, have been staged in what could be described as "developing countries" (see Table 8.1).

The challenges of hosting mega-events in the developing world have been noted, as history shows that such events are frequently mired by organizational deficiencies, poor budget management, unstable national politics, and local poverty (e.g. Horne, 2010; Lorde, Greenidge and Devonish, 2011). Moreover, despite

TABLE 8.1 Cricket World Cups: location and competition structure

Year	Host	Teams	Matches	Duration (days)
1975	England	8	15	14
1979	England	8	15	14
1983	England	8	27	16
1987	India–Pakistan	8	27	31
1992	Australia	9	39	31
1996	India–Pakistan–Sri Lanka	12	37	31
1999	England	12	42	36
2003	South Africa–Zimbabwe–Kenya	14	54	42
2007	Caribbean	16	51	46
2011	India–Bangladesh–Sri Lanka	14	49	42
2015	Australia–New Zealand	14	49	43

Source: Data extracted from Arnold and Wynne-Thomas (2009) and ESPN cricinfo websites.

increasing claims for cricket's globalization (Rumford and Wagg, 2010), it remains the case that the CWC event is *quasi*-global, with participants invariably limited to members of the former British Empire. Although claimed to be the third most watched sports event in the world (Sturm, 2015b), the CWC compares unfavourably with other first order mega-events on account of its restricted geographical appeal and, consequently, its limited commercial market (particularly in Europe, South East Asia and the Americas). Indicative of this are the commercial links the CWC attracts, for although global companies including Pepsi, LG, Hyundai, Castrol, Moneygram, Emirates Airways and Reebok were official 2015 sponsors, two further sponsors (the Reliance Group and MRF Tyres) are essentially national (Indian) organizations.

Underpinning questions about the CWC's status as a megamediasport event, therefore, is the sport's peculiar international structure. As Table 8.1 illustrates, CWCs manifest ongoing tension between global reach and meaningful competition; between tournament size and quality. Initially tournaments were held in England and took about two weeks to complete.[2] The 1975 competitors were ICC Full members (England, Australia, West Indies, New Zealand, India, Pakistan) plus Sri Lanka and a composite "East Africa" side (an explicit example of juggling globalizing and competition imperatives). Tournaments initially consisted of 15 matches (60 overs per side) played in traditional white outfits and with a red ball. The 50-over-per-side format was introduced for the 1987 CWC due to the shorter daylight hours in India and Pakistan but, by this point, tournaments consisted of 27 matches extended over four weeks. The steady increase in the number of competitors, matches played, and tournament duration is fundamentally structured by the traditional hierarchy of member countries, as "Full member" nations are joined by a varying number of "Associates". Tournament formats have been "tweaked" from simple group and elimination phases (1975–1987), to a round-robin format (1992), "super-sixes" (1999–2003) and "super-eights" (2007) (essentially two interlinking sets of round-robin matches) as a way of providing opportunities for emerging countries while protecting the participatory and commercial interests of the established. Many suggested that the CWC had become too protracted, especially the group stages of the competition (Rumford, 2011), but, baulking trends in the tournament's development, the 2015 event featured just 14 teams. There are proposals for the 2019 event to be reduced further to ten teams.

These issues formed a major strand of the 2015 ICC CWC narrative. The ICC's CEO David Richardson was quoted as saying that the world governing body would like to create "a bigger, better, global game" particularly involving the US (Wigmore, 2015). Conversely Tony Irish, Executive Chairman of the International Players' Union, argued that the proposed future exclusion of "minnows" defied the "global view" the game needed (Booth, 2015). The Western press attributed the potential changes to the failure of India to qualify for the latter stages of the 2007 CWC and the subsequent lost revenue, but future amendments were portrayed as "effectively making it less a World Cup than a continuation of a members' club … the ICC is alienating the smaller countries that it should be cherishing" (Brenkley, 2015, p. 6). The logic that fewer teams equals more competitive equals more spectator-friendly events, was problematized during the 2015 ICC CWC by Ireland's victories over two "Full members" (the West Indies and Zimbabwe), England's elimination following the group stages, and the view that "some of the closest and most engaging matches at this World Cup have been between Associate nations" (ibid., p. 9). The logics of global expansion were compromised by commercial interests and complicated by cricket's historical legacies.

While some aspects of the media critiqued this sense of cricket being a private members' club (Booth, 2015; Brenkley, 2015), others served to replicate the status quo. In keeping with the peculiar structure of international cricket, broadcasters shared output and in so doing drew on an unusually non-partisan pool of commentators. During the tournament it was not unusual for a combination of Indian (Sanjay Manjrekar), English (Michael Atherton), Australian (Shane Warne) and New Zealand (Ian Smith) commentators to be deployed for a single match. Uniquely perhaps, the anchor presenter for the host Australian broadcaster (Mark Nicholas), is a former player from their greatest rivals, England.

Discussions about the format of future tournaments continue. A central dynamic is commercial revenue and the value the media can extract from particular types of fixture involving particular teams. However all such debates remain contoured by the hierarchical structure of the international game which itself stems from cricket's Imperial past.

Presentation of the 2015 ICC men's Cricket World Cup

Contrary to previous concerns over the sustainability of a 50-over format, the 2015 ICC CWC offered a degree of redemption, producing "a more entertaining spectacle" (Sturm, 2015b, p. 236). The success of the event was attributed to exhilarating on-field performances. A significant number of new records were set: the highest team score (417: Australia); the fastest score of 50 (18 balls: Brendon

McCullum, New Zealand), and fastest 150 (62 balls: AB de Villiers, South Africa); the two highest individual scores (215, Chris Gayle, West Indies; 237, Martin Guptil, New Zealand); the first player to score four consecutive CWC centuries (Kumar Sangakara, Sri Lanka); the first team to post consecutive scores in excess of 400 (South Africa). What we saw at the 2015 CWC were tactical innovations that were perceived to transplant the "best" aspects of Test match (attacking bowling) cricket and the flair of Twenty20 batting into the 50-overs format. Such records suggested that this format could continue to improve.

These statistical achievements were intertwined with the success of the media-tized representation. While one of the media's key advantages is to "bring the mass audience closer" to the individuals and action (Frandsen, 2014, p. 535), the fine margins adjudicated in cricket make the sport particularly amenable to media-tization. For example, Sturm (2015b) has detailed how matches would typically utilize approximately 30 cameras and microphones positioned at fixed locations within and outside the stadia, around the perimeter/boundary, and even within the stumps at the centre of the playing area. However, the event also made use of more mobile cameras: steadicams operated from Segways, spidercams suspended on wires above the playing area, and cameras mounted on drones. These, and the deploy-ment of innovative framing and technologies, transported the viewers into the heart of the action and in order to "navigate the spaces and competitors of live sport in a fluid and free-floating manner" (ibid., p. 237). For Sturm, the 2015 CWC demonstrated. "a marked shift and stylistic orientation towards navigating the cricketing terrain … furnishing exploratory, roaming and free-floating visual representations of diverse aspects of cricket and its surrounds" (ibid., p. 237).

A second key feature of this presentation was what Sturm (2015a, p. 86) calls the repositioning of the viewer as an "*idealised omniscient observer*". In addition to the multiple perspectives offered, omniscience was generated via the extensive use of televisual technology employed in the adjudication of umpiring decisions. For the 2015 ICC CWC the decision review system (DRS) "tools" consisted of various slow motion and ultra-slow motion replays, "Hawk-Eye" ball-tracking technology and modelling software which predicts the potential path of the ball, and the "real time sound" system which uses an audio recording to indicate impacts between bat, ball and body. The 2015 ICC CWC did not employ the widely used "hotspot" (thermal imaging which detects friction-induced heat caused by the impact of the ball or bat), but innovated with "the Flashing Wicket System", in which red lights indicate separation of the bails and cricket stumps, to enable viewers to judge run-out and stumping decisions.

While Sturm (2015b) argues that a central consequence of this technological deployment is the democratization of the game, in many ways it also reaffirms the complexity of cricket. Indeed, mirroring the game's traditional veneration of statistics, it was not unusual for the televised coverage to display no less than 13 pieces of information at any one time including: each batsman's total runs and balls faced, which batsman is "facing" the bowling, the bowler's number of wickets, runs conceded and speed of last ball, whether the game was in a "power play" (periods of mandatory fielding restrictions), the score and number of overs bowled, the current rate at which runs had been scored, and the number of runs needed to win. Other graphic displays included the sequences of runs a batsman had scored, a count of the total number of "sixes" in the tournament, the distance the last "six" travelled, a 360 degree image ("wagon wheel") of where the ball had been hit during a batter's innings, the "Manhattan" bar graph showing the rate of runs per over as the innings progressed, and the "worm" which compared the scoring trajectories of the two sides. While all are designed to provide the viewer with "infotainment", the quantity and complexity of media represented data makes the game impenetrable to the uninitiated viewer.

This level of complexity was epitomized by the technologies employed to clarify umpiring decisions. For example, as part of the deployment of DRS on leg before wicket (LBW) decisions, Hawk-Eye is used to establish whether or not the ball would have hit the stumps (had the batsman's legs not intervened). However, partly in recognition of an inherent margin for error, but partly also due to the traditions of the sovereignty of the umpire, the system employs an "umpire's call" clause such that in marginal cases the umpire's initial decision overrides the technologically derived evidence. Similarly confusing is the partial use of DRS (e.g. teams have a limited number of reviews and umpires can only review certain types of decision) such that, at times, viewers can see that the umpires have mistakenly called a player (not) out. This occurred during a quarter-final when the umpire's decision to declare India's Suresh Raina not out was shown to be erroneous. Indeed, the DRS regulations are so complex that, during the England–Australia fixture the umpires used it incorrectly. Finally, in one incident the flashing wicket system indicated that the bails and stumps of an Irish player (Ed Joyce) had separated. However, as the bails re-landed on the stumps without human interference, by the laws of the game he remained "not out".

The technology introduced to "infotain" spectators had considerable potential to create confusion rather than simplify proceedings; it could merely expose the viewer to more complex aspects of the game's laws and nuances. Thus while media technology has been deeply integrated into the game – and has to a large extent been driven by commercial imperatives – the contextual logics of cricket continue to define the way the game is played, viewed and consumed.

Conclusion

Cricket, like most other sports, has become highly mediatized. The overriding principle behind this mediatization is the technological framing of how consumers engage both with cultural forms and each other, by promoting the value of "speed, immediacy, interactivity, and bespoke consumption as cultural aesthetics" (Axford and Huggins, 2010, pp. 1328–1329). Indeed, the way cricket is now packaged for television is unrecognizable compared to even a decade ago. This was exemplified in 2015 by the Tui promotion whereby spectators who took a one-handed catch while wearing a T-shirt purchased from the sponsor won a share of up to NZ $1 million. Sturm (2015b, p. 240) writes that cricket is packaged as "entertainment, complemented by lavish displays of technology, commerce and (trans)national identities". The term "infotainment" acknowledges that while there has clearly been a cultural shift in the way cricket is packaged, delivered and consumed, it still maintains a curious obsession with statistics, a peculiar international structure and a multi-game format that limits its appeal to newcomers. Cricket therefore is an excellent example of the non-uniformity of mediatization processes (Frandsen, 2014).

Contemporary cricket representations are thus hybrid: an attempt to satisfy both the purist's thirst for information and statistics, and the interloper's quest for excitement and spectacle. These representations are commercially slick and marketable to sponsors but for many, this hybridization has come at a cost to the overall integrity of the sport. Sturm (2015b) for example, warns how many of the recent technological innovations in cricket, while celebrated for their ability to get audiences "closer" to the action, are somewhat superfluous to the on-field action taking place. From an audience perspective, while it is clearly interesting to be able to hear directly from our idols on the pitch via microphone, and many cricketers and non-cricketers alike might appreciate experiencing a 90+ mph bouncer from Mitchell Johnson via "Helmet-cam"; in reality, none of these are really aimed at cricket "purists", but in (perhaps misguided) attempts to appeal to a wider audience. These developments are aimed at audiences who are less invested in the specifics of the competition, reflecting the contemporary transformation of cricket via its "remediation as a mass television sport that emphasises attracting, entertaining and retaining audiences through slick productions, technological innovations and commercial imperatives" (ibid., p. 82).

Movement towards entertainment and spectacle are not confined to cricket, or even sport in general, rather, according to Axford and Huggins (2011, p. 1327), they are frequently rehearsed in the kind of "cultural pessimism that attaches to a good deal of commentary on the mediatization of social life". They continue, arguing that the main threat to social life posed by new media is their focus on "speed", "interaction", "immediacy" and "reflexivity", and warn that we are entitled to feel anxious about the "reductive simplicity" of media whose primary attribute is speed.

While criticisms of the viability of the CWC should be considered in this light, in a number of respects the CWC will remain a "second class" megamediasport event for the foreseeable future. Despite exponential growth of consumption on the Indian subcontinent, the CWC will not enter the first order of mega-events until it casts off its Imperial legacies and penetrates European and North American markets (or perhaps China). As long as the game retains its peculiarly historical orientation and continues to celebrate traditional and longer forms of the game, the CWC will remain second class in the cricket nomenclature. And while other formats are commercially more profitable and more readily consumed in emerging markets, the CWC will remain second class in terms of income-generation as well.

Notes

1   We recognize the problems of only explicitly gendering the "ICC Women's Cricket World Cup", but for sake of readability will not consistently refer to the "men's" competition here.
2   Underlining the peculiarity of the CWC a women's version pre-dated the men's event by 2 years (Velija, 2015).

References

Ammon, E. (2015). Sky bids £40m for rights to city-based domestic Twenty20 tournament. *The Guardian*, July 25. Retrieved from www.theguardian.com/sport/2015/jul/25/sky-ecb-twenty20-cricket-colin-graves (accessed 24 November 2016).

Arnold, P. and Wynne-Thomas, P. (2009). *The complete encyclopedia of cricket*. Dubai: Carlton Books.

Axford, B. and Huggins, R. (2010). The telemediatization of cricket: commerce, connectivity and culture in the post-television age. In C. Rumford and S. Wagg (eds), *Cricket and globalization* (pp. 122–151). Newcastle upon Tyne: Cambridge Scholars Press.

Axford, B. and Huggins, R. (2011). Cricket for the people who don't like cricket?: Twenty20 as expression of the cultural and media zeitgeist. *Sport in Society*, *14*(10), 1326–1340.

Bandyopadhyay, K. (2013). Cricket as nationalist obsession. ICC World Cup 2011 and Bangladesh as co-host. *Sport in Society*, *16*(1), 19–32.

Booth, L. (2015). A 10-team ICC Cricket World Cup that excludes minnows defies the "global view" the game needs, says international players' union boss Tony Irish. *The Daily Mail*, 11 March. Retrieved from www.dailymail.co.uk/sport/cricket/article-2990401/A-10-team-ICC-Cricket-World-Cup-excludes-minnows-defies-global-view-game-needs-says-players-union-boss.html (accessed 24 November 2016).

Brenkley, S. (2015). Cricket World Cup: Why ICC attitude to minnows is "bonkers". *The Independent*, 5 March. Retrieved from www.independent.co.uk/sport/cricket/cricket-world-cup-ireland-can-prove-icc-strategy-is-bonkers-10089166.html (accessed 24 November 2016).

Cashman, R. (2011). The Packer cricket war. In A. Bateman and J. Hill (eds), *The Cambridge companion to cricket* (pp. 100–115). Cambridge: Cambridge University Press.

Fletcher, T. (2015). Cricket, migration and diasporic communities. *Identities: Global Studies in Culture and Power*, *22*(2), 141–153.

Frandsen, K. (2014). Mediatization of sports. In K. Lundby (ed.), *Mediatization of communication* (pp. 525–543). Berlin: Mouton de Gruyter.

Gupta, A. (2010). India: the epicentre of global cricket? In C. Rumford and S. Wagg (eds), *Cricket and globalization* (pp. 41–59). Newcastle upon Tyne: Cambridge Scholars Press.

Harriss, I. (1990). Packer, cricket and postmodernism. In D. Rowe and G. Lawrence (eds), *Sport and leisure: Trends in Australian popular culture* (pp. 109–121). Sydney: Harcourt Brace Jovanovich.

Holden, R. (2010). International cricket – the hegemony of commerce, the decline of government interest and the end of morality? In D. Malcolm, J. Gemmell and N. Mehta (eds), *The changing face of cricket: From imperial to global game* (pp. 213–226). London: Routledge.

Horne, J. (2010). Cricket in consumer culture: Notes on the 2007 Cricket World Cup. *American Behavioral Scientist*, *53*(10), 1549–1568.

ICC (2015a). ICC president Mustafa Kamal threatens to reveal "mischievous things" taking place at governing body. *The Telegraph*, 30 March. Retrieved from www.telegraph. co.uk/sport/cricket/cricket-world-cup/11503979/ICC-president-Mustafa-Kamal-threatens-to-reveal-mischievous-things-taking-place-at-governing-body.html (accessed 24 November 2016).

ICC (2015b). ICC Cricket World Cup: Breaking records and capturing hearts. 28 March. Retrieved from www.icc-cricket.com/cricket-world-cup/news/2015/media-releases/87514/icc-cricket-world-cup-2015-breaking-records-and-capturing-hearts (accessed 24 November 2016).

ICC (undated). Members overview. Retrieved from www.icc-cricket.com/about/96/icc-members/overview (accessed 24 November 2016).

Lorde, T., Greenidge, D. and Devonish, D. (2011). Local residents' perceptions of the impacts of the ICC Cricket World Cup 2007 on Barbados: Comparisons of pre- and post-games. *Tourism Management, 32*, 349–356.

Madeley, G. (2015). Top Scottish World Cup cricketer is sent home from the tournament after "racist tweet" row when he was dropped from squad for latest match. *The Daily Mail*, 12 March. Retrieved from www.dailymail.co.uk/news/article-2991053/Top-Scottish-World-Cup-cricketer-sent-home-tournament-racist-tweet-row-dropped-squad-latest-match.html (accessed 24 November 2016).

Malcolm, D. (2013). *Globalizing cricket*. London: Bloomsbury.

Malcolm, D. and Waldman, D. (2017). The politics of international cricket. In A. Bairner, J. Kelly and J.-W. Lee (eds), *Handbook of sport and politics*. (pp. 520–531). London: Routledge.

Malcolm, D., Bairner, A. and Curry, G. (2010). "Woolmergate": Sport and the representation of Islam and Muslims in the British Press, *Journal of Sport and Social Issues, 34*(2), 215–235.

MCC (2010). *The laws of cricket*. London: Gardners Books.

Mehta, N. (2009). Batting for the flag: Cricket, television and globalization in India. *Sport in Society, 12*(4–5), 579–599.

Mehta, N., Gemmell, J. and Malcolm, D. (2009). "Bombay Sport Exchange": Cricket, globalization and the future. *Sport in Society, 12*(4–5), 694–707.

Premachandran, D. (2015). Chris Gayle didn't just batter Zimbabwe – his Twitter critics were routed too. *The Guardian*, 24 February. Retrieved from www.theguardian.com/sport/blog/2015/feb/24/chris-gayle-west-indies-cricket-world-cup-zimbabwe-record (accessed 24 November 2016).

Roche, M. (2000). *Mega-events and modernity*. London: Routledge.

Roche, M. (2008). Putting the London 2012 Olympics into perspective: The challenge of understanding mega-events. *Twenty-First Century Society, 3*(3), 285–290.

Rumford, C. (2007). More than a game: Globalization and the post-Westernization of world cricket. *Global Networks*, 7(2): 107–247.

Rumford, C. (2011). Introduction: Twenty20 and the future of cricket. *Sport in Society, 14*(10), 1311–1315.

Rumford, C. and Wagg, S. (2010). Introduction: Cricket and globalization. In C. Rumford and S. Wagg (eds), *Cricket and globalization* (pp. 1–17). Newcastle upon Tyne: Cambridge Scholars Press.

Samiuddin, O. (2009). PCB issues legal notice to ICC for World Cup exclusion. Retrieved from www.espncricinfo.com/pakistan/content/story/403690.html (accessed 28 October 2015).

Sarkar, M. (2015). #IndvsPak cricket: A billion viewers expected to have tuned in. *CNN*, 15 February. Retrieved from http://edition.cnn.com/2015/02/15/sport/india-pakistan-cricket (accessed 24 November 2016).

Shah, J. (2015). World Cup 2015 to affect March box office. *The Hindustan Times*, 18 February. Retrieved from www.hindustantimes.com/bollywood/world-cup-2015-to-affect-march-box-office/story-URjJdKAoIo9u24MLFrLDQJ.html (accessed 24 November 2016).

Sinclair, L. (2015). World Cup win breaks ratings record. *The Australian*, 30 March. Retrieved from www.theaustralian.com.au/business/media/cricket-world-cup-win-breaksratings-records/story-e6frg996-1227284674453 (accessed 24 November 2016).

Sturm, D. (2015a). Smash and bash cricket? Affective technological innovations in the Big Bash. *Media International Australia, 155,* 80–88.

Sturm, D. (2015b). "Fluid spectator-tourists": Innovative televisual technologies, global audiences and the 2015 Cricket World Cup. *Comunicazioni Sociali, 2,* 230–240.

Velija, P. (2015). *Women's cricket and global processes: The emergence and development of women's cricket as a global game.* London: Macmillan.

Wigmore, T. (2015). Cricket, looking to grow, keeps shrinking World Cup. *The New York Times*, 25 February. Retrieved from www.nytimes.com/2015/02/25/sports/cricket/cricket-looking-to-grow-keeps-shrinking-world-cup.html?_r=0 (accessed 24 November 2016).

Wilson, A. (2014). World Test Championship set to be shelved due to lukewarm interest. *The Guardian*, 13 January. Retrieved from www.theguardian.com/sport/2014/jan/13/world-test-championship-shelved-england-cricket (accessed 24 November 2016).

Wright, G. (1994). *Betrayal: Struggle for cricket's soul.* London: H.F. & G. Witherby.

9

WIMBLEDON

A megamediasport tradition

Eileen Kennedy, Laura Hills and Alistair John

- Strengthen and enhance Wimbledon as a world class sporting venue of national and international significance.
- Conserve Wimbledon's unique and special heritage.
- Guided by "Tennis in an English Garden", develop the finest setting and facilities for the entertainment and enjoyment of all visitors.

Wimbledon Master Plan (AELTC, 2013)

The Wimbledon Master Plan describes the ethos of Wimbledon as "Tennis in an English Garden" – evoking the mannered, upper middle-class Victorian origins of the lawn tennis championships. This is Wimbledon logic – the apparent triumph of tradition over change. Set in its dedicated grounds in "the lush suburb of Wimbledon" (Holt, 1990, p. 125), the grass of the courts is cultivated all year to achieve the perfect playing surface for two weeks in summer. Aside from the Championships, the All England Club remains preserved year round as if in aspic, largely accessible only to the private members practising on a few outer courts and to closely chaperoned tour parties and museum visitors (Kennedy and Hills, 2009). Meanwhile, the Wimbledon website too lays in wait, showing videos of Tim Henman and the Road to Wimbledon, and yet to be activated links to the live scores, video and radio coverage of the following year's competition. Passing by the ground during the rest of year, however, there seems to be continual construction going on. Wimbledon has an excess of time to get ready – as the post on Wimbledon's Facebook page on 6 February 2016 with the hashtag "#141days to go" communicated, next to a photo of two groundsmen pushing lawnmowers in Centre Court.

When the time comes, Wimbledon presents itself in time-honoured tradition, the flowers in Wimbledon colours (purple, white, gold), everything else in green, green, green, strawberries and cream on sale and queues that back up almost to

Southfields tube station, coiling slowly around Wimbledon Park. The good behaviour of the crowds of well-dressed, polite spectators standing in line seem to suggest Wimbledon has preserved tennis's role as a social occasion that "bridged the upper and middle classes" in nineteenth century England (Holt, 1990, p. 126).

Holt (ibid.) maintains that the country sports journal, *The Field*, had much to do with the popularization of tennis in the late 1800s. More contemporary media seem to have a similarly important role to play now. In fact, it could be argued that the logic of Wimbledon has meshed inextricably with media logic to present the audience with a thoroughly mediatized experience. So, while Wimbledon appears to be anachronistic as a sporting spectacle, the old fashioned cousin to the other three Grand Slam events in the tennis calendar, its dependence on media to sustain its carefully constructed traditions puts it firmly in the contemporary era.

In this chapter, we will consider the mediatization of Wimbledon from the perspective of the spectator, analysing both media content and the live/mediated audience experience, as well as considering the institutional logic manifested in the particularity of this sporting mega-event. We will present a series of examples of the interweaving of media and tradition in the social construction of Wimbledon as a mega-event drawn from analysis of the mediation of one day's play during the 2015 Championships along with observations of the audience at the live and mediated event, and reflections on our own experiences as spectators. Television, Internet, social media, digital and material advertising and promotional artefacts were all examined, and we observed spectators and officials in the town of Wimbledon, the queue, the grounds and at courtside. We noted our own responses as we travelled to Wimbledon, engaged with the advertising, social media, televised coverage and watched the live tennis. We will show the way that the live experience of Wimbledon is inseparable from the mediated experience, or in Hjarvard's (2008, p. 110) terms "[n]on-mediated reality and forms of interaction still exist" at Wimbledon "but mediatization means that they, too, are affected by the presence of media". For Hjarvard, however, the influence of the media stems not just from their integration into the way other institutions operate, but also from their growing independence and autonomy, which means that they start to force other institutions "to greater or lesser degrees, to submit to their logic" (ibid., p. 106). The question at the heart of this chapter is, therefore, to what extent can Wimbledon be said to have submitted to the logic of media, or does the logic of Wimbledon still hold sway?

Getting there: a mediatized journey to Wimbledon

At Wimbledon train station a banner positioned above the ticket office was emblazoned with the straplines, "Wimbledon Awaits", "Tradition Awaits" and "Fashion Awaits" inscribed over a succession of images: manicured lawn, purple flowers, strawberries and cream, and a black and white photograph of Bunny Austin, the first player to wear shorts at Wimbledon. Large billboards advertising Evian with the slogan "live young" and "share your reaction #wimblewatch", mixed images of Sharapova as a child and adult with images of unidentified spectators.

(Field notes, 2 July 2015)

Our journey to Wimbledon presented us with multiple examples of mediatization. The official Wimbledon logo was imprinted on the stairway and station walls, and upon leaving the station there was a large arch with the repeated motif "Wimbledon Awaits" and instructions for getting to the ground (which required a bus, taxi or tube ride). The route provided more advertising opportunities. On the station forecourt, for example, were further billboards, and a tennis "information" hut and an image of the trophies on a background of leafy green for "selfies". Queue barriers covered with Wimbledon imagery and words like "history" were laid out in anticipation of crowds returning to the station after the event. Wimbledon town centre entered into the swing of things by erecting a large screen and striped deckchairs on artificial turf outside the Morrisons supermarket. The faint hearted might just stop there and watch, along with shoppers and locals, a mediated Championships in Wimbledon but not actually at Wimbledon.

At Southfields, the closest tube station to Wimbledon, a carpet of artificial grass covered the normally grey concrete floor, and the now seemingly ubiquitous "Wimbledon Awaits" signage adorned the walls and seats. Joining a mass of people, we followed the sign reading "The queue 5 minutes", giving assurance that we were getting closer all the time, and we could only expect to see more purple and green from here on in. When we arrived at the famous Wimbledon queue for the evening sessions, we entered via a series of arches constructed of green Wimbledon Awaits banners which made it feel as if our Wimbledon experience had begun. A green walkway protected the grass and white and purple displays of flowers decorated the path. The walkway was bounded by fences resembling tennis court nets and more "Wimbledon Awaits" billboards. Pictures on the billboards showed the interior of the Wimbledon space, the flowers, the seats, and the courts as well as photographs of tennis players in action.

Following Couldry (2014), Jansson (2015, p. 58) observes that mediatization is a meta-process, operating in "non-linear and transversal ways, meaning that it exercises different kinds of influence within different fields". The very peculiar ways in which Wimbledon has become mediatized point to the specific logic of the field of Wimbledon. Jansson (ibid.) argues that media can become part of the communicational doxa of a given field in three ways. This "triple articulation" of the media involve "technics" (the functional dependencies media create); properties (or symbolic markers required to express the identity of an institution) and textures (or the integration of media within the "taken for granted material environment and temporal rhythms of everyday life"; ibid., p. 58). It is possible to observe these articulations of the media at Wimbledon, and together they communicate not just mediatization but the way the essence of Wimbledon endures.

The queue was made to feel part of the experience. Key rules were highlighted en route, like road signs: "No selfie sticks, cash only, one bag, one ticket per person". One of the "honourable stewards" (as his badge read) distributed the "guide to queuing" – a small booklet explaining the etiquette of the line. Spectators received this "gift" with delight. A range of other Wimbledon themed entertainment and refreshments was provided by advertisers. HSBC bank hosted a tennis tournament on a small court lined with flower boxes, HSBC-red Wellington boots and white picket fencing. Lavazza served coffee in purple and green cups. The order of play was shown on a large screen framed in wood like a garden shed. A hedge-themed decoration read @wimbledon in topiary mixing tradition and technology in Wimbledon green. After an hour, we submitted our queue cards to the steward and we were allowed to head to the ticket booth, following a reprimand arising from a failure to display on demand the queue card in timely enough fashion. We left the initial queue and joined a much shorter queue to purchase our tickets into the ground.

(Field notes, 2 July 2015)

While the technics of the media have become a functional necessity for much of the audience's access to Wimbledon, this does not extend to everything. The experience of queuing at Wimbledon brought us into contact with very traditional communication formats as we were handed hard copies of the guide to queuing and paper cards that showed our place in the queue. Rules were enforced by stewards who ensured that the queue was orderly and moving and that everyone displayed their queue card at all times. One of our party was disciplined by a steward for not displaying the queue card quickly enough – learning early on in our visit, the importance of regulation of the body at Wimbledon, and the British historical legacy of moral control through the correct cultivation of pleasures (Rojek, 1991).

The various signs and advertisements we encountered in the queue also revealed Wimbledon's dependence on the media to communicate symbolically its properties. Lavazza, the Italian coffee company, was handing out free mini-cappuccinos. Lavazza has been an "official supplier" to Wimbledon since 2011. Wimbledon's logic of official suppliers enables it to maintain its allure as far removed from the brash commercialization of contemporary media sporting spectacles, eschewing the sponsorship that would see its traditional look and feel overwritten by external marketing campaigns, in favour of a select few of what the Wimbledon website (www.wimbledon.com) calls "blue chip brands", who supply various amenities whilst adding the often high-brow connotations of their products to the overall image of the Championships. These include Slazenger (tennis balls), Robinsons (soft drinks), IBM (IT), Lanson (champagne), Ralph Lauren (outfitter), Evian (water) and Jacob's Creek (wine) and Rolex as the "official timekeeper". Instead of imprinting their logos on Wimbledon, the suppliers are permitted to use Wimbledon's brand in their advertising, following strict guidelines. Whannel (1992, p. 179) observed the deftness of Wimbledon's move to "preserve the aura of exclusivity" by rejecting title, competition and arena sponsorship in this way. Nevertheless, during the Championships these brands pepper the grounds and adorn the most prominent advertising sites in London, as well as running high profile television and Internet campaigns, which simultaneously, therefore, promote Wimbledon. These brands' success in meshing the Wimbledon look with their own brand image could be seen as a triumph of mediatization of Wimbledon. Nevertheless, it is also a triumph for Wimbledon's traditional values. However, the much-touted values of Wimbledon are underpinned by social hierarchies, which may be seen as "exclusive" in a traditional, almost romantic way, but can also be seen as divisive, continuing to support a somatic norm for Wimbledon as male, upper class and white (Hills and Kennedy, 2006). The media actively construct the Wimbledon habitus through providing sources "of historical knowledge about the norms and behavior of yesterday" (Hjarvard 2013, p. 147), but this historical knowledge is "interpreted within a contemporary framework".

The celebration of social hierarchy can be seen in Lavazza's outdoor advertising campaign in London during Wimbledon in 2013 (Lavazza, 2016). The tagline from the campaign was "The New Tradition", which featured billboard posters throughout the London Underground. Three real-life Wimbledon officials in blazers, a man flanked by two women, each hold a Lavazza espresso cup. As the two women look into the distance, their haughty gazes directed off to the side, the man in centre stage literally looks down his nose at the camera, and by extension, the audience itself. While officials may not in fact occupy the top of the Wimbledon hierarchy, they have a symbolic association with it, as keepers of Wimbledon rules and regulations. The New Tradition offered by Lavazza, then, is one where everyone knows their place and rigid social positions are strictly enforced. The only thing that is new is the coffee being served.

In the next section, we will explore the different ways that Wimbledon engages the media to communicate, examining the mediatization of the event on the web, TV and social media as well as the incorporation of media during the live event. We will show how media is central to the experience of Wimbledon both from afar and at the site of the mega-event itself.

Watching the play: feeling Wimbledon wherever you are

The BBC's Wimbledon title sequence for 2015 began with a white screen gradually tinting sky blue to reveal two halves of a sphere coming together, travelling at speed – indicated by sound of rushing air – clothed mid-flight in the yellow felt of a tennis ball, before being hit by a tennis racket. The signature brass sounds of the BBC's Wimbledon theme tune announced themselves as the sequence showed the All England Club being computer-generated, piece by piece. First, trees and the spire of St Mary's Church popped up and squares of green turf started to cover the ground. Nets and green seating sprang up, the ball bounced on the white line, and centre court was assembled around a glittering procession of players who appeared to bat the ball back and forth, including Serena Williams, Roger Federer, Rafael Nadal, Andy Murray, Maria Sharapova, Novak Djokovic, Eugenie Bouchard, and Petra Kvitová. The sequence drew to a close with Kvitová holding the Ladies Singles 2014 winner's silver salver and Djokovic kissing the Gentlemen's winner's trophy as it glints in the sun. An aerial view of the fully assembled club ground, the final buildings and bushes jumped into place, became the background to the "Wimbledon 2015" and "BBC Sport" graphics announcing the televised action.

A mix of old and new indicated the tension between the logic of Wimbledon with its greens and yellows, its seemingly ancient traditions (underscored by the image of the neighbouring twelfth-century church), the recognizable and unchanging sounds, setting and cast of characters, and the logic of the media, emphasizing the new – computer graphics, speed, effects, sporting celebrity, unpredictable winners. Within the BBC opening sequence, the first seamlessly became the second, as the hyper-local space of Wimbledon, tucked away in suburban London, where no one lacking local knowledge might ever find it, was mediatized as a global mega-event, without ever losing its traditional "essence".

> When we got to the front of the line we entered the tunnel and waited patiently at the top of the stairs for a break in play. When we were allowed to go in we could not see three seats together immediately and, as play was about to start, we were hustled back into the tunnel to wait for the next break in action. As we waited, the group behind us in the queue were cautioned for making too much noise. On the next attempt we were successful and ensconced ourselves on three seats near the middle of the court. Between points the crowd chanted "Ali, Ali, Ali – oy, oy, oy" at the Slovenian-born British player Aljaz Bedene, reminiscent of football chants in Britain. The crowd talking quietly and a mobile phone ringing during a point elicited a gasp of amused disapproval. From our vantage we could see across Wimbledon into 4 other courts. There was evidence of media – seven TV cameras and a large number of photographers, there were also 2 TV cameras across the court and a media centre was positioned above the baseline. The scoreboards doubled as TV screens which were used to replay points and for Hawk-Eye. During changeovers scores from other matches were shown. It was possible to observe a subtle array of sponsors but all were embedded into the colour schemes of Wimbledon. Wimbledon.com was on the scoreboard, Jaguar and IBM on the service speed board, Slazenger on the back of the nets, Rolex on the scoreboard and bottles of Robinson positioned on the umpire chairs.
>
> *(Field notes, 2 July 2015)*

The complex relationship between media and tradition is observable at the live event. Hawk-Eye, "a multifarious computer system used in cricket, tennis and other sports to visually track the path of the ball and display a record of its most statistically likely path as a moving image" (Singh Bal and Dureja, 2012, p. 108), was initially developed as a television replay tool for cricket broadcasting. First used at Wimbledon on the Centre and Number 1 Courts in 2006, the electronic line calling system now operates across all six show courts. Not only providing milli-metre accurate ball-tracking capabilities, Hawk-Eye innovations (2015) claim to be able to "generate huge volumes of data which enables Hawk-Eye to deliver analysis and insights that truly enhance the fan experience and helps to tell the story across broadcast and online channels" including ball-tracking, ball spin speed/revolutions and athlete running distance. Despite unfavourable challenge success rates (in the 2015 singles competitions, men successfully challenged decisions 26.5 per cent of the time while women successfully challenged 27 per cent of calls (AELTC, 2015)), the employment of the tool has modified both the live and mediated experience with the crowd engaging in the ritualistic "slow-clap" in the lead-up to the moving image of a tennis ball imposed on a digital "Wimbledon" tennis court clean of any corporate logos other than the Wimbledon Tennis logo on side-hoardings. As the ball moves towards the white line a Rolex sponsored "box" indicates the "official review" before determining if the ball has landed "in" or "out"; which subsequently causes the crowd to applaud or groan depending on their affiliation. In many ways, the media technology that Hawk-Eye represents appears to contrast with the "English Tennis in a Country Garden" ethos that the Wimbledon Master Plan embraces. It also seems at odds with the unashamedly anti-consumerist approach to spectators who are expected to wait in queue after queue, even when they have already gained entry to the grounds, and to watch in silence. Yet, the integration of Hawk-Eye into the Wimbledon spectacle has been so successful that it has become one of the audience's few allowed moments of animated expression accompanying the computerized visualization of the point. Indeed, other than the engagement or laughter at "Ali, Ali, Ali, oy, oy, oy" chants, Hawk-Eye provided the clearest example of crowd excitement during our visit to Wimbledon.

Hawk-Eye has become part of the texture of Wimbledon, like the giant screen TV installed in 1997 on Aorangi Terrace. This outside picnic area became popularly known as "Henman Hill" after the British player, Tim Henman, who would draw enormous crowds and is now known also as Murray Mound. This testament to the mediatization of Wimbledon shows how the media have become part of the rhythm of Wimbledon and have normalized "certain expectations of positionality and regularity with regards to media practices" (Jansson, 2015, p. 21). The screen on the manmade grass bank adjacent to the Number 1 Court provides a strong sense of "place" or "topophilia" (Bale, 1993) to the hundreds of thousands of spectators attending during the fortnight, illustrated by the affectionate names bestowed upon the landscape. The hill also features heavily in the televising of the event. TV journalists often conduct on the spot interviews and "vox pops" (opinion pieces) with spectators on the hill and TV cameras frequently sweep across the site to illustrate crowd interest in specific matches. In a strangely circular homage to media, as spectators notice themselves on the big screen, they cheer or wave, creating more media–spectator interaction.

TV images of the hill draw spectators at the event, eager to relive the fun – a place where the body can be indulged – eating, speaking, shouting, laughing, standing up and lying down are all permitted. Our own experience on the hill, however, did not quite live up to its media reputation. Hoping to watch some of the match between Dustin Brown and Rafa Nadal on the big screen, we looked for a spot to sit on the hill. The sheer size of the crowd made the site almost impossible to navigate, however, and there was not an inch of spare ground anywhere. Security guards policed the area, preventing people from sitting on the unmarked "walkway" and passing under their gaze between so many people produced more topophobia than topophilia. Out of options, we eventually came to rest behind a building that blocked our view of the big screen and streamed the match on an iPad. Ironically, such experiences may only serve to reinforce the success of mediatization of Wimbledon, as the range of media formats available to the Wimbledon spectator (both at the live event and outside) are part of the media's attempt to comply with audience demand for content and orientation that reflect their lifestyle (Hjarvard, 2013).

The functional aspects of mediatization like Hawk-Eye and Henman Hill have become comingled with tradition. It feels as if people always slow clapped while Hawk-Eye showed us whether the ball was in or out, and people always congregated on Henman Hill to watch marquee matches on one of the largest outdoor screens in Europe. The media technics have merged with the textures and rhythms of Wimbledon, and it is these mediated live experiences that the media offer to their audiences. Wimbledon is a particular mediatized sociospatial entity. Jansson (2013) has discussed mediatization as a sociospatial concept. The process of mediatization of Wimbledon transforms the social space of Wimbledon by offering itself up for the consumption of the masses, but "the *shape* of these alterations are dependent on pre-existing sociospatial social arrangements, which are, in turn saturated with deep-seated values, or metaphysics, related to space/place, mobility, and communication" (ibid., p. 280).

Jansson references five media trends that show the "close relationship between mediatization and sociospatial transformations" (ibid., p. 280). These are mediated/mediatized mobility, technological convergence, interactivity, new interfaces (bringing media closer to the body) and the automation of surveillance. These media trends are observable in the increasing use of social media as part of the mediatization of Wimbledon.

For example, a campaign launched by Jaguar, another Wimbledon supplier, attempted to use new media technologies to communicate the textures of the Wimbledon live experience to audiences located at home. The campaign brought mobile media in close contact with Wimbledon spectators' bodies, adopting convergent platforms, user interactivity, intimate surveillance, while mining social media for more participant data. On Jaguar's "Feel Wimbledon" website (jaguar.wimbledon.com), the presenter of a video summary of the campaign described their mission in the following terms: "Jaguar have been there every step of the way to bring you all the emotion – as it happened". The "Feel Wimbledon" campaign endeavoured to gauge the intensity of the feelings around Wimbledon by taking three measurements from the live crowd. Jaguar referred to these as biometric (fans were given wearable technology to record their heart rate) atmospheric (movement and other sensors were set around the space of Wimbledon) and sociometric (Twitter was monitored for trending tweets). Jaguar described the combination and visualization of the data from these sources in highly technical terms: they formed an "intelligence engine", using "bespoke algorithms" and the expertise of "information specialists and neuroscientists". The technical explanation on their promotional webpages at jaguar.wimbledon.com emphasized its complexity and positioned the prospective reader as possessing excessive technological understanding: "Do you speak Geek?"

The visualization of the emotion of Wimbledon that resulted from the project showed heart rate variability in a wave form graph in bright Wimbledon colours, which peaked as the heart rate of "superfans" rose at key moments, and the audio of fans on Henman Hill got louder. Neither measurement was at all surprising, however, or provided the promised new insight into what it feels like to attend Wimbledon. This was the media's version of science as discourse – superficial explanations which simply affirmed what we already know from watching Wimbledon – the crowd gets excited. The output from the myriad of sensors and monitors adorning "superfans" and recording the crowd obeys media logic – it was aesthetic and fun but ultimately formulaic, and allowed an easy transposition of the technological expertise from the data visualizations onto the Jaguar brand. Wimbledon logic is there too, however, in the illusory promise of access to an exclusive live experience. Watching the excitement of the privileged through the lens of Jaguar simply confirms the distance between having a ticket to Centre Court and consumption of the event at a distance. After all, not everybody's experience has the same chance of being represented in the media: "[w]hether or not a given segment of the population will be served by the media – and have its lifestyle represented in magazines, websites, or television programs – depends on the economic attractiveness of the particular segment" (Hjarvard, 2013, p. 148).

Another mobile media advertising strategy used Twitter and participant engagement to bring about a mediatized transformation of the elite space of Wimbledon to the democratized space of the many and was evident in the advertising campaign of one of Wimbledon's oldest sponsors, the soft drink manufacturer, Robinson's. Accompanying the Championship, Robinson's hired the Oliver agency to create a Twitter competition to mark their 80 years as a Wimbledon official supplier. It is possible that this kind of contemporary social media campaign might hope to obscure the anachronism of their brand association with a mega-sport event. While Robinson's traces the origins of their drink as a response to Wimbledon players' hydration needs in 1935, their barley "squash" seems antiquated in an age of high-tech sports drinks. However, in 2015, having been bought out by Britvic, Robinson's withdrew its original recipe in favour of a "no-added sugar" product line aimed at the new health-conscious consumer. Robinson's use of Twitter therefore marked a step in its own mediatized transformation, since "audience maximization" by catering to consumers' changing lifestyle choices "has become an important logic of the media" (Hjarvard, 2013, 148).

The Twitter competition rewarded participants who discovered giant tennis balls hidden in 14 different locations deemed "significant to the Wimbledon royalty" around the UK. Twitter was used to release clues using the hashtag #Huntfor Wimbledon, and participants tweeted photos and "selfies" with the balls to win a prize. For example, @DrinkRobinsons tweeted a video clip of the former British tennis player Tim Henman next to the Fred Perry statue in the Wimbledon ground to send participants to Perry's family home (in Stockport in the north of England) where they then tweeted photos of an enormous tennis ball stuck on the outside of the house to enter a prize draw. As Hjarvard (2013, p. 147) observes, the media "produce a continuous representation of our contemporary society that is accessible for everybody in almost all social institutions". @DrinkRobinsons represented the Wimbledon experience within the local space of everyone, not just the elite few who gained entry to the AELTC.

The marketing agency, Oliver (2015), reported that "@DrinkRobinsons followers grew by a massive 46% with nearly 12 million unique users reached during the 2 week period" of the campaign. The campaign team sent 1,212 replies to fans and argued that the "quality" of these replies enabled Robinson's to top the list of the best UK sports sponsorship. This kind of relationship marketing epitomizes mediatization, since it merges meaningful interpersonal communication flows with social media. The campaign wove together participants' active engagement with the experience of Wimbledon within their personal locale with the Robinson's brand, extending Robinson's merchandise into the fabric of their lives by blending it with the sporting experience of Wimbledon. On the final day of the Championship, @DrinkRobinsons invited participation in a "spot the ball" competition on Twitter, offering Twitter as one of the media audience's potential multiscreen experiences, which would provide an affective "feedback loop" (Dean, 2010) with tangible rewards in the form of tickets for next year's Championships. This is the "playful sociability" that Hjarvard (2013, p. 149) argues has become "the preferred mode of interaction" of social networking media. Through mediatization Wimbledon is able to expand the space of Wimbledon into the personal, meaningful and emotional geographies of its media audiences, whilst preserving the exclusivity of the live event.

Going home: reflecting on Wimbledon

There is a large scoreboard showing all of the matches played and scores that is updated by hand. As we pass by a steward is perched on a ladder slotting in the score of a recently completed match. These lived practices harken to a pre-digital era, feeling quaint and endearing. And we are somehow pleased to see that it appears to be part of an enduring tradition.

(Field notes, 2 July 2015)

The Wimbledon experience – either live or mediated – is an experience of mediatization. Jansson (2013) has urged us to consider mediatization in terms of sociospatial transformations. The media trends Jansson identifies with such a transformation are very much in evidence at Wimbledon. Mediatized mobility, blurring text and context, is observable in @DrinkRobinsons' Twitter competitions and Lavazza coffee cups, making "the settings of media use (production and consumption) increasingly fluid" (ibid., p. 280). Similarly, "technological convergence" is ever present as Wimbledon media flow through more and more platforms and formats to provide multiscreen experiences. "Interactivity" creates opportunities for Wimbledon viewers to feel like they are taking part, and "new interfaces" bring the media closer to the body (Jaguar's biometrics measurements from wearable technology). In turn, this creates an "automation of surveillance" as the data from watching Wimbledon bodies everywhere is recycled into new mediatized campaigns. Jansson (ibid., p. 281) argues that an analysis of mediatization should "start out from the transformations, as well as the maintenance, of certain sociospatial arrangements, including the amalgamation of various mediated practices within these arrangements". This is what we have tried to show in Wimbledon – the way the media has become part of the texture of the space, and is able to invite distant, mediated audiences in to share those textures, wherever they are.

Mediatization theorizes how the character of institutions has changed as a result of the media. Yet, mediatization does not operate in the same way for all institutions. Mediatization is not independent of the character of the institution. While we have pointed to media logic in multiple aspects of Wimbledon, it does not make sense to think of Wimbledon as having had "to submit to their logic" (Hjarvard, 2008). Wimbledon has its own logic that is discernible in all aspects of its mediatization. The mediatization of Wimbledon is a testament to its enduring character. Wimbledon has to a certain extent adapted to changing media conventions. Yet, it has also been highly successful in incorporating media into the existing rhythms of the Championships, preserving the old textures in the new.

References

AELTC. (2013). *The Wimbledon master plan.* Wimbledon: AELTC.

AELTC. (2015). Facts and figures/FAQ. Retrieved from www.wimbledon.com/en_GB/atoz/faq_and_facts_and_figures.html (accessed 10 February 2016).

Bale, J. (1993). *Sport, space and the city.* London: Routledge.

Couldry, N. (2014). Mediatization and the future of field theory. In K. Lundby (ed.), *Mediatization of communication* (pp. 227–245). Berlin: Mouton de Gruyter.

Dean, J. (2010). *Blog theory: Feedback and capture in the circuits of drive.* Cambridge: Polity.

Hawk-Eye Innovations (2015). Hawk-Eye in tennis. Retrieved from www.hawkeyeinnovations.co.uk/sports/tennis (accessed 10 February 2016).

Hills, L. and Kennedy, E. (2006). Space invaders at Wimbledon: Televised sport and deterritorialization. *Sociology of Sport Journal, 23*(4), 419–437.

Hjarvard, S. (2008). The mediatization of society. *Nordicom Review, 29,* 105–134.

Hjarvard, S. (2013). *The mediatization of culture and society*. London: Routledge.

Holt, R. (1990). *Sport and the British*. Oxford: Oxford University Press.

Jansson, A. (2013). Mediatization and social space: Reconstructing mediatization for the transmedia age. *Communication Theory, 23*(3), 279–296.

Jansson, A. (2015). Using Bourdieu in critical mediatization research: Communicational doxa and osmotic pressures. *MedieKultur, 58*, 13–29.

Kennedy, E. and Hills, L. (2009). *Sport, media and society*. Oxford: Berg.

Lavazza (2016). Advertising history – The past and present. Retrieved from www.lavazza.co. uk/uk/lavazza-world/advertising/advertising_history (accessed 24 November 2016).

Oliver (2015). Robinsons – #HuntForWimbledon. Retrieved from www.oliver.agency/en/ work/robinsons-huntforwimbledon (accessed 5 January 2017).

Rojek, C. (1991). *Ways of escape: Modern transformations of leisure and travel*. Glasgow: University of Glasgow.

Singh Bal, B. and Dureja, G. (2012). Hawk Eye: A logical innovative technology use in sports for effective decision making. *Sport Science Review, 21*(1–2), 107–119.

Whannel, G. (1992). *Fields in vision: Television sport and cultural transformation*. London: Routledge.

10

THE MASTERS GOLF TOURNAMENT

Media mega-event, the environment and the emergence of Augusta National syndrome

Brad Millington and Brian Wilson

In this chapter, we examine and reflect on the emergence of Augusta National syndrome, an "illness" said to "afflict" golfers who have viewed television broadcasts of the Masters golf tournament, held annually in the splendour of Augusta National Golf Club in Augusta, Georgia. Afflicted golfers are those who, upon viewing the Masters, demand Augusta's idyllic playing conditions at their own local courses. While this would be a significant development in any context, in the post-war years the golf industry acquired tremendously powerful tools to help create and maintain the golf-landscapes that are so enticing for audiences of the Masters. By "tools", we are referring especially to machinery for re-shaping natural landscapes and chemicals for doing away with unwanted pests. Although the golf industry's history of pursuing rationalization as a way of making the game "better" (i.e. modernizing the sport) pre-dates the post-war period, the arrival of Augusta National syndrome – which coincided with the earliest colour television broadcasts of the Masters in the early 1960s – led to heightened pressures on golf course superintendents to maintain their courses at an exceptionally high standard. Thus, it is especially pertinent in this context that these same superintendents had the *capacity* to pursue a "perfect" golf course aesthetic.

In this sense, while focused on golf in particular, this chapter illuminates a broader story about the interconnections between sport, the environment, media, and modernization. It is well known that sport and media have developed a close relationship over the years, particularly in the age of televised sport (see Boyle and Haynes, 2009). It is well known too that sport can be impactful in a material sense when it comes to its relationship with the ecosystems in which games are played (Wilson and Millington, 2013, 2015). Less attention has been paid, however, to how the mediasport complex and environmental issues such as chemical use, excessive watering, and aggressive landscape manipulation on golf courses are interconnected. We thus adopt a broad focus in this chapter, and in doing so respond to calls from scholars like Frandsen (2014) for increased sensitivity to the "interrelated processes" at work in and around media (also see Hjarvard, 2009). Indeed, in *de-centring* media herein, we are able to consider all three areas of the mediasport triumvirate: institutions and production are considered as we assess the role of both Augusta National and the TV network CBS in televising the Masters; media content is considered as we discuss the presentation of Augusta National Golf Club on TV; reception is considered as we discuss how presumptions about audience interpretations of Masters programming are, to a great extent, what spurred the "birth" of Augusta National syndrome. At the same time, we also assess how factors such as the televising of golf spiral together with wider factors such as the growing use of technology in golf course management – the outcome being significant social, cultural, and, in particular, environmental changes.

On this basis, we are well positioned in this chapter to engage especially with key aspects of the concept of mediatization – a concept that is useful for both illuminating and inspiring critical analysis of "the interrelation between changes in media and communications on the one hand, and changes in culture and society on the other" (Couldry and Hepp, 2013, p. 197). Mediatization is integral to this chapter as our broader goal here is to consider changes in media over time in relation to changes in golf courses and golf course maintenance techniques as a way of considering questions of "how golf changed television" and "how television changed golf". Furthermore, we will note in our conclusion how the interrela-tionships between these developments, while striking in their own right, also provide a rich backdrop to contemporary developments in the mediatization of sport and environment relationships more generally, including the emergence of digitally enabled environmentalist movements related to golf and a range of mega-events.

Our analysis in this chapter draws from a larger study of golf and the environment (see Millington and Wilson, 2016). This research looked at the golf industry's developing environmental sensibilities across the twentieth and early twenty-first centuries, with a focus primarily on the United States and Canada. Our references to the golf industry below pertain mainly to these two countries. By "golf industry", we mean those involved in the process of developing and maintaining golf courses (e.g., course owners, architects, designers, and superintendents). In the following sections, we draw from a range of sources that were part of our wider project in assessing the emergence of Augusta National syndrome and its sustained existence in the post-war years. These include two book publications historicizing the Masters (Owen, 2003; Sampson, 1999), Masters architect Alistair Mackenzie's (1920) book on golf course construction, news media reports on Augusta National syndrome, and articles from industry trade publications from organizations such as the Golf Course Superintendents Association of America (GCSAA) and United States Golf Association (USGA) that we studied in a systematic way as part of our work.

With this background in place, in the following section we describe and contextualize the making of Augusta National Golf Club, juxtaposing this with wider developments in golf in the early 1900s. We then describe the process whereby the Masters made its way onto TV, and eventually developed a rather curious place within the mediasport complex. Again, we contextualize this by considering wider developments in golf at the time. From there, we turn our attention to Augusta National syndrome specifically, examining cases of this syndrome at work while considering who is responsible for its continued existence. Finally, we conclude by reflecting on the significance of our analysis as it pertains to golf, media, and the process of modernizing sport in general.

The golf course as camouflage: the birth of Augusta National Golf Club

Augusta National Golf Club was built in the early 1930s on a plot of land called Fruitlands – an antebellum plantation that, in the mid-nineteenth century, was turned into Fruitland Nurseries. As the name would suggest, Fruitlands was fertile territory; as Owen (2003) recounts, in 1861, Fruitlands' owner Prosper Berckmans "reported that his test gardens contained more than thirteen hundred varieties of pears, nine hundred varieties of apples, three hundred varieties of grapes, and a hundred varieties of azaleas – a plant that Berckmans was largely responsible for making popular in [the United States]" (Owen, 2003, p. 51; also see Nps.gov, undated). Augusta National designer (and famed golfer) Robert (Bobby) T. Jones, Jr. was allegedly captivated upon seeing this landscape in 1930: "I knew instantly it was the kind of terrain I had always hoped to find" (cited in Wind, 1955).

Jones arrived at the Fruitlands site with help from Clifford Roberts, an investment banker who would eventually serve as Masters Chairman. The Scotsman Alistair Mackenzie was hired as course architect. Surely, Mackenzie's impressive résumé was a key reason for this, though Sampson (1999, p. 19) suggests that Mackenzie's emphasis on the artistic qualities of golf course construction "spoke directly to Bobby Jones's heart", and that his simultaneous focus on *efficiency* in course development spoke to the Depression-era need for cost-effective construction. Indeed, Mackenzie's concern for efficiency was laid bare in his book, *Golf Architecture: Economy in Course Construction and Green-Keeping* (1920). Among the important elements in achieving "economy in course construction" was the availability of time- and labour-saving technologies:

> By introducing labour-saving machinery we have recently been getting better results at less than pre-war cost. If work on a large scale is being done, the steam navvy or grab might be tried for excavating and making hummocks, etc.; traction engines are useful in uprooting small trees, and larger ones can with advantage be blown up by dynamite. I recently used blasting charges for the purpose of assisting to make bunkers.
>
> *(Mackenzie, 1920, pp. 68–69)*

As Sampson (1999) writes, Augusta National was, unsurprisingly, efficient in its design. In one sense, for example, it featured a relative dearth of (expensive) sand traps. In another sense, machine technology was indeed leveraged in course construction:

> A small fleet of Caterpillar track-driven tractors pushed over trees, graded fairways, and pushed up or hollowed out the heavy clay soil for greens, tees, valleys, and mounds. Georgalina Tractor Company supplied three Cat Sixties (sixty horsepower), three Thirties, a Twenty, and two Fifteens. The big one, the Sixty, looked substantially like a modern earthmover, except its engine was slung forward, like the hood on a Buick.
>
> *(Sampson, 1999, p. 27)*

Thus, Augusta National was born as a modern course. Indeed, we can contextualize its emergence in a way that reflects our interest in how the Masters became a mega-event with environmental implications ranging beyond the tournament itself. In our research into golf's relationship with the environment we have documented how, in the early decades of the 1900s, golf was undergoing a process of rationalization (Millington and Wilson, 2015a, 2016). Before "migrating" from Europe to North America in the 1800s, golf was subject to the whims of the earth. "Links" courses in Scotland generally followed the contours of the land, with little done by way of modification. As Mackenzie observed in his book *Golf Architecture*, "In the old days, many golf courses were designed by prominent players, who after a preliminary inspection of the course simply placed pegs to represent the position of the sites for the suggested tees, greens, bunkers, etc." (Mackenzie, 1920, p. 127). The whole process, he added, could be done in a few hours. By contrast, in the twentieth century, the earth was increasingly subject to the whims of the game. Mackenzie continues: "The modern designer, on the other hand, is likely to achieve the most perfect results and make the fullest use of all the natural features by more up-to-date methods" (ibid.).

What underpinned this transition from "pre-modern" to modern golf? In one sense, the methods and tools available to key stakeholders in golf – architects, designers, and greenkeepers, for example – were changing, as suggested in Sampson's above description of "earthmoving" at Augusta National. Beyond sculpting the land during course construction, greenkeepers were experimenting with pesticides for combatting irksome insects and weeds. In the early 1920s, for example, B.R. Leach (1921) of the United States Department of Agriculture, writing in a prominent USGA publication, expressed concern over Japanese beetle infestations on golf courses in the American northeast. Just a few years later, however, he remarked that the hysteria surrounding this issue had subsided: a carbon disulphide emulsion – applied broadly via a "proportioning machine" – was doing wonders in solving the problem (Leach, 1925).

In another sense, consumer demand – or, at least, the *perception* of demand – was evidently a driving force behind golf's modernizing imperative. The first issue of *The Golf Course*, a golf industry publication featuring sections such as "Modern

Golf Chats", made clear that golfers were becoming "critical" and "fastidious": "no longer are they content with the primitive courses of early days" (Anon, 1916a, p. 2). Later in the same year, a similar sentiment was expressed in this same publication: "The mediocre Golf Course will no longer do, and it naturally follows that the best talent obtainable is being sought to carry out the work which confronts a new club or an established one where an improved course is required" (Anon, 1916b, p. 114).

A question remains as to how this modern, scientific sensibility could be squared away with Mackenzie's and Jones's more romantic view of golf course construction as art. Mackenzie makes a comparison that is telling in this regard. Golf course construction, he writes, is not unlike military camouflage. To escape the enemy's attention, a gun emplacement must be indistinguishable from its surroundings. "And what can appear more innocent than the natural undulations of the ground?" (Mackenzie, 1920, p. 129). Thus, in both camouflage and in golf course construction, "the ability to imitate natural undulations successfully is of special importance" (ibid.). In the modern age, the golf course was not real so much as *hyperreal*: an artificial landscape perfectly mimicking its original analogue.

A technological wonder: Augusta National in the post-war context

In 1934, the inaugural Augusta National Invitational was held. In 1939, this event was given a new name: the Masters. In 1956, another milestone: the Masters was first broadcast on television. That the Masters would *succeed* on TV, however, was far from a foregone conclusion.

Indeed, as Owen (2003) recounts, the first TV broadcast of a golf tournament in 1947 was not a great success. "Golf was poorly suited to the TV technology of the day," Owen writes, "since the game was played outdoors in unpredictable lighting, and the competitors roamed over an area that was hard to cover with stationary cameras" (ibid., p. 184). Moreover, Masters Chairman Clifford Roberts was allegedly wary of television due to its power to shape perceptions (Cossar, 2005; Sampson, 1999). As described below, protecting the image of the Masters was of vital importance.

Despite this, by Owen's account, Roberts pressed forward on the matter of televising the annual Masters event, seeing this as an opportunity to bolster the tournament's prize offerings, making golfers into true professional athletes. The first Masters TV broadcast in 1956 was ultimately a hit, attracting an estimated ten million viewers (Owen, 2003, p. 184). Broadcast technology only advanced from there. As Barclay (1992, p. 451) writes, by the mid-1960s, broadcasters had gone from a small number of cameras and technicians to "a dozen fixed cameras plus portables, mobile and stationary platforms, dozens of directors, and hundreds of technicians". In this same decade, the Masters was broadcast on colour TV – something that again was realized through pressure from Augusta National.

Of course, it need be remembered here that this was not just any tournament being broadcast on television, and eventually colour television. By the 1960s the Masters was one of men's golf's four major tournaments. More to the point, Augusta National itself was remarkable in its appearance. Writing in *Sports Illustrated* in 1955, Herbert Warren Wind gushed over Augusta's "green, green grass" and bright blue water hazards. Visitors to Augusta taking in the hill-top view that once won over Bobby Jones were sure to be equally impressed: "There are few first-timers who, upon experiencing that view, do not exclaim either aloud or to themselves, 'Yes, it's all it's cracked up to be and more'" (Wind, 1955).

Effusive praise of this kind is still common to this day. It can be found, for example, in Hodgetts's (2014) view that Augusta is "punctuated by explosions of colour from banks of azaleas and framed by towering pines" and in Golf Channel contributor Hawkins's (2014) assertion that Augusta "assumes a heaven-on-earth type of quality". And so when the Masters was first broadcast on colour TV it was not just the competition but the course itself and the Fruitlands landscape that suddenly had an audience numbering in the millions. Writes Oosthoek (2012), "starting in the late 1960s, colour broadcasts of the Masters Tournament at the Augusta National Golf Club in Georgia showed the world a meticulously-maintained course shimmering like an ethereal Emerald City. Golfers turned green with envy" (see also Millington and Wilson, 2014, 2016).

These post-war developments in Masters history can again be contextualized with the aim of assessing their significance. That golf was televised in the post-war years is no surprise, even acknowledging the logistical difficulties this presented. This was a time when sport and media were growing ever more entangled. As Frandsen (2014) writes, the relationship that would emerge between sport and TV is one of shared obligations and reciprocal support. What is interesting in this arrangement as it pertains to the Masters, however, is how much power Augusta National has held in its relationship with the broadcaster CBS.

Clifford Roberts, the long-time Masters Chairman, has a complicated legacy. Augusta National's exclusionary history is well known; "As long as I'm alive," Roberts has been quoted as saying, "all the golfers will be white and all the caddies will be black" (Crouse, 2012). But when it comes to media, Roberts was an in-novative figure. He sought, for example, to dramatize production by suggesting that golf shots should be tracked from the player's point of view, thus showing the ball's trajectory to the audience (Owen, 2003). The TV-friendly convention of showing fans a scoreboard with competitors' overall scores against par was likewise Roberts's idea (Cossar, 2005). More significant to these purposes, with Roberts's under-standing of the power of media in mind, Augusta National held tremendous sway over how the Masters was portrayed to television audiences at home. It was Augusta National, not the network CBS, who picked the Masters' sponsors and determined what they would pay and the amount of airtime they would receive (Owen, 2003, p. 197; Sampson, 1999, p. 205). As Sampson (ibid.) recounts, only "dignified" sponsors were considered. Broadcast language was scrutinized too (Cossar, 2005; Myers, 2014).

Thus, in the post-war years, golf and the Masters became part of the mediasport complex, though Augusta National retained more control than usual in its relationship with the media. The trade-off for extra control was and is rights fees; it is generally assumed that the Masters earns less in this regard than the market could otherwise yield (see Boudway, 2013). Of course, this "compromise" might be seen as a way of strategically managing an "under-commercialized" brand – itself a commercially driven approach. As Owen (2003, p. xxvi) observes, part of the appeal of the Masters is its ostensible "purity": "Sandwiches cost just a buck and a half, pairing sheets and parking are free, and the whole place is devoid of advertising". For this analysis, the key point is that Augusta National's "dignified" presentation on TV fits together hand and glove with the course's "perfect" aesthetic qualities. Augusta National is heaven; "Presumably there are no ads for hemorrhoid cream in heaven" (Sampson, 1999, p. 210).

At the same time, the Masters' rise to prominence in the post-war years can also be explained in relation to wider developments in the golf industry at the time. We saw above how in the early decades of the 1900s, golf industry representatives had new tools and methods at their disposal – earthmoving machinery and pesticides, for example. In the post-war years, golf course architects and designers were further emboldened in their ability to re-shape the land (see Strawn, Barger and Rogers, 2011). Greenkeepers, now more commonly known as superintendents in reflection of their ongoing professionalization, had more potent chemicals at their disposal than ever before – the best case in point being the powerful insecticide DDT. Indeed, as a product of wartime research, DDT could be applied to great effect in fending off "problem" pests. It could also be applied quite liberally thanks to the chemical application technology of the time. Golf course superintendent Joseph Valentine (1947), writing in the superintendent publication *Golfdom*, articulated both of these points in reviewing his own course management practices in Pennsylvania:

> we applied insecticides, using a dusting machine that operates with a blower through tubes under a large canvas. The duster is sixteen feet wide. On some fairways both DDT and lead arsenate were applied, on others DDT was used alone and on a third group lead arsenate alone was applied.
>
> *(Valentine, 1947, p. 70)*

In the post-war years, then, the golf industry could exert control over nature unlike ever before. And whereas Alistair Mackenzie (1920) described a delicate balance between human intervention and natural features – like military camouflage, human engineering should be made to appear natural on the golf course – Augusta National eventually developed a reputation not just for its beauty but for its *fabricated* beauty. Indeed, the Masters course is thought to benefit from an atypically large workforce and from a maintenance budget that far outstrips that of a regular course (though budgetary details are not well known). As Sterba (2001) writes, this allows a remarkable level of care: on one level, the finest of details can be attended to; on a larger scale, Augusta National, "boasts the latest in golf-course technology" such as underground pipes for drying putting surfaces from below (also see Klein, 2013; Shackelford, 2012).

From this perspective, to say Augusta National is like military camouflage does not go far enough: it is a nature simulacrum, and a transparent one at that. Even Herbert Warren Wind, so effusive in praising Augusta National's beauty in 1955, seemed aware of its fabricated elements. Among the "sundry 'little touches' that spring from [Clifford] Roberts' passion for efficiency and order" was the fact that "the brown water in the [water] hazards is touched up into a bright blue by adding a Calcozine dye" (Wind, 1955).

Augusta National syndrome

From a critical perspective, in the post-war years, the rationalizing of golf reached an *irrational* point. Golf had become a modern game, characterized by standard-ization (e.g. of rules, equipment, and technique) and efficiency (e.g. via scientific and technologically enhanced methods in course construction and maintenance). This is not an uncommon trajectory for sport. Nor is it uncommon for television to exacerbate the need for standardization – or at least the perception thereof. As Horne *et al.* write:

> As audiences around the world become accustomed to receiving top quality live broadcasts of major sport events [in the 1970s], so the television industry became concerned with uniformity. The conventions already established in the leading television nations of North America and Europe were extended to the rest of the world ... Regional diversity and specificity began to decline and by the 1980s even the internal geography of stadium design was tending towards a universality of style.
>
> *(Horne et al., 2013, p. 152)*

But efficiency in golf, at least in part, meant efficiency in deploying incredibly potent chemicals and efficiency in unsettling nature. In hindsight, carpet-spraying golf courses with DDT can be seen as rationalization reaching an irrational point; indeed, this type of practice has been questioned within the golf industry *itself* in recent years (Millington and Wilson, 2013). What is important too is that standard-ization in golf involved the view that golf's "stadiums" should tend towards a highly manicured style in particular.

This is where the phrase "Augusta National syndrome" becomes relevant. Recall Oosthoek's (2012) above-noted point that, when the Masters tournament was shown on colour TV, "Golfers turned green with envy." Augusta National, set in the inimitable Fruitlands terrain, maintained through a perhaps-inimitable level of care, and earning media coverage unlike any other course, nonetheless became a standard-bearer for the golf industry as a whole. In 1982, James A. Wyllie, president of the Golf Course Superintendents Association of America, went so far as to entitle his monthly address to superintendents in the pages of the trade publication *Golf Course Management*: "The Masters, A Visible Standard".

To be specific, it is *golfers* who were – and at times still are – generally deemed to be "afflicted" with Augusta National syndrome. Golfers apparently turned green with envy because they saw Augusta National as a representation of how a golf course can and should appear. Sharp (2000) lays out a hypothetical case along these lines, one that allegedly happens each year across the United States. Having watched the Masters on TV, you – the amateur golfer – then head out to the local course:

> But on the first tee, reality comes crashing in … your golf swing is one only a mother could love, your short game is long on miscalculations, and the conditions at your favorite course in no way resemble those of Bobby Jones' and Alister Mackenzie's masterpiece amidst the azaleas and dogwoods. Sure, you may blame yourself for not having the game that will enable you to break 90, but should you be putting so much pressure on your superintendent to maintain Augusta-like course conditions?
>
> *(Sharp, 2000, p. 20)*

Likewise, ahead of the 2002 Masters, Rubenstein (2009) commented on the ramifications of golfers' unrealistic expectations – "intense water usage and application of chemicals" among them (p. 104). Just as in the early 1900s, then, in the post-war years golfers were seen as critical and fastidious, the difference being that later in the century the golf industry could do even more to appease its finicky consumers, enacting an even greater toll on the earth in doing so.

Of course, whether Augusta National syndrome actually exists is an open question. On the one hand, the golf industry has responded to criticism of its environmental practices by stressing that golf courses are now far more responsible than in the past in using chemicals and water and in upsetting local ecosystems. We have dubbed this golf's "responsible" turn (Millington and Wilson, 2016). Even Augusta National has been said to be "greener" than usually thought: "Contrary to popular opinion, the club does not apply heavy doses of fertilizer or pesticides to keep appearances up … In fact, the opposite is true" (Boyette, 2012). On the other hand, evidence that golfers are insistent on "perfect" playing conditions to the point that an illness metaphor is appropriate is scarce at best. Perhaps to the contrary, a recent *Golf Digest* survey found that 64 per cent of golfers surveyed were willing "to play golf under less manicured conditions to minimize the use of pesticides on the course" (Barton, 2008).

At the very least, Augusta National syndrome is a *perceived* problem. For Rubenstein (2009), it could be solved "if only" golfers could realize the façade that is Augusta National's spectacular appearance. The "sick" are both afflicted by and causing their "condition".

But Augusta National syndrome can equally be construed as an industry construction. From this perspective, it is a product of both the golf industry's willingness to pursue the "Augusta standard" through their course management practices and the promotion of this standard through media outlets of various kinds. In other words, from this view, blame lies with architects, superintendents, and TV producers, who together conspire towards an unrealistic norm. Writing in the USGA publication the *Green Section Record* in 1993, TV commentator and course designer Jerry Pate convincingly made this point. Low-cut fairways, exceedingly fast putting greens, year-round weed-free grass, and perfect playing conditions: "Television has marketed these qualities to the golfing public, and today's golfers now want these conditions for their own courses" (Pate, 1993, p. 19). For Pate, superintendents were partly responsible for this, as were course architects. To say that Augusta National syndrome is an industry construction is, in essence, to say that *demand* is constructed. As McChesney (2015) argues with respect to corporate media, the notion that corporate media – and in this case, corporate media working together with the golf industry – simply respond to consumer needs is a mythology.

Rather than an illness that afflicts one group or another, we would argue that Augusta National syndrome is better understood as Augusta National *ideology*: it is a body of ideas that has no one specific "owner", and is perhaps not even wholeheartedly believed by those impacted by it, but that nonetheless serves to normalize a particular aesthetic and related set of practices. Indeed, the idea that the golf industry has embraced an environmental ethic and done away with its most damaging environmental practices still sits uncomfortably against the lingering image of how a golf course "should" present itself to the golfing public. The 2015 men's US Open presented the golf industry with the perfect chance to celebrate its newly developed environmental credentials. The tournament was held at Chambers Bay in Washington State, a former sand and gravel pit that had earned certification as a Silver Signature Sanctuary from the environmental organization Audubon International. By our reading, however, what unfolded over the four days of the US Open was nothing short of Augusta National syndrome rearing its head (see Millington and Wilson, 2015b). By the accounts of broadcasters and players alike, the course was too brown, and the putting surfaces were not of a proper quality. When golfer Henrik Stenson called the putting greens "borderline laughable" and compared them to broccoli and the surface of the moon (Murray, 2015), fellow golfer Rory McIlroy humorously amended this view: "I don't think [the greens are] as green as broccoli ... I think they're more like cauliflower" (Pennington, 2015).

Conclusion: unravelling modern sport

In this chapter, we examined and contextualized Augusta National syndrome, an ideology that, while emerging from a particular sporting mega-event, has been deemed impactful across the golf industry in general. In doing so, we also illuminated ways that golf, and the Masters especially, influenced media – and how media, and the development of colour TV especially, influenced golf and golf's relationship with the environment. While surveying these influences and interrelationships we were consistently reminded of the mediatization concept – as a term that recognizes the pervasiveness of media and the diffuse and heterogeneous character of contemporary media's influence (Couldry and Hepp, 2013) – and, in the context of our research, the media's role in the reproduction of golf and environment-related discourses.

We came to this point from an analysis that focused initially on social and cultural changes around golf beginning in the early 1900s – a time when golf industry representatives were evidently keen to modernize the sport so as to meet the demands of golf's critical and fastidious consumer market. The Augusta National course, eventual home of the Masters, was in this sense a product of its time, though architect Alistair Mackenzie was of the view that modern methods were still compatible with nature. In the post-war years, the golf industry had the capacity to radically manipulate the earth thanks to chemicals like DDT and technologies like broad-based chemical applicators. Augusta National again was representative of this change in the sense that it came to be viewed as the most manicured of all courses, maintained to what was and remains an impossible standard for many. But even with its many advantages, Augusta National nonetheless became a standard in the industry. Augusta National syndrome allegedly puts false expectations in the minds of consumers and places pressure on those building and maintaining courses to meet these expectations. If the effectiveness of the superintendent's chemical "toolkit" was not reason enough to put this toolkit to use, the idea that a golf course *should* be weed-free and perfectly green further rationalized such activity.

The emergence of Augusta National syndrome is of course significant for golf – and, as said above, what is interesting in this regard is how the representation of one particular course and mega-event in media can generate effects across an industry writ large. But there is equally a lesson about sport in general given our analysis herein. The narrative outlined in this chapter is suggestive of how difficult it can be to undo the negative effects of modernization in sport in a context where sport and media are so tightly bound together – where golf influences media and media influences golf and course development. From an optimist's perspective, the golf industry has indeed sought in recent years to redress the environmental failings of modernization – for example, by leveraging science and technology towards the safer application of chemicals. We have criticised these measures in the past for being far less rigorous than they could be (Millington and Wilson, 2013, 2016). But even if one accepts that the golf industry adopted a new, "responsible" environmental ethic beginning roughly in the 1980s, it would seem that the lingering *image* of golf in the public imagination makes even moderate changes in course management quite difficult to enact. The post-war years were a time not just when golf course developers and managers could radically manipulate the earth, but when television helped show the perfectly green golf course as normal – indeed, rational. Environmental "best practices" in this sense compete with the "best image" of golf on TV.

Indeed, in Rubenstein's commentary on Augusta National syndrome, he cites golf architecture critic Brad Klein's view that "Green is beautiful, but brown is better" (Rubenstein, 2009, p. 105). As Rubenstein writes, "The way to counteract the Augusta National syndrome is to allow a course to go brown" (ibid.). Perhaps over time this would in fact be a successful strategy. Perhaps golf can be rationalized in a way where irrational practices are avoided. But the case of Chambers Bay and the 2015 US Open suggests how difficult it is to counteract Augusta National syndrome in the immediate term. The golf course-as-cauliflower is still not an acceptable look.

At the same time, and reflecting on Frandsen's (2014) recognition of the role of digital media in mediatization, it is important to consider, on one hand, ways that Augusta National's landscapes are now accessed, promoted, and consumed through "new" media (e.g. video games, golf promotional websites) – and, on the other hand, how responses to golf-related environmental problems, and indeed environmental issues pertaining to sport mega-events more generally, have become the focus of Internet and social media-driven activist campaigns intended to raise awareness of, and sometimes resist, the sort of developments that were largely taken-for-granted and unchallenged at other moments in time. The Global Anti-Golf Movement is but one especially relevant example of a group that benefitted from the emergence of the Internet and more sophisticated forms of social media-driven activism (Millington and Wilson, 2016). While we recognize that even with activist-friendly media, there are no guarantees that there will be a full "recovery" from Augusta National syndrome – at least the potential for pro-environment changes seems to be enhanced in the current social and cultural context (Wilson, 2007). Such is the value of the mediatization concept here, as a guide for asking questions about the shifting relationships between always-changing media and always-changing social and cultural contexts, within and outside the realm of sport and mega-events.

References

Anon. (1916a). [No title.] *The Golf Course*, January, 2.
Anon. (1916b). [No title.] *The Golf Course*, November, 114.
Barclay, J.A. (1992). *Golf in Canada: A history.* Toronto: McClelland & Stewart.
Barton, J. (2008). How green is golf? *Golf Digest.* Retrieved from www.golfdigest.com/magazine/2008-05/environment_intro (accessed July 2014).
Boudway, I. (2013). The Masters: A sponsorship tradition unlike any other. *Bloomberg.* Retrieved from www.bloomberg.com/bw/articles/2013-04-12/the-masters-a-sponsorship-tradition-unlike-any-other (accessed February 2016).
Boyette, J. (2012). Augusta National Golf Club: Nothing cosmetic. *The Augusta Chronicle.* Retrieved from www.augusta.com/node/45 (accessed February 2016).
Boyle, R. and Haynes, R. (2009). *Power play: Sport, the media and popular culture.* Edinburgh: Edinburgh University Press.
Cossar, H. (2005). Televised golf and the creation of narrative. *Film and History: An Interdisciplinary Journal of Film and Television Studies, 35*(1), 52–59.

Couldry, N. and Hepp, A. (2013). Conceptualizing mediatization: Contexts, traditions, arguments. *Communication Theory, 23*(3), 191–202.

Crouse, K. (2012). Treasure of golf's sad past, black caddies vanish in era of riches. *New York Times*, 3 April. Retrieved from www.nytimes.com/2012/04/03/sports/golf/from-a-symbol-of-segregation-to-a-victim-of-golfs-success.html?_r=3 (accessed February 2016).

Frandsen, K. (2014). Mediatization of sports. In K. Lundby (ed.), *Mediatization of communication* (pp. 525–543). Berlin: Mouton de Gruyter.

Hawkins, J. (2014). Hawk's nest: 10 reasons why we love the Masters. *Golf Channel*. Retrieved from www.golfchannel.com/news/john-hawkins/hawks-nest-10-reasons-why-we-love-masters (accessed December 2014).

Hjarvard, S. (2009). The meditization of society: A theory of the media as agents of social and cultural change. *Nordicom Review, 29*(2), 105–134.

Hodgetts, R. (2014). Masters 2014: 18 reasons to love Augusta – golf's unique event. *BBC*. Retrieved from www.bbc.com/sport/0/golf/26887265 (accessed December 2014).

Horne, J., Tomlinson, A., Whannel, G. and Woodward, K. (2013). *Understanding sport: A socio-cultural analysis* (2nd ed.). New York: Routledge.

Klein, B.S. (2013). Green with envy? Don't be. *Golfweek*. Retrieved from http://golfweek.com/news/2012/apr/01/green-envy-dont-be-augusta-national-unique (accessed February 2016).

Leach, B.R. (1921). The Japanese beetle in relation to golf grounds. *Bulletin of the Green Section of the US Golf Association*, October, 210–211.

Leach, B.R. (1925). Improvements in the method of treating golf greens for the control of the Japanese beetle. *Bulletin of the Green Section of the US Golf Association*, May, 100–102.

Mackenzie, A. (1920). *Golf architecture: Economy in course construction and green-keeping*. London: Simpkin, Marshall, Hamilton, Kent & Co.

McChesney, R.W. (2015). *Rich media, poor democracy: Communication politics in dubious times*. New York: The New Press.

Millington, B. and Wilson, B. (2013). Super intentions: Golf course management and the evolution of environmental responsibility. *Sociological Quarterly, 54*(3), 450–475.

Millington, B. and Wilson, B. (2014). The masters of nature: Golf, non-humans, and consumer culture. In J. Gillett and M. Gilbert (eds), *Sport, animals and society* (pp. 52–66). New York: Routledge.

Millington, B. and Wilson, B. (2015a). Golf and the environmental politics of modernization. *Geoforum, 66*, 37–40.

Millington, B. and Wilson, B. (2015b). Eco-friendly golf means not worrying if the grass is greener on the other course. Retrieved from http://theconversation.com/eco-friendly-golf-means-not-worrying-if-the-grass-is-greener-on-the-other-course-44688 (accessed February 2016).

Millington, B. and Wilson, B. (2016). *The greening of golf: Sport, globalization and the environment*. Manchester: Manchester University Press.

Murray, E. (2015). US Open: Chambers Bay greens cause red faces but finest will prevail. *The Guardian*. Retrieved from www.theguardian.com/sport/2015/jun/20/us-open-chambers-bay-greens-red-faces (accessed February 2015).

Myers, A. (2014). Recalling that time Gary McCord was banned from the Masters (Oh, and Tiger Woods won his first of three straight US Amateurs). *Golf Digest*. Retrieved from www.golfdigest.com/story/tiger-woods-gary-mccord-cbs-masters (accessed February 2016).

Nps.gov. (undated). Fruitlands/Augusta National Golf Club. *National Park Service*. Retrieved from www.nps.gov/nr/travel/augusta/fruitlands.html (accessed February 2016).

Oosthoek, S. (2012). How golf courses are getting greener. *The Globe and Mail.* Retrieved from www.theglobeandmail.com/report-on-business/careers/top-employers/how-golf-courses-are-getting-greener/article577697 (accessed October 2012).

Owen, D. (2003). *The making of the Masters: Clifford Roberts, Augusta National, and golf's most prestigious tournament.* New York: Simon & Schuster.

Pate, J. (1993). Television golf and the golf course superintendent. *USGA Green Section Record*, May/June, 19–21.

Pennington, B. (2015). "Like putting on broccoli," or cauliflower, and results are bumpy. *New York Times*, 21 June. Retrieved from www.nytimes.com/2015/06/21/sports/golf/like-putting-on-broccoli-or-cauliflower-and-results-are-bumpy.html?_r=0 (accessed February 2016).

Rubenstein, L. (2009). *This round's on me: Lorne Rubenstein on golf.* Toronto: McClelland & Stewart.

Sampson, C. (1999). *The Masters: Golf, money, and power in Augusta, Georgia.* New York: Random House.

Shackelford, G. (2012). The Augusta syndrome revisited. Retrieved from www.golfdigest-canada.ca/courses-and-travel/the-augusta-syndrome-revisited (accessed October 2012).

Sharp, S. (2000). Great expectations. Battling the dreaded "Augusta National syndrome". *Golfdom*, May, 20–24.

Sterba, J.P. (2001). Augusta National's hyper green leads to copycats and critics. *Wall Street Journal.* Retrieved from www.wsj.com/articles/SB98650267594856710 (accessed February 2016).

Strawn, J., Barger, J. and Rogers, J.D. (2011). Earth as medium: The art and engineering of golf course construction. In S.D. Brunn (ed.), *Engineering earth: The impacts of mega-engineering projects, Volume 1* (pp. 1159–1190). London: Springer.

Valentine, J. (1947). Efficiency is keynote of better course management. *Golfdom*, Fall, 68–70.

Wheeler, K. and Nauright, J. (2006). A global perspective on the environmental impact of golf. *Sport in Society, 9*(3), 427–443.

Wilson, B. (2007). New media, social movements, and global sport studies: A revolutionary moment and the sociology of sport. *Sociology of Sport Journal, 24*(4), 457–477.

Wilson, B. and Millington, B. (2013). Sport, ecological modernization, and the environment. In D. Andrews and B. Carrington (eds), *A companion to sport* (pp. 129–142). Malden, MA: Blackwell Publishing.

Wilson, B. and Millington, B. (2015). Sport and environmentalism. In R. Giulianotti (ed.), *Routledge handbook of the sociology of sport* (pp. 366–376). New York: Routledge.

Wind, H.W. (1955). The Masters. *Sports Illustrated*, 4 April. Retrieved from www.si.com/vault/1955/04/04/605310/the-masters (accessed December 2014).

Wyllie, J.A. (1982). Message from your president: The Masters, a visible standard. *Golf Course Management*, May, 5.

11

TOUR DE FRANCE

Mediatization of sport and place

Kirsten Frandsen

The Tour de France is an annual cycling race which has taken place on the roads of France since 1903. For many decades, it was mainly considered a national French event, though it has involved riders and teams most typically from neighboring European countries and also received regular coverage in international newspapers over the years (Reed, 2015). However, especially since the 1980s, it has been steadily globalized in terms of the teams, riders and sponsors taking part, and most notably regarding media coverage (Reed, 2003; Palmer, 2010). As a sporting mega-event, the Tour de France stands out in terms of how it is organized in time and space, and this chapter will center on how such framing causes a particular process of mediatization, where tourism blends in distinctive ways with sport and affects both the event and the media coverage.

Mediatization is about the interrelations of media with other social and cultural domains and how they contribute to structural changes in a long-term perspective (Frandsen, 2014). As we shall see, there have been ties and mutual interests between media, sport and tourism in the Tour de France for many years. The mixture of local and regional political and economic interests behind hosting major sports events, the intention of using events as tools for branding places and economic development, and the overall impact of these efforts have also been widely documented and debated. In fact, these complex interrelated interests have become one of the defining elements of a "mega-event" (Horne and Manzenreiter, 2006; Müller, 2015; Roche, 2000). Indeed, the merits of hosting mega-events as "hallmark" events and using them as "image builders of modern tourism" (Bull and Lovell, 2010, p. 232) have received much scholarly scrutiny in recent years.

In the case of the Tour de France, the relationship between sport and geographical space has been essential in defining the event's meaning. Compared to many other major events where the visibility and identity of the host locations tend to disappear or have a more marginal status in the coverage when competition starts

(Evans, 2014), "geography" is in many ways the foundation on which any understanding of the Tour de France rests. Since the advent of television, the event has developed into a suggestive audiovisual spectacle, with the meaning of places produced and articulated being married to the meaning of the sporting action in a very distinctive manner. In recent years, this symbiosis has made the Tour de France a special promotional vehicle not only for a wide spectrum of corporate sponsorships in cycling, but also for a tourist industry that is increasingly seeking global exposure.

However, as a globally distributed event, the Tour de France is not a "collective." It has both a "core" and a "periphery" (Evans, 2014; Puijk, 2000). The French context and organizers Amaury Sport Organisation (ASO) – formerly La Société de Tour de France – provide a core production in the form of a race and an audiovisual signal produced by French television for all broadcasters with the right to transmit the event. However, this product is widely customized by the respective broadcasters in order to advance strategic goals sensitive to local contexts for audiences that define diverse "peripheries" for the event. Thus, the production of this mega-event is a complex and multilayered process, involving many agents from media, sports, corporate businesses, and authorities. This will be illustrated briefly at the end of this chapter by way of a Danish case showing how the media are agents of cultural and social change in the periphery of a sporting mega-event.

A sporting mega-event with distinct characteristics

Currently, the Tour de France is the largest free annual sporting event in the world, accumulating 10–15 million spectators along the roads every year (Andreff, 2016). With an average total distance of around 3,664 kilometers in three weeks, it has a touch of the extreme. Twenty-two teams, each with nine riders, participated in the 2015 event and approximately 4,500 people (organizers, teams, media, partners, the advertising caravan and service providers) traveled with the race on the route each day. The modern media coverage of the Tour involves around 2,000 accredited media professionals, and the race is broadcast in 190 countries. French television (France Télévisions) is the official broadcast partner that produces the international signal, and in 2015 they broadcast eight out of 21 stages in full, and provided in total 80 hours of live broadcasts to international broadcasters with the right to transmit the event. The organizers, ASO, expected more than 2,400 hours of television coverage. Global viewership has been on the rise for several decades, but its exact size remains highly uncertain because it consists of many different national and regional ratings. For some years, the ASO's own official estimations have been around 3.5 billion, whereas the official sponsor, Skoda, estimated in 2014 that global viewership for the 2013 event was 1.4 billion (Skoda, 2014; Tour de France, 2015; VeloNews, 2015a).

The Tour de France has three characteristics that make it an essential case to consider in understanding how the media are agents of change alongside other macro-social cultural processes like commercialization and globalization. First, the event was – just like several other cycling races at that time – invented by the press (Reed, 2015; Thompson, 2008) when the French sports newspaper *L'Auto* wanted to increase summer circulation to beat a competing sports newspaper. Thus, right from the beginning, the underlying basis for the event was driven by the practical and commercial needs of French media in a nationalized context. The Tour de France emerged primarily as an object for media coverage, but throughout the twentieth century its popularity gave its French organizers both "formal and informal power to shape the global sport" (Reed, 2015, p. 4). Commercialization of the press intertwined with commercial interest from a flourishing cycle manufacturing industry, which supported the race because it could use these races, the accompanying press coverage and the ads as promotional instruments (ibid.; Thompson, 2008; Wille, 2003). As such, the Tour de France is a prominent early example of what has increasingly been seen as a "mediatized" event (rather than a "media event"), one that recognizes that the role of the media is much more far-reaching than just mediating a real-life event (Evans, 2014; Livingstone, 2009). The Tour de France notably illustrates how the media were historically engaged in the very shaping of modern sport. It was at the ground floor of the first wave of mediatization of cycling – one that contributed to the formation of professional cycling as one of the oldest professional sports (Desbordes, 2006). Founded for profit in times of a booming market economy, the first two decades of the race were organized around teams sponsored by the bicycle industry.

Second, the Tour de France is a mobile event that establishes a distinct relationship between sport and geographical space. The founders were highly influenced by matters of national identity: "The association of the Tour with national identity is thus not only a contemporary fact, but a historical intention on the part of its founders" (Campos, 2003, p. 153). The event was also designed with a pedagogical and ideological intention of contributing to the identity formation of the French people. After a humiliating defeat in the Franco-Prussian War in 1870, at the start of the twentieth century French politicians were still seeking to reinforce the sense of national identity. They sought to establish France as "a land unit having a strong cultural tradition" (ibid., p. 151). At the same time the country faced social unrest and cultural tensions as industrialization and urbanization expanded. The Tour de France also became popular and commercially successful because it showcased the variety of the nation by visiting various towns and regions, and the event established a bond between industrial, modern France (the bike and the city workers) and the rural areas (Thompson, 2008).

As a mobile event, the sporting activities of the Tour de France have never been confined to or dependent on large stadiums with only restricted access for the public. Because the Tour de France takes place on public roads in the villages, towns and open landscapes of France and its neighboring countries, it offers the public a unique, intimate, but ephemeral experience of the sporting action. The absence of physical barriers between the spectators and the riders not only makes it "the greatest free sporting event in the world" (Wille, 2003, p. 128), but also supports the creation of an intense, intimate, and varied spectacle – even though the spectators' experiences of the sporting action are restricted to short glimpses of the riders passing by.

Because "getting the 'big picture' of competition" is so difficult for spectators at the scene of the race, the media have become vital for the event in two related respects. First, the spectators by the roadside cannot experience the race in a cohesive way. Their experience is quite different than that of a restricted group of organizers, VIP guests, team coaches, mechanics, trainers, and medical assistants who follow the riders on the roads on each stage. Everyone else, including the bulk of accredited reporters and commentators, is reliant on information about live sporting action on the roads from the audiovisual constructions used in broadcasting coverage and a dedicated radio channel used for internal event communication. Second, as there are no ticket sales, the media, with their ability to facilitate and structure public attention and exposure, play an essential role in the financial structure and success of the event.

Third, as an annual event, the Tour de France has been inexorably marked by the summer holiday atmosphere surrounding it. From the start, it has attracted throngs of spectators along the roadside and, as a result, has become intimately linked to tourism activities. The coverage in *L'Auto* was initially characterized by narrative styles associated with tourist guides and early coverage even described the experiences of some of the racers as similar to those of tourists. In the first two decades of the event, newspapers started offering travel packages to the event for fans in collaboration with tourist agencies and railroad companies (Thompson, 2008). In the 1920s, the commercial value of the event led host cities to offer the Tour organizers subsidies in order to attract the race. This revenue became increasingly important for the organizers as the growth in the bicycle industry subsided in the same period. As a result, starting in 1930, a new business model for the race was launched. The race was now organized around national teams from France, Belgium, Italy, Spain and Germany (selected and organized by the chief editor of *L'Auto*). The suspension of corporate team sponsorships from the bicycle industry, tire manufacturers and producers of bicycle accessories increased the demand for new incomes dramatically as *L'Auto* now had to cover all expenses for accommodation, bicycles, etc. Therefore a publicity caravan was created in which "anyone who was willing to pay the entry fee could join" (Reed, 2015, p. 39) and publicize their product from a vehicle. This arrangement opened up for a wide spectrum of sponsorships in the 1930s, representing more than 13 different categories of products and businesses, including in particular alcoholic beverages, food, bicycles/automobile related equipment – but also furniture/houseware and clothing and the entertainment business. Right from the beginning many of these businesses sought to convey their messages in creative and festive ways, using decorations and music, and thus the publicity caravan gained a "carnivalesque quality" (ibid., p. 40) for the many roadside spectators.

This new model for the event also entailed a heavy increase in the subsidy payments now demanded by organizers. In 1938, subsidies from stage towns provided 21 percent of the total event budget (ibid., p. 42). Thus, a good case may be made that a mediatized cycling event, the Tour de France, had become a significant engine in the mediatization of tourism in provincial France.

Producing a hybrid of drama and "gaze"

Tourism is "a kind of organized retreat from the temporal and spatial features of labor practices and everydayness" (Jansson, 2002, p. 431). From Jansson's perspective, mediatization has to be understood as a process in which people's cultural frameworks are increasingly based on media consumption. Being a tourist involves a particular kind of "gaze," "through which the tourist objectifies and interprets the place that he or she visits" (ibid., p. 431), a gaze that has become increasingly intertwined with the consumption of media images.

The Tour de France produces a "mediatized gaze" (Lamont and McKay, 2012), albeit a particular one, as it links the experience of geography and places together with a long-running, dramatic sporting experience. As such, it is a hybrid that serves other interests than those of cycling: "we are basically – involuntarily and indirectly – great ambassadors for certain aspects of our country, notably tourism" (Marchetti, 2003, p. 46). Because the event is mobile, it furthermore produces an experience of always being on the move, which, according to Lamont and McKay (2012), is a key component in tourism today. Because the Tour de France repeatedly takes place at the same time of the year and the organizers are very careful not to make major changes in the basic design of the race route, it becomes a strong communicative structure of attention that gradually molds the audience's cultural framework with regard to both France and cycling. And for many this imaginary hybrid has become an integral part of taking a break from everyday life throughout three weeks of prime European holiday time.

The production of this experience is a matter of both spatial planning and mediation. Palmer (2010) has described how the current organizer of the Tour de France, ASO, operates the event with regard to its spatial dimension. An important part of the production is the route design and the spatial transformations of host towns and villages before the race arrives. The pre-planning begins 2 years before the actual race with a bidding session from towns who wish to host a stage start or finish. Here, local interests in attracting tourists and getting exposure, the highlighting of key narratives and images of "Frenchness," the history of the Tour itself, economic incentives, and the pragmatics of organization all tie together in shaping the logistical and cultural frameworks for producing the event. On the basis of the bids received (there are often more than 200 of them, Andreff, 2016), the organizers draft a route choosing stage towns (which pay €50,000–100,000 for the privilege with 12 months' notice to prepare for the event). For the towns involved, besides making practical arrangements for everything from telecommunication to flowers, preparations may also include alterations to spatial infrastructure like roundabouts and cobblestones, transforming public gardens into start areas, converting buildings into media centers, and installing temporary food, beverage, and merchandise stands. On the one hand, the transformation of these towns is a process where "the civic space of the stage villages is transformed and recast as the space of the Tour" (Palmer, 2010, p. 875). On the other hand, people and organizations articulate local and regional identities in numerous ways along the route.

The Tour de France is produced through an interlocking network of actors, agents and associations. Organizers in the ASO constitute key agents, deciding not only the route and spatial logistics, but also which teams can participate and which media are accredited. Palmer (2000) stresses that the ASO group is dominated by people with a background as media professionals; thus, the event's logic is driven by a highly mediatized sporting organization (Frandsen, 2016). However, other media organizations, local officials, corporate promoters and team coaches are also important contributors to the production of the core event.

The rest of this chapter focuses on the role of television as a particularly influential and notably complex agent in producing the Tour de France as an event. The transformative power of television is illustrated by the ways in which it brings the Tour de France and its locales into contact with the audience, and by the nature of its interplay with other macro-structural forces, most notably commercialism and globalization.

Imagery visualized as live and on the move

The relationship between television and the Tour de France was established in the wake of the Second World War. The widespread popularity of the event made it a strategic tool for French state-run television to attract audiences, fuel television sales, and encourage experiences with the new technology (Dunne, 2002). Coverage of the final stage in Paris in 1948 was the object of one of the first live broadcasts on French television, and coverage of the Tour was an essential element in the launching of news programs in summer 1949 (ibid.). Early on, French producers were keen experimenters with television technology – filming from the rear of motorbikes, and optimizing transport and editing processes for footage to facilitate the prompt delivery of images to the audience. Production was a "veritable rolling laboratory and testing ground for new television technologies and filming techniques" (ibid., p. 31). Though mountain stages provided important testing grounds for distribution technology, a consistent focus was on creating intimacy for French viewers by relying on mobile shots of both the race and its riders. This facilitated an insider perspective on the event which, in many respects, was better than the short glimpses gained by roadside spectators. At the same time geographical diversity provided "added value" of a larger backdrop for those watching the coverage (Wille, 2003).

Exposure of corporate interests

At the start of the 1960s, television had become such a powerful factor that it indirectly prompted profound changes in both the organization of the race and its business model. After the Second World War the Tour de France faced increasing financial difficulties, with the newspaper and bicycle industries both suffering from declining sales. However, at the same time France experienced an economic boom, and advertisers sought new promotional channels. In order to overcome some of the financial difficulties for professional cycling, the governing body of French cycling supported a demand for increased sponsorship by allowing advertisements on riders' jerseys and shorts. Marketers regarded the Tour de France and its teams as optimal vehicles for gaining exposure as television brought the event straight into people's living rooms across France, and, with the advent of the Eurovision network in 1954, across borders. At this time, the Tour director had become increasingly concerned that the event should be seen as a "powerful symbol of French heritage" (Reed, 2003, p. 111), and, in facilitating competition between national teams, that it should be seen as sharing characteristics of the Olympic Games. In this, he saw a particular responsibility to safeguard this piece of French culture and French cycling from further commercialization.

Nevertheless, throughout the 1950s financial difficulties in tandem with the growing popularity of television and its coverage of the Tour fueled commercial pressures for a return to corporate teams. Some of the new sponsors in cycling from outside cycling's traditional business partners (often referred to as "extra-sportifs") regarded the race as lacking commercial value because of the national teams formula. Thus, several leading riders who were sponsored by those sponsors did not participate in the race in the late 1950s and early 1960s.

Finally, in the early 1960s the Tour management gave in on the issue. Corporate teams were reintroduced from 1962 – but now including both the bicycle industry and new business partners as team sponsors. With this model television gained an important role for the future of the event and for cycling in general. The founding financial structure, with the sporting event being used to increase circulation and advertising revenue by the newspaper that organized it, was gradually abandoned in favor of a model based on the unique ability of television to give audiovisual national (and eventually international) exposure to corporate sponsor messages, cycling, and the places featured on the Tour route. Given that advertisements were not allowed on French television until 1968, producing the event constituted an "attractive advertising loophole" (Dunne, 2002, p. 316). In this way the Tour de France not only influenced French television as a driver of technological innovation and development, but also served as an instigator of commercialization in French television (Reed, 2003; Wille, 2003).

In 1962, against this backdrop of increasing commercialization and the reintroduction of corporate sponsored teams, French television planned to introduce live coverage. Overcoming objections from the regional press, French television offered live coverage of the final parts of every stage from 1963 (Wille, 2003), ushering in a new era. In order to accommodate corporate demand for television exposure, organizers increased the number of teams in the race from 11 to 13, new categories of official sponsorships for the race were introduced, and a number of new sponsor-financed prizes and awards were implemented (Reed, 2003). All this prompted an increased competitive pressure in the race. Teams were (and still are) fully financed by corporate sponsorships. Television and the increasing number of teams competing for both wins and presence and exposure in front of the cameras have made the race faster. For this reason, television has also been regarded as a factor behind doping (Mignon, 2003).

Rights fees as an economic booster

The next turning point in the relations between the Tour de France and television was initiated by developments in the early 1980s, when satellites and a liberal market orientation facilitated new processes of globalization amidst the deregulation of television in Europe. Though French television had always paid a small fee for its broadcast rights, it was not until the late 1980s, when a competitive television system had been introduced all over western Europe, that television rights became a significant source of income for Tour organizers. The need for popular content on an increasing number of both national and international television channels in Europe was instrumental for turning rights fees into a new, all-important source of income. As former event director Jean-Marie Leblanc noted about the prioritization of television: "Today we are concerned with the press, I won't say less, but proportionally compared to television it's not very important" (Marchetti, 2003, p. 37). In 1960, rights fees accounted for 1.5 percent of the event's budget. By 1992, fees had increased to 26 percent of the budget, and by 2010 they edged up to about 44 percent of the event budget (Andreff, 2016; Reed, 2003).

Thus, market-driven television continued to change the financial structure of the Tour de France, making broadcasting rights a major source of income on a par with corporate sponsorships (Marchetti, 2003). Revenues from television broadcasting rights multiplied by 65 from 1980 to the late 1990s (from €250,000 to €16 million; Andreff, 2016). Since the beginning of the 2000s, they have constituted 45–50 percent of a budget that skyrocketed from €5 million in 1980 to €130 million in 2013 (Andreff, 2016; Marchetti, 2003; Reed, 2015).

The relative importance of subsidies from stage cities decreased from 40 percent of the budget in 1952 to 5 percent in 2010 (Andreff, 2016). However, places remain important as they have become significant ingredients in the production of a televisual spectacle.

Competition within the European television market was paralleled by increased focus by organizers on the prospects of global distribution of the Tour de France. With this, the event changed in several respects. Since the early 1980s the management has taken several initiatives to support an interest in road cycling in affluent media markets outside Europe, seeking to strategically expand the market for rights and grow the audience (Reed, 2003). At the same time, the number of teams, riders and accredited media has increased and infrastructural, logistical concerns have gained higher priority when routes are charted. According to Palmer (2010), this transformation into a more globalized event gained momentum from the late 1990s. More foreign riders and international teams participated, resulting in only 4 out of the 22 teams in 2015 being sponsored by French companies. More teams wished to participate, and more team owners and sponsors built teams around their Tour de France performance (Marchetti, 2003). The event is now characterized by intensified competition and the increasingly international nature of the media accredited to cover it. In 2002, only 40 percent of the accredited journalists were French (ibid.). By 2015, evidence suggested that interest in the event was growing worldwide, but decreasing in France (VeloNews, 2015b).

Turning sports viewers into "armchair tourists"

Since 1954, the start of the Tour has regularly been organized in one of the neighboring countries, but since the late 1990s this has happened more frequently. In 2007 the managing director, Christian Prudhomme, said he expected the "grand départs" outside France to become a higher priority, estimating that three out of five future starts would take place abroad. This shift is underpinned by a general interest in boosting tourism through the hosting of major sports events. In the case of the Tour de France, this is a well-established strategic concern, but owing to the primacy of television, it has been heightened in two ways. First, since 1992 technology has allowed French television to feature high-quality images of the race and the attractiveness of its sites through the use of aerial cameras (Wille, 2003). Second, the transition to a booming economy based on the combination of corporate exposure *and* rights has prompted a self-perpetuating increase in live coverage on television, where images of places have become a crucial asset. Increased prizes for the rights are accompanied by increased demand for as many hours of high-quality broadcasting as possible (John Jäger, personal communication, June 12, 2015; Marchetti, 2003). Well-paying hosts of "grand départs" abroad and team sponsors push for more exposure as well. In response, and for these reasons, French television has constantly increased and improved the live coverage. More stages, including flat ones, are covered fully, as are stages not traditionally marked by dramatic competition.

With increased coverage, geographical and cultural-historical contexts for the race have gained in importance. The lack of constant sporting action has been compensated for by providing a growing number of spectacular images of landscapes, castles, bridges and monuments, which are quite often supplemented by images of the spectacular crowds along the roadsides. Studies of the aesthetics in comparable transmissions from flat stages in northern France in 1995 and 2015 illustrate this. The relative amount of time spent on images where the focus clearly shifts from the race to the landscape, buildings or monuments increases from 6 to 13 percent over that period. By 2015, the geography and places were no longer considered only as scenic backdrops for sporting action. Providing context has, in definitive ways, become an integral element in fashioning a more complex audio-visual spectacle. As such, coverage of the Tour de France has taken on some of the qualities of travel and landscape programming that has been described as a combination of "slow" and "spectacular" television (Wheatley, 2011). However, in covering the Tour, the "travelogue" imagery is interspersed with coverage of competition and the crowd. Prominent visual attention is given to the spectators along the route, diverse performances aimed at those spectators, the race as it passes them by, and their recognition of the television audience. All of this becomes part of the mediation of the event. To some extent, the spectacle is co-produced through and by the spectators and places along the route.

The enhanced aesthetic integration of landscapes, landmarks, buildings and people is bolstered by other types of informative material made available to those telling the broadcasters' "story." Today, a historical guide to the Tour de France, a tourist guide to the visited regions, a commentators' book and a roadbook are sent to international broadcasters in advance of the event. The last two of these contain not only practical tips about safe driving, the location of gas stations, parking facilities at team hotels, the routes for each stage, and the handling of rubbish, but also comprehensive, detailed demographic, historical and cultural information about the sites, places and regions of each stage. This information is provided partly by the stage cities and partly by French television and the ASO. From its initiation in the 1990s, the roadbook was provided only in French; but since the mid-2000s, the ASO has provided it in English to accommodate the international media. For each stage, the roadbook points out select culturally and historically significant buildings, monuments and landscapes that French television plans to stress in its visuals from helicopters. This footage "objectifies and interprets the place" (Jansson, 2002, p. 431), offering the sports viewers an exclusive opportunity to become "armchair tourists" (Waade, 2008). Following Wheatley's (2011) work on "landscape" programs, the focus of such images likely explains why the Tour de France, compared with other sports events, attracts a "less working-class" and "bit less 'young'" media audience (John Jäger, personal communication, June 12, 2015; Marchetti, 2003, p. 39).

The sound of summer on the periphery

As briefly touched upon in the introduction, the Tour de France is not solely produced by the ASO and French television. The television audience's experience is also shaped by the various broadcasters and their national or local strategic interests. The national broadcasters are co-producers of the event, as they provide commentary, interviews and features in various forms of pre- and post-programs. They re-contextualize the event, and may even add new layers of meaning. Accordingly, Puijk (2000) and Evans (2014) stress that it is analytically useful to differentiate between a "core" and a "periphery" of an event – in terms of both viewers and production. In considering a Danish case, it can been seen that attention is focused on "localizing" aspects of the production of the Tour de France. This particular case provides an illustration of how mediatization is a multilayered process of change. Mediatization is both a process in which the media actively shape people's cultural frameworks regarding cycling and France, and a transformative process in which the institutions of sport, media and tourism mutually influence each other – even at the local level of production.

The Tour de France has been covered live on Danish national television since 1990. This coverage provided one of the first successes for a new national public service channel, TV 2. Since then, the channel has covered the event extensively every year, and the Tour de France is now considered essential to the service's brand strategy by the chief editor of TV 2 Sport:

> The Tour de France is one of the few sports events that people associate with a particular television station. It is part of TV 2's identity. It takes place in summertime, when it is difficult to make people watch television. That is why it is so important for us. … We own the summer because of the Tour de France. … The melody that we associate with the Tour de France – it's the sound of summer.
>
> *(John Jäger, personal communication, June 12, 2015)*

One of the main reasons for this success was that TV 2 deliberately chose to give more attention to the context of the event. They engaged a Danish artist, long known for his passion about sports and well known for his journalistic and creative works, as an expert commentator. He provided the viewers with expressive and dramatic interpretations of the race, with riders and their strategies linked to local geographies, culture, and history. For Danish TV 2, the Tour de France became a means to showcase itself as a quality channel that was innovative in covering sports, one that attracted (for the first time in Danish television) a broader audience for international cycling coverage. From 1993, this approach was reinforced by culturally oriented prime-time programs that blended features and interviews with Danes passionate about or living in France, with a focus on French lifestyles, gastronomy and art connected to regions on the race route.

Since 2000, TV 2 has shared the rights with another Danish broadcaster and has been limited to covering the Tour de France via live transmissions. However, in 2014 they launched a new program, *TV 2 on Tour*, scheduled each day before live coverage. But *TV 2 on Tour* is more than a television program. It also involves local cycling events for kids and adults that are organized in ten different towns in Denmark by TV 2 in collaboration with local authorities, tourism agencies and cycling organizations. As such it is a social and cultural event where various forms of interest merge and seek to take advantage of the Tour de France. At the same time, it provides an alternative story about cycling – a story about cycling as a localized, recreational, family and leisure-related activity. The program *TV 2 on Tour* covers the junior and senior races and performances by local mayors who compete using cycle simulators on the legendary Alpe d'Huez stage. All this takes place in a reconstructed Tour space where symbols and signs (from the hosts and reporters to the graphics and set design and the prominent use of the color yellow) that are well known from the Tour de France coverage are used to build a relationship between this local alternative cycling event, its television coverage, and the sporting mega-event.

Following the program, spectators are offered Tour de France coverage on large screens on the local set. In this manner, Danish television situates itself as the co-organizer of a sports event where the intention is to "bring the Alps to the Danish summer towns" (www.tv2.dk). Besides stimulating tourist interest in visiting the host towns and regions, the program supports a booming interest in self-organized recreational cycling that has developed in Denmark since the 1990s. Above all, however, the initiative functions as image branding for the channel, building good rapport with ordinary Danes across Denmark by demonstrating an interest in cycling that is both original and relates to the mega-event. Thus, the media heightening of the Tour de France event provides a "mediated structure of attention" for other agents to connect with, thereby reproducing the processes of mediatization of sport and tourism on a more local level.

Final remarks

This chapter has focused on how the media – most particularly television – have been active in shaping and changing the formation and production of the Tour de France. In many respects, the Tour de France provides a very early example of how "everything" has become increasingly mediatized. At this point, it is no longer sufficient in studying an event of this sort to consider only its relation to media institutions and processes.

Founded by a newspaper, the Tour de France is an excellent example of how the field of sport has been challenged and enriched by the larger processes of mediatization, a continuous process whereby the media saturate and influence diverse social and cultural domains. The founding newspaper, *L'Auto*, was a sports newspaper, so it may be argued that in the Tour de France, the relationship of media to event is, above all, characterized by an interrelatedness of mutual and complex processes of the mediatization of cycling and the commercialization and differentiation of media.

Furthermore, the Tour de France is distinctive with regard to its organization of time and space. The media have not only transformed the experience of the event. Indeed, for the audience, the media have become a prerequisite for experiencing the event in full. Increasingly, over time, the audience's social relation with the event and its riders has been shaped by media organizations, strategies, and technologies.

Through its communicative characteristics, television has been an exceptional driver in changing how we understand what was once a more modest national cycling event. Much of this influence stems from the strong macro-social forces of commercialization and globalization. Taking the long view, television has been instrumental not only in changing the financial and organizational structures of the Tour. It has also changed the whole way our cultural imagination about sport and places may be interlinked through a communicative hybrid which is unique and exclusive to the Tour de France, with the impact of its "media logic" growing along with its international audience.

References

Andreff, W. (2016). The Tour de France: A success story in spite of competitive imbalance and doping. In D. Van Reeth and D.J. Larson (eds), *The economics of professional road cycling* (pp. 233–255). Heidelberg: Springer.

Bull, C. and Lovell, J. (2010). The impact of hosting major sporting events on local residents: An analysis of the views and perceptions of Canterbury residents in relation to the Tour de France 2007. *Journal of Sport and Tourism, 12*, 229–248.

Campos, C. (2003). Beating the bounds: The Tour de France and national identity. In H. Dauncy and G. Hare (eds), *The Tour de France 1903–2003* (pp. 149–174). London: Routledge.

Desbordes, M. (2006). The economics of cycling. In W.A. and S. Szymanski (eds), *Handbook on the economics of sport* (pp. 398–410). Cheltenham: Edward Elgar Publishing.

Dunne. K. (2002). Sport as media propaganda vehicle: The Tour de France and French television, 1948-62. *French Cultural Studies, 13*, 309–317.

Evans, C. (2014). The discursive representation of host locations in a sports media event: Locating the "real site" of Formula One. *Interactions: Studies in Communication and Culture, 5*, 231–245.

Frandsen, K. (2014). Mediatization of sports. In K. Lundby (ed.), *Handbook of communications sciences, vol. 21: Mediatization of communication* (pp. 525–543). Berlin: Mouton de Gruyter.

Frandsen, K. (2016). Sports organizations in a new wave of mediatization. *Communication and Sport, 4*(4), 385–400.

Horne, J. and Manzenreiter, W. (2006). An introduction to the sociology of sports mega-events. *The Sociological Review, 54*(s2), 1–24.

Jansson, A. (2002). Spatial phantasmagoria. The mediatization of tourism experience. *European Journal of Communication, 17*, 429–443.

Lamont, M. and McKay, J. (2012). Intimations of postmodernity in sports tourism at the Tour de France. *Journal of Sport and Tourism, 17*, 313–331.

Livingstone, S. (2009). Foreword: Coming to terms with "mediatization." In K.T. Lundby (ed.), *Mediatization. Concept, changes, consequences* (pp. ix–xi). Bonn: Peter Lang.

Marchetti, D. (2003). The changing organization of the Tour de France and its media coverage – an interview with Jean-Marie Leblanc. In H. Dauncy and G. Hare (eds), *The Tour de France 1903–2003* (pp. 33–56). London: Routledge.

Mignon, P. (2003). The Tour de France and the doping issue. In H. Dauncy and G. Hare (eds), *The Tour de France 1903–2003* (pp. 227–245). London: Routledge.

Müller, M. (2015). What makes an event a mega-event? Definitions and sizes. *Leisure Studies, 34*(6), 627–642.

Palmer, C. (2000). Spin doctors and sportsbrokers: Researching elites in contemporary sport – a research note on the Tour de France. *International Review for the Sociology of Sport, 35*, 364–377.

Palmer, C. (2010). "We close towns down for a living": Spatial transformation and the Tour de France. *Social and Cultural Geography, 11*, 865–881.

Puijk, R. (2000). A global media event? Coverage of the 1994 Lillehammer Olympic Games. *International Reviews for the Sociology of Sport, 35*, 309–330.

Reed, E. (2003). The economics of the Tour, 1930–2003. In H. Dauncy and G. Hare (eds), *The Tour de France 1903–2003* (pp. 103–127). London: Routledge.

Reed, E. (2015). *Selling the yellow jersey.* Chicago, IL: University of Chicago Press.

Roche, M. (2000). *Mega-events and modernity.* London: Routledge.

Skoda (2014) Skoda – official Tour de France partner until 2018. March 4. Retrieved from www.skoda-auto.com/en/mobile/newsdetail?newsid=369&nids=373,372,371,370,

369,368,367,366,365,364&lurl=www.skoda-auto.com/en/mobile/Pages/news.aspx?
pageindex=5 (accessed 24 November 2016).

Thompson, C.S. (2008). *The Tour de France*. Berkeley, CA: University of California Press.

Tour de France (2015). Infographic: Tour de France 2015 interesting facts and stats. Retrieved from www.tourdefrance2015live.com/2015/06/infographic-tour-de-france-2015-facts-stats.html (accessed 24 November 2016).

VeloNews (2015a). The 2015 Tour de France by the numbers. *VeloNews*, June 24. Retrieved from www.velonews.competitor.com/2015/06/tour-de-france/the-2015-tour-de-france-by-the-numbers_375008 (accessed 24 November 2016).

VeloNews (2015b). Tour de France fan numbers grow … but not in France. *VeloNews*, July 22. Retrieved from www.velonews.competitor.com/2015/07/news/tour-de-france-fan-numbers-grow-but-not-in-france_379225 (accessed 24 November 2016).

Waade, A.M. (2008). Travel as TV entertainment. Paper presented to the annual meeting of European Communication Research and Education, Barcelona 2008.

Wheatley, H. (2011). Beautiful images in spectacular clarity: Spectacular television, landscape programming and the question of (tele)visual pleasure. *Screen*, *52*, 233–248.

Wille, F. (2003). The Tour de France as an agent of change in media production. In H. Dauncy and G. Hare (eds), *The Tour de France 1903–2003* (pp. 128–146). London: Routledge.

12

THE MONACO GRAND PRIX AND INDIANAPOLIS 500

Projecting European glamour and global Americana

Damion Sturm

The Monaco Grand Prix and Indianapolis 500 (Indy 500) are globally renowned as pinnacle annual events on the international motor-racing calendar. Although one-off races within their larger series (Formula One and IndyCar respectively), they are revered as the stand-out events on their specific racing calendars. Indeed, to some degree, they seemingly operate as stand-alone events (particularly the Indy 500) given the prominence, pre-eminence and global attention they are accorded. For example, O'Kane asserts that:

> In open-wheel racing the Monaco Grand Prix, which is the "jewel in the crown" of the Formula One world championship, alongside the famous Indianapolis 500-mile race, held annually at the Indianapolis Motor Speedway in the USA, represent the most desirable open wheel race victories in the world.
>
> *(O'Kane, 2011, p. 282)*

O'Kane continues by noting that, "arguably these races are viewed as being more important and prestigious than the … separate racing series that they incorporate" and that to win either race "attracts fame, prestige, wealth and respect among drivers and motor racing enthusiasts" (ibid.). Of course, it is easy to overstate the relevance and significance of both races. Unravelling some of their mythical tapestry offers insights into these racing events.

In a literal and figurative sense, both races represent, reproduce and reify mythic projections around notions of tradition, glamour, prestige, history and grandeur. The sense of occasion for both races is immense, evoking grandiose histories that span 100 years for the Indianapolis 500 and over 85 years at Monaco (65 years for staging Formula One races). As such, these histories have afforded the formulation and cementing of traditions that have endured, such as the winning driver drinking milk at Indianapolis.

Much of the prestige of the Monaco Grand Prix and Indy 500 as major events stems from the unique settings of their sites, which draws attention to their histories and to the surroundings that convey speed, risk and danger in contrasting ways. For Monaco, it is the narrow, tight, twisting street circuit that is instantly recognizable on Formula One's global telecasts that reach 500 million television viewers annually (Sturm, 2014). Reportedly, the Monaco Grand Prix has averaged above four million viewers in the United Kingdom alone since 2013 (F1 Broadcasting, 2015). For drivers, this allows no respite or margin for error as they race around the tiny principality inches from metal barriers and walls, and speed through the darkened tunnel into bright light. Despite its comparatively low speeds, it is generally regarded as the most dangerous circuit on the Formula One calendar due to its complexity. Former three-time world champion Nelson Piquet described racing at Monaco as "like trying to ride your bicycle around your living room" (Widdows, 2011).

In contradistinction, the Indy 500 offers 33 cars racing at full throttle for the majority of the race. At the Indianapolis Motor Speedway, the cars consistently race in excess of 225 mph around the large four kilometre oval. Its "megamediasport" event status is less assured. American television viewing figures have lingered around 4–6 million since 2013, almost half the reported 7–10 million viewers reportedly tuning in during the 1990s and 2000s (Sports Media Watch, 2014). While global figures are notoriously difficult to access, evidence of less than 50,000 television viewers in the United Kingdom in 2015 suggests limited global popularity for the Indy 500 (F1 Broadcasting, 2015). Nevertheless, the size and scale of the facility, its reputed annual crowds of between 250,000–400,000 (O'Kane, 2011) and its long-serving legacy as one of the oldest and grandest races serves to reaffirm its status in American and global sport. Specifically, when combined with the Le Mans 24 hour endurance sports-car race staged in Le Mans, France, these three races form part of the unofficial "Triple Crown" that is revered as the ultimate accomplishment in elite global car racing (O'Kane, 2011). Historically, only one driver, Englishman Graham Hill, has accomplished the feat of winning the Indy 500, Monaco Grand Prix and Le Mans.

Origins of Formula One and IndyCar

Contemporary motorsport not long pre-dates the Indianapolis 500, beginning in France in the 1890s. Historians dispute whether the 1894 Paris to Rouen event was a race or mere reliability trial for the 1895 Paris to Bordeaux race (Hughes, 2004; Rendall, 2000). Nevertheless, two key aspects emerged from these events. First, as Frandsen (2014, p. 531) reminds us, many sports were developed in unison with modern mass media, particularly as "newspapers would organise sports events in order to both build up interest in the sports and consumption of the papers". Owner of the *New York Herald*, American James Gordon Bennett, sponsored the annual Gordon Bennett Cup for motor-races staged in Europe between 1900 and 1905, a pre-runner to the first "Grand Prix" of 1906 (Rendall,

2000). The history of motorsports would be shaped by media and commercial influences that became more pronounced in later coverage of Formula One and the Indianapolis 500.

Second, deaths to competitors and spectators during the 1903 Paris-to-Madrid race forced the French government to ban road racing, a pattern replicated in other nations (Hughes, 2004). Yet motorsport remained popular. Europe focused on designing closed "road-like" circuits to maintain a semblance of road racing. In America, where road racing had never been permitted, the construction of the Indianapolis Motor Speedway in 1909 provided an enormous banked oval to race and test cars (Rendall, 2000). Collectively, the construction of ovals and circuits also revealed the commercial potential of motorsport; being able to accommodate and charge large audiences (Sturm, 2013).

The origins of both IndyCar racing and Formula One were steeped in amateurism. Based upon the European Grand Prix series of the 1920s and 1930s, the Formula One World Championship was established in 1950, with seven "official" races that included the Monaco Grand Prix and Indianapolis 500 (Rendall, 2000). In America, with the Indianapolis 500 as its centrepiece from 1911, Shaw (2014, p. 20) notes that "the American Automobile Association oversaw the majority of motor racing activities in the US from the beginning of the 20th century". A national championship ran intermittently from 1916 although, arguably, IndyCar's origins were more pronounced when the United States Auto Club (USAC) took control from 1955 (ibid.). Collectively, both series comprised "privateers" or "enthusiasts" during their formative years, competitors who would often manufacture and fund their own cars (Sturm, 2013). From the late 1960s, the advent of car sponsorship by large (primarily tobacco) companies, as well as the increased involvement of car manufacturers saw costs escalate, literally driving many privateers out (ibid.).

Monaco Grand Prix as megamediasport event?

In light of these historical developments, can the Monaco Grand Prix and Indianapolis 500 be considered "megamediasport" events? Roche (2000, p. 1) asserts that, "'mega-events' are large-scale cultural (including commercial and sporting) events which have a dramatic character, mass popular appeal and international significance". The Monaco Grand Prix needs to be assessed in the context of the annual Formula One World Championship. Sturm (2014) posits that Formula One would appear to fit Roche's (2000, p. 69) criteria "through its sheer scale, global exposure, elite positioning, vast commercial and corporate interests, and the mass media attention that it garners". Whether Formula One adheres to Horne's (2010) "first-order" of mega-events, such as the Summer Olympic Games or Men's Football World Cup, is debatable. Horne's (ibid.) "second-order" events include other World Championships and World Cups in relation to international athletes, rugby, cricket and the Winter Olympics. Arguably, Formula One would be best situated alongside these "second-order" events in Horne's typology.

The impacts and legacies of mega-events, in terms of cultural, economic and political significance for host localities, both pre- and post-event, is another salient factor (Horne, 2010; Roche, 2008). This also extends to the scope, scale and reach of the event (Roche, 2000). The "mega" component to Formula One appears irrefutable. It is disseminated to over 500 million television viewers across 185 countries, cost over US$2 billion per season in the 2000s (Sturm, 2014) and currently is staged in 21 global locations. Localities pay over US$400 million annually to obtain host-nation status (Lefebvre and Roult, 2011). The sport has also expanded beyond its European origins to Asia and the Middle East (Bromber and Krawietz, 2013; Silk and Manley, 2012). Arguably these orientations are "grobal" rather than global; reflecting an imperialistic grobal ambition for Formula One to realize economic and media interests in non-traditional locales (Andrews and Ritzer, 2007). The localities also harness the assumed global prestige and reach of Formula One; using the sport's media and marketing platform as symbols of progress, pride and to boost tourism (Bromber and Krawietz, 2013; Silk and Manley, 2012).

The Monaco Grand Prix remains elevated as Formula One's "jewel in the crown" (O'Kane, 2011). By offering prize money of 100,000 francs for the winning driver in 1929, the Monaco Grand Prix cemented its place on the European motorsport calendar (ibid.). Monaco became a permanent fixture in Formula One from 1955 (Rendall, 2000). Associations with prestige, complexity and evocations of glamour have permeated its history. Discussing Formula One in the 2000s, Lefebvre and Roult (2011) note, "this sport's audience was mostly composed of a Western urban elite. A few emblematic urban destinations symbolized the entire sport, such as the Monte Carlo or the Monza Grand Prix" (ibid., p. 330). Monaco gets especial attention as the "event" on the Formula One calendar. The scope and impact of the Monaco Grand Prix as a mega-event is also evident in the global, non-Western shift for Formula One. New circuits in Abu Dhabi and Singapore have imitated Monaco's prestigious components, with Singapore hailed for its "glitz and glamour" as the "Monaco of the East" (Silk and Manley, 2012). The Monaco Grand Prix showcases Formula One's notions of elitism, wealth and glamour; aspects that will be further developed later in the chapter.

Indianapolis 500 as megamediasport event?

Assessing the Indianapolis 500 as a "megamediasport" event is more problematic. As a spectator event, it remains popular. The Indy 500 is touted as being the largest single day sporting event in the world, with crowds exceeding 400,000 (O'Kane, 2011). Contemporary attendance has stabilized at 250,000-300,000, due to recent seating reductions (Cavin, 2013). Historical divisions and exclusions have diluted its mega-event status. Shaw (2014, p. 21) notes that the USAC's "one-dimensional focus on the Indy 500" was the catalyst for existing teams to form a rival Championship Auto Racing Teams (CART) series in 1978. A CART/USAC divide remained from 1983 to 1995. The USAC sanctioned the Indy 500; CART teams participated but ran their separate championship. This split became more divisive in 1996. Tony George, president of the Indianapolis Motorway Speedway, created a rival Indy Racing League (IRL) which excluded many CART teams from the Indy 500 (ibid.). Eventually, CART and the IRL re-unified as the IndyCar Racing series in 2008.

Arguably the Indy 500 has oscillated as a "second"- and "third-order mega-event" (Horne, 2010). Crawford (1999, p. 195) asserts, "up until the 1960s the Indianapolis 500 remained the greatest auto race in America". Then, with victories by British Formula One drivers, "the Indianapolis 500 became the world's most famous car chase" (ibid., p. 196). Its mega-event status was further solidified in the 1980s and 1990s. Shaw (2014, p. 21) observes that the inclusion of international manufacturers and increased transnational sponsors "led more international drivers to consider CART as a viable alternative to F1". High-profile drivers competed in and won the Indy 500, such as Brazilian Emerson Fittipaldi and Canadian Jacques Villeneuve (Crawford, 1999). At its peak, the Indy 500 and championship offered a significant counterpoint to the supremacy of Formula One (O'Kane, 2011), with coverage televised in 120 countries (Shaw, 2014).

The IRL/CART division affected the contemporary status and impact of the Indy 500. IndyCar became more insular and American-focused (despite its international drivers) in terms of locations and sponsors. Domestically, stock-car racing surpassed its popularity. During the mid-2000s, Newman (2007, p. 292) observes that, after American Football, NASCAR was "the second most popular spectator sport in North America (in terms of television ratings and per event attendance)". Although NASCAR's television ratings and attendance figures may have plateaued, the series attracts greater commercial investment and media coverage than IndyCar (Newman and Beissel, 2009). This includes flagship events. The Indy 500 attracts a larger American television audience compared to the NASCAR Coco-Cola 600 staged the same day; with 2016 figures of 6 million to 5.7 million viewers respectively (Sports Media Watch, 2016). Comparatively, NASCAR's major event, the Daytona 500, attracted 11.6 million in 2016 (ibid.). In light of steady if not declining television audiences, the Indy 500 arguably meshes with Horne's (2010) "third-order" events, which includes America's Cup sailing and the Asian and Pan American Games. The future international scope, scale and impact of the Indy 500 as a mega-event remains uncertain.

Mediation and mediatization

Beyond being significant sporting events in their own right, the Monaco Grand Prix and Indy 500 are transformed as mediated events. Global mediations serve to inform, entertain and retain the socio-cultural and economic significance of the historical running of these two distinctive motor-races. However, Frandsen (2014) cautions against media-centric approaches that often treat sports as generic commodities. Citing "interrelation processes" (ibid., p. 529), Frandsen notes "mediatization is a social process, where media exert a growing influence on society to the extent that they seem to play a role in the transformation of social and cultural fields" (ibid.).

Scholars have also highlighted the inter-dependence of sport, media, culture, commerce and politics (Horne, 2010; Hutchins and Rowe, 2012, 2013; Whannel, 1992). Specifically Wenner's (1998) term "MediaSport" points to the institutional interpenetration of media and sport in social and cultural spheres. Sporting structures and fields also have their own variations, complexities and nuances. Frandsen asserts:

> Profound reflections on the specificities of the field of sport, of television, and on differences and historical changes in terms of media systemic and sports systemic contexts are therefore informative musts if we want to understand the role of media in relation to sports.
>
> *(Frandsen, 2014, p. 530)*

Historical distinctions in the organization of the Monaco Grand Prix and Indianapolis 500 revealed some of their nuanced contexts. Both races are also infused with social and cultural interrelation processes that reflect their respective European and American origins. These localized elements and symbols are incorporated in the media representations. Specifically, television coverage projects a joint global spectacle of speed that encapsulates either European glamour for Monaco or "global Americana" for the Indy 500. Each event will be given race-specific treatment later in the chapter.

Hutchins and Rowe (2012) suggest that as media technologies become more intricate, they provide profound changes to the contours of "real" sporting practices and social relations. Technological permutations afford "new" interactive capacities and innovations to sport; its representation, its consumption and within its own structures (Whannel, 2014). This includes experiences and expressions of fandom (Hutchins and Rowe, 2012). Representationally, however, digital technologies often reproduce and supplement aspects of the television coverage (Hutchins and Rowe, 2013). In an alleged "post-broadcast" era, contemporary live televised sport still has the capacity for attracting global audiences, enticing sponsors and selling audiences to advertisers (Whannel, 2014).

Sturm (2014, p. 69) suggests that Formula One was repackaged in the 1980s "as an event *for* the media". This included negotiating global television rights, currently valued at $600 million per year (ibid.). Formula One has remained resistant to the encroachment of new media. The televised race broadcasts are privileged, resulting in non-sanctioned or fan-produced content forcibly policed and removed online (ibid.). The prime area of innovation has been the annual globally released *F1* video games from Codemasters, which reproduce simulations of Formula One circuits with striking realism (Conway and Finn, 2014). The IndyCar series caters to both television and online viewership. Title sponsor, Verizon Communications, provides various live streaming options and promotes the series through social media platforms. Surprisingly, IndyCar has not released branded video-games since

IndyCar Series 2005. In terms of television spectatorship, the sport has limited or cable access in some global localities. Domestically, IndyCar's audience has increased, albeit averaging less than one million per race when compared to rival NASCAR's estimated five million (Schoettle, 2014).

Reproducing mediated racing spectacles

Reliant on traditional broadcast media forms for their global circulation and consumption, the Monaco Grand Prix and the Indy 500 are re-cast as televised spectacles of speed. Describing what is involved in the transformation of a live sporting event to television spectacle, Gruneau (1989, p. 135) notes that "a wide range of processes of visual and narrative representation – choices regarding the images, language, camera positioning, and story line are required to translate "what happened" into a program that makes "good television". Such processes aim to inform and entertain the viewer; projecting the speed and drama of the racing spectacle (Whannel, 1992). The televised spectacle also attempts to sustain an aura of liveness and immediacy for global audiences by rendering experiential elements of the "live" first-hand event as witnessed by in-situ spectators (Billings, 2010).

The Monaco Grand Prix and Indy 500 share many overlapping representational strategies. Both races (and series) are framed via the highly mobilized fluidity discernible in Formula One (Sturm, 2014). Representationally, the coverage adheres to Whannel's (1992, p. 98) "highly mobile ideal spectator", affording a "perfect view" for television viewers via continuous trackside transitions and perspectives that are not available to live attendees. The use of frequent cuts, transitions and the juxtaposition of camera angles and perspectives, seeks to maintain interest in what, at times, can become monotonous motor-racing events. For example, barring a crash, driver error or technical issue, the Monaco Grand Prix tends to be processional. With the drivers often unable to pass on this narrow and twisting circuit, by-and-large they usually run in the same race order for most of the 78 laps. In turn, while the Indy 500 facilitates more regular over-taking, in reality watching cars continually circulate around four banked turns for 200 laps arguably also can have a limited appeal. However, these representational techniques vitiate against rendering the "real" speed experienced trackside by live event attendees (Whannel, 1992).

To combat this, regular transitions from stationary wall-mounted cameras to the driver perspectives are used to show how close the cars are running to barriers at Monaco or to the other drivers at Indianapolis. Providing these perspectives attempts to convey the immense speed at which drivers must operate as they nimbly negotiate the swimming pool complex in Monaco or race in excess of 230 mph in close formation down long Indy straights. Additionally, the sense of occasion is heightened by using frequent long shots and dramatic angles from elevated cranes or helicopters. Such shots continually reinforce the glamorous setting for the Grand Prix as we see historical buildings, the harbour and the wealthy of Monaco. At Indianapolis, on one hand, the long one kilometre straights are foreshortened through using telephoto lenses with zoom techniques to easily follow the racing action. On the other hand, helicopters flying above the speedway render and reinforce the immense size and scale of the facility, as seemingly tiny cars circulate before zoom techniques or other transitions return viewers to close views of the race.

Collectively, these techniques reflect and reinforce the duality of informing and entertaining the televised viewers. The techniques afford "pleasure points" that focus on the racing action, allowing the viewer to take in dramatic moments and provide intimacy with star drivers to frame the races as marketable televisual commodities with attributes attractive to delivering large audiences (Whannel, 2014). The use of informative and entertaining production techniques underpins the representations of both races. However, production for the Indy 500 is less focused on Formula One's emphasis on glamour and reliance on special "high-tech" effects (Sturm, 2014). Rather, producing this race builds on traditions and pageantry that idealize American values. Both events interplay with representational techniques that evoke their historical and prestigious mantle within global motorsport. A closer analysis of these distinctive spectacles of speed is now provided.

The "jewel in the crown": the Monaco Grand Prix as European glamour

Frandsen (2014, p. 533) reminds us that "as staged events sports games are forms that communicate certain meanings, which are powerful forces in the relationship. They have their own cultural value." The Monaco Grand Prix projects notions of European "glamour" and sophistication through an assemblage of iconic global images that are suggestive of wealth, prestige, elitism and symbols of excess (for example, celebrities, yachts, fashion, jewellery and stereotypically beautiful females). It is difficult to not resort to a series of clichés to account for the "glamorous" images and excessive displays. O'Kane's description of the significance of Monaco is imbued with such sentiments:

> The Monaco Grand Prix has long been viewed as the "jewel in the crown" of the Formula One world championship and one of the most prestigious motor races in the world … The Monaco Grand Prix is the most important race in the Formula One calendar due to its history and prestige and also its glamorous location … Monaco is famous for its conspicuous consumption, its wealth as well as its gambling centre of Monte Carlo. The fact that the principality is a tax haven makes it the playground of the rich and famous and for many the perfect venue for the high-octane sport of Formula One motor racing.
>
> *(O'Kane, 2011, p. 287)*

Monaco, as a location, reaffirms the glamorous and elitist underpinnings of Formula One. Monaco also represents and reifies what Giardina (2001) labels an "aura of Europeanness", with this aura being "a cross between old world, nineteenth-century charm and its twentieth century counterpoint: the high-tech, jet-set glamour that exemplifies London, Paris and Milan" (ibid., p. 210). A "Europeanness" of character also pervades, with a "'worldly' image, cultured tastes, and fashionable image" providing "a powerful signifier of sophistication" (ibid.). As a harbinger of "Europeanness", transmitting images of Monaco's wealth, luxury and "glamour" dovetails with Formula One's socio-cultural structures that evoke expense and elitism, promote a jet-set lifestyle and utilize localities as extravagant backdrops for hi-tech racing projectiles (Sturm, 2014).

The exacerbated projection of glamour contributes to the aura of Monaco. Racing fast cars through affluent city streets provides an idyllic setting; further furnished with the stunning background of historic buildings and an expensive array of yachts in the harbour. Moreover, the rich and celebrated are also shown in attendance, facilitating a mediatized cocktail that mixes celebrities, fashion, corporate sponsors, luxury yachts and beauty in a way that complements and often supersedes screen images of fast cars racing. The treatment of the sport seems meant to facilitate heroic understandings of these racing men as the noble drivers who "vanquish" opponents and "conquer" Monaco's narrow streets through the exceptional display of skill, replete with a royal reception from Monaco's monarchy for the victorious. Kennedy (2000, p. 65) observes that the Monaco Grand Prix is particularly reliant on heroic depictions of the male driver as a "knight going into battle" with the beautiful women, symbolically at least, included in the "spoils of victory" for the winning driver via their explicitly sexualized representations dismissively codified as "glamour" (see Sturm, 2014).

Beyond gendered notions of the heroic driver demonstrating his skill and bravado to supposedly "tame" the circuit, much of the aura of Monaco takes place off the challenging race track. Indeed, much in the Monaco Grand Prix's "jewel in the crown" reputation does not come from racing per se but from its symbolic linking of glamour, wealth and luxury in association with Formula One. In tandem, Monaco Grand Prix features many opportunities to facilitate commerce. Many of the teams use the event for publicity, as an opportunity to "schmooze" significant clients, and advance business deals. Indeed, the Monaco Grand Prix is the only Formula One event that conducts practice on a Thursday (Friday is officially a "rest day"), primarily to furnish greater commercial opportunities, while catering to other off-track activities, promotions and events across the race weekend. Through-out, fashion shows, designer jewellery displays and sponsor-intensive functions are staged and teams participate in corporate tie-ins that have included placing diamonds in driver helmets (e.g. Lewis Hamilton in 2007 and 2008) and mounting them in the cars (e.g. Jaguar Racing in 2004).

With Formula One fundamentally Eurocentric in design and financed by major transnational corporations, the sport disseminates a highly mediated, commodified and consumable homogenized spectacle for its global audience (Sturm, 2014). Media representations make glowing reference to Monaco's significance, history, tradition and prestige on the calendar. Accordingly, Monaco provides the extravagant template for projecting a myopic, global "vision" of Formula One as affluent and aspirational. Monaco's impact and legacy are evinced by emerging localities buying-in to these characteristics.

Despite lacking either the history or tradition of Monaco, newer circuits in Singapore and Abu Dhabi have adopted and replicated elements of its setting to provide explicitly self-referential promotional techniques. By-and-large successful, both localities produce idealized images of what Silk and Manley (2012, p. 475) refer to as a "stylized global exotic". Singapore stages races at night against a brightly lit materialistic backdrop of city landmarks and skyscrapers to produce its global media spectacle. For Abu Dhabi's "galactic vision" (Bromber and Krawietz, 2013, p. 200) futuristic hotels and expensive yachts are prominent on the purpose-built artificial island that houses the track.

As a mega-event, the Monaco Grand Prix retains its global pre-eminence and "jewel"-like status in motorsport. The venue and race embodies, encapsulates and emboldens Formula One's prestige, history and tradition as its original, highly complex street circuit. O'Kane observes:

> The Monaco Grand Prix is representative of everything that attracts drivers and spectators to motor racing – speed, glamour, excitement and prestige …
> Monaco is the one Grand Prix that every driver wants to win above all the rest of the races on the Formula One calendar.
>
> *(O'Kane, 2011, p. 292)*

Staging the race among a backdrop of royalty and palaces, casinos and high-stakes gambling, luxury yachts adorned with the celebrated and the beautiful, and the principality as a moneyed tax haven in the sun-soaked south of France, the Monaco Grand Prix collectively projects and reifies lavish aspirational motifs of European glamour.

The "greatest spectacle in racing": the Indianapolis 500 as global Americana

In different ways, the Indianapolis 500 also attempts to project prestige and grandeur in presenting the race as a long-established historical event. The casting of the Indy 500 offers a global snapshot of Americana by painting an imagined and mediated portrait of America in its characterization of event traditions. Much of the hue and grandeur associated with this event stems from its grandiose and history laden site. The sheer size and scale of the Indianapolis Motor Speedway (IMS) is striking. The colossal sporting facility is its own spectacle and this is amplified by cars rocketing around 60 foot banked ovals. Located in suburban Indianapolis, the IMS facility sits on 80 acres of land, comprising of a 2.5-mile (or four-kilometre) four-cornered banked oval. The facility also houses a golf course, hotel and even a separate track within its infield. Its 235,000 permanent seating capacity makes it the largest capacity sports venue in the world (Cavin, 2013), and there is room for expansion.

Rituals buttress the staging of this event and contribute to its longevity as a predominantly spectator sport. 2016 featured the 100th running of the Indy 500, a prestigious and unprecedented milestone in international motorsport. With history permeating this iconic facility, the cyclic and repeated traditions continue to draw crowds back to Indianapolis. O'Kane notes:

> The race holds an important place in American culture and has become an annual pilgrimage for many American families … pre-race ceremonies and traditions take some time and help build up the atmosphere among the 400,000-plus crowd. This all plays a part in establishing the race as the cultural reservoir that it has now become within the American psyche.
>
> *(O'Kane, 2011, p. 284)*

This cultural reservoir hints at how sporting rituals can provide social functions and cultural connections for communities or, indeed, nations (Butterworth, 2005; Newman, 2007). The sense of occasion associated with the Indy 500 as a vicarious lived experience, as well as the IMS as a memorable site, are further underscored by its familiarity.

For in-situ spectators and televised viewers, numerous iconic moments have become folkloric traditions celebrated in association with the race. In turn, such iconic moments have become expected rituals trackside, while being framed as significant focal points for the event's mediation. For example, "Gentlemen start your engines" has been an enduring feature of the Indy 500 (O'Kane, 2011), revised since 1977 to "Ladies and Gentlemen start your engines" as more female drivers have come to compete. At the conclusion of the race, the winning driver also enacts a series of ceremonial performances for the spectators, sponsors and media. Notably recognizable is the drinking of milk by the winning driver, a ritual that dates back to 1936 where three-time winner Lou Meyer requested and drank buttermilk (O'Kane, 2011). Today, drinking milk in celebration has become a profitable marketing exercise, evidenced by the American Dairy Company paying the winning driver $10,000 for the rights to associate its product with victory (Jenkins, 2015).

Other rituals and performances envelope the Indy 500. Many of these reveal the complexity of "interrelation processes" (Frandsen, 2014, p. 529) while pointing to the political and ideological undercurrents of the Indy 500 as a cultural institution. On race day, the prescribed set of rituals that take place are carefully framed by the media to further contribute to the Indy 500 spectacle and pageantry. Staged as it is on Memorial Day weekend, the race is situated to build on linkages to American tradition and folklore. Many of these ceremonies reek of American patriotism by linking church, military and the state.

With the race run on a Sunday, a Roman Catholic religious invocation has opened the proceedings, blessing the military, drivers and event, since 1974. Next, a celebration of the military is championed through the rendition of "Taps", a fly-by of military aircraft and a public address from a key military or government official as part of the remembrance and honouring for those who served. Fervent patriotism is further embellished by a series of celebratory songs, with local celebrity Florence Henderson (of *The Brady Bunch* fame) often singing *America the Beautiful* and *God Bless America* before the National Anthem is sung by another famous American guest singer. The final song reflects distinctly Indianapolis origins, with *Back Home Again in Indiana* having been sung since 1946, most frequently by Jim Nabors (of *Gomer Pyle* fame) from 1972 to 2014. Drivers are then instructed to go to their vehicles, await the "start your engines" command while a celebrity guest waves the green flag to signify the start of the race (O'Kane, 2011).

These performances arguably mesh with other American sports, notably baseball and NASCAR, in terms of their patriotic displays (Butterworth, 2005; Newman, 2007; Newman and Beissel, 2009). For example, NASCAR's rituals appear more categorically patriotic by aligning Christianity, the Religious Right, the military and predominantly conservative, white and Southern values. Newman (2007) suggests that these pre-race rituals serve to "spectacularize the preferred, hyper-militaristic, neoconservative identity politics of NASCAR Nation" (p. 302). By privileging similar conservative values and ideologies, the Indy 500 ceremonies seem to be highly contentious. Nevertheless, they are represented in an unquestioned and unproblematic manner. Paradoxically, despite the American focus of the race (and series), the Indy 500 is explicitly international. Of the 33 race entrants, only 11 in 2014 and 12 in 2015 were American. This international dimension is neither acknowledged nor incorporated into the pre-race customs, despite comprising of past winners or series champions. While this is troublesome, increased "foreign" driver participation may partially account for a recent downturn in American television viewing of the race, as occurred in NASCAR (Newman and Beissel, 2009). Alternatively, it may be that the reliance on proclamations about Americana and capitalist ideologies may partially account for reduced contemporary global television viewing figures for the Indy 500.

Despite being a significant global sporting event composed of an international field, the mediated representations of the Indy 500 and its set of pre-race ceremonies idealizes the ideologics behind an array of American traditions, proclamations and endless evocations of Americana. O'Kane (2011) asserts that "the traditions that have grown up around the race have contributed greatly to its popularity and enduring appeal. Many fans see the customs and rituals that the race generates as representative of a particular form of American spirit" (ibid., p. 283). In many ways, this is the essence of the Indy 500 – even if its enduring appeal is becoming more questionable. Despite the need to grow a global audience, despite the international field of drivers and despite contemporary forms of multiculturalism, the Indy 500 has retained an insular, durable, and almost singular focus on quintessential proclamations of Americana. The Indy 500 projects, protects and reifies these idealized expressions of American traditions and conservative ideals via its narrow preoccupation with American patriotic values.

Concluding remarks

As two of the most significant annual events on the international motor-racing calendar, the Monaco Grand Prix and the Indianapolis 500 collectively reify their heightened status by reinforcing unique rich traditions, distinct forms of prestige and legendary histories. In turn, these sensibilities are re-codified for global audiences through mediated processes that reproduce their aura and allure as "spectacles of speed".Televisual technologies and representations draw upon highly stylized and fluid forms to frame race competition at Monaco and Indianapolis, amplifying and flavouring the racing experience through an array of production techniques and a focus on the local. Conversely, while being framed through complementary techniques, distinctive versions of the "essence" of the spectacle for these separate events are also being globally disseminated.

The Monaco Grand Prix imparts elitist, aspirational motifs of Formula One to its already global audience. European glamour is projected through an assemblage of iconic images and associated symbols that reiterate its status, privilege, luxury and conspicuous consumption. Monaco's illusions of European glamour dovetail seamlessly with Formula One's prestigious global image and maintain its "mega-mediasport" event status. Alternatively, the Indy 500 resiliently relies on an insular vision of Americana while attempting to build an event with global appeal. Through its pre-race pageantry, ceremonies and rituals, the Indy 500 projects, celebrates and retains a persistent and ethno-centric American emphasis built around idealized American values and fervent patriotism. Arguably, this remains enduring and endearing to a core domestic fan base, many of whom still attend in large numbers. However, its more recent television viewing figures indicate that this myopic vision of "Americana" may be hindering the Indy 500's prestigious status as a global "megamediasport" event.

References

Andrews, D. and Ritzer, G. (2007).The grobal in the sporting glocal. In R. Giulianotti and R. Robertson (eds), *Globalization and sport* (pp. 28–45). Oxford: Blackwell.

Billings, A. (2010). *Communicating about sports media: Cultures collide.* Barcelona: Aresta.

Bromber, K. and Krawietz, B. (2013). The United Arab Emirates, Qatar and Bahrain as a modern sport hub. In K. Bromber, B. Krawietz and J. Maguire (eds), *Sport across Asia: Politics, cultures and identities* (pp. 189–211). New York: Routledge.

Butterworth, M. (2005). Ritual in the "church of baseball": Suppressing the discourse of democracy after 9/11. *Communication and Critical/Cultural Studies, 2*(2) 107–129.

Cavin, C. (2013). Indy 500 will have smallest capacity since 2000. *USA Today,* 16 May. Retrieved from www.usatoday.com/story/sports/motor/indycar/2013/05/15/indianapolis-motor-speedway-indy-500-seating-capacity/2164499/# (accessed 24 November 2016).

Conway, S. and Finn, M. (2014). Carnival mirrors: Sport and digital games. In B. Hutchins and D. Rowe (eds), *Digital media sport: Technology, power and culture in the network society* (pp. 219–234). London: Routledge.

Crawford, S. (1999). Indy auto racing. In D. Levinson and K. Christiansen (eds), *Encyclopedia of world sport* (pp. 195–197). New York: Oxford University Press.

F1 Broadcasting (2015). Monaco Grand Prix remains above 4 million. *The F1 Broadcasting Blog*, 25 May. Retrieved from http://f1broadcasting.co/2015/05/25/monaco-grand-prix-remains-above-4-million (accessed 24 November 2016).

Frandsen, K. (2014). Mediatization of sports. In K. Lundby (ed.), *Mediatization of communication* (pp. 525–543). Berlin: Mouton de Gruyter.

Giardina, M. (2001). Global Hingis: Flexible citizenship and the transnational celebrity. In D. Andrews and S. Jackson (eds), *Sport stars. The cultural politics of sporting celebrity* (pp. 201–217). New York: Routledge.

Gruneau, R. (1989). Making spectacle: A case study in television sports production. In L.A. Wenner (ed.), *Media, sports, and society* (pp. 134–154). Thousand Oaks, CA: Sage.

Horne, J. (2010). Cricket in consumer culture: Notes on the 2007 Cricket World Cup. *American Behavioral Scientist*, *53*(10), 1549–1568.

Hughes, M. (2004). *The unofficial Formula One encyclopedia*. London: Anness.

Hutchins, B. and Rowe, D. (2012). *Sport beyond television: The Internet, digital media and the rise of networked media sport*. London: Routledge.

Hutchins, B. and Rowe, D. (eds), (2013). *Digital media sport: Technology, power and culture in the network society*. New York: Routledge.

Jenkins, C. (2015). Why does the Indy 500 winner drink milk? *USA Today*, May 24. Retrieved from http://ftw.usatoday.com/2015/05/indy-500-milk-2# (accessed 24 November 2016).

Kennedy, E. (2000). Bad boys and gentlemen: Gendered narrative in televised sport. *International Review for the Sociology of Sport*, *35*(1) 59–73.

Lefebvre, S. and Roult, R. (2011). Formula One's new urban economies. *Cities*, *28*(4) 330–339.

Newman, J. (2007). A detour through "NASCAR Nation": Ethnographic articulations of a neoliberal sporting spectacle. *International Review for the Sociology of Sport*, *42*(3) 289–308.

Newman, J. and Beissel, A. (2009). The limits to "NASCAR Nation": Sport and the "recovery movement" in disjunctural times. *Sociology of Sport Journal*, *26*(4) 517–539.

O'Kane, P. (2011). A history of the "Triple Crown" of motor racing: The Indianapolis 500, the Le Mans 24 Hours and the Monaco Grand Prix. *The International Journal of the History of Sport*, *28*(2), 281–299.

Rendall, I. (2000). *The power game: The history of Formula 1 and the world championship*. London: Cassell & Co.

Roche, M. (2000). *Mega-events and modernity*. London: Routledge.

Roche, M. (2008). Putting the London 2012 Olympics into perspective: The challenge of understanding mega-events. *Twenty-First Century Society*, *3*(3), 285–290.

Schoettle, A. (2014). Indy 500 TV ratings tick up, but Miles still has miles to go. *Indianapolis Business Journal*, 27 May. Retrieved from www.ibj.com/blogs/4-the-score/post/47853-indy-500-tv-ratings-tick-up-but-miles-still-has-miles-to-go (accessed 24 November 2016).

Shaw, J. (2014). The full story of America's F1 rival. *Autosport*, 14 August, 20–24.

Silk, M. and Manley, A. (2012). Globalization, urbanization and sporting spectacle in Pacific Asia: places, peoples and pastness. *Sociology of Sport Journal*, *29*(4) 455–484.

Sports Media Watch (2014). Indy 500 TV ratings up slightly, but third-lowest ever. *Sports Media Watch*, 28 May. Retrieved from www.sportsmediawatch.com/2014/05/indy-500-tv-ratings-up-slightly-but-third-lowest-ever (accessed 24 November 2016).

Sports Media Watch (2016). Indy 500 hits three-year low, but edges NASCAR's Coke 600. *Sports Media Watch*, 1 June. Retrieved from www.sportsmediawatch.com/2016/06/indy-500-ratings-down-abc-viewership-tops-nascar (accessed 24 November 2016).

Sturm, D. (2013). Motorvehicle sports: Formula One racing. In D. Levinson and G. Pfister (eds), *Berkshire encyclopedia of world sport* (3rd ed.), (pp. 830–837). Great Barrington, MA: Berkshire.

Sturm, D. (2014). A glamorous and high-tech global spectacle of speed: Formula One motor racing as mediated, global and corporate spectacle. In K. Dashper, T. Fletcher and N. McCullough (eds). *Sports events, society and culture* (pp. 68–82). London: Routledge.

Wenner, L.A. (ed.) (1998). *MediaSport*. New York: Routledge.

Whannel, G. (1992). *Fields in vision: Television sport and cultural transformation*. London: Routledge.

Whannel, G. (2014). The paradoxical character of live television sport in the twenty-first century. *Television and New Media, 15*(8), 769–776.

Widdows, R. (2011). Monaco challenge remains unique. *Motorsport Magazine*, 24 May. Retrieved from www.motorsportmagazine.com/f1/monaco-challenge-remains-unique (accessed 24 November 2016).

13

THE AFC ASIAN CUP

Continental competition, global disposition

David Rowe

Introduction: continental or global?

Precisely what constitutes a global sports spectacle may not be as obvious as commonly assumed. While the Summer Olympic Games and the Fédération Internationale de Football Association (FIFA) World Cup come as close to legitimate global status as any current cultural phenomena, many other mediasport (following the neologism of Wenner, 1998) events can claim to be in some sense global through a combination of scale, media coverage and dispersed interest among global diasporas. The Asian Football Confederation (AFC) Asian Cup is precisely such an event. It is one of the world's largest association football (soccer) tournaments, with the Australian Federal Minister for Sport prior to its 2015 edition in that country estimating that, "a [presumably cumulative] global TV audience of more than 2.5 billion people [is] expected" (Lundy, cited in AFC, 2013a). Although the actual measured global TV audience for the tournament was, as is conventional, rather inexact, it was estimated [again, presumably a cumulative figure] to have been "in excess of one billion" (Jump Media and Marketing, 2015, para. 7). In particular, by attracting the interest of television viewers from across the globe, both among football fans and, especially, among Asian and Australian diasporas in all other continents, the AFC Asian Cup is simultaneously continental and global. It is for this reason that I describe the event in terms of both continental competition and global disposition. Like other spatially specific mega-mediasport events such as the Super Bowl and Grand Slam tennis tournaments, the AFC Asian Cup marks itself variously in terms of nation, continent, region and the globe.

This chapter assesses the place of the AFC Asian Cup within contemporary mega-mediasport, focusing on the role of the media and event promoters in the representation of the 2015 tournament that took place in the perhaps geopolitically unlikely location of Australia for the first time after 15 previous tournaments in other locations. It explores, in particular, the manner in which the media produce and propose ways of seeing sport events, and the societies that host and participate in them, as part of a wider negotiation of identity and power at a variety of levels and in a range of contexts.

Of specific concern is the power of the process of mediatization to draw and redraw symbolic existential boundaries through the treatment of sport. This process should not be confused with the simple (though it is never just that) mass mediation of sports events, because the very act of mediation profoundly affects what is being communicated about and its relationships with other socio-cultural phenomena. As Frandsen (2014, p. 527) notes with regard to the mediatization of sport, the "collaboration between television and sport has resulted in programmes and events where former boundaries between the sports event, the mediated representation of this event and third-party commercial interests have been blurred". In the specific instance of the AFC Asian Cup, the media are integral to the symbolic and material fashioning of a sport event that is global because it involves the "world game" of association football, marked as continental within the framework of FIFA's confederated governmental structure (in one case emphasized later, Australia, spanning continents), and then split into regional blocs and animated by conceptions of nation that are crucial to the logic of an international competitive sports tournament. This is not to argue, of course, that the media create sports events out of thin air; rather, they work with and on the available material for a range of different purposes – social, cultural, political and economic. With regard to the AFC Asian Cup, this communicative work includes what it means to be Asian, and how an event can be made to resonate within and outside the shifting terrain that is nominated as Asia while being projected into the global sphere.

Towards the Orient

Although the AFC once constitutionally required its members to be spatially part of Asia, the relaxation of this qualification means that the AFC Asian Cup now involves the non-Asian nation of Australia, which in 2006 left the Oceania Football Confederation to join the larger AFC. However, while the AFC admitted a non-Asian nation in the early twenty-first century, it lost a continental member in 1974 after excluding Israel (host and winner of the 1964 AFC Asian Cup), while gaining the aspirant nation-state Palestine (which, in 2012, was accorded non-member observer state status by the United Nations) in 1998, the same year in which Palestine became a member of the world governing body, FIFA. Formed in 1954, the AFC's headquarters are in Kuala Lumpur, Malaysia, from which it oversees the administration of 46 member associations and one associate member entity (the Northern Mariana Islands). Divided into the West, Central, South, East and South East Asia regions (with Australia in the last), the AFC ranges across a vast, diverse area incorporating northern and southern hemispheres, many time zones and separate land masses, thereby revealing the relatively arbitrary nature of continental classification, while also indicating Asia's global significance in terms of population (over four billion, approximately 60 per cent of the world's population) and land area (over 44 million square kilometres, approximately 30 per cent of the world's land mass).

The almost ungovernable scale and diversity of the AFC, therefore, gives to its premier competition, the AFC Asian Cup, a "proto-global" status with regard to spatial footprint and socio-cultural complexity. Thus, like the FIFA World Cup and the Summer and Winter Olympics, it is held only every 4 years. Since 2007 the men's AFC Asian Cup has been held in a non-Olympic year and in the year following the FIFA World Cup, scheduling that enables avoidance of mega-sport event congestion. The AFC Women's Asia Cup – which is not for reasons of space and scope discussed in detail in this chapter – ran every 2 or 3 years between 1975 and 2010, but since 2014 is held every fourth year in order to accommodate qualification for the FIFA Women's World Cup, which has been held every 4 years since 1991 (and so now occurs in the same years as the men's AFC Asian Cup). Asia is of increasing importance to global sport, just as it is to the broad domains of economics and politics, and for similar reasons. Although at an uneven rate, the balance of global power has been shifting from West to East in what is now commonly referred to as the "Asian Century" (Australian Government, 2012; Kohli, Sharma and Sood, 2011), with a particular emphasis on the rise of China as an empire capable of challenging – and even gaining ascendancy over – the United States (Enright, Scott and Chang, 2005). The advancement of Asia has meant not only an extension of its political influence, but the attraction of Western capital to new opportunities in growing, "underdeveloped" Asian consumer markets.

In the specific domain of sport, mature and increasingly saturated mediasport markets in North America and Europe have seen systematic attempts to cultivate sports and fans in populous, economically advancing Asian contexts. The 2008 Beijing and 2020 Tokyo Summer Olympics and 2018 PyeongChang and 2020 Beijing Winter Olympics, are all prominent examples of global multi-sport mega-events hosted within Asia, which has held the now-substantial four-yearly Asian Games since 1951. But with regard to single sport events, the AFC Asian Cup is of particular importance in Asia's embracing of a football code that advances the most plausible claim to be the premier world sport commonly played and followed closely – unlike, for example, cricket or baseball – in virtually every Asian country.

Association football is widely regarded as having considerable unfilled potential in Asia. Although Korea and Japan – both of which have strong domestic club-based leagues – held the FIFA World Cup in 2002 and (controversially) Qatar has been chosen to host the 2022 edition (Manfred, 2014), the development of the sport in Asia has been by no means consistent. A key reason for this sometimes-faltering progress has been a particular problem with the establishment and maintenance of strong domestic leagues for a range of reasons, including wide-spread corruption and the crucial brand advantage of European clubs like Manchester United, Real Madrid, Arsenal, Barcelona, Juventus, Chelsea and AC Milan, which has caused many football fans in Asia to prefer watching the major European leagues on television than attend league matches in their own countries

(Rowe and Gilmour, 2010). In seeking to counter this trend, China, for example, has run an anti-corruption drive in football and has developed a plan, with the enthusiastic support of President Xi Jinping, intended to make that country the world's largest sport market by 2025 and which includes hosting the FIFA World Cup (Chadwick, 2015a). The scale of this ambition is signified by Chinese expenditure on improving its domestic standard of football by recruiting leading footballers from around the world:

> The influx of investment into Shanghai SIPG [Shanghai International Port Group] is no standalone story, though it is one occurring in clubs across the country. While Jiangsu Suning are making worldwide headlines with the signing of Ramires and Alex Teixeira, who turned down Liverpool for a life in Nanjing, perhaps more telling is this fact: in the winter transfer window, the Chinese Super League spent more than any other in the world. Second was the English Premier League. Third? China League One.
>
> *(Kelly, 2016)*

Although of lesser magnitude than China's investment in football, the establishment of the Indian Super League in 2014 in the world's second most populous country has been described by Kushai Das, General Secretary of the All India Football Federation (AIFF), as signifying "a giant that has finally woken up" which is "ready to get out of bed and conquer the world" (Wilson, 2014, paras 32–33). Indeed, Chinese capital, heavily supported as noted by the state (the ultimate owners of Shanghai SIPG) has attempted this task more literally by investing in European football (Chadwick, 2015b), as have major Middle Eastern companies (East, 2015). Thus, it is apparent that the global circulation of sports, clubs, players, brands, images and money enables a multidirectional exchange that reinforces sport in some locations and destabilizes it in others (Rowe, 2011). A regional mega-event like the AFC Asian Cup, therefore, inevitably extends beyond a single continent because it is already embedded in a web of global interconnections. Hence, it is marked by tensions over matters of identity and diffusion, and between notions of "Asianness" and globality.

FIFA and the AFC

In his account of the role of the AFC in the development of football in Asia, Weinberg (2012) presents a core–periphery model in which Europe, home of FIFA (founded in 1904 with an initially small and exclusively continental European membership) and the game's most powerful national associations, has sought to retain control over the game as it spread across the globe. Thus, for example, while South America could claim that it has had multiple FIFA World Cup winners in Argentina, Brazil and Uruguay (including the inaugural World Cup trophy victory by host nation Uruguay in 1930), the FIFA Presidency and the centre of power remained securely in Europe until the 1970s. Asia and Africa, with their still-developing football systems operating across large territories and amid considerable division, diversity and, in several cases, turmoil (see Cho, 2015), had little initial capacity to reposition themselves beyond a condition of institutional dependency. However, as is the case with the most renowned supranational body, the United Nations – itself a force for the global advancement of sport through, for example, its Sport for Development and Peace initiative (United Nations, 2016) – the mobilization of geo-political power blocs of members which, on their own, could exercise little political efficacy, can have a significant impact on governmental power. The United Nations currently has 193 member states, whereas FIFA has 209 national associations (not all, as noted, nation-states and with two members, Kuwait and Indonesia, currently suspended) and the International Olympic Committee has 206 National Olympic Committees. While power in such organizations tends to be concentrated within the core group of founding and most prominent members, the democratization of governance structures enables some dispersal of that power, in both legitimate and illegitimate forms as, of course, can occur in the core (see Tomlinson, 2014 for a comprehensive critical historical analysis of FIFA).

In the case of FIFA, its longest serving President (1974–1998), the Brazilian João Havelange, artfully wrested control from his predecessor, the Englishman Stanley Rous, through active lobbying outside Western Europe, where most presidential votes were located. Havelange activated a range of "liberationist" rhetorics to gain support from regional federations like the AFC and the Confederation of African Football (CAF) and their constituent members, including opposition to the reinstatement of the apartheid-era South Africa national association (banned in 1963), more World Cup places, opportunities to host this and other major football events, and more FIFA funding to support the game in regions and countries outside Europe. As Sugden and Tomlinson have argued:

> The Third World countries were restless. They wanted Eurocentric soccer to give them some respect. They hadn't the resources to fight their own battle, so the challenge was led by the cosmopolitan Havelange from the Second World. As he traded in the rhetoric of anti-imperialism, few noticed at the time that Havelange was backed by tough capitalists in Europe and America.
> *(Sugden and Tomlinson, 1999, pp. 14–15)*

Havelange "concentrated his campaigning on Africa and Asia", telling them that it "was time to break the stranglehold of the former colonial masters" (ibid., p. 31). This accentuation of the global political dimension of FIFA, however, required to be underpinned by the commercial global capital that funded his campaign promises. It was at this point – as occurred with the IOC under the presidency (1980–2001) of Juan Antonio Samaranch – that global (especially media) capital became critical to the operation of FIFA through the success of sports marketer Patrick Nally and the founder of the Adidas sport leisurewear and marketing company, Horst Dassler, in creating the conditions for major investment as FIFA partners by US-based global corporations such as Coca-Cola and McDonald's, and of rights-purchasing broadcast organizations such as FOX, Telemundo, and the European Broadcasting Union. These global interconnections would, of necessity, tie the development of regional association football not only to FIFA as the governing body, but to the web of financial relationships that would, in time, include major Asian corporate brands such as Hyundai-Kia, Emirates, Toshiba, and Sony.

The AFC had been founded in Manila, the Philippines in 1954, two decades before Havelange became FIFA president at a meeting attended only by "representatives from Afghanistan, Burma, Taiwan, Hong Kong, India, Indonesia, Japan, South Korea, Pakistan, the Philippines and Vietnam" (Weinberg, 2012, p. 537). The inaugural AFC Asian Cup followed 2 years later in Hong Kong (in 1956) but, as is clear from the above discussion, the initial development of the AFC was faltering (see, for example, Straits Times, 1964) and, hence, its members were receptive to Havelange's invitation. Of particular concern was its belief that it was under-represented in FIFA's committee system, especially in the pivotal Executive Committee, as well as various disputes with FIFA over the AFC's position on the politically sensitive matters of inclusion/exclusion of Israel, the People's Republic of China, and Taiwan/Chinese Taipei. Hosting the 2002 FIFA World Cup in Korea and Japan consolidated the place of Asia in world football, as did the strength of the domestic leagues in those countries (K-League and J-League) and the increasing interest of China, the world's most important developing trade economy, in becoming a football power.

Thus, since its inception, the AFC has overseen an expanding range of sex-, age-, format- and ability-based competitions (AFC, 2016) and now runs three major developmental programs (Vision Asia, Aid27 and Dream Asia) as part of its declared commitment to "social responsibility" (see, for example, AFC, 2015a). It has also grown in size and influence, especially under the presidency (2002–2011) of the Qatari Mohamed bin Hammam, who oversaw the 2006 admission of Australia to the AFC. Indeed, the extension of the AFC's influence is indicated by two of its representatives, respectively bin Hammam in 2011 and Prince Ali bin al-Hussein (President of the Jordan Football Association and founder and president of the West Asian Football Federation) in 2015, standing against Havelange's successor and protégé Joseph Sepp Blatter in FIFA presidential elections. Although the former withdrew and was subsequently banned from FIFA for life on ethical grounds and the latter did not proceed after losing the first round of the election (having not been supported by the AFC), their candidature can be interpreted as indicative of the opening of new leadership possibilities within FIFA.

Following Blatter's well-documented fall from grace (Moyer, 2015), both al-Hussein and AFC president (since 2013) Sheikh Salman bin Ebrahim al-Khalifa of Bahrain announced their intention to succeed him as FIFA president at its congress in late February, 2016. That the AFC had two candidates (out of six) for the FIFA presidency both demonstrates the emerging power of the Confederation and a relative lack of unity given its Executive Committee's declared support for al-Khalifa (AFC, 2015b). While its governmental position within FIFA is important, for Asia's legitimacy in global association football it is also essential that it be recognized as a region where some of the world's best football is played. Of particular weight here is how consistently competitive national teams from Asia can be in the FIFA World Cup. This record has been underwhelming, with no Asian team having won the tournament or played in its final, and with a particularly poor contribution to the 2014 FIFA World Cup in Brazil, where the AFC (represented by Australia, Korea, Japan and Iran) was the only confederation without a single winning team or one that progressed past the group stage. But if Asia cannot perform well at the World Cup, its own regional tournament must at least impress in terms of scale, event management quality, media audiences and footballing spectacle. These subjects are the focus of the following discussion of the 2015 AFC Asian Cup in Australia, as well as its identity as both a regional and global sporting event.

The AFC Asian Cup

Each FIFA Confederation has a competition both for clubs and nations. The former is annual and spread over a lengthy period and involves multiple home and away fixtures. The prestige and profile of club competitions is connected closely to the global standing of the clubs involved. Hence, for example, the UEFA Champions League, usually featuring Europe's most famous clubs, attracts attention well beyond Europe – not least, as noted, in Asia. Thus, the 2015 UEFA Champions League final in Berlin between Barcelona and Juventus (Ashby, 2015), "captivated hundreds of millions of supporters across the globe as fans watched the action and shared their views on social media" (Ashby, 2015, para. 1) according to UEFA. Its "status as the world's most watched annual sporting event" drew an "estimated global TV audience of 180 million in over 200 territories" with an "estimated global reach of 400m viewers", while Indonesia was the third of the Top six countries "buzzing about the match" on Facebook (ibid.). By contrast, the AFC Champions League, which does not involve global club "brands" of the calibre of Real Madrid or Chelsea, is more dependent on attracting viewers from within Asia. For example, when in 2013 Guangzhou Evergrande played FC Seoul at its home stadium in the second leg of the final (the format being different than that of UEFA Champions League), the AFC (2013b) placed emphasis on it being the "largest TV audience for a sporting event in China this year, with an average audience totalling over 30 million" and "the total reach for the second leg of the final across all channels [was] nearly 120 million".

The mediated spectatorial dynamic is, however, different for an event like the AFC Asian Cup, which involves 16 national teams assembling every 4 years in one of those nations for a tournament lasting about three weeks and with a single "knockout" final as its culmination (as is the case with the FIFA World Cup). This arrangement, combining temporal and spatial concentration and overt nationalism, is more conducive to making the tournament a mega-event as influentially defined by Roche, through a combination of scale, drama, "mass popular appeal and international significance" (Roche, 2000, p. 1). Asia is a large enough entity to construct a sport mega-event in its own right provided that it attracts sufficient simultaneous co-present and mediated audience interest, although the precise definitional characteristics of a mega-event are elusive (Horne and Manzenreiter, 2006). But, there is a tension between the mega-event having a delimited character (a competition between eligible continental confederation members) and an expansionary impulse to register as significant well beyond its own governmental footprint. Even Confederation membership may be controversial, with Australia's aforementioned admission to the AFC in 2006 not universally popular among some (especially west) Asian nations, leading to an embarrassing news story just before the 2015 AFC Asian Cup final of a move to oust Australia attributed to – though denied by – AFC President al-Khalifa (Hassett, 2015). At issue here is what it means to be Asian, whether Australia is essentially a "White nation" that sees itself as the United States' "Deputy Sheriff" in the Asia-Pacific region, and is seen by Asian nations as a White, Western "supremacist" power (Carniel, 2012; Rowe, 2015a). However, such issues of identity and governance (applying in various ways also to ex-AFC members Israel, New Zealand and Kazakhstan) are probably less significant than the global growth imperative of recognition as more than a Confederation event. So, just as the UEFA European Championship (and to a lesser degree the African Cup of Nations and the Copa América) are sport mega-events with global reach (for example, the 2012 final in Kiev between Spain and Italy was watched by an "official television audience of 299 million viewers worldwide"; Associated Press, 2013), the AFC seeks comparable TV viewing figures from well beyond Asia – including, of course, by Asian diasporas.

Those responsible for "producing" the AFC Asian Cup must present its credentials in a variety of ways, while the host needs to justify the cost and effort of staging the event. With regard to the 2015 edition, this case is made in the context of *Building Australia's Football Community: A Review into the Sustainability of Football* (Commonwealth of Australia, 2011), a report commissioned by the federal government which had, not coincidentally, allocated "AU$45.6 million (excluding GST [goods and services tax] to FFA [Football Federation Australia] to facilitate a bid to host the FIFA World Cup" (Football Federation Australia, 2011, p. 5). Notoriously, Australia's bid to host the 2022 World Cup resulted in only one FIFA Executive Committee vote (Rowe, 2015b). Given that hosting the 2015 AFC Asian Cup involved support from the Commonwealth, New South Wales, Victorian, Queensland and Australian Capital Territory governments, whose collective liability was up to AU$61 million, there was understandable sensitivity to criticism that more public resources would be "wasted" on association football.

The benefits of hosting the Cup in 2015 were, then, presented as multi-faceted. First, there is its continental prestige and global ambition – "The Asian Cup is regarded as the premier sporting event in Asia. It is a contest between the sixteen best teams in Asia, which include a number of highly ranked nations comprising world class players ... AFC has ambitions to see the event take its place among the most prestigious of tournaments in world football" (Commonwealth of Australia,

2011, p. 37). Second, it is argued (ironically, in view of the aforementioned mooted move against Australia by some AFC members) that it would "cement" Australia's "place in the Asian football community" while also advantaging its domestic game. Third, in terms of wider (that is, non-football related) benefits to "the Australian economy and community", there is mention of "major international exposure through television audiences that could be up to one billion", up to 1,000 new local jobs, half a million spectators, and other preferential economic benefits "leveraged" from a "tourism, trade and foreign relations perspective". Finally, there are claimed social policy advantages, including "increased grassroots participation and social inclusion", such as "opportunities to link with other government supported initiatives such as Street Soccer" (ibid., pp. 37–38).

Here, it can be seen that, as with all sport mega-events, there is both an internal and external promotional discourse, with economic and social benefits to the host nation accompanied by those that encompass regional, international and global factors. The role of the media is especially emphasized, despite "commercial rights to the Asian Cup [being] owned by [exclusive AFC marketing partner] World Sports Group – including all broadcast and sponsorship", leading to a local reliance on ticket sales, "which have historically been modest" (ibid., p. 40). The event itself took place in a relatively remote, medium-sized country, meaning that it was deeply reliant on the process of mediation to signify its importance beyond the realms of football and nation. As Couldry (2008) argues, mediation and mediatization are not synonymous in that the former refers more generally to the "take up" of socio-cultural phenomena like sport by the institution of the media, and the latter describes a more thoroughgoing transformation of a diverse range of those phenomena which, because of their increasing dependency on the media, can be regarded as increasingly made in their own image. Both processes, it should be noted, can co-exist and operate in different ways according to context. Here, the emphasis is on mediatization as a process that, in the case of a mega-event like the AFC Asian Cup, deploys a media logic of rhetorically appealing to the global.

Thus, the AFC Asian Cup is produced as a mega-media event that connects diverse audiences via media to sponsors. Official Asian regional broadcasters (free-to-air and subscription) such as China's Beijing TV, Iran's IRIB and Thailand's Channel 7 (BBTV), combined with coverage of the Middle East and North Africa (BeIn Sport and Al Kass), operate as bridges to what the AFC describes as the "Rest of the World": South America through Brazil's TV Globo, Europe via Eurosport, New Zealand (SkyNZ) and the US and Canada (One World Sports). To be added to this list of broadcast outlets are those which, legally and illegally, carry AFC Asian Cup-related texts across digital and mobile platforms, and the many in-stadium and other fans who upload their own captured and relayed content. Similarly, many sponsors and advertisers, including those who "ambush" audiences by associating themselves with the event without paying for the privilege, use multiple media vectors to raise their brand profile. The company that managed the media operation from Australia estimated, as noted above, that there was a "global TV audience in excess of one billion for the tournament" (Jump Media and Marketing, 2015, para. 7). In specific countries, viewing figures were remarkable, such as that 37 per cent of South Koreans watched that country's semi-final with Iraq (ibid.). Similarly, a study of Australia's presence in South Korean online news over a six-month period found that, "Although we anticipated that there would be much interest in the Asian Football Cup (AFC), culminating with Australia and South Korea competing in the final match in January 2015, we did not foresee the dramatic spike in news coverage that ensued" (Spry and Dwyer, 2016, p. 5).

These viewers encounter the football tournament and its "Official Sponsors" and "Official Supporters", which for 2015 consisted mainly of large Asian (mostly Japanese) corporations with a reach well beyond the region in terms of company subsidiaries and products/services, as well as one each from the USA and Europe. Of the sixteen official sponsors/supporters of AFC Asian Cup 2015, ten are Japanese (Asahi Shimbun, Credit Saison, Epson, Family Mart, Makita, Nikon, Kirin, Konica Minolta, Toshiba, Toyota) and two are Korean (Hyundai, Samsung), with the remainder from the United Arab Emirates (Emirates), Qatar (Qatar Petroleum), Germany (Continental) and USA (Nike). An FFA report of the AFC Congress in Bahrain in late April, 2015 – only three months after the final in Sydney – demonstrated the constant interplay of grounded place and mediated space, traversing national, regional and global environments:

> During the main meeting, giant video screens showed plenty of action from the tournament, with facts and figures flashing up to remind delegates, including FIFA president Sepp Blatter, of the success on and off the pitch.
>
> Circa 650,000 fans came to the stadiums and there were 85 goals, 275 shots on target, 150,000 app downloads, 12.7 million minutes watched on YouTube – the list went on.
>
> *(Duerden, 2015, paras 2–3).*

Populous, the US-based sport architectural company, revealed this synthetic, multimedia dependence of the AFC Asian Cup (and of other mega-sport events) in discussing the relationship between stadium design and global communication. Paul Henry (2015), one of its senior architects, described watching the China–Australia quarter-final with 50,000 co-present others, observing that "it was fascinating to reflect that more than 20 million people were also watching that same match on television in China" in a display of "the true intersection between the live and remote audience during a major sporting match in today's digitally connected world and the real global connectivity sporting events offer to a city" (ibid., para. 1). He noted that "the official #AC2015 Twitter hashtag reach was 3.1 billion by the end of the tournament" (ibid., para. 2), to which it can be added that many more would have communicated about the event without using it. Stadium design, broadcast technology and social media communication are now expected to be in harmony, allowing multidirectional communication and experiential exchange. Although the sport stadium is rigorously enclosed and its physical boundaries policed, those responsible for managing the sport events within them are refining ways of making stadiums "even more accessible to the international broadcaster at the event, so they can better tell the away team story and make the Game more relevant for the fans sitting back home in Beijing or Seoul, New York or Paris" (Henry, 2015, para. 5). This is mediatization clearly exposed, with designers of the stadium space of the AFC Asian Cup, along with those who represent it by audio-visual means, concentrating as much on far-distant others – many beyond the boundaries of Asia – as on those in physical attendance.

Conclusion: Asia beyond Asia

In the 2016 FIFA presidential election addressed earlier, neither AFC candidate was successful and Swiss-born UEFA General Secretary Gianni Infantino was elected. Australia, notably, did not support the AFC-endorsed al-Khalifa and opted instead, as it had in 2015, for al-Hussein. This outcome was a disappointment for the AFC, because an Asia-based presidency would have increased its power and profile, including attracting more attention to the AFC Asian Cup. The lesson that can be drawn here regarding sport and mediatization is that a mega-event like the AFC Asian Cup may be large and successful (as in Australia in 2015); it may operate effectively at the national-cultural level, enhance regional and continental connectivity (both positively and negatively), and have global reach. But, no matter how professionally packaged and marketed, and despite increasing availability through (especially digital media) (Hutchins and Rowe, 2012, 2013), sport mediatization of one event inevitably takes place under conditions of multiple-event mediatizations, and where other resources of power are differentially distributed.

Regarding association football, Europe currently has a hold on governmental power within FIFA (irrespective of its one member, one vote constitution) and, despite large-scale investment in the game in Asia (especially in China), the best players in the world and the largest media audiences, including in Asia, are drawn to its prestigious, brand-rich inter/national club and country competitions. The biggest event of all, the FIFA World Cup, which has guaranteed Asian team involvement and, as currently planned, will be hosted again there in 2022 (and, it should be noted, by the Eurasian nation of Russia in 2018), has generally confirmed the superiority of European and South American football over that of the other confederations. The AFC Asian Cup is a legitimate sport mega-event that is available for global viewing but there are limits to its appeal beyond Asia, where it attracts interest from Asian diasporas and, ironically, from fans who track Europe-based elite club footballers, such as South Korea's Son Heung-Min of Bayer Leverkusen in the Bundesliga and, before him, Park Ji-Sung at Manchester United in the English Premier League, back to their "home" tournament. Asia's domestic leagues and international club/country competitions, it appears, will require many more years of investment and development before they reverse this sporting–performative imbalance and spectatorial flow (Gilmour and Rowe, 2012; Weinberg, 2012).

Thus, as the specific case of the AFC Asian Cup illuminates, the broad concept of the mega-event may obscure significant variations among those events that technically qualify for that status. Furthermore, the process of mediatization in sport proceeds on multiple, competitive fronts that, like sport itself, creates winners and losers whose prospects are shaped by historically inherited global dynamics of power that cannot be overcome automatically by even a powerful combination of capital investment, population size, economic potential, sporting ambition and media reach.

References

AFC (2013a). Australia 2015 venues and match schedule unveiled. 26 March. Retrieved from www.the-afc.com/asian-cup-2015-news/australia-2015-venues-and-match-sched ule-unveiled (accessed 24 November 2016).

AFC (2013b). ACL final attracts record TV viewers. 13 November 1. Retrieved from www.the-afc.com/marketing-afc-champions-league-2013/acl-final-attracts-record-tv-viewers (accessed 24 November 2016).

AFC (2015a). AFC Dream Asia award winners announced. 5 October. Retrieved from www.the-afc.com/social-responsibility/afc-dream-asia-award-winners-announced (accessed 24 November 2016).

AFC (2015b). AFC Executive Committee backs Shaikh Salman for FIFA presidency. 27 November. Retrieved from www.the-afc.com/afc-president/afc-executive-committee-backs-shaikh-salman-for-fifa-presidency (accessed 24 November 2016).

AFC (2016). All competitions. Retrieved from www.the-afc.com/all-competitions (accessed 24 November 2016).

Ashby, K. (2015). Berlin final captures the world's imagination. 8 June. Retrieved from www.uefa.com/uefachampionsleague/news/newsid=2255318.html (accessed 24 November 2016).

Associated Press (2013). UEFA reports TV audience of 299 million for Euro 2012 final, 167 million for Champions League. 23 January. Retrieved from www.timescolonist.com/entertainment/television/uefa-reports-tv-audience-of-299-million-for-euro-2012-final-167-million-for-champions-league-1.54426#sthash.uN7DVeEA.dpuf (accessed 24 November 2016).

Australian Government (2012). *Australia in the Asian Century White Paper.* Canberra: Department of the Prime Minister and Cabinet. Retrieved from www.murdoch.edu.au/ALTC-Fellowship/_document/Resources/australia-in-the-asian-century-white-paper.pdf (accessed 24 November 2016).

Carniel, J. (2012). Reflections on race, regionalism and geopolitical trends via Australian soccer. *The International Journal of the History of Sport, 29*(17), 2405–2420.

Chadwick, S. (2015a). Football and China's World Cup goal. *Asia and the Pacific Policy Society Policy Forum,* 23 September. Retrieved from www.policyforum.net/football-and-chinas-world-cup-goal (accessed 24 November 2016).

Chadwick, S. (2015b). Football's "bamboo revolution". *Asia and the Pacific Policy Society Policy Forum,* 3 December. Retrieved from www.policyforum.net/footballs-bamboo-revolution (accessed 24 November 2016).

Cho, Y. (ed.) (2015). *Football in Asia: History, culture and business.* Abingdon: Routledge.

Commonwealth of Australia (2011). *Building Australia's football community: A review into the sustainability of football* (authored by W. Smith). Canberra: Commonwealth of Australia.

Retrieved from www.ausport.gov.au/__data/assets/pdf_file/0020/624161/FFA_
sustainability_report.pdf (accessed 24 November 2016).

Couldry, N. (2008). Mediatization or mediation? Alternative understandings of the emergent
space of digital storytelling. *New Media and Society, 10*(3), 373–391.

Duerden, J. (2015). AFC leaders in awe of Australia's Asian Cup. 1 May. Retrieved from
www.footballaustralia.com.au/article/afc-leaders-in-awe-of-australias-asian-cup/je5qsf
125fdb1e4ym8ysws3z8#qXhp0wgMa5jKvzc3.99 (accessed 24 November 2016).

East, S. (2015). Middle East millions fueling European football, *CNN*, 12 January. Retrieved
from http://edition.cnn.com/2015/01/12/football/qatar-uae-sponsor-football-europe
(accessed 24 November 2016).

Enright, M.J., Scott, E.E. and Chang, K. (2005). *Regional powerhouse: The Greater Pearl River
Delta and the rise of China*. Singapore: John Wiley & Sons (Asia).

Fédération Internationale de Football Association (2016). Governance. Retrieved from
www.fifa.com/governance/index.html (accessed 24 November 2016).

Football Federation Australia (2011). *Bidding nation Australia: Final report*. Sydney: FFA.

Frandsen, K. (2014). Mediatization of sports. In K. Lundby (ed.), *Mediatization of communication* (pp. 523–543). Berlin: Mouton de Gruyter.

Gilmour, C. and Rowe, D. (2012). Sport in Malaysia: National imperatives and Western
seductions. *Sociology of Sport Journal, 29*(4), 485–505.

Hassett, S. (2015). Angry Gulf nations leading charge to kick Australia out of Asian
Football Confederation. *The Sydney Morning Herald*, 29 January. Retrieved from
www.smh.com.au/sport/soccer/afc-asian-cup/angry-gulf-nations-leading-charge-to-
kick-australia-out-of-asian-football-confederation-20150129-131e5g.html (accessed 24
November 2016).

Henry, P. (2015). The AFC Asian Cup was one of the most talked about football events ever
in Asia. What does that mean for the future of stadium design? *Populous*, 23 February.
Retrieved from http://populous.com/posts/the-afc-asian-cup-was-one-of-the-most-
talked-about-football-events-ever-in-asia-what-does-that-mean-for-the-future-of-
stadium-design (accessed 24 November 2016).

Horne, J. and Manzenreiter, W. (2006). *Sports mega-events: Social scientific analyses of a global
phenomenon*. Oxford: Blackwell.

Hutchins, B. and Rowe, D. (2012). *Sport beyond television: The Internet, digital media and the rise
of networked media sport*. New York: Routledge.

Hutchins, B. and Rowe, D. (eds) (2013). *Digital media sport: Technology, power and culture in the
network society*. New York: Routledge.

Jump Media and Marketing (2015). AFC Asian Cup Australia 2015. Retrieved from www.
jumpmedia.com.au/projects/afc-asian-cup-australia-2015 (accessed 24 November 2016).

Kelly, N. (2016). Revealed: How one man's obsession is turning China into a football
superpower. *The Telegraph*, 8 February. Retrieved from www.telegraph.co.uk/sport/
football/12146017/Revealed-How-one-mans-obsession-is-turning-China-into-a-
football-superpower.html (accessed 24 November 2016).

Kohli, H.S., Sharma, A. and Sood, A. (2011). *Asia 2050: Realizing the Asian century*. New
Delhi: Sage.

Manfred, T. (2014) 14 Reasons why the Qatar World Cup is going to be a disaster. *Business
Insider Australia*, 22 April. Retrieved from www.businessinsider.com.au/qatar-world-cup-
problems-2014-4?r=US&IR=T (accessed 24 November 2016).

Moyer, J.M. (2015). Soccer czar Sepp Blatter banned from FIFA for 8 years. *The Washington
Post*, 21 December. Retrieved from www.washingtonpost.com/news/morning-
mix/wp/2015/12/21/former-soccer-czar-sepp-blatter-banned-from-fifa-for-8-years
(accessed 24 November 2016).

Roche, M. (2000). *Mega-Events and modernity: Olympics and expos in the growth of global culture.* New York: Routledge.

Rowe, D. (2011). *Global media sport: Flows, forms and futures.* London: Bloomsbury Academic.

Rowe, D. (2015a). Sport, diplomacy and Australia in the Asian Century: The case of the 2015 AFC Asian Cup. Unpublished paper delivered at Sport and Diplomacy Colloquium: Message, Mode and Metaphor?, Centre for International Studies and Diplomacy, School of Oriental and African Studies, University of London, 3 July.

Rowe, D. (2015b). The player played: Frank Lowy and Australia's failed World Cup bid. *The Conversation*, 18 November. Retrieved from https://theconversation.com/the-player-played-frank-lowy-and-australias-failed-world-cup-bid-50007 (accessed 24 November 2016).

Rowe, D. and Gilmour, C. (2010). Sport, media and consumption in Asia: A merchandized milieu. *American Behavioral Scientist, 53*(10), 1530–1548.

Spry, D. and Dwyer, T. (2016). *The Representation of Australia in South Korean online news: October 2014–April 2015. A report for the Australia–Korea Foundation.* Sydney: University of Sydney. Retrieved from www.academia.edu/20423611/The_Representation_of_Australia_in_South_Korean_Online_News_October_2014_April_2015 (accessed 24 November 2016).

Straits Times (1964). AFC tells Indonesia: Pay or be sacked. *The Straits Times*, 28 August. Retrieved from http://eresources.nlb.gov.sg/newspapers/Digitised/Article/straitstimes19640828-1.2.130.6.aspx (accessed 24 November 2016).

Sugden, J. and Tomlinson, A. (1999). *Great balls of fire: How big money is hijacking world football.* Edinburgh: Mainstream.

Tomlinson, A. (2014). *FIFA (Fédération Internationale de Football Association): The men, the myths and the money.* Abingdon: Routledge.

United Nations (2016). Sport for development and peace. Retrieved from www.un.org/wcm/content/site/sport/home/unplayers/goodwillambassadors (accessed 24 November 2016).

Weinberg, B. (2012). "The future is Asia?" The role of the Asian Football Confederation in the governance and development of football in Asia. *International Journal of the History of Sport, 29*(4), 535–552.

Wenner, L. (ed.) (1998). *MediaSport.* London: Routledge.

Wilson, B. (2014). Indian Super League to waken football "sleeping giant". *BBC News Business*, 8 September. Retrieved from www.bbc.com/news/business-29110757 (accessed 24 November 2016).

14

SUPER BOWL

Mythic spectacle revisited

Michael R. Real and Lawrence A. Wenner

> The structural values of the Super Bowl can be summarized succinctly: North American football is an aggressive, strictly regulated team game fought between males who use both violence and technology to gain control of property for the economic gain of individuals within a nationalistic entertainment context. The Super Bowl propagates these values by elevating one game to the level of a spectacle of American ideology collectively celebrated.
>
> *(Real, 1975, p. 42)*

> The more things change, the more they stay the same.
>
> *French proverb*

Reflecting upon the Super Bowl's 50th anniversary in 2016, we begin with twin observations. The first revisits the closing summary of one of the first studies (Real, 1975) in the field of communication to take the Super Bowl – and more broadly the increasing cultural importance of mediated sport – seriously. That study of 1974's Super Bowl VII told a larger tale of how the myths and spectacle of America's premier homegrown sporting mega-event revealed much about the nation's sensibilities. By calling on the second statement, commonly voiced as an ironic truism – that while much seemingly changes, much does not – we signal that much about the mythic and cultural functioning of the Super Bowl continues to hold true today. Yet, change is inevitable. Thus, in this chapter, we revisit those aspects of the Super Bowl that are deep and stable, and assess change from commodification, mediatization, and digitization. To set the stage, we consider "the super" as context, event, and logic.

The super context

Over its first half-century, the Super Bowl has increasingly come to dominate the American cultural landscape as the ultimate national celebration. More Americans join together at one time in watching the Super Bowl each year than in any other single activity. Advertisers spend more money per second to access those attentive eyeballs than for any other event. The Super Bowl is not just *a* big event, it is *the* *biggest*. It is not just the final game, it is the ultimate spectacle. In the US, the Super Bowl is what Christmas is to shopping, Thanksgiving is to eating, New Year's Eve is to champagne and hangovers, and the Fourth of July is to patriotism and fireworks. In combining all these attributes, the Super Bowl has become America's most complete celebration of itself.

Named as "super" on its third incarnation in 1969, when little was "super" apart from supermarkets and a comic book hero, it was clear that the institutionalization of the championship game between the winners of the National (NFL) and American (AFL) football leagues had both aspirations and pretensions. Aiming for more than the large, huge, or great of "mega," the "super" of the Super Bowl announced its intent to be above and beyond all else in American sport. Ushering in the era and signaling the disposition of "super media" (Real, 1989), it swaggered, using Roman numerals to tautologically assert its self-importance and infuse successive years of a nascent event with the permanence and significance of history.

While the first championship game in 1967, televised using primitive production techniques that revealed many empty seats, was clearly not so "super" (Sandomir, 2016a), the event's tentacles have grown in magnitude and significance. The Super Bowl's self-congratulatory historicism led the NFL in 2016 to finally reassemble the pieces of the first championship game and air the result on the league's own channel, refusing in the process to pay the requested fee for the only known copy of the original broadcast (Sandomir, 2016b). Fueled by increasingly huge television ratings for the game, the number of commodified "festivities" that have been built around it have convincingly positioned it as America's premier cultural event.

2016's Super Bowl 50 was landmark in key ways. Upon having reached its "golden anniversary," the trumped-up historicization of naming each year's event with Roman numerals was for the first time abandoned. While the NFL touted the change as a way to "elevate and celebrate the historic" anniversary, the move to the modern "logo-friendly" Arabic numeral 50 may have been less befuddling than marketing Super Bowl "L" (Garcia, 2015, ¶3).

Yet, the game itself, featuring the NFL's conference champions, the Carolina Panthers and Denver Broncos, was no different in many regards than any other. For the record, the Broncos won the game over the Panthers 24-10. Although the Nielsen total of 112 million US viewers for the game telecast, known historically for dominating lists of the most highly rated programs in American television history, fell just shy of the record audiences for the two previous Super Bowls (Kissell, 2016), its global audience of 160 million grew (Whittle, 2016). While "super" for a peculiarly American form of football, these figures are overshadowed by recent World Cup final audience estimates of 695 million in-home viewers and over one billion watching for more than a minute if out-of-home viewing is included (FIFA, 2015).

Still, with evidence that about half of US homes were tuned to the game and factoring in the many more viewing at bars and public places and millions more streaming the game, it is undeniable that the Super Bowl is as big as a sporting mega-event gets in America (Breech, 2015). And in upping the ante in "celebration" of Super Bowl 50, the NFL, and its many ancillary arms and partners, were not going to miss an opportunity to further "super-size" and monetize the event.

The super event

Since our earliest dissections of the Super Bowl's functioning in culture and commerce (Real, 1975; Wenner, 1989), considerable scholarly attention has been given to the study of large cultural events in the media age. There has been much recognition that media, and more importantly, the broadening use of "media logic" as a way to "see" and interpret culture, were game changers (Altheide and Snow, 1979). Many scholars saw the rhythm of ritual and the heroes of myth inexorably altered in the face of "media events" (Dayan and Katz, 1992) becoming routinized, spectacularized, and commodified (Real, 2013).

Because these features are so integral in Eastman, Newton, and Pack's (1994) characterization of "megasports" as important sporting events that masses put on their calendar, it is not surprising that sporting mega-events dominate mega-event studies (Gruneau and Horne, 2016). Certainly, the Super Bowl meets Roche's (2000, p. 1) criteria that mega-events are "large-scale cultural (including commercial and sporting events), which have dramatic character, mass popular appeal, and international significance". Still, with rapt hold in the US but limited – albeit growing – global appeal, the Super Bowl may best be characterized as a "third-order" mega (Horne, 2010) or "major" sporting event (Müller, 2015), along with others having regional or niche appeal.

While debatable, the Super Bowl's ranking on the international sporting mega-event scale may be moot. On two key criteria, having "significant consequences for the host city, region or nation in which they occur" and in attracting "considerable media coverage" (Horne and Manzenreiter, 2006, p. 1), the Super Bowl excels. This has been driven by a two-week onslaught of media "superhype" (Wenner, 1989) that comes strategically during a mid-winter cultural and sports "dead zone," after the holidays and end of college football, and before the basketball playoffs and start of the baseball season.

Situated thus, the Super Bowl as media mega-event is perched to build success around three conditions necessary for the modern manufacture of mythic spectacle:

1 technological infrastructure that can reach a national audience, live and with sound, motion, and color;
2 stories that the public can relate to, that are lively and convey strong emotions to capture the popular imagination; and
3 stories that in their presentation connect to the deepest meanings in the American culture, ones that encapsulate and vivify the nation's shared basic values (Real, 1977).

Indeed, the Super Bowl's event construction, as a mythic spectacle that speaks for a culture and binds together its members, recalls tribal spectacles which celebrate membership and meaning in diverse traditional cultures (Geertz, 1973).

These constituent features have allowed the Super Bowl to become not only a "media beast" but a cultural season marked by a manufactured "high holy day" (Dayan and Katz, 1992) featuring rituals celebrating its spectacularity. In this, the Super Bowl spectacle has become a poster child for the "superseding" of reality with apparition that Baudrillard (1981/2006) has called *simulacra*. Indeed, today's Super Bowl "activities" have become emblematic of the larger colonization of social life by commodities and their logic that Debord (1967/1995) sees encapsulating a contemporary culture defined through spectacle. As the naturalization of such "super logics" is integral to our analysis of the Super Bowl, we turn to two related schools of thought.

The super logic

In melding attributes of the mega-event, media event, ritual, and myth in spectacle, the Super Bowl relies on the broader twin logics of commodification and mediatization that theorists increasingly have seen as the tent poles of the postmodern condition. The rise of consumer culture theory (Arnould and Thompson, 2005; Smart, 2010) amplifies Debord's (1967/1995, p. 29) observations about the society of the spectacle residing in a "world of the commodity." Of key influence has been Bauman's characterization of postmodern "liquid modern life" as one enveloped by a "consumer sociality" where pleasures rule and we act on choices within an obligatory "market-mediated mode of life" dominated by a "consumerist attitude" or "syndrome" that views existence as a series of marketplace challenges (Bauman, 2007; Blackshaw, 2008). For Bauman, consumer culture "is a *circulum vitiosus*, magic circle with an osmotic circumference – easy entrance, no exit" (quoted in Rojek, 2004, p. 304).

Indeed, the degree to which mega-events, such as the Super Bowl, have worked to fashion a *circulum vitiosus* and make the logic of consumption omnipresent is striking, even to observers particularly attuned to this tendency.

> [A]s aware as I was of its commercial obsessions, I would never have guessed, for example, that the National Football League (NFL) would sell naming rights to the pregame coin toss replete with football celebrities to orchestrate

it. What was in 1974, a 4-hour telecast now knows no limits in time and channel domination. ESPN, nonexistent then, now provides 24/7 coverage of every aspect of the lead-up to the Super Bowl, with the NFL channel, along with whichever major network owns the rights in a given year, providing pre-Super Bowl specials, variety shows, mini-documentaries, cross-promotional insertions and so much more. It was the biggest spectacle in 1974 and it has only gotten bigger in the interim.

(Real, 2013, pp. 236–237)

Such "hypercommodification" of the contemporary mega-event is not just pervasive but integral. Debord, Bauman and many others have recognized that the logic of commodification that drives spectacle would not be possible without media. Indeed, Horne and Manzenreiter (2006, p. 2) assert that "an unmediated mega-event would be a contradiction in terms."

In recognition of this, we embrace contemporary thinking about how the "logic" of media intersects with understanding and experiencing everyday life. The recent turn to "mediatization" (Hepp, 2013; Hjarvard, 2013; Lundby, 2009) as a theoretical frame to understand the contemporary cultural condition builds on important earlier work about "media logic" (Altheide and Snow, 1979). Cognizant not only of how the forces of "super media" (as articulated in spectacularized media events) have come to make the "super" a frame for interpreting the common (Real, 1989), the lens focuses on the "mediatization of everything" (Livingstone, 2009). Mediatization recognizes "how social institutions and cultural processes have changed character, function, and structure in response to the omnipresence of media" (Hjarvard, 2013, p. 2). Following Frandsen's (2014) arguments that mediatization processes related to sport – particularly in their mega-incarnations – spread their own "logic," we consider how sensibilities about the Super Bowl transact with other quarters of social, cultural, and mediated life.

In framing our analysis, we note that if one were to look at Super Bowl 50 "by the numbers," one might think much has changed since the event's early days. Indeed, key indicators have been "super-sized," resulting in stratospheric ticket packages, the most expensive television advertising, and an ever-growing number of tie-in events. Yet, much about how the Super Bowl functions mythically and is structurally contained and constrained remains relatively stable. Thus in the next sections, we revisit the Super Bowl event's mythic and structural formations, relying on categories used earlier (Real, 1975, 1977) to assess stability amidst change fueled by increased commodification, mediatization, and digitization.

The mythic

Mythic activity, "the collective reenactment of symbolic archetypes that express the shared emotions and ideals of a given culture," and its powers as "regulatory and directing mechanisms" (Real, 1977, pp. 96–97) are catalyzed through the Super Bowl in interlocking ways that historically have made myth captivating and powerful. While the basic contours of the Super Bowl's mythic functioning – to build personal identification through heroic archetypes to drive a communal focus, as well as to regulate time, space, and economic ecology – remain stable, changes abound, most particularly in the commodification of cultural experiences that facilitate community and aestheticize narratives of consumption.

Personal identification

In advancing identification to facilitate engagement, the Super Bowl continues to build upon a potpourri of identity "anchors" that underlie fanship and facilitate vicarious participation. Media narratives – from those fashioned by the NFL through its diverse media machines to those told by media covering the rollup to the game to those "hyping" derivative "special" television programming and carnivalesque parties and expos that bask in the mediated glow of the Super Bowl light – provide symbolic "hooks" for identity and engagement. As such commodity-driven understandings about who to root for and the significance of the event itself are embraced, naturalized, and amplified through the "echo chambers" of social media, the mediatized terms of participation, identification, and meaning associated with the Super Bowl reveal the displacement in the locus of human relations that Ellul (1964) sees defining a technological society.

Heroic archetypes

The Super Bowl continues to provide America's grandest stage for celebrating a notion of the sports hero rooted in both mythology and romanticism (Crepeau, 1981). The sports hero narrative, commonly seen as driving the mythic functioning of American athletics and often blending "greatness" in both situational action and admirable character, has come to dominate contemporary heroic space (Allison and Goethels, 2011). Building on football as "America's Game," the NFL, populated by the game's "greatest" players, has strategically built its elite brand by portraying a compelling "holiness" to a ubiquitous heroic. Through its own media outlets and brands, such as NFL Films and the NFL Network, the historicized heroic logics valorized in its own Hall of Fame are extended and naturalized. The league's "broadcast partners" advance this by framing "stars" in key game action as heroic, a predilection elevated when the stakes are the highest as they are in the Super Bowl.

Communal focus

Collective participation in ritualized activities enable a sharing of experience and concerns beyond the individual that are at the heart of mythical belief (Cassirer, 1944). In the US, no event commands communal attention more than the Super Bowl. Today, in an era where media is fragmented and micro-audiences disperse and time shift to specialty programming, the Super Bowl remains the biggest cultural tent with more people "sharing" in the live experience than any other. Beyond being a television ratings juggernaut displacing other cultural activities and curbing traffic, Super Bowl Sunday is a "high holy day." Friends and family come together in localized rites and rituals of consumption and engagement, anchored in food, drink, and betting.

The 43 million fans that come together for in-home parties to "share" in the Super Bowl experience continue to provide the broadest base for the event's mythic functioning. Stimulated by a panoply of feature stories and online guides to aid hosting at-home parties, Super Bowl Sunday has become an engine for consumption. In recent years, adult beverage sales have spiked to new levels before the game, and with Super Bowl Sunday the top day for consuming pizza and chicken wings, it is second only to Thanksgiving in terms of food consumption (Earls, 2016; Nielsen, 2016). In recent years the push to communally experience the Super Bowl as a "first class" celebration has become increasingly subject to commodification schemes, many of which exist to service the elite and the corporate. At the local level, especially in cities that have "home" teams playing in the Super Bowl in a given year, "parties" and special events are "hosted" in bars and restaurants, many of which offer pricey "packages" to groups of fans looking to upgrade from homespun gatherings.

Nowhere is the upgrade more evident than in sport tourism's servicing the elite who have the resources or connections that privilege their ability to attend the Super Bowl game itself. With avenues for US$850–2500 "walk-up" tickets largely closed off, resale market tickets averaging US$5000 and pricey "all inclusive" Super Bowl packages (that include four- and five-star hotel stays, game tickets, and entry to exclusive parties and events) in the range of US$10,000 per person, the "community" that "focuses" on the game festivities "up close and personal" is quite different than those reliant on media performances (Fortune Editors, 2016). Other points of entry into this community come to those privileged to be wined and dined by corporations looking to advance their influence by "entertaining" clients while claiming a business expense.

Facilitated for Super Bowl 50 by a local hosting committee looking to boost the San Francisco Bay Area economy by US$220 million (to offset the considerable added costs of providing public safety services), some 50 public events throughout the region anchored communal focus through carnivalesque celebrations (Wagner, 2016). Growing from the mediated popularity of the Super Bowl, fan-centric events such as the "NFL Experience," "Super Bowl Fan Express," "Super Bowl Opening Night," "Super Bowl Media Day," and many more also served as "backdrops" for media feature stories that further built "hype" for and legitimized the Super Bowl myth. While the myriad events vary from those with free admission to those with costly entry to "hot" private parties (with exclusive entry by invitation only), what is shared is that, through media coverage, they offered a way to showcase to fans at home how the privileged conspicuously consume the Super Bowl.

Marking time and space

As postmodern urban existence has moved humans further from nature, sport seasons have increasingly taken on mythic functions of marking time and space (Real, 1977). In strategically calendaring the Super Bowl amidst a mid-winter lull with end-of-year holidays and competing major sports concluded (or in mid-season doldrums), the NFL has facilitated what Eliade (1959) might call a "sacred" time and space for the event amidst everyday "profane" existence. This "uncluttered" sacred space continues to provide the Super Bowl a unique cultural opening to fashion a primordial media-driven event resplendent with commodified ritual activities and marketable heroic archetypes.

Ecologically regulatory mechanisms

Just as myth and ritual patterns in rural and tribal cultures serve to pragmatically regulate environmental and relational practices towards sustainability (Rappaport, 1968), a key regulatory function of the Super Bowl is to advance the economic system by selling products and services. While in the early days, the Super Bowl, as a marketing platform, was no more extraordinary than many other sports events or media products, today it is unparalleled as America's most visible and venerated celebration of unrepentant commercialism. While much is made of the cost of Super Bowl game broadcast advertising, reaching US$5 million for 30 seconds, more telling is the shift of figure-ground relationships in the focus for many viewing the game. In keeping with Debord's (1967/1995) observations about spectacle residing in a "world of commodity," today more people (39 percent) cite the commercials rather than the game itself (28 percent) as their "favorite thing about the Super Bowl" (Garibian, 2013).

This change in figure-ground relationships that has come to prioritize the Super Bowl as a "commercial celebration" (McAllister, 2001) stems from Super Bowl advertising having become a niche cultural industry. Here, advertisers strategize how to produce the "best" (and often most expensive) commercials to enable products and services to make a big (and well-received) splash on the stage of America's most spectacular event. The competition among advertisers, not only to "break through the clutter" of competing messages, but to have their commercial narratives aesthetically evaluated has been formalized as "a 'game within the game' seen as the 'Super Bowl of Advertising'" (Wenner, 2015, p. 26). This game is spurred on by media watching, scorekeeping, and valorizing advertising efforts, thus raising this exercise to the level of spectacle. Adding to pundits' abundant assessments of these commercials, institutionalized media ventures such as *USA Today*'s Admeter, YouTube's AdBlitz, and CBS's two-hour "Super Bowl's Greatest Commercial 2016" primetime special, engage consumers by encouraging their voices to be heard through "voting" for commercials they judge to be aesthetically "the best." It would be difficult to find a cultural process that more clearly embraces Marx's (1867/1981) notion of "commodity fetishism" through the celebration of what

Haug (1986) termed "commodity aesthetics." Noting Debord's (1967/1995) observations about a society of the spectacle, Wenner (2015, p. 26) sees this state of affairs "as 'end stage spectacle' because the spectacle is not just a vehicle upon which commodification catches a ride, but rather a spectacle that is comprised of the commercials themselves."

The structural

Consistent with the mythic functioning of the Super Bowl, stability overshadows change in the event's structural dimensions. In affirming that "the Super Bowl is a formal analog of the institutional and ideological structure of the American society and culture it is 'about'" (Real, 1977, p. 103), we revisit how the structuration of territoriality and property, labor, management, action motivation, infrastructure, and packaging draws and contains spectacle. While many contour shifts are evident, we call special attention to key dimensions in motivation stimulated by "gamblification" and how packaging has advanced with strategic branding in companion with digital and social media.

Territoriality and property

As with capitalism, football is about gain through competition. Further, football, like war, essentializes using force to advance into enemy territory towards ultimately seizing it. The touchdown, marked by penetration into the opponent's end zone, symbolizes accumulation, and the team that controls production and commandeers the most property wins (Paolantonio, 2008). Spectacularized celebrations of nationalism and support for the military, frequently featured in Super Bowl pre-game and half-time performances, provide engrained thematic reinforcement (Swanson, 2016).

Time

Much has been made (Durslag, 1976) about the finding (Real, 1975) that 1974's Super Bowl VII featured less than seven minutes of actual live-play action. Overshadowed by game commentary, pre-and post-game shows and advertising, time devoted to live-play action constituted only 3 percent of that event's broadcast time. With today's 12-hour parade of pre- and post-game "specials" and extended time for advertising, live play in today's event programming easily shrinks to less than 1 percent of broadcast running time. Yet, at its core, football is about "using time" (regulated externally and precisely by technology) efficiently in 4–9-second bursts of discontinuous action in separate "plays." Given constant attention in Super Bowl game commentary, the event teaches and celebrates efficiency in using time.

Labor

The labor on display during the Super Bowl game continues to be a poor reflection of diversity and opportunity in America. While the NFL celebrates that women now make up 45 percent of their fans (Beahm, 2015), both women and men worship exclusively male athletic achievement on the Super Bowl's cultural stage. In this male bastion, few women are seen as either field commanders (coaching and support staff) or commentariat (apart from the occasional sideline reporter) in the Super Bowl's cultural performance. The most visible women continue to be sexy entertainers, such as Beyoncé, available for the male gaze during gender "appropriate" half-time and pre-game festivities. A racial divide is seen on other labor fronts. While NFL head coaches of color are down from a high of eight in 2011, the proportion of African-American players has risen to almost 70 percent, resulting in disproportionately Black gladiators warring before diverse television audiences and strikingly White privileged audiences in the stands. Beyond Black and White players, the combined percentage of NFL players from other racial categories totals only 3.7 percent (Lapchick and Robinson, 2015).

Management

Super Bowl teams and their supporting corporate structures continue to be direct analogs of the American corporate business system. The Super Bowl brings together two teams, each large corporations, that "compete" while sharing in a larger cooperative and monopolistic NFL cartel. The reduced risk environment, fueled by long-term television rights contracts (that yield each of the league's 32 teams more than US$200 million every year before a ticket is sold) has led to individual franchise values exceeding US$4 billion with average revenue in the US$300–500 million range (Badenshausen, 2011; Forbes, 2016). With operating budgets often over US$100 million, these are complex corporations with valued top executives at every turn, from head coaches to experts heading scouting, training, marketing, communication, facilities, and game operations, backed by an army of attorneys and accountants.

Action

This fusion of management and labor combines to produce marketable "action." In today's Super Bowl coverage, the sights and sounds of physical contact (ranging from 300-pound-plus linemen warring in "the pit" to head-on full speed collisions) remain a key focus facilitating spectator engagement and are celebrated in replays. Today's gladiators are super-sized in comparison to the average six foot two (188 cm) and 225-pound (102 kg) player seen in 1974's Super Bowl (Real, 1977). Modern speed players, such as the Carolina Panther's six foot five (196 cm), 250-pound (113 kg) quarterback Cam Newton, dwarf linemen of earlier eras (Gaines, 2015). In service of spectacle, action is faster, hits harder, and injuries frequent.

Sullying the purity of this action performance as entertainment has been increased attention given to collateral damage that includes the normalization of life-long injuries and widespread chronic traumatic encephalopathy found later among former players (Beck, 2015).

Motivation

While recreational athletes may play for the "love of the game" or the "thrill of competition," the playing of professional football and winning the Super Bowl is most motivated by money. While winning and losing team players receive more today (respectively US$97,000 and $49,000) than for playing in the 1974 Super Bowl (US$15,000 and $7,500), such game "bonuses" are a far smaller piece of the motivational pie, especially given the US$2.1 million average salary among NFL players (Gerencer, 2016; Real, 1975; Reimer, 2016). Motivation for victory is more stimulated by the considerable value added to the market worth of both players and teams as winning "brands" (Badenhausen, Ozanian, and Settimi, 2015).

While the motivation for NFL, and its teams and players, is clear, they are not the only ones motivated by a money game. As Geertz (1973) has vividly chronicled in his study of Balinese cockfighting, entire communities of fans have long enjoyed having "skin" in the game. Geertz suggests that involvement in sport through betting is driven by "deep play," as the possible winnings do not justify the risk taken. More importantly, Schimmel (2006, p. 160) argues, is that the money at stake deepens the play, facilitating a "migration of status hierarchies into the body of the event." It is not surprising then, driven by the mega-media primacy of the Super Bowl, that virtually every assessment characterizes the game as "the single biggest betting event every single year," with estimates suggesting that some 200 million people wager as much as US$10 billion on the contest annually (e.g. see www.superbowlbets.com). Even in a climate where much online betting is illegal in countries such as the United States and where 97 percent of bets placed were illegal, evidence suggests an 8 percent increase in betting on the Super Bowl in 2016 over the previous year (Fortune Editors, 2016). Fueled by the ease of placing wagers via now ubiquitous offshore gambling sites in conjunction with what is increasingly called the "gamblification" of sport (Pillsbury, 2015), a phenomenon driven by social media in conjunction with "an intricate web of surveillance and targeted advertising exposure by information technology corporations such as Google and Facebook" (Rowe, 2015, p. 151), Super Bowl betting has become one of the more notable mediatization effects of the event. These effects are obviously compounded by the dysfunctions and social costs associated with compulsive gambling.

Infrastructure

Earlier consideration of the "infrastructure" of the Super Bowl grew from the observation that "The institutional organization is not *like* American business; it *is*

American business" (Real, 1975, p. 40). While teams (as business entities) and the NFL (as a sophisticated cartel) continue to reproduce themselves and the Super Bowl event as amoeba in an orgy of corporate excess, what is most notable is how the event is seen to play on local economies and psyches of communities hosting the event. Cities, both their governments and business communities, engage in "place wars" (Haider, 1992) in bidding to host the Super Bowl and bask in its glory and perceived benefits. Entry requirements typically mandate offering up expensive new stadiums to showcase the game and places to wine and dine the privileged who attend the many corporate-sponsored football fan carnivals. While the costs to insure required infrastructure, from five-star hotels to robust technological backbones, can be daunting, gleeful reports of yields, such as US$220 million coming to the San Francisco Bay Area as a result of hosting Super Bowl 50 (Wagner, 2016) overshadow well-documented "economic irrationality" (Schimmel, 2006).

Packaging

While the infrastructure requirements for packaging the Super Bowl experience are considerable, their value and very existence as human experiences in a local community would not be possible without the constancy and cohesion of the media forces promoting and surrounding the Super Bowl. At the heart of the media package is a "broadcast day" that, in its bare bones, includes a pre-game show, the game broadcast, and a post-game show produced by the television network holding the rights in a given year. While 1974's broadcast day featured what seems today a modest half-hour pre-game show (Real, 1975), CBS's broadcast schedule leading up to Super Bowl 50 stretched to seven and a half-hours and featured five pre-game shows: one, *The Super Bowl Today*, lasting four hours, and two, *Super Bowl 50: Before They Were Pros* and *Road to the Super Bowl*, produced by NFL Films, the in-house promotional arm of the league that exists to tell the NFL's story in historic and heroic terms. When one adds the increasingly spectacular half-time show, also owned by the NFL, one can see the broadcast day as an unrepentant NFL package wrapped in a pretty bow by a media partner that has paid for the privilege to do so.

While this extended calendar of programs shown on its broadcast partner's network may be seen as evolutionary, it is only one part in a larger packaging ecosystem that facilitates ubiquity for the Super Bowl brand. In the two weeks in advance of the game, three forces – amplification, echoes, and reverberation – combine to facilitate the Super Bowl's dominating the media space.

The now multi-faceted media arms of both the NFL and its broadcast partner (CBS in the instance of Super Bowl 50) take the lead, amplifying the significance of the event and more broadly celebrating the cultural importance of NFL football. Here, diverse programming from NFL Films, chronicling both Super Bowl's past and celebrating NFL heroism as worthy and noble, is spread, almost as fairy dust, across broadcast schedules of the NFL Network, CBS/Viacom's Showtime and

Nicktoon channels, and featured on ESPN and Fox Sports outlets. Further amplification comes from NFL Communications (2016, ¶3) whose commandeering efforts to blanket the digital space with "wall-to-wall coverage and exclusive content" is featured on its NFL.com and SuperBowl.com websites and via digital partners such as NFL Mobile from Verizon and NFL on Xbox. In the week leading to the game, the CBS primetime schedule featured three hours of specials valorizing *Super Bowl's Greatest Commercials*, and two two-hour specials, produced by the NFL, one celebrating *Super Bowl's Greatest Halftime Shows* and the other, *5th Annual NFL Honors*, valorizing noteworthy play.

Echoing the core media narratives offered by the NFL and CBS is a large media chorus that "covers" and discusses "breaking news" concerning the "big game." Led by the gargantuan voices of diverse multi-platform sport-centric giant brands ESPN and FOX Sports (who have skin in the larger game as NFL partners), the echo chamber is supportive, loud and dominant. Individually smaller, but collectively considerable, an army of sport-centric commercial coverage, from daily newspapers to local television news to print and web sport publications, that in principle can offer more "detached" coverage, mostly fan the flames, both not to be seen as "out of step" by missing the Super Bowl's "big story" and to use the allure of the game to attract their own viewers and readers.

A relatively new addition to an increasingly digitized media packaging ecosystem for the Super Bowl comes in the form of voices from citizens and corporations engaging social media. Here, through Twitter, Facebook and other social media platforms, fans engage with a plethora of accounts "branded" in association with all variants of "Super Bowl," from the event in the generic to Super Bowl 50 in the particular to Super Bowl commercials to Super Bowl parties and food recipes. When social media accounts following Super Bowl teams and players are added to the mix, the reverberation is considerable. Still, as Wenner (2014, p. 734) notes "new and social media, just like 'pre-digital' social communication, functions largely as ripples emanating from the splash [of dominant media], courtesy, in this instance, of bloggers and tweeters vying to become opinion leaders about the larger agenda that has been set by the media–big sport combine that dominates the mediasport production complex." As such, the reverberations from social media largely serve to further advance the Super Bowl package towards spectacle.

The super spectacle

In earlier analyses (Real, 1975, 1977), "spectacle" was treated as a final structural characteristic of the Super Bowl. In taking stock of the advance of commodification and mediatization on the Super Bowl as a unique articulation of the sporting mega-event, the analyses here suggest that spectacle needs to be recognized as much more than a structural element. It strikes us as more appropriate today to see the spectacle of the Super Bowl as an "end game" that is a result of its unique mythic functioning and structures coming together to shape sensibilities. In that game, we suggest that three overarching and interlocking forces – technology, history, and nation – continue to play an outsized role in the Super Bowl spectacle being able to command cultural influence.

First, the worthiness of the Super Bowl spectacle is signaled by the use of extensive and cutting edge technology. For Super Bowl 50, joining the all-time high of 70 cameras used to capture the game, were "whiz-bang" technologies such as Eye Vision 360 replay cameras capable of freezing then encircling continuous play, end zone corner pylon cameras to capture high definition video and audio, and improved Sportvision video technology to superimpose "first and ten" lines on the field seen on television screens from any angle. Beyond television, spectacle was facilitated through the 400 miles of fiber and copper cable and the 1200 Wi-Fi access points in Levi's stadium driving event-related social media posts, and apps, such as Road to 50, enhancing fan engagement whether at the stadium, bar, or home (Basile, 2016).

Second, the spectacular significance of the event is reinforced by a constant onslaught of media celebrating select constructions of the history of the Super Bowl and its heroes. Each Super Bowl reifies its place in the present by marking its historical trajectory in "our" collective past, providing continuity and ritual. This tautological exercise is facilitated by the NFL through stories promoted by its media arms and partners, and through feature stories across platforms by media outlets seeing the great game myth as a way to attract consumers. While aided and abetted by "sport-centric" media outlets such as ESPN, Fox Sports, SB Nation, and a parade of fan-pitched websites, the overarching "media logic" is driven by the NFL. For Super Bowl 50, NFL Films offered a vast catalogue of museum-quality programming. Ranging from *Super Bowl Memories* to *50 Super Bowl Stories* to specials devoted to each Super Bowl, playoff, and season, this programming dominated the schedules of not only the NFL Network and its CBS broadcast partner's networks, but those of the ESPN and Fox Sports brand outlets. When combined with the NFL's traveling exhibit "Gridiron Glory: The Best of the Pro Football Hall of Fame" being featured at an art museum near the stadium and in trotting out a parade of former Super Bowl MVPs to celebrate the start of its 50th anniversary game, it is clear that the NFL takes its sense of history seriously.

Third, the legitimacy of the Super Bowl is facilitated by the strategic pairing of its history and significance with that of nation. The NFL's boastful claim that "For decades the NFL and the military have had a close relationship at the Super Bowl" (National Football League, 2011, ¶3) has received well-chronicled criticism. Critics note a problematic leap of logic in the NFL's attempts to synergize the connection between celebrating the Super Bowl, as the penultimate show of "America Game" as one of ritualized force, with celebrations of the American military and support for the force it wields in war (King, 2008; Schimmel, 2012). What is less well known is that the US military actually pays the NFL for the privilege of appearing in the Super Bowl (Swanson, 2016).

In celebrating the Super Bowl's 50th anniversary, "the might of the American empire was on full display" (Lazare, 2016, ¶1). Building on a tradition of spectacularized pre-game and half-time displays, spectators were asked to "take pride" in the military by cheering performances such as the Armed Forces Chorus singing "America the Beautiful," during which CBS intercut footage, bannered as "United States Forces Afghanistan," of uniformed troops at attention on stadium and television screens. Following Lady Gaga's performance of the national anthem, the familiar ritual of a "flyover" the stadium by the US Navy Blue Angels was rewarded with cheers from spectators for its ritualistic "shock and awe" display. In a post-9/11 era, the militarization of the Super Bowl event has extended beyond media to stadium security (Schimmel, 2012). As a US Department of Homeland Security Level 1 security event, US Air Force F-15 Eagles patrolled the airspace over the stadium. On the ground, metal detectors were everywhere, and a massive deployment of police and troops featured the armed march of military personnel into the security zone next to the media entrance and throngs of camouflaged Humvees with roof gun mounts patrolling the perimeter (Swanson, 2016).

Final gun

At the heart of its cultural force, the spectacle that is the Super Bowl grows from this powerful triad marrying the new of cutting edge technology with the stable mythic allure of history and powerful pull and force of nation. In many regards, it is these elements that enable the fusion of all the other mythic and structural elements of the Super Bowl to combine in a way that is greater than the sum of their parts. As such, the Super Bowl remains an ever-updatable case study in the workings of mediatization set amidst the larger logics of commodification. While it is easy to see how some of the dynamics behind its workings have necessarily adjusted to and embraced changes endemic in today's digitized and social media era, the bulk of the evidence in our analysis supports the truism that "the more things change, the more they stay the same."

At the same time, the analysis here provides a reminder of the malleable nature of media, mediatization processes, and, above all, the forces of commodification embedded in a larger capitalist logic. In many ways, our findings concerning the Super Bowl are largely confirmatory. Confirmatory evidence is seen on many fronts on matters as diverse as McLuhan's (1964) notion that new media repurposes the old, Dayan and Katz's (1992) recognition that media events become "high holy days" with their own rituals celebrating their own spectacularity, Baudrillard's (1981/2006) assertions that *simulacra* will routinely supersede the real, Bauman's (2007) characterization of consumer culture as a *circulum vitiosus* where an obligatory "market-mediated mode of life" is internalized, and Debord's (1967/1995) observations about how the colonization of cultural life by commodities has created a society of the spectacle.

To our mind, the evidence here goes beyond mere mediatization. This is not to say that the lens of mediatization (Hjarvard, 2013), with its focus on how the omnipresence of media has changed social institutions, cultural processes and everyday life, is not relevant here. Indeed, our analysis showcases many examples displaying these tendencies. Rather, we would like to argue, as many of the scholars noted above have in line with the core arguments of the Frankfurt School (Wiggerhaus, 1995), that the popular needs to be taken seriously and interrogated as ideology. As Silverstone (1999, p. 152) reminds those analyzing media: "it's all about power." And given that case studies of sports mega-events, such as this one about the Super Bowl, necessarily employ two of Althusser's (1971/2001) most important ideological state apparatuses (or ISAs) – sport and media – to hail us in service of their "logics," contextualizing mediatization in this light seems essential. All of this should serve to remind us that the Super Bowl – whose mediatization rides on the strategic command of technology, characterization of history, and invocation of nation in the context of building identification through heroic archetypes to command communal focus to naturally situate itself as America's largest spectacle in a larger world of commodity – is powerful indeed.

References

Allison, S.T. and Goethels, G.R. (2011). *Heroes: What they do and why we need them.* New York: Oxford University Press.

Altheide, D.L. and Snow, R.P. (1979). *Media logic.* Beverly Hills, CA: Sage.

Althusser, L. (1971/2001). *Lenin and philosophy and other essays* (trans. B. Brewster). New York: Monthly Review Press.

Arnould, E.J. and Thompson, C.J. (2005). Consumer culture theory (CCT): Twenty years of research. *Journal of Consumer Research, 31,* 868–882.

Badenshausen, K. (2011). The NFL signs TV deals worth $27 billion. *Forbes,* December 14. Retrieved from www.forbes.com/sites/kurtbadenhausen/2011/12/14/the-nfl-signs-tv-deals-worth-26-billion/#6c56668c2a67 (accessed 24 November 2016).

Badenshausen, K., Ozanian, M. and Settimi, C. (2015). The business of football. *Forbes,* September 14. Retrieved from www.forbes.com/nfl-valuations/ (accessed 24 November 2016).

Basile, D. (2016). The evolving technology of the Super Bowl. *Tech Crunch,* February 7. Retrieved from http://techcrunch.com/2016/02/07/the-evolving-technology-of-the-super-bowl (accessed 24 November 2016).

Baudrillard, J. (1981/2006). *Simulacra and simulation* (trans. S.F. Glaser). Ann Arbor, MI: University of Michigan Press.

Bauman, Z. (2007). *Consuming life.* Cambridge: Polity.

Beahm, D. (2015). For NFL teams, treating women like real fans can offer big payoff. *Sporting News,* September 30. Retrieved from www.sportingnews.com/nfl/news/nfl-fan-clubs-women-roger-goodell-buccaneers-red-colts-patriots-steelers-packers/175qo1qlsfwu51u4zk27ikhzkx (accessed 24 November 2016).

Beck, J. (2015). The NFL's continuing concussion nightmare. *The Atlantic,* September 21. Retrieved from www.theatlantic.com/health/archive/2015/09/researchers-find-brain-damage-in-96-percent-of-former-nfl-players/406462 (accessed 24 November 2016).

Blackshaw, T. (2008). Bauman on consumerism: Living the market-mediated life. In M.H. Jacobsen and P. Poder (eds), *The sociology of Zygmunt Bauman: Challenges and critiques* (pp. 117–135). London: Routledge.

Breech, J. (2015). Super Bowl 49 watched by 114.4M, sets US TV viewership record. *CBS Sports,* February 15. Retrieved from www.cbssports.com/nfl/eye-on-football/25019076/super-bowl-49-watched-by-1144m-sets-us-tv-viewership-record (accessed 24 November 2016).

Cassirer, E. (1944). *Essay on man*. New Haven, CT: Yale University Press.

Crepeau, R.C. (1981). Sport, heroes and myth. *Journal of Sport and Social Issues*, 5(1), 23–31.

Dayan, D. and Katz, E. (1992) *Media events: The live broadcasting of history*. Cambridge, MA: Harvard University Press.

Debord, G. (1967/1995) *The society of the spectacle* (trans. D. Nicholson-Smith). New York: Zone Books.

Durslag, M. (1976). Two weeks of ballyhoo, seven minutes of action. *TV Guide*, January 17, 14–16.

Earls, S. (2016). Super Bowl 50: By the numbers – the wagers, the people, the wings and the pizza. *The Gazette*, February 7. Retrieved from http://gazette.com/super-bowl-50-by-the-numbers-the-wagers-the-people-the-wings-and-pizza/article/1569425 (accessed 24 November 2016).

Eastman, S.T., Newton, G.D. and Pack, L. (1996). Promoting prime-time programs in megasporting events. *Journal of Broadcasting and Electronic Media*, 40, 366–388.

Eliade, M. (1959) *The sacred and the profane*. New York: Harper & Row.

Ellul, J. (1964). *Technological society*. New York: Knopf.

FIFA (2015). 2014 FIFA World Cup reached 3.2 billion viewers, one billion watched final. FIFA.com, December 16. Retrieved from www.fifa.com/worldcup/news/y=2015/m=12/news=2014-fifa-world-cuptm-reached-3-2-billion-viewers-one-billion-watched—2745519.html (accessed 24 November 2016).

Forbes (2016). NFL team values 2015. *Forbes*. Retrieved from www.forbes.com/pictures/mlm45fljdi/nfl-team-values-2015/#74a691064e36 (accessed 24 November 2016).

Fortune Editors (2016). Super Bowl by the numbers. *Fortune*, February 7. Retrieved from http://fortune.com/super-bowl-by-the-numbers (accessed 24 November 2016).

Frandsen, K. (2014). Mediatization of sports. In K. Lundby (ed.), *The handbook of mediatization of communication* (pp. 525–543). Berlin: Mouton de Gruyter.

Gaines, C. (2015). NFL lineman weren't always so enormous. *Business Insider*, September 13. Retrieved from www.businessinsider.com/nfl-offensive-lineman-are-big-2011-10 (accessed 24 November 2016).

Garcia, A. (2015). NFL ditches Roman numerals for Super Bowl 50. *CNN Money*, September 10. Retrieved from http://money.cnn.com/2015/09/10/news/companies/super-bowl-50-nfl/ (accessed 24 November 2016).

Garibian, L. (2013). Super Bowl ads more popular than game action. Retrieved from www.marketingprofs.com/charts/2013/9990/super-bowl-ads-more-popular-than-game-action (accessed 24 November 2016).

Geertz, C. (1973). *The interpretation of cultures*. New York: Basic Books.

Gerencer, T. (2016). How much money do NFL players make? *Money Nation*, January 5. Retrieved from http://moneynation.com/how-much-money-do-nfl-players-make (accessed 24 November 2016).

Gruneau, R. and Horne, J. (eds) (2016). *Mega-events and globalization: Capital and spectacle in a changing world order*. London: Routledge.

Haider, D. (1992). Place wars: New realities of the 1990s. *Economic Development Quarterly*, 6, 588–601.

Haug, W.F. (1986). *Critique of commodity aesthetics: Appearance, sexuality, and advertising in capitalist society*. Minneapolis, MN: University of Minnesota Press.

Hepp, A. (2013). *Cultures of mediatization*. Cambridge: Polity.

Hjarvard, S. (2013). *The mediatization of culture and society*. London: Routledge.

Horne, J. (2010). Cricket in consumer culture: Notes on the 2007 Cricket World Cup. *American Behavioral Scientist*, 53, 1549–1568.

Horne, J. and Manzenreiter, W. (2006). An introduction to the sociology of mega-events. *Sociological Review, 54*(suppl. s2), 1–24.

King, S. (2008). Offensive lines: Sport–state synergy in an era of perpetual war. *Cultural Studies Critical Methodologies, 8*, 527–539.

Kissell, R. (2016). Super Bowl 50 ratings: CBS draws third largest audience on record. *Variety*, February 8. Retrieved from http://variety.com/2016/tv/news/super-bowl-50-ratings-cbs-third-largest-audience-on-record-1201699814 (accessed 24 November 2016).

Lapchick, R. and Robinson, L. (2015). *The 2015 racial and gender report card: National Football League*. Orlando, FL: Institute for Diversity and Ethics in Sport. Retrieved from www.tidesport.org/nfl-rgrc.html (accessed 24 November 2016).

Lazare, S. (2016). The might of the American empire was on full display at Super Bowl 50: A bizarre war spectacle extraordinaire. *Alternet*, February 8. Retrieved from www.alternet.org/civil-liberties/might-american-empire-was-full-display-super-bowl-50-bizarre-war-spectacle (accessed 24 November 2016).

Livingston, S. (2009). On the mediation of everything. *Journal of Communication, 59*, 1–18.

Lundby, K. (ed.) (2009). *Mediatization: Concept, changes, consequences.* New York: Peter Lang.

Marx, K. (1867/1981). *Capital, Volume 1: A critique of political economy.* London: Penguin.

McAllister, M. (2001). Super Bowl advertising as commercial celebration. *The Communication Review, 3*, 403–428.

McLuhan, M. (1964). *Understanding media.* New York: McGraw-Hill.

Müller, M. (2015). What makes an event a mega-event? Definitions and sizes. *Leisure Studies, 34*, 627–642.

National Football League (2011). NFL and the military event outreach. October 25. Retrieved from www.nfl.com/news/story/09000d5d8237c745/article/nfl-and-the-military-event-outreach (accessed 24 November 2016).

NFL Communications (2016). NFL digital media celebrates Super Bowl 50 with wall-to-wall coverage and exclusive content. February 7. Retrieved from https://nflcomm unications.com/Pages/NFL-Digital-Media-Celebrates-Super-Bowl-50-With-Wall-To-Wall-Coverage-and-Exclusive-Content.aspx (accessed 24 November 2016).

Nielsen (2016). Super Bowl Sunday is no longer just a beer holiday. *Nielsen Insights*, February 3. Retrieved from www.nielsen.com/us/en/insights/news/2016/super-bowl-sunday-is-no-longer-just-a-beer-holiday.html (accessed 24 November 2016).

Paolantonio, S. (2008). *How football explains America.* Chicago, IL: Triumph Books.

Pillsbury (2015). Gamblification: An overview of legal issues with gambling in social games and social media. Retrieved from www.pillsburylaw.com/siteFiles/MDT/FACTSHEET _SMG_Gamblification_011714.pdf (accessed 24 November 2016).

Rappaport, R.A. (1968) *Pigs for the ancestors: Ritual in the ecology of a New Guinea people.* New Haven, CT: Yale University Press.

Real, M.R. (1975). The Super Bowl: Mythic spectacle. *Journal of Communication, 25*, 31–43.

Real, M.R. (1977). *Mass-mediated culture.* Englewood Cliffs, NJ: Prentice-Hall.

Real, M.R. (1989). *Super media: A cultural studies approach.* Newbury Park, CA: Sage.

Real, M.R. (2013). Reflections on communication and sport: On spectacle and mega-events. *Communication and Sport, 1*, 30–42.

Reimer, A. (2016). Super Bowl 2016: Winning shares of $97K is low in comparison to other sports. *SB Nation*, February 7. Retrieved from www.sbnation.com/nfl/2016/2/7/10930756/2016-super-bowl-50-winner-shares-broncos-panthers (accessed 24 November 2016).

Roche, M. (2000). *Mega-events and modernity: Olympics and expos in the growth of global culture.* London: Routledge.

Rojek, C. (2004). The consumerist syndrome in contemporary society. *Journal of Consumer Culture*, *4*, 291–312.

Rowe, D. (2015). Afterword: Media sport – coming to a screen near and on you. *Media International Australia*, *155* (May), 149–152.

Sandomir, R. (2016a) For broadcast of Super Bowl I, NFL Network picks excess over tact. *New York Times*, January 16. Retrieved from www.nytimes.com/2016/01/17/ sports/football/for-broadcast-of-super-bowl-i-nfl-network-picks-excess-over-tact.html (accessed 29 January 2016).

Sandomir, R. (2016b). Out of a rare Super Bowl I recording, a clash with the NFL unspools. *The New York Times*, February 2. Retrieved from www.nytimes.com/2016/02/03/ sports/football/super-bowl-i-recording-broadcast-nfl-troy-haupt.html (accessed 7 February 2016).

Schimmel, K. (2006). Deep play: Sport mega-events and urban social conditions in the USA. *Sociological Review*, *54*(Supplement), 160–174.

Schimmel, K. (2012). Protecting the NFL/militarizing the homeland: Citzen soldiers and urban resilience in post-9/11 America, *International Review for the Sociology of Sport*, *47*, 338–337.

Silverstone, R. (1999). *Why study the media?* London: Sage.

Smart, B. (2010). *Consumer society: Critical issues and environmental consequences.* London: Sage.

Swanson, D. (2016). The Super Bowl promotes war. February 16. Retrieved from www.films foraction.org/articles/the-super-bowl-promotes-war (accessed 24 November 2016).

Wagner, S. (2016). Forget Carolina and Denver: The real Super Bowl winner is the Bay Area. *Bloomberg Business*, February 4. Retrieved from www.bloomberg.com/news/articles/ 2016-02-04/forget-carolina-and-denver-the-real-super-bowl-winner-is-the-bay-area (accessed 24 November 2016).

Wenner, L.A. (1989). The Super Bowl pregame show: Cultural fantasies and political subtext. In L.A. Wenner (ed.), *Media, sports, and society* (pp. 157–179). Newbury Park, CA: Sage.

Wenner, L.A. (2014). On the limits of the new and the lasting power of the mediasport interpellation. *Television and New Media*, *15*, 732–740.

Wenner, L.A. (2015). Connecting events to advertising: Narrative strategies and dirty logics in Super Bowl commercials. In K. Dashper, T. Fletcher and N. McCullough (eds), *Sports events, society and culture* (pp. 25–39). London: Routledge.

Whittle, M. (2016). The $5m question: What does Super Bowl 50 offer to advertisers? *The Guardian*, February 4. Retrieved from www.nytimes.com/2016/02/03/sports/football/ super-bowl-i-recording-broadcast-nfl-troy-haupt.html (accessed 24 November 2016).

Wiggerhaus, R. (1995). *The Frankfurt School: Its history, theories, and political significance.* Cambridge: Polity.

15

THE WORLD SERIES

Baseball, American exceptionalism and media ritual

Michael L. Butterworth

On November 3, 2015, members of the Kansas City Royals appeared before an estimated 800,000 fans to celebrate their victory over the New York Mets in the World Series of Major League Baseball (MLB). It was Kansas City's first championship in 30 years, made all the more satisfying by the symbolism of a small-market franchise from the nation's heartland triumphing over a big-spending opponent from the coast. Understood as a myth, the heartland "provides a shorthand cultural common sense framework for 'all-American' identification, redeeming goodness, face-to-face community, sanctity, and emplaced ideals to which a desirous and nostalgic public discourse repeatedly returns" (Johnson, 2008, p. 5). This middle-American ethos was on full display during a parade that featured various symbols of national identity: thousands lined the sun-bathed streets, and a fire engine and Chevrolet pick-up led the procession. An observer might have assumed the event was an Independence Day celebration, except the American red, white, and blue flag was largely replaced by royal blue. The collection of images presented an "All-American" snapshot, evoking the familiar mythology of baseball that ties it to the innocence and purity of America's presumed agrarian origins and affirming the middle-American values symbolized by the heartland.

While the parade imagery offered the familiar threads that subtly weave together baseball with the very fabric of American identity, another moment from the World Series celebration captured a far bolder approach. Jonny Gomes, who appeared in only 12 of 162 games for Kansas City in 2015 and was not on the World Series roster, was among the team members who addressed the crowd during a rally at Union Station. Gomes delivered his speech about teamwork and perseverance with almost manic enthusiasm, and he stalked the stage carrying an enormous American flag. Despite baseball's symbolic standing as the "national pastime," there was no particular need for the Stars and Stripes. Nevertheless, Gomes held it proudly and, as he paced the stage, he "planted" it each time he referenced the award-winning players on the teams vanquished by the Royals on the way to a championship. It was, in the words of *Huffington Post* columnist Justin Block (2015, ¶ 2), "the most impassioned speech invoking American exceptionalism since the president's in 'Independence Day.'"

American exceptionalism is most often understood as an expression of the superiority of the United States. In the words of Weiss and Edwards (2011, p. 1), "Champions of American exceptionalism hold that because of its national credo, historical evolution, and unique origins, America is a special nation with a special role – possibly ordained by God – to play in human history." Just about everything associated with the World Series might be understood in terms of American exceptionalism, and so I view Gomes's performance as an invitation to consider the symbolic associations between this foundational national myth and one of the nation's most enduring cultural institutions. More specifically, I focus on the mediated production of the annual "fall classic," which has been broadcast by FOX since 2000 and will remain with the network until at least 2021 (Newman, 2012).

The World Series is baseball's signature media event, and its best-of-seven format supplies multiple opportunities for media rituals to affirm the values presumably inherent to the national pastime. Moreover, like other sports mega-events, the World Series is situated within a dramatically and rapidly changing media land-scape. As Rowe describes it:

> the economics of the media sports cultural complex and the patterns of practice across it are shifting as, for example, the mediated experience of major sports events like the Super Bowl and the FIFA World Cup can, simul-taneously, involve broadcast television, mobile viewing, social networking, micro-blogging, and so on.
>
> *(Rowe, 2013, p. 73)*

In this passage, he hails the tradition of scholarship rooted in ideas of the "sports/media complex" (Jhally, 1984) or "mediasport" (Wenner, 1998). These constructs have served media and communication scholars well, but several scholars (Frandsen, 2014; Hjarvard, 2013; Hutchins, 2016) contend that "mediatization" is a term that provides a more contemporary and nuanced means by which we can assess the relationship between the logic of media, the overarching sensibilities manifest in its content, and the meanings created for audiences.

Frandsen (2014) worries that the prevailing approach to research on media and sport has too often isolated case studies and is limited by the historical context of the 1980s and 1990s. She finds mediatization a productive direction, then, because it is a social and historical process, one situated in relationship to other processes such as globalization and commercialization. As she explains, mediatization is "characterized by both continuity and change and sometimes even contradiction" (ibid., p. 529). Although some scholars (Couldry, 2008; Deacon and Stayner, 2014) express concern that mediatization can be used as a universal or reductionist conceptual framework, Hjarvard (2013, p. 17) insists that can be understood "as a conceptual shorthand for the various institutional, aesthetic, and technological *modus operandi* of the media." Sport, specifically, is a productive site for understanding mediatization because of the "symbiotic relationship between professional (mostly men's) sports and the mass media that developed over the course of the 20th Century" (Hutchins, 2016, p. 423). The World Series, then, is a useful site for thinking through mediatization because its evolution spotlights tensions between continuity and change. Indeed, as of 2014, FOX streams games online and, in the words of FOX Sports Executive Vice President of Production John Entz, the network aims to provide "the most technically comprehensive World Series we've ever done" (Barr, 2014, ¶ 19). At the same time, many of the efforts to promote the series and describe the action on the field rely on familiar baseball mythologies that emphasize the game's history and nostalgia for the past. In particular, baseball, as it often has been, is a vehicle through which American exceptionalism finds ritual expression. Yet, at the same time, the World Series is exceptionalist in another sense of the word – that is, its commitment to myth and nostalgia marks it as a distinct site within the mega-event landscape. As a result, the World Series broadcast is unquestionably a product of both contemporary media practices and historical traditions that contextualize contemporary events.

In this chapter, I evaluate the ways that World Series media ritual (Real, 1989) enacts the myth of American exceptionalism. To begin, I engage in a genealogy of this myth as it articulates with baseball and its fall classic. Next, I situate the World Series in the scholarly discussion about mega-events and mediatization. Finally, I attend to broadcast coverage in recent years to identify the ritualized expressions of American exceptionalism, with a particular interest in the use of nostalgia. Finally, I assess the role of baseball and the World Series as an exemplar of mediatization and sport in the contemporary, global age.

Baseball and American exceptionalism

In my book, *Baseball and Rhetorics of Purity*, I argue that baseball served during the "war on terror" as a rhetorical resource for the purification of American national identity, and that the articulations of the national pastime with politics "constituted Americans as innocent and virtuous, thereby amplifying the myth of American exceptionalism that has long characterized US identity" (Butterworth, 2010, p. 2). As a rhetorical scholar, I am concerned less with "myth" as a statement of fiction and more with it as a symbolic means of inducing attitudes and behaviors in a given community. Myths are narratives but they are not merely clever stories; rather, they *"explain* the world" (Robertson, 1980, p. xvii) and "serve as a moral guide to proper actions" (Hart, 1990, p. 305). Because they are "complex blends of archetypal and rhetorical elements" (Rushing, 1989, p. 2), they have broad, sometimes universal, appeal. Indeed, Fisher (1984, p. 160) concludes that the "most compelling, most persuasive stories are mythic in form."

Hughes (2004, p. 5) suggests that the United States has five foundational myths, all of which are "rooted in a religious understanding of reality." These five myths – that the US is a chosen nation, populated by a chosen people, who have been granted natural rights, who are collectively innocent, and will bring about a millennial age of freedom – each express dimensions of what is more commonly condensed into a singular myth of American exceptionalism. This myth, which technically marks the United States simply as "being different, not necessarily better" (Lipset, 1996), more often defines Americans "as a people morally separate from other nations" (Motter, 2010, p. 512). As Weiss and Edwards (2011, p. 2) conclude, the ubiquity of American exceptionalist discourse across cultural, political, and social institutions in the United States suggests the myth "is a fundamental, perhaps even primary, characteristic of US political and social culture."

In his historical account of American exceptionalism (and its decline), Pease (2009) argues that the rhetorical evolution of this myth is rooted in twentieth century geopolitics and nationalist discourses that affirmed the global mission of the United States. As he explains, especially during the Cold War, "the interpretive assumptions embedded within this foundational term have supplied American citizens with the images and beliefs that have regulated the production, transmission, and maintenance of their understanding of what it means to be an American" (ibid., p. 8). Intensified declarations of American exceptionalism therefore correspond with the period of time during which baseball was supplanted by football as the most popular sport in the United States. As has been obvious in more recent years, however, baseball's diminished popularity seems only to have reinforced its symbolic "significance as a cultural resource that dramatizes the best hopes of the nation" (Butterworth, 2010, p. 53).

If it is true that political culture in the United States is increasingly characterized by doubts about its exceptionality (Pease, 2009), then we might anticipate this anxiety to be met with nostalgic discourses and ritual performances of, purportedly, distinctly American values. In the case of baseball, "people have been hailing baseball as the very essence of America since the game emerged in the middle of the nineteenth century" (Springwood, 1996, p. 1). In 1856, the *New York Mercury* hailed baseball as the "national pastime," and an 1860 Currier and Ives cartoon referred to it as "The National Game" (Tygiel, 2000, p. 4). By the turn of the twentieth century, the game was fully professionalized and wildly popular. Given its symbolic status, it was also seen as a mechanism for affirming the nation's status as an emerging world power. In his book, *The Empire Strikes Out*, Robert Elias (2010) details the various ways the national pastime projected American identity beyond its national borders. As he observes:

> Predicated on notions of US exceptionalism, it assumed America was superior to all other nations. Baseball soon shared this jingoistic spirit. In his book *America's National Game*, Albert Spalding provided a chauvinistic history of US baseball. America's internal sense of superiority cultivated external visions of how the United States should make the world over in its own image.
>
> *(Elias, 2010, pp. 12–13)*

The figure of Spalding was particularly important, given his role in fashioning the myth that Abner Doubleday invented baseball in 1839 in Cooperstown, New York. As has now been well documented, Spalding organized the Mills Commission, which was charged with discovering the uniquely American origins of the game. Although it is likely Doubleday never even played baseball, let alone invented it, this creation myth was solidified by the discovery of the so-called "Doubleday baseball" in a Cooperstown attic (Springwood, 1996, p. 39). Granting the game a mythic birthplace in the pastoral New York village that was home to a Civil War hero, the Mills Commission concluded definitively, "That Baseball had its origins in the United States" (Lieb, 1950, p. 13). At around the same time, in 1903, the National and American Leagues concluded their seasons with a championship event: the *World* Series. Of course, despite missionary tours that attempted to spread the game across the globe, Major League Baseball was contained to a northeastern region of the United States. As Elias suggests:

> [S]ince various missions had sought to spread the sport around the globe, the "World" Series might have been only a premature label for a hoped-for future. But the name's implications likely went further, reflecting the emerging spirit of the times – outside of baseball. America was already viewing itself as a world player and burgeoning empire. So of course the US baseball championship would also be viewed as the world's baseball championship.
>
> *(Elias, 2010, p. 75)*

Baseball had become a definitive symbol of national pride and, as the United States found itself drawn into the First World War, "The government became an active participant and catalyst in mobilizing the patriotic movement and in promoting a particularly intolerant and authoritarian brand of patriotism" (O'Leary, 1999, p. 221). The national pastime was a prominent vehicle for this mobilization, and the First World War-era witnessed the introduction or expansion of many of the gestures we now accept as commonplace: military personnel and veterans were given free admission to games, uniforms were adorned with American flag patches and red, white, and blue trim, and, during the 1918 World Series, the "Star-Spangled Banner" become a highlight when sung by the crowd during the seventh-inning stretch. Subsequent performances of the song were so popular that Elias (2010, p. 95) suggests baseball could be "given most of the credit" for the successful ratification of the "Star Spangled Banner" as the US national anthem in 1931. By the time that Franklin D. Roosevelt penned his famous "Green Light Letter," in which he urged MLB Commissioner Kenesaw Mountain Landis to preserve the 1942 season, in spite of the attack on Pearl Harbor, it was obvious that the national pastime was inextricably linked with national identity.

Mediatization and ritual

This truncated history omits many details, but it nevertheless captures some of the mythic contours of baseball's articulation with American exceptionalism, many of which continue to resonate in an era defined by the 9/11 attacks and the subsequent responses by the US government and military. Over the course of its history, baseball mythology has been expressed in various ways – for example, literature and film, the canonization of heroic figures in the Hall of Fame, and, of course, media coverage. As Trujillo and Ekdom (1985) suggest, from its earliest days sportswriting was a means to affirm cultural values. Much of that early media content was specifically about baseball mythology, grounded in the effort to "promote the game and its players while commodifying heroes to sell more newspapers" (Roessner, 2009, p. 40). Consistent with this tradition, contemporary sportswriting trades on mythic portrayals of the game and its stars, often through frames that affirm biases regarding white, masculine identity (Butterworth, 2007) or a myopic nostalgia that celebrates baseball's virtues while eliding its historical exclusions (Aden, 1995; Von Burg and Johnson, 2009).

Despite the foundational significance of sportswriting, it is television and, increasingly, online media, that now largely facilitates the ritual production of baseball mythology. Indeed, when we shift our focus from baseball, generally, to the World Series, specifically, television has long defined the relationship between the game and its rituals. As Rowe (2013, p. 65) reminds us, in spite of the substantial influence of the Internet and social media, television "is unquestionably at [the] heart" of the sport/media complex. Jhally (1984) was the first to name something called the "sport/media complex," and subsequent critical scholars have either applied it or, in the case of Wenner's (1998) "mediasport," adapted it. Reflecting on nearly 30 years of scholarship in this tradition, Wenner (2013, p. 83) explains, "In its contemporary hypercommodified form, the ideological contours and ethical sensibilities of the mediasportscape dominate the cultural meanings that are associated with sport." In particular, highly commercialized, visually spectacular sporting events are powerful stages for the rehearsal of communal myths, especially those that express national identity (Rowe, 1999).

The "spectacular" nature of major sporting events has captured the attention of media scholars interested in "mega-events," such as the Olympic Games and World Cup. Roche (2000, p. 1) defines mega-events as "large-scale cultural (including commercial and sporting) events, which have a dramatic character, mass popular appeal and international significance." In keeping with the critical scholarship situated in the mediasportscape literature, Horne and Manzenreiter (2006, p. 1) argue that "sports mega-events and global sport culture are central to late modern capitalist societies," and add that such events have a significant impact on a local city and attract substantial media attention. By this definition, it is not clear whether or not MLB's World Series can be understood as a "mega-event" (certainly, the relatively young World Baseball Classic might). Nevertheless, the scope of and media coverage dedicated to the World Series directs us to similar questions and concerns – mainly, that the heavily mediated, and carefully ritualized, championship series is a compelling rhetoric perform-ance of American myth.

If baseball's World Series complicates the notion of the mega-event, it similarly invites us to pause over judgments made about the changing nature of media. Yes, online streaming, user-generated content, and social media are all transforming the production and consumption of mediated sport; yet, televised baseball continues to depend on mythologies that are heavy on nostalgia. This ambiguity provokes us to consider the production of the World Series in terms of "mediatization," a term in media studies that aims to capture the transitional state of media's evolution. Hjarvard notes an important distinction when he suggests:

> Media and communication research has primarily been occupied with the study of "mediation," that is, the use of media for communicative practices, whereas the study of "mediatization" is concerned with the long-term influence of media on cultural and social structures and agency.
>
> *(Hjarvard, 2016, p. 9)*

Frandsen (2014, p. 530) further emphasizes that mediatization is both a social and historical process, one that is "related to other socio-historical processes like global-ization, individualization, and commercialization." Without question, MLB is engaged in these processes, especially through its efforts to expand its global reach (Klein, 2006). MLB's influence over the World Baseball Classic, for example, recalls baseball's missionary efforts in the late nineteenth and early twentieth centuries. Those expeditions, which "were framed by the mythology of American exception-alism" (Butterworth, 2010, p. 134), are symbolically referenced by efforts to exert control over other nations. Given this legacy, and that the WBC was developed in the midst of the US-led "war on terror," it was no accident that one Japanese official suggested, "This whole thing smacks of imperialism on the part of MLB" (Klein, 2006, p. 246).

As I have detailed above, baseball generally and the World Series specifically have featured the myth of American exceptionalism through conspicuous rituals, including national anthem performances and red, white, and blue decorations. As compelling as these repeated iterations are, it is a moment of disruption that demonstrates how powerfully these rituals can reinforce communal myths. Prior to Game 5 of the 1968 World Series – in the midst of the Vietnam War – Puerto Rican-born singer José Feliciano performed what may have been the first non-traditional interpretation of the national anthem. His soulful, creative rendition seems innocent enough by today's standards, but at a time of intense cultural conflict Feliciano provoked scorn and outrage. For many of the estimated 55 million viewers who watched on television, the performance represented "a patriotic ritual bent to the breaking point" (Zang, 2001, p. 7).

One of the common lessons of the Vietnam War is to be sure never to repeat the "mistakes" made during that era, in which those deemed "unpatriotic" –

whether they be singers or protestors – undermined American resolve at home and in combat. By the 1980s, then, at the height of the Cold War and Reagan's muscular nationalism, this kind of "rhetoric dovetailed with a narrative propagated in the 1980s that suggested Vietnam was lost not on the battlefield but rather on the home front by media, politicians, and protestors" (Stahl, 2010, p. 29). Given this emphasis, it is not surprising that sporting events – from Super Bowl XV in New Orleans, to the Team USA "Dream Team" in the 1992 Olympics, to performances of "God Bless America" in baseball stadiums after 9/11 – have amplified the mythology of American exceptionalism. As I have demonstrated elsewhere, especially in the years since 9/11, ritual enactments of American identity have become commonplace in baseball (and other sports) to the point that they have become "normal" (Butterworth, 2014), consistent with Rowe's observation that myth "demonstrates the power of particular symbols and narratives in expressing widely, unconsciously and deeply held beliefs as 'natural' in any given society" (Rowe, 1999, p. 85).

Media ritual in the World Series

Much suggests that José Feliciano's interpretive anthem performance is now, 48 years later, remembered fondly. Official baseball narratives often tend to work that way – there is no better case than the public memorializing of Jackie Robinson, whose transcendent status from being the first African-American major leaguer in the modern era is commonly used as a symbol of problems no longer relevant to our community; indeed, baseball is celebrated not as an institution that prohibited African-Americans from participating for more than six decades but as the noble institution that "broke the color barrier" that should never have existed in the first place. All of this is to say that baseball mythologizing uses ritual to draw upon the game's rich history and pastoral imagery, to valorize the ideals of "home," and to absorb even the nation's failures into an ultimate story of triumph. In this section, I focus on contemporary examples from the World Series, giving particular focus to the televised coverage that has been controlled by FOX since 2000.

As I have noted, the terrorist attacks of 9/11 elicited dramatic responses from MLB and other sports leagues in the United States. Here, baseball was the first of the major sports to return to play – six days after the attacks. Arguably, however, the definitive mythic moment happened nearly two months later, when President George W. Bush threw out the first pitch during Game 3 of the World Series in Yankee Stadium. This moment has been symbolically linked to President Bush's leadership and the resolve of the nation that it is possible to conclude "baseball not only shaped the Bush administration, it *defined* it" (Butterworth, 2010, p. 5). It has been documented in several places, most recently in an ESPN 30 for 30 short film, *First Pitch*. *Grantland* writer Louisa Thomas (2015) interviewed President Bush about the pitch and the film. Commenting on how those events are remembered, she writes:

For some, memories were fading. Others were too young to remember at all. The way [Bush] described it sheds light on his understanding of American history, American exceptionalism, and American prerogatives in the present day. "There's a whole bunch of people in America now, and there's going to be obviously a lot more as time goes on, that view 9/11 like Pearl Harbor, as a moment and a paragraph in a history book," he went on. "But the problem is that the evil is still real. And so this movie – to the extent that it reminds people about kind of the realities of the world in which we live – is important."

(Thomas, 2015, ¶ 25)

The importance of Bush's first pitch, and its enactment of American exceptionalism, is set in the context of other enhanced patriotic and militaristic rituals. Now, several years after 9/11, some of the fervor has diminished. However, special occasions such as the World Series reveal the continued need for dramatic expressions of American identity. Perhaps the most obvious of these rituals are the performances of the national anthem before the game and "God Bless America" during the seventh-inning stretch. The anthem is the most sacred of the "church of baseball's" hymns, but in the post-9/11 era "God Bless America" seems to have earned almost equal status. The song was seen as so essential to promoting unity that MLB Commissioner Bud Selig mandated in 2002 that it be performed at all games. This is no longer the case, but it is significant that FOX's coverage – and FOX is the only network to have broadcast the World Series since 9/11 – always includes the performance of "God Bless America," whereas typical broadcasts favor commercials over the seventh-inning stretch's usual fare of "Take Me Out to the Ballgame." In addition, the performances provide an endless supply of military personnel and first responders with golden singing voices (perhaps inspired by the widespread praise for New York's Daniel Rodriguez, known as the "singing policeman"; Henson, 2011).

Whereas the national anthem might be sung by a famous musician – John Legend at Game 1 of the 2010 World Series in San Francisco, for example – "God Bless America" always provides a nod to patriotism and militarism. Back in San Francisco for Game 1 of the 2012 World Series, the song was performed by Sergeant Jerry D'Arcy of the San Francisco Police Department; in 2013, Game 6 at Fenway Park, it was the US Air Force Heritage of American Band; and at Game 1 in 2014 at Kaufman Stadium, the crowd heard from Retired Navy Petty Officer First Class, Generald Wilson. In addition, the performances are punctuated by various crowd shots that show flag-waving fans, or live images of military personnel stationed overseas, such as the Combined Joint Task Force 10 at Bagram Airfield in Afghanistan in 2014. More than simply highlighting national identity through a song that is explicitly exceptionalist – "God Bless *America*," after all – the broadcasts also fulfill an important commercial function. Masked in the language of a charitable effort, in both 2013 and 2014 FOX play-by-play analyst Joe Buck announced the efforts of Bank of America to donate $1 million to non-profit organizations that assist veterans, such as the Wounded Warriors Project. The articulation of Bank of America comes both before and after the performance of "God Bless America," thus reinforcing the merger of capitalism and patriotism. The broadcasts feature a range of other symbolic rituals – enormous American flags appear in center field during the national anthem, some games, such as Game 1 in 2010, feature a military flyover, military personnel often appear on the field, and military and political figures throw out ceremonial first pitches.

It is also commonplace to see former players invited for the first pitch ritual. For example, at Game 1 of the 2015 World Series in Kansas City, Royals legend George Brett was on hand for the ritual. The New York Mets countered in Game 3 with their own former great, Mike Piazza. In fact, the mediated production of World Series games commonly features tributes to the game's history. A montage that preceded Game 1 of the 2012 World Series highlighted a number of iconic World Series moments – Willie Mays' over-the-shoulder catch in Game 1 in 1954; Bill Mazeroski's series-winning home run in 1960; Carlton Fisk's game-winning Game 6 home run in 1975. These carefully edited packages lean heavily on baseball nostalgia, honoring a time and place many viewers can remember, perhaps mistakenly, as simpler and happier. The broadcasters themselves routinely fall into similar patterns. In just one example, commentator Harold Reynolds responded to the first at-bat by David Murphy of the Mets in Game 1 of the 2015 World Series, "Regardless of what they try to do, if you've been following the playoffs, you've got to be excited to watch this guy hit. It has been some kind of run. It takes you back to your childhood, Reggie Jackson-type stuff." Anyone with a minimal knowledge of baseball history is likely to recall Jackson's three-home-run perform-ance in Game 6 of the 1977 World Series – the game that cemented his status as "Mr. October." References such as these are built on a repository of baseball memories that celebrate the game and, by extension, the nation. In the words of the film *Field of Dreams* character Terence Mann, baseball "reminds us of all that once was good, and it could be again" (Robinson, 1989).

One additional moment especially emphasizes the ritualistic turn to nostalgia that characterizes even the most contemporary and technologically advanced FOX broadcasts. The 2010 World Series was introduced by a two-minute short film based on a Ken Burns poem called, simply, *Home* (Burns, 2010). Burns's tenth-inning addition to his acclaimed nine-inning documentary, *Baseball*, had been released approximately one month earlier, and the production of his poem evokes the same strands of longing and sentimentality. *Home* is two minutes of unapolo-getic nostalgia: narrative nods to baseball as "timeless," images of children and connections to family, claims to baseball's egalitarian inclusiveness, and cinematography that bathes ballfields in amber waves of sunlight. The narration celebrates the national pastime as "the place we always come back to: home." To be clear, I greatly enjoy the short film, but I also see it as an explicit judgment about baseball's capacity to represent an idealized America. The emphasis of the film is on "home," not as a literal dwelling but as a shared symbolic space, an "imagined community" (Anderson, 1991), a merger of pastime and nation that is unlike any other. From such a view, baseball's nationalist exceptionalism justifies its exception from the mega-event, mediatization landscape. In other words, the game's mythic status alone seems to claim that the rules that govern the production of other mega-events need not apply in the case of America's national pastime.

The decline of exceptionalism?

Former MLB Commissioner Bart Giamatti provides one of the signature romantic interpretations of baseball:

> It breaks your heart. It is designed to break your heart. The game begins in the spring, when everything else begins again, and it blossoms in the summer, filling the afternoons and evenings, and then as soon as the chill rains come, it stops and leaves you to face the fall alone. You count on it, rely on it to buffer the passage of time, to keep the memory of sunshine and high skies alive, and then just when the days are all twilight, when you need it most, it stops. ... And summer [is] gone.
>
> *(Berkow, 1989, ¶1–2)*

This eloquent metaphor for life and death might apply equally well to the nation. In a chapter about American exceptionalism and the recent surge of interest in soccer in the United States, Farred (2013, p. 482) spotlights an apparent irony, suggesting, "In the age of America as a declining imperial power ... the United States is respected in international football circles." Perhaps more striking than the recognition that the US can be taken seriously as a soccer country is the implication that the nation's best days are in the past. Indeed, many Americans fear this to be the case, the "sunshine and high skies" of the American Century have given way to the fall. Some academics (Noble, 2002; Pease, 2009) also conclude that it is no longer possible to define the United States with a discourse of exceptionalism.

Even if we cannot say with certainty that the United States is a nation in decline, we can assuredly say it is in transition. Neoliberal capitalism, globalization, and mediatization have all converged to complicate what once was a fairly simple narrative – the United States, an exceptional nation chosen by God, has achieved the greatest democracy in the history of the planet and brought freedom to millions of others around the globe. That powerful myth has been bolstered by the nation's cultural institutions, not least of which is baseball. Given the game's history, and the ritualized rehearsal of baseball nostalgia, it is no wonder that we see American exceptionalism on display at a rally to celebrate a World Series champion.

Yet, if the national pastime demonstrates mythic resilience in this era of mediatization, then it does so only precariously. After all, during Game 1 of the 2015 World Series, FOX had technical difficulties that resulted in losing the broadcast. As a result, viewers briefly missed the action on the field before the broadcast switched to MLB International coverage. Much of the audience, at least those viewers who also use sites such as Twitter, appeared to prefer the switch (Nathan, 2015). Perhaps the reaction is more a product of fatigue with announcer

Joe Buck than it is a metaphor for a game or nation in decline. Nevertheless, it does highlight the fragility of the current mediasportscape – a global, technologically sophisticated, highly commercialized enterprise, all of which can be diminished by a human mistake or a computer glitch. This is all the more relevant given the twin exceptionalisms of the World Series – both in its persistent mythologizing of American identity in an era of geopolitical change and its marginal status as a mega-event. The World Series thus represents the symbolic possibilities of media ritual and the material limitations of American exceptionalism in a globalized, mediatized world. Indeed, it highlights the precarious state of exception in which Americans find themselves in the early twenty-first century. Increasingly, such uncertainty is as American as a championship parade.

References

Aden, R.C. (1995). Nostalgic communication as temporal escape: *When it was a game's* reconstruction of a baseball/work community. *Western Journal of Communication, 59,* 20–38.

Anderson, B. (1991). *Imagined communities: Reflections on the origin and spread of nationalism.* London: Verso.

Barr, J. (2014). Fox Sports president on future of World Series broadcast. *PoliticoMedia,* October 21. Retrieved from www.capitalnewyork.com/article/media/2014/10/855 4928/fox-sports-president-future-world-series-broadcast (accessed 31 January 2016).

Berkow, I. (1989). The green fields of Bart's mind. *New York Times,* September 2. Retrieved from www.nytimes.com/1989/09/02/sports/sports-of-the-times-the-green-fields-of-bart-s-mind.html (accessed 3 February 2016).

Block, J. (2015). Kansas City Royals' Jonny Gomes delivers patriotic and confrontational World Series victory speech. *Huffington Post,* November 4. Retrieved from www.huffing tonpost.com/entry/kansas-city-royals-jonny-gomes-parade-speech_us_563a0e3ee4 b0b24aee48254b (accessed 30 January 2016).

Burns, K. (2010). *Home.* October 28. Retrieved from http://m.mlb.com/video/topic/ 6479266/v12919391/ken-burns-poem-opens-the-2010-world-series (accessed 29 January 2016).

Butterworth, M.L. (2007). Race in "the race": Mark McGwire, Sammy Sosa, and heroic constructions of whiteness. *Critical Studies in Media Communication, 24,* 228–244.

Butterworth, M.L. (2010). *Baseball and rhetorics of purity: The national pastime and American identity during the war on terror.* Tuscaloosa, AL: University of Alabama Press.

Butterworth, M.L. (2014). Public memorializing in the stadium: Mediated sport, the 10th anniversary of 9/11, and the illusion of democracy. *Communication and Sport, 2,* 203–224.

Couldry, N. (2008). Mediatization or mediation? Alternative understandings of the emergent space of digital storytelling. *New Media and Society, 10,* 373–391.

Deacon, D. and Stayner, J. (2014). Mediatization: Key concept or conceptual bandwagon? *Media, Culture and Society, 36,* 1032–1044.

Elias, R. (2010). *The empire strikes out: How baseball sold US foreign policy and promoted the American way abroad.* New York: New Press.

Farred, G. (2013). To be like everyone else, only better: The U.S. men's football team and the World Cup. In D.L. Andrews and B. Carrington (eds), *A companion to sport* (pp. 481–492). Malden, MA: Wiley Blackwell.

Fisher, W. (1984). Narration as human communication paradigm: The case of public moral argument. *Communication Monographs, 51*, 1–22.

Frandsen, K. (2014). Mediatization of sports. In K. Lundby (ed.), *Mediatization of communication* (pp. 525–543). Berlin: Mouton de Gruyter.

Hart, R. (1990). *Modern rhetorical criticism*. Glenview, IL: Scott Foresman.

Henson, S. (2011). Singing tenors helped healing process, one 7th-inning stretch at a time. *Yahoo! Sports*, September 5. Retrieved from www.yahoo.com/news/9-11-mlb-ronan-tynan-daniel-rodriguez-god-bless-america.html (accessed 20 June 2016).

Hjarvard, S. (2013). *The mediatization of culture and society*. London: Routledge.

Hjarvard, S. (2016). Mediatization and the changing authority of religion. *Media, Culture and Society, 38*, 8–17.

Horne, J. and Manzenreiter, W. (eds) (2006). *Sports mega-events: Social scientific analyses of a global phenomenon*. Oxford: Blackwell.

Hughes, R. (2004). *Myths America lives by*. Urbana, IL: University of Illinois Press.

Hutchins, B. (2016). "We don't need no stinkin' smartphones!" Live stadium sports events, mediatization, and the non-use of mobile media. *Media, Culture and Society, 38*, 420–436.

Jhally, S. (1984). The spectacle of accumulation: Material and cultural factors in the evolution of the sports/media complex. *Insurgent Sociologist, 12*, 41–57.

Johnson, V.E. (2008). *Heartland TV: Prime time television and the struggle for US identity*. New York: New York University Press.

Klein, A.M. (2006). *Growing the game: The globalization of major league baseball*. New Haven, CT: Yale University Press.

Lieb, F.G. (1950). *The baseball story*. New York: G.P. Putnam's Sons.

Lipset, S.M. (1996). *American exceptionalism: A double-edged sword*. New York: W.W. Norton & Co.

Motter, J. (2010). American exceptionalism and the rhetoric of humanitarian militarism: The case of the 2004 Indian Ocean tsunami relief effort. *Communication Studies, 61*, 507–525.

Nathan, A. (2015). Twitter reacts to World Series Game 1 delay due to Fox technical issues. *Bleacher Report*, October 27. Retrieved from http://bleacherreport.com/articles/25834 63-twitter-reacts-to-world-series-game-1-delay-due-to-fox-technical-issues (accessed 29 January 2016).

Newman, M. (2012). MLB reaches eight-year agreement with FOX, Turner. *MLB.com*, October 2. Retrieved from http://m.mlb.com/news/article/39362362 (accessed 31 January 2016).

Noble, D.W. (2002). *Death of a nation: American culture and the end of exceptionalism*. Minneapolis, MN: University of Minnesota Press.

O'Leary, C.E. (1999). *To die for: The paradox of American patriotism*. Princeton, NJ: Princeton University Press.

Pease, D.E. (2009). *The new American exceptionalism*. Minneapolis, MN: University of Minnesota Press.

Real, M.R. (1989). *Super media: A cultural studies approach*. Newbury Park, CA: Sage.

Robertson, J.O. (1980). *American myth, American reality*. New York: Hill & Wang.

Robinson, P.A. (director and writer). (1989). *Field of dreams* [movie]. Hollywood, CA: Universal Pictures.

Roche, M. (2000). *Mega-events and modernity*. London: Routledge.

Roessner, L.A. (2009). Hero crafting in *Sporting Life*, an early baseball journal. *American Journalism, 26*, 39–65.

Rowe, D. (1999). *Sport, culture, and the media: The unruly trinity*. Buckingham: Open University Press.

Rowe, D. (2013). The sport/media complex: Formation, flowering, and future. In D.L. Andrews and B. Carrington (eds), *A companion to sport* (pp. 61–77). Malden, MA: Wiley Blackwell.

Rushing, J.H. (1989). Evolution of "The New Frontier" in *Alien* and *Aliens*: Patriarchal co-optation of the feminine archetype. *Quarterly Journal of Speech, 75*, 1–24.

Springwood, C.F. (1996). *Cooperstown to Dyersville: A geography of baseball nostalgia.* Boulder, CO: Westview Press.

Stahl, R. (2010). *Militainment, inc.: War, media, and popular culture.* New York: Routledge.

Thomas, L. (2015). The pitch. *Grantland*, September 11. Retrieved from http://grantland.com/features/the-pitch (accessed 3 February 2016).

Trujillo, N. and Ekdom, L.R. (1985). Sportswriting and American cultural values: The 1984 Chicago Cubs. *Critical Studies in Mass Communication, 2*, 262–281.

Tygiel, J. (2000). *Past time: Baseball as history.* Oxford: Oxford University Press.

Von Burg, R. and Johnson, P.E. (2009). Yearning for a past that never was: Baseball, steroids, and the anxiety of the American dream. *Critical Studies in Media Communication, 26*, 351–371.

Weiss, D. and Edwards, J.A. (2011). Introduction: American exceptionalism's champions and challengers. In J.A. Edwards and D. Weiss (eds), *The rhetoric of American exceptionalism: Critical essays* (pp. 1–10). Jefferson, NC: McFarland.

Wenner, L.A. (ed.) (1998). *MediaSport.* London: Routledge.

Wenner, L.A. (2013). The mediasport interpellation: Gender, fanship, and consumer culture. *Sociology of Sport Journal, 30*, 83–103.

Zang, D.W. (2001). *Sportswars: Athletes in the age of aquarius.* Fayetteville, AR: University of Arkansas Press.

16

THE NCAA BASKETBALL CHAMPIONSHIPS

March Madness goes global

Bryan E. Denham

On March 19, 1966, one of the most important sporting events of the twentieth century took place in Cole Field House at the University of Maryland. The event, the NCAA men's basketball championship game, featured an all-White Kentucky Wildcat team coached by Adolph Rupp against a predominantly Black Texas Western squad, coached by Don Haskins. Played less than 2 years after US President Lyndon Johnson signed the Civil Rights Act of 1964, and 2 years prior to the assassination of civil rights leader Martin Luther King, Jr., the athletic contest would come to symbolize the struggle of Black Americans to be recognized and respected as members of a racial minority. As author Frank Fitzpatrick (1999) recalled, sportswriters had expected a highly disciplined Kentucky team to defeat Texas Western by using sound fundamentals on both the offensive and defensive ends. In contrast, writers expected Texas Western to play an undisciplined "run-and-gun" type of game that would ultimately prove no match for the seasoned Wildcats. But as Fitzpatrick recounted, Texas Western played with poise and focus, its guards walking the ball up the court, controlling the pace and leading the Miners to a 72–65 victory over the heavily favored Wildcats. Future professional coach Pat Riley, a member of the Kentucky team, referred to the championship game as the "Emancipation Proclamation of 1966" (Fitzpatrick, 1999, p. 25).

Indeed, the Miner victory transcended Cole Field House and empowered Black Americans during a time of social unrest in the United States. College basketball had been a segregated sport in the American South (Martin, 1993; Smith, Kilgo, and Jenkins, 1999), with Rupp, in particular, refusing to recruit Black athletes. But, as Riley noted, Texas Western recorded an historic victory, and the Miners made a bold statement in the process: Provided an even playing field (or court), Black athletes could perform as well as – or better than – White athletes. For helping to prove that point, Haskins received some 40,000 pieces of hate mail (Price, 1991).

The year 2016 marked the 50th anniversary of the Kentucky–Texas Western championship game, and while the outcome of that contest represented a turning point in sport and society, relatively few people actually saw it. As Fitzpatrick (2003) noted, "Its starting time was 10:00 p.m. [EST], it wasn't covered by a major network, and it was televised only on a taped-delayed basis in several American cities." Much of its impact occurred the following day, as news of the outcome spread through word of mouth. ESPN and other sports networks did not exist, nor did the Internet and cellular phone applications. Viewing segments of the 1966 contest on YouTube, one observes grainy black-and-white footage of a bygone era. Moviegoers did get to experience a dramatization of the championship game when Buena Vista Pictures distributed the 2006 film *Glory Road* to movie theaters nationwide.

In the five decades since the Kentucky–Texas Western contest, NCAA basketball tourneys have grown into mega media events. Roche (2000) suggested such events contain at least three elements: Drama, mass popular appeal, and international significance (see also, Giulianotti *et al.*, 2015; Horne and Manzenreiter, 2006; Maennig and Zimbalist, 2012). "March Madness," an all-encompassing term used to promote NCAA basketball tournaments, contains each element Roche identified; live-action games offer drama to millions of basketball fans throughout the nation and the world (see, for general discussion, Feinstein, 1998, 2006). In 2015, an average of 28.3 million viewers in the United States watched Duke defeat Wisconsin to win its fifth national championship in men's college basketball, with an average of 33.4 million tuning in during the final moments of the CBS broadcast (Pallotta, 2015). The average audience of 28.3 million made the 2015 contest the most-watched championship game in 18 years. As CNN reported (ibid.), NCAA March Madness Live, the tournament streaming application, generated 80.7 million live video streams, and among social media, more than 350 million impressions appeared on Facebook and Twitter (a 45 percent increase over 2014). ESPN International televised the 2015 Men's Final Four in 179 countries and territories across 26 networks outside the United States (Humes, 2015). On the women's side, the 2015 national championship game between Connecticut and Notre Dame drew 3.1 million viewers (Paulsen, 2015), with the ESPN family of networks carrying all 63 games of the tournament (Siegal, 2015). ESPN International offered Final Four coverage through ESPN2 Australia, ESPN Brazil HD, ESPN Caribbean, ESPN Latin North, ESPN Tres North, ESPN Tres South, and ESPN UK. ESPN also used social media to supplement coverage of the 2015 Women's Final Four (ibid.).

The overall impact of March Madness can be observed through its annual *advertising effect*, which Smith (2008, p. 387) explained as "a successful branding in which the college or university has been able to translate its sporting prowess into tangible benefits for the school's academic mission." McCormick and Tinsley (1987) initiated this area of study, observing a positive relationship between athletic success and quality of academics. Pope and Pope (2009, 2014) found that success in college sports, including appearances in NCAA basketball tournaments, leads to an increase in student applications. This appears especially true among males,

African-Americans, out-of-state students, and students who played sports in high school. Toma and Cross (1998) had previously observed slight increases in applications following a championship season in basketball, with Mixon (1995) finding a positive relationship between basketball success and Scholastic Aptitude Test (SAT) scores. Rishe (2003) found that athletic success helped to predict graduation rates among student-athletes and other undergraduates; Trenkamp (2009) observed an association between basketball success and academic rankings; and Baade and Sundberg (1996) found a positive relationship between basketball tournament appearances and gifts to public universities. Getz and Siegfried (2010) summarized the direct and indirect benefits associated with athletic success.

Although some studies have not observed advertising effects (Bremmer and Kesselring, 1993; Smith, 2008; Tucker, 2004), March Madness does offer universities national exposure; as sportswriter John Feinstein (2006) pointed out, more than 1,400 credentialed journalists cover the men's Final Four basketball championships. Additionally, participation in March Madness offers universities video content for promotional efforts. As Rowe (2004, p. 74) explained, "Media sports texts are particularly valuable assets because of their flexibility and interconnectedness. A single sports 'live' TV broadcast can be shown in 'real time' and endlessly afterwards, and can be cut up and packaged in myriad ways." Universities often "cut up" broadcast material for use in promotional messages, and as Depken (2010) explained, success (and mediated reinforcement of success) often proves contagious, resulting in larger numbers of attendees at subsequent sporting events. The NCAA also benefits, as TV revenues from the men's tournament, in particular, play a significant role in the financial stability of the organization (Mondello, 2006, p. 292).

This chapter examines March Madness as a mega media event that includes both male and female athletes performing in the elite ranks of sport. The chapter explains how the men's and women's NCAA tournaments have contributed to the global expansion of basketball, which in turn has impacted the rosters of teams that compete each year, and by extension, the content of televised sport. Mediatization, conceptualized here as a process in which media treatment of an event influences perceptions of the social reality surrounding it (see Frandsen, 2014), in turn impacting future iterations of the event itself, offers theoretical guidance.

Mediatization

In the United States, individuals frequently attend sporting events in person, but those living in other parts of the world may experience such events solely through media channels. Before mass media offered international telecasts of college basketball, and long before the Internet allowed international audiences to stream sporting events held in the United States, audiences abroad had little access to major US competitions. International athletes could read about what happened at a US sporting event, but they could not watch live action, limiting their ability to emulate elite athletes. With advancements in technology, spatial distances have become less important, as individuals in London, England can watch the same sporting events as individuals in London, Kentucky.

Schulz (2004) discussed mediatization in the context of social change, suggesting that media engage in *extension, substitution, amalgamation* and *accommodation*. Schulz observed that human communication is limited by factors such as space and time, but mass media have the capacity to extend communication – "to bridge spatial and temporal distances" (ibid., p. 88). Regarding substitution, Schulz argued that media coverage of an event changes its character; especially pertinent to the current chapter is the capacity of media to assign symbolic meaning to a major sporting competition. As an example, scholars have observed intersections between medi- ated sport and patriotism (see Butterworth, 2014), and March Madness symbolizes pursuit of the American dream through its implicit message that anyone can achieve success through dedication and hard work. In NCAA basketball tourna- ments, teams from conferences that receive little national exposure (e.g., Horizon, Patriot League, Sun Belt, and Colonial Athletic Association) compete against teams representing major conferences such as the Atlantic Coast Conference (ACC), the Big Ten, the Big East, and the Pac-12.

To qualify for an NCAA basketball tournament, a team must win its conference tournament or receive an at-large bid. In recent years, the men's tournament has added four "play-in" games, with four teams from smaller conferences and the four lowest-ranked at-large teams competing to advance in the field of 64. Teams competing at this stage hope to become "Cinderellas," arriving at "The Dance" amid modest expectations but then overachieving and advancing past the initial rounds of play. Cinderella teams tend to appear more frequently in the men's tournament, largely because of parity among teams. In women's college basketball, a relatively small number of teams (i.e., Connecticut, Tennessee, Baylor) have dominated the game for the past three decades (see Hersh, 2015). In fact, in the twenty-first century, Connecticut had won the national championship nine times by the time of this writing.

Amateur basketball players worldwide observe male and female NCAA athletes competing for championships before thousands of fans, receiving adulation in the press, and signing lucrative professional contracts. Not surprisingly, many foreign- born athletes seek to emulate and ultimately join their NCAA counterparts by receiving a scholarship and attempting to play professionally. In this context, mediatization intersects conceptually with globalization, which, Maguire (2006, p. 436) explained, can be understood as "The flow of leisure styles, customs, and practices from one part of the world to another."

According to Schulz (2004), mediated reality and social reality tend to merge, or amalgamate, through processes of mediatization. "For example," Schulz noted, "we listen to the radio while driving, read the newspaper in the metro, watch television during dinner, and have a date at the movies" (ibid., p. 89). Regarding March Madness, in particular, labor analyses reveal that employers stand to lose as much as $1.9 billion in wages during the respective tournaments, with some 60 million individuals viewing at least some tourney action while at work (Bukszpan, 2015). In

2015, Purdum (2015) reported, the American Gaming Association estimated that 40 million individuals would complete as many as 70 million tournament brackets, with total wagers expected to exceed $9 billion (see also Real, 2013, p. 35).

Lastly, Schulz (2004) suggested, mass media require accommodation from economic and political actors, who are often dependent on media representations (see also Giulianotti *et al.*, 2015). Regarding participation, NCAA policies concerning eligibility among international athletes have undergone significant change, as have processes for obtaining student visas (see Greer, 2013; Kosmider, 2014); both have facilitated greater participation among athletes born in other nations. In the 1990s, the NCAA imposed restrictions on athletes who had been involved with international basketball academies, but after clarifications on the definition of "amateur," officials later relaxed certain standards for participation, allowing more athletes to compete in the United States.

Growing the game

Data gathered by the NCAA show appreciable increases in "nonresident alien basketball student-athletes" during the first decade of the twenty-first century and into the second.[1] From the 1999–2000 season to the 2014–2015 campaign, foreign-born male competitors increased from 3.0 to 7.1 percent in Division I basketball. In 1999–2000, 140 foreign-born male athletes competed in Division I, compared to 358 in 2014–2015. Combining Division I frequencies with those from Divisions II and III, 272 male athletes competed in 1999–2000 compared to 692 foreign-born basketball players in 2014–2015. Among females, from 1999–2000 to 2014–2015, foreign-born competitors increased from 2.6 percent ($n = 110$) to 5.1 percent ($n = 236$) in Division I basketball. Combining Division I frequencies with those from Divisions II and III, 173 female athletes competed in 1999–2000 compared to 388 foreign-born female basketball players in 2014–2015. Thus, among both males and females, foreign-born basketball players more than doubled across the two time periods.

Figure 16.1 provides a conceptual representation of how mediated sport, in this case March Madness, can influence perceptions of US college basketball among international athletes, and how international athletes who ultimately enroll and succeed in college basketball affect the content of the televised package and implicitly encourage additional international athletes to pursue college sports in the United States. The model positions established international players as role models for rising athletes, some of whom will develop skills strong enough for Division I basketball. Rising athletes may receive significant press coverage in their home nations and they also may use available technology such as YouTube to create highlight videos for coaches and scouts. Based on their needs (i.e., guards, forwards or centers), coaches may recruit athletes they observe through media channels. In fact, outlets such as ESPN and the *New York Times* have reported on how college basketball coaches have used new media such as YouTube, as well as social media platforms such as Facebook and Twitter, to gain an edge in both national and international recruiting (Medcalf, 2012; Thamel, 2011). Some recruits will join US college basketball teams and become established players, continuing the cycle in Figure 16.1. As discussed below, athletes from Africa and Europe helped to set this process in motion.

Before starring with the Houston Rockets in the National Basketball Association (NBA), Hakeem Olajuwon played in three Final Fours with the University of Houston Cougars, becoming a consensus All-American in 1984. In the early 1980s, relatively few players in major college basketball had been born in other parts of the world, and until Olajuwon appeared on the court, virtually none had become superstars. But Olajuwon, who had emigrated from Lagos, Nigeria, altered that pattern, arriving in the United States alone, developing a basketball skill set, and eventually proving himself a standout on the court. As he recalled in his autobiography (Olajuwon and Knobler, 1996), the change in cultures proved challenging, in part because few individuals had chosen a similar athletic path.

Indeed, during the 1980s, just two additional athletes from African nations played college basketball in the United States. Born in what is now South Sudan, 7'7" Manute Bol played the 1984–1985 season at the University of Bridgeport in

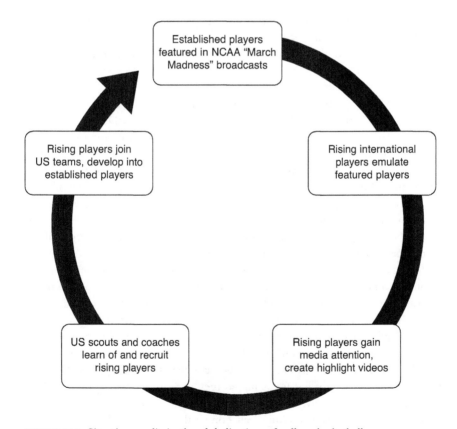

FIGURE 16.1 Situating media in the globalization of college basketball

Connecticut before joining the Washington Bullets in the National Basketball Association. From the Democratic Republic of Congo, Dikembe Mutombo played for the Georgetown Hoyas from 1988 to 1991 and also enjoyed success as an eight-time NBA All-Star. As Washburn (2015) pointed out, Olajuwon, Bol and Mutombo demonstrated that basketball players from African nations could compete at the highest levels in the United States, and in fact more than 30 players from African countries have now reached the NBA, including recent top-ten draft picks Jahlil Okafor (Duke) and Victor Oladipo (Indiana).

Shifting continents, Detlef Schrempf emigrated from Leverkusen, (West) Germany to Washington state in 1980, arriving in time for his senior year of high school. Schrempf then played basketball at the University of Washington from 1981 until 1985, reaching the NCAA Sweet 16 in 1984. Following his collegiate career, he played 16 seasons in the NBA, making the All-Star team three times. Country-man Christian Welp played at Washington from 1983 until 1987, combining with Schrempf for two Pac-10 regular-season titles. A third German athlete, Uwe Blab, born in Munich, played at Indiana University from 1981 until 1985, helping the Hoosiers reach the NCAA Elite Eight in 1984. Upward of 35 athletes from Germany have now competed in US college basketball, with most appearing after Schrempf and others demonstrated that success could be achieved. Athletes in other Western and Eastern European nations have followed suit, as have athletes from Asia, Australia and South America. When the University of Connecticut won the men's national championship in 2014, its roster included two players from Germany, one from Ghana, and one from Jamaica.

Discussing the impact of international athletes on US college basketball, Kosmider (2014) noted that Metropolitan State University in Denver, Colorado boasted 6′10″ Bounama Keita from Senegal. Observing a role for mass media, Kosmider noted "Bounama Keita's older brother, Baye Moussa Keita, played at Syracuse, and Bounama marveled at being able to see so many of his brother's games on ESPN." International broadcasts of US sporting events have allowed athletes such as Bounama Keita to emulate players who appear on television and, in some instances, on Internet sites such as YouTube. As indicated, athletes overseas frequently post highlight videos on YouTube, demonstrating their athletic abilities for coaches in the United States. In this regard, a basketball player in Africa may watch and emulate a certain player during the course of a season, learning to model the athlete on both the offensive and defensive ends of the court; at a certain point, the player may post a highlight video online, seeking to attract the attention of a coach. As Kazadi (2013) reported, Arizona Western women's coach Patrick Cunningham landed Congolese recruits Emilie Muanandibu and Lisette Longomo after observing their abilities on YouTube.

Although international athletes have not competed in the upper echelon of women's college basketball as frequently as they have in the men's game, foreign-born players certainly have not been absent. As an example, Russian forward Svetlana Abrosimova won All-American honors three times at the University of Connecticut, helping to lead UConn to a national championship in 2000

(Auriemma and MacMullan, 2006). At Baylor University in Waco, Texas, coach Kim Mulkey recruited Sophia Young, who became an All-American at Baylor, from Evangel Christian School in Shreveport, Louisiana, where Young had been a foreign exchange student (Mulkey and May, 2007). Mulkey also recruited Abiola Wabara from Parma, Italy, and both Young and Wabara contributed to Baylor's 2005 NCAA national championship. Advancing 10 years to the women's national championship game in 2015, Canadian guard Kia Nurse contributed a tenth national championship for the UConn Huskies. As Brady (2015) reported, 20 Canadian athletes competed in the 2015 women's national basketball tournament.

While the women's basketball program at the University of Idaho has not received as much acclaim as the program at UConn, it recently became one of four universities with at least seven international basketball players on one team (Idaho Athletics, 2015). Athletes from three continents and five countries appeared on its 2014–2015 roster, with four of those players from Australia. Other team members came from Bosnia, Norway and Spain.

International athletes on "Sweet 16" rosters in 2015

Men's tournament

Table 16.1 identifies international athletes who competed in the 2015 men's "Sweet 16." As the table indicates, athletes came from the following countries and territories: Australia, Austria, the Bahamas, Canada, Egypt, Estonia, France, Germany, Hungary, Kenya, Lithuania, Nigeria, Norway, Poland, Puerto Rico, and Serbia. In addition to home nation, the table also includes the height of each player and his position on the court, giving rise to quantitative analyses of professional basketball in the United States, specifically the National Basketball Association (NBA). Scholars have examined increases in foreign-born players from the standpoint of economics and markets, with height, in particular, conceived as a scarce resource (see Eschker, Perez, and Siegler, 2004; Lee and Berri, 2008). As Berri *et al.* (2005, p. 1037) noted, "For the 2003–04 season, nineteen players who were at least seven feet tall played substantial minutes in the NBA. Of these, nine, or 47 percent, were born in a country other than the United States."

Examining Table 16.1, it appears that multiple teams in the elite ranks of men's college basketball recruited international athletes to play center or power forward. Although schools such as Gonzaga and Utah boast strong programs, they may not attract as many US high-school stars as perennial basketball powerhouses do. From a media standpoint, games that begin at 8:00 p.m. in the Western United States do not start until 11:00 p.m. in the East, well after ESPN and other sports networks have covered basketball scores for primetime audiences. Fewer recruits in Eastern and Midwestern population centers may view games in the West, and even fewer may consider the programs viable options. Friends and family might have to travel 2,000 miles to watch a game in person. Accordingly, in some cases, coaches at schools such as Gonzaga and Utah may follow the lead of the NBA and search the international

TABLE 16.1 International players on 2015 "Sweet 16" teams in NCAA men's basketball

Team	Players
Arizona	Dusan Ristic, 7-0 center, Novi Sad, Serbia
Duke	Sean Obi, 6-9 forward, Kaduna, Nigeria
Gonzaga	Kevin Pangos, 6-2 guard, Holland Landing, Ontario, Canada
	Domantas Sabonis, 6-10 forward, Kaunas, Lithuania
	Przemek Karnowski, 7-1 center, Torun, Poland
	Dustin Triano, 6-3 guard, Vancouver, British Columbia, Canada
Louisville	Matz Stockman, 7-0 center, Oslo, Norway
	Mangok Mathiang, 6-10 center, Melbourne, Australia
	Anas Mahmoud, 7-0 forward, Cairo, Egypt
Michigan State	Lourawls Nairn, Jr., 5-10 guard, Nassau, Bahamas
Notre Dame	Eric Katenda, 6-9 forward, Paris, France
	Martinas Geben, 6-9 forward, Vilnius, Lithuania
Oklahoma	Buddy Hield, 6-4 guard, Freeport, Bahamas
	Dinjiyl Walker, 6-1 guard, Vaughan, Ontario, Canada
Utah	Dallin Bachynski, 7-0 center, Calgary, Alberta, Canada
	Kenneth Ogbe, 6-6 guard, Munich, Germany
	Jakob Poeltl, 7-0 forward, Vienna, Austria
West Virginia	Gary Browne, 6-1 guard, San Juan, Puerto Rico
Wichita State	Rauno Nurger, 6-10 center, Keila, Estonia
	Tom Wamukota, 6–11 center, Bungoma, Kenya
UCLA	Gyorgy Goloman, 6-10 forward, Kormend, Hungary
	Jonah Bolden, 6–10 guard, Sydney, Australia

Note: Teams that did not list international players on rosters included Kentucky, North Carolina, North Carolina State, Wisconsin, and Xavier.

talent pool for athletes at a certain position. Teams such as Kentucky and North Carolina can select the best high-school players in the United States, many of whom grew up dreaming of becoming a Wildcat or a Tar Heel. International players tend to be less selective; many of these athletes may have grown up dreaming of competing in the United States, and plenty of schools apart from Kentucky and North Carolina offer strong competition and exposure before professional scouts.

But sometimes even the most elite programs cannot escape market forces. For instance, in the United States, athletes cannot compete in the NBA until they have played at least one season at the college level (or until they have reached age 19). This "one and done" rule allows exceptional athletes to consider the college game a type of prep school for professional basketball. In 2015, a record seven underclassmen from the University of Kentucky entered the NBA draft (Associated Press, 2015), leaving Coach John Calipari with relatively few players. Calipari looked to the global talent pool and added four international players to his roster for 2015–2016: Isaac Humphries, a 7'0" forward from Sydney, Australia; Skal Labissiere, a

6'11" forward from Port-au-Prince, Haiti; Mychal Mulder, a 6'4" guard from Windsor, Canada; and Jamal Murray, a 6'4" guard from Kitchener, Canada. For Calipari, recruiting foreign-born athletes made the task of replacing seven stars less daunting.

Indeed, with foreign-born players capable of competing at the Division I level, the recruiting pool has increased to a point at which nearly constant turnover does not prove disruptive. With NCAA basketball games viewable worldwide, international athletes can study and emulate international players who compete in the elite ranks, demonstrating that opportunities exist for those with the necessary skill sets. To wit, more than three decades after Hakeem Olajuwon arrived at the University of Houston, Ikenna Okwarabizie, also from Lagos, Nigeria, joined the storied basketball program at UCLA.

Women's tournament

Table 16.2 identifies international athletes who competed in the 2015 women's "Sweet 16." As the table indicates, athletes came from the following nations: Australia, Canada, Croatia, France, Germany, and Spain. Foreign-born players appeared most frequently on teams such as Dayton, Florida State and Gonzaga, showing a pattern similar to the men's rosters in Table 16.1. While few would dismiss the accomplishments of these teams, the rosters of perennial champions Connecticut, Tennessee and Notre Dame contained no foreign-born athletes apart from Connecticut guard Kia Nurse. Regarding player position, international athletes played center or power forward on five of the seven teams with foreign-born talent, and 10 of the 16 athletes included in Table 16.2 stood at least 6'0" tall. The three players at Dayton were 6'3", 6'4" and 6'5".

Examining the rosters of the 2015 Sweet 16 teams the following season, Florida State added Maria Conde, from Madrid, Spain, as well as Rachel Antoniadou, from Ripplebrook, Victoria, Australia, giving the team five international players. Additionally, four teams that included no foreign-born athletes in the 2015 tournament – Duke, South Carolina, Stanford and Texas – each added at least one international player. Thus, in the aggregate, while women's rosters include fewer international players, Division I coaches are clearly interested in foreign-born talent, especially from Australia, Canada and Germany.

Concluding comments

Positioning March Madness as a mega media event, this chapter considered international coverage of NCAA college basketball tournaments as a contributor to global expansion of the sport. March Madness, the chapter suggested, influences perceptions of US college basketball among international athletes, some of whom will eventually play in the United States and, in doing so, affect televised sport content. International athletes who excel implicitly (and sometimes explicitly) encourage additional foreign-born athletes to pursue college basketball

TABLE 16.2 International players on 2015 "Sweet 16" teams in NCAA women's basketball

Team	Players
Arizona State University	Isidora Purkovic, 5-11 guard, Calgary, Alberta, Canada Quinn Dornstauder, 6-4 center, Regina, Saskatchewan, Canada
Baylor	Kristy Wallace, 5-11 guard, Loganholme, Queensland, Australia
Florida State University	Adut Bulgak, 6-4 center, Edmonton, Alberta, Canada Ama Degbeon, 6-2 center, Grunberg, Germany Leticia Romero, 5-8 guard, Las Palmas, Spain
Gonzaga	Kacie Bosch, 5-9 guard, Lethbridge, Alberta, Canada Georgia Stirton, 5-8 guard, Melbourne, Australia Emma Wolfram, 6-5 center, Kamloops, British Columbia, Canada Sunny Greinacher, 6-4 forward, Essen, Germany Emma Stach, 5-9 guard, Buchholz, Germany
University of Connecticut	Kia Nurse, 6-0 guard, Hamilton, Ontario, Canada
University of Dayton	Andrijana Cvitkovic, 6-3 forward, Kraljevica, Croatia Jodie Cornelie-Sigmundova, 6-4 center, Strasbourg, France Saicha Grant-Allen, 6-5 center, Hamilton, Ontario, Canada
University of Iowa	Christina Buttenham, 6-0 forward, Hamilton, Ontario, Canada

Note: Teams that did not list international players on rosters included Duke, Stanford, Louisville, Maryland, North Carolina, Notre Dame, South Carolina, Tennessee, and Texas.

opportunities in the United States, and the cycle remains in motion. The chapter discussed this process in the context of mediatization, conceptualized as a process in which media treatment of an event influences perceptions of the social reality surrounding it, in turn impacting future iterations of the event itself.

Of course, one should appreciate that coaches and other recruiters log thousands of miles visiting players in countries throughout the world, and the enterprise of college basketball does not rely solely on media portrayals of NCAA tournaments. Scouting trips remain popular and allow coaches to evaluate players in person. Still, with international athletes posting highlight reels on YouTube and coaches staying in touch with athletes via social media outlets such as Facebook and Twitter, the impact of media on college basketball recruiting and actual performance seems apparent. In terms of recruiting, media channels provide both recruits and their prospective coaches with communicative options, as Medcalf (2012) noted in an article for ESPN: "A shy kid may not like to talk on the phone. Another prospect might prefer phone calls because he's sick of letters. And some kids just want to see a direct message in their Twitter inboxes."

Overall, increased international participation in college basketball has expanded the recruiting pool and has the potential to increase parity in competition. Universities that may not attract the very best players in the United States may recruit exceptional players from overseas, as shown by the impressive number of athletes identified in Tables 16.1 and 16.2. Many of these international athletes played key roles in guiding teams to the NCAA tournaments in 2015, making them role models for additional athletes. The cycle continues.

Note

1   The NCAA provides an online database for identifying statistical trends in collegiate sports. The database can be accessed at http://web1.ncaa.org/rgdSearch/exec/saSearch. Allowing for random variation, percentages generally moved along a linear ascent for both male and female foreign-born basketball players.

References

Associated Press (2015). Kentucky breaks record with seven players declaring for NBA draft. Fox Sports, April 9. Retrieved from www.foxsports.com/college-basketball/story/kentucky-wildcats-break-record-with-seven-players-declaring-for-nba-draft-040915 (accessed 24 November 2016).

Auriemma, G. and MacMullan, J. (2006). *Geno: In pursuit of perfection*. New York: Warner Books.

Baade, R.A. and Sundberg, J.O. (1996). Fourth down and gold to go? Assessing the link between athletics and alumni giving. *Social Science Quarterly*, 77, 789–803.

Berri, D.J., Brook, S.L., Frick, B., Fenn, A.J. and Vicente-Mayoral, R. (2005). The short supply of tall people: Competitive imbalance and the National Basketball Association. *Journal of Economic Issues*, 39, 1029–1041.

Brady, R. (2015). UConn freshman charges way to the top. *The Globe and Mail*, April 4, p. 56.

Bremmer, D.S. and Kesselring, R.G. (1993). The advertising effect of university athletic success: A reappraisal of the evidence. *Quarterly Review of Economics and Finance*, 33, 409–421. doi:10.1016/1062-9769(93)90006-6

Bukszpan, D. (2015). Guess how much money employers lose during March Madness. *Fortune*, March 13. Retrieved from http://fortune.com/2015/03/13/march-madness-employers-lost-productivity (accessed 24 November 2016).

Butterworth, M.L. (2014). Public memorializing in the stadium: Mediated sport, the 10th anniversary of 9/11, and the illusion of democracy. *Communication and Sport*, 2, 203–224. doi:10.1177/2167479513485735

Depken, C.A., II. (2010). Is March Madness contagious? Post-season play and attendance in NCAA Division I basketball. In L.H. Kahane and S. Shmanske (eds), *The Oxford handbook of sports economics, Volume I: The economics of sports* (pp. 373–399). Oxford: Oxford University Press.

Eschker, E., Perez, S.J. and Siegler, M.V. (2004). The NBA and the influx of international basketball players. *Applied Economics*, 36, 1009–1020. doi:10.1080/00036840420002 46713

Feinstein, J. (1998). *A march to madness: The view from the floor in the Atlantic Coast Conference*. Boston, MA: Little, Brown & Company.

Feinstein, J. (2006). *Last dance: Behind the scenes at the Final Four*. New York: Little, Brown & Company.

Fitzpatrick, F. (1999). *And the walls came tumbling down: Kentucky, Texas Western, and the game that changed American sports*. New York: Simon & Schuster.

Fitzpatrick, F. (2003). Texas Western's 1966 title left lasting legacy. *ESPN Classic*, November 19. Retrieved from http://espn.go.com/classic/s/013101_texas_ western_fitzpatrick.html (accessed 24 November 2016).

Frandsen, K. (2014). Mediatization of sports. In K. Lundby (ed.), *Mediatization of communication* (pp. 525–543). Berlin: Mouton de Gruyter.

Getz, M. and Siegfried, J. (2010). What does intercollegiate athletics do to or form colleges and universities? In L.H. Kahane and S. Shmanske (eds), *The Oxford handbook of sports economics, volume I: The economics of sports* (pp. 349–372). Oxford: Oxford University Press.

Giulianotti, R., Armstrong, G., Hales, G. and Hobbs, D. (2015). Sports mega-events and public opposition: A sociological study of the London 2012 Olympics. *Journal of Sport and Social Issues, 39*, 99–119. doi:10.1177/01937235|4530565

Greer, J. (2013). Foreign-born players becoming more commonplace in college basketball. *Louisville Courier-Journal*, December 25. Retrieved from www.courier-journal.com /story/sports/college/louisville/2013/12/25/foreign-born-players-becoming-more-commonplace-in-college-basketball/4201751 (accessed 24 November 2016).

Hersh, P. (2015). Northwestern, DePaul, Notre Dame into women's NCAA basketball tournaments. *Chicago Tribune*. Retrieved from www.chicagotribune.com/sports/college/ ct-ncaa-womens-tournament-spt-0317-story.html (accessed 24 November 2016).

Horne, J. and Manzenreiter, W. (2006). An introduction to the sociology of sports mega-events. *Sociological Review, 54*, 1–24. doi:10.1111/j.1467-954X.2006.00650.x

Humes, M. (2015). ESPN live from Indianapolis for men's Final Four beginning April 2. *ESPN MediaZone*, March 31. Retrieved from http://espnmediazone.com/us/press-releases/2015/03/espn-live-indianapolis-mens-final-four-beginning-april-2 (accessed 24 November 2016).

Idaho Athletics (2015). International flavor: Idaho roster covers five countries, three continents. News release, January 30. Retrieved from www.ncaa.com/news/basketball-women/article/2015-01-30/international-flavor (accessed 24 November 2016).

Kazadi, S.M. (2013). Hoops dreams; two athletes bring their talent from Congo to the American court. *Newsweek*, March 1, p. 1.

Kosmider, N. (2014). College basketball becoming global. *Denver Post*, December 28, p. 1CC.

Lee, Y.H. and Berri, D. (2008). A re-examination of production functions and efficiency estimates for the National Basketball Association. *Scottish Journal of Political Economy, 55*, 51–66. doi:10.1111/j.1467-9485.2008.00443.x

Maennig, W. and Zimbalist, A. (2012). What is a mega sporting event? In W. Maennig and A. Zimbalist (eds), *International handbook on the economics of mega sporting events* (pp. 9–14). Northampton, MA: Edward Elgar Publishing.

Maguire, J. (2006). Sports and globalization: Key issues, phases, and trends. In A.A. Raney and J. Bryant (eds), *Handbook of sports and media* (pp. 435–446). Mahwah, NJ: Erlbaum.

Martin, C.H. (1993). Jim Crow in the gymnasium: The integration of college basketball in the American South. *International Journal of the History of Sport, 10*, 68–86. doi:10.1080/ 09523369308713814

McCormick, R.E. and Tinsley, M. (1987). Athletics versus academics? Evidence from SAT scores. *Journal of Political Economy, 95*, 1103–1116.

Medcalf, M. (2012). The revolution will be recruited. August 5. Retrieved from http://espn.go.com/mens-college-basketball/story/_/id/8229423/recruiting-social-media-effect-men-college-basketball (accessed 24 November 2016).

Mixon, F.G. (1995). Athletics versus academics? Evidence from SAT scores. *Education Economics*, *3*, 227–234. doi:10.1080/09645299500000025

Mondello, M. (2006). Sports economics and the media. In A.A. Raney and J. Bryant (eds), *Handbook of sports and media* (pp. 277–294). Mahwah, NJ: Erlbaum.

Mulkey, K. and May, P. (2007). *Won't back down: Team, dreams, and family*. Philadelphia, PA: Da Capo Press.

Olajuwon, H. and Knobler, P. (1996). *Living the dream*. Boston, MA: Little, Brown & Company.

Pallotta, F. (2015). March Madness is a TV slam dunk: Highest ratings in 22 years. *CNN Money*, April 7. Retrieved from http://money.cnn.com/2015/04/07/media/march-madness-tv-ratings (accessed 24 November 2016).

Paulsen (2015). Six-year low for UConn's latest coronation. *Sports Media Watch*, April 8. Retrieved from www.sportsmediawatch.com/2015/04/womens-final-four-ratings-uconn-notre-dame-viewership-down-espn-semifinals-up-ncaa-tournament (accessed 24 November 2016).

Pope, D.G. and Pope, J.C. (2009). The impact of sports success on the quantity and quality of student applications. *Southern Economic Journal*, *75*, 750–780.

Pope, D.G. and Pope, J.C. (2014). Understanding college application decisions: Why college sports success matters. *Journal of Sports Economics*, *15*, 107–131. doi:10.1177/1527002512445569

Price, J.L. (1991). The Final Four and final judgment: The cultural significance of the NCAA basketball championship. *Journal of Popular Culture*, *24*(4), 49–58. doi:10.1111/j.0022-3840.1991.2404_49.x

Purdum, D. (2015). Estimated 40 million fill out brackets. March 12. Retrieved from http://espn.go.com/chalk/story/_/id/12465741/estimated-70-million-brackets-9-million-bets-ncaa-tournament (accessed 24 November 2016).

Real, M. (2013). Reflections on communication and sport: On spectacle and mega-events. *Communication and Sport*, *1*, 30–42. doi:10.1177/2167479512471188

Rishe, P.J. (2003). A reexamination of how athletic success impacts graduation rates: Comparing student-athletes to all other undergraduates. *American Journal of Economics and Sociology*, *62*, 407–421. doi:10.1111/1536-7150.00219

Roche, M. (2000). *Mega-events and modernity*. London: Routledge.

Rowe, D. (2004). *Sport, culture and the media* (2nd ed.). Maidenhead: Open University Press.

Schulz, W. (2004). Reconstructing mediatization as an analytical concept. *European Journal of Communication*, *19*, 87–101. doi:10.1177/0267323104040696

Siegal, R.M. (2015). ESPN 2015 NCAA women's Final Four fact sheet – April 5 and 7. *ESPN MediaZone*, April 3. Retrieved from http://espnmediazone.com/us/press-releases/2015/04/espn-2015-ncaa-womens-final-four-fact-sheet-april-5-7 (accessed 24 November 2016).

Smith, D.R. (2008). Big-time college basketball and the advertising effect: Does success really matter? *Journal of Sports Economics*, *9*, 387–406. doi:10.1177/152700250 7310805

Smith, D., Kilgo, J. and Jenkins, S. (1999). *A coach's life*. New York: Random House.

Thamel, P. (2011). Coaches' new friends. *New York Times*, August 9. Retrieved from www.nytimes.com/2011/08/10/sports/facebook-and-twitter-become-the-norm-in-recruiting.html?_r=0 (accessed 24 November 2016).

Toma, J.D. and Cross, M.E. (1998). Intercollegiate athletics and student college choice: Exploring the impact of championship seasons on undergraduate applications. *Research in Higher Education*, *39*, 633–661.

Trenkamp, B.A. (2009). Does the advertising effect of athletics impact academic rankings? *Applied Economic Letters*, *16*, 373–378. doi:10.1080/13504850601018585

Tucker, I.B. (2004). A reexamination of the effect of big-time football and basketball success on graduation rates and alumni giving rates. *Economics of Education Review*, *23*, 655–661. doi:10.1016/j.econedurev.2004.03.001

Washburn, G. (2015). Dikembe Mutombo a true pioneer en route to the Hall of Fame. *Boston Globe*, September 13. Retrieved from www.bostonglobe.com/sports/2015/09/12/dikembe-mutombo-true-pioneer-route-hall-fame/B0dhdXBxPUwvkIdvbYmdbL/story.html (accessed 24 November 2016).

17

THE X GAMES

Re-imagining youth and sport

Holly Thorpe and Belinda Wheaton

The term "action sports" broadly refers to a wide range of mostly individualized activities such as BMX, kite-surfing, skateboarding, surfing, and snowboarding, that differed – at least in their early phases of development – from traditional rule-bound, competitive, regulated Western "achievement" sport cultures. Many action sports gained popularity initially in North America during the new leisure trends of the 1960s and 1970s, and increasingly attracted alternative youth who appropriated these activities and infused them with a set of hedonistic and carefree philosophies and subcultural styles. While each action sport has its own unique history, identity, and development patterns, early participants sought risks and thrills, touting anti-establishment and do-it-yourself philosophies; core members saw their culture as "different" to the traditional rule-bound, competitive, regulated Western institutionalized sport cultures (Beal, 1995; Booth and Thorpe, 2007; Humphreys, 1997; Thorpe and Wheaton, 2013; Wheaton, 2004).

Since the 1960s, action sports have experienced unprecedented growth both in participation and in their increased visibility across mediated spaces (see, for example, Booth and Thorpe, 2007; Rinehart, 2000; Thorpe, 2011; Wheaton, 2004). Many of these activities were already gaining popularity when American-based cable television network ESPN (Entertainment and Sports Programming Network, owned by ABC, itself a division of the Walt Disney Group) saw in them the potential to tap into the hard to reach young male consumer group. ESPN broadcast the first Summer X Games in mid-1995. Staged at Newport, Providence, and Middletown (Rhode Island), and Mount Snow (Vermont), the inaugural games featured 27 events in nine categories: bungee jumping, eco-challenge, in-line skating, skateboarding, skysurfing, sport climbing, street luge, biking, and water sports (Booth and Thorpe, 2007). Twelve months later, X Games II attracted around 200,000 spectators, and early in 1997 ESPN staged the first Winter X Games at Snow Summit Mountain (California) Resort (Pickert, 2009). The X Games quickly garnered an international audience, and by 2002 the Summer X Games were broadcast on ABC, and ESPN to a record 63 million viewers (Wong, 2013). Backed by a range of transnational corporate sponsors, the X Games – the self-defined "worldwide leader" in action sports – have played a significant role in the global diffusion and expansion of the action sport industry and culture (Rinehart, 2000), and in redefining how sporting mega-events appeal to younger viewers.

As a "recurring spectacular commercial media festival" (Smart, 2007, p. 130), we argue that the X Games constitutes an action sports focused "mega-event". With the aim of examining the impact of the X Games on the contemporary sport–media–industry complex, this chapter consists of two parts. We begin with a discussion of the X Games as a choreographed effort on the part of ESPN to reach new audiences, and how action sport cultural audiences' responses to this event changed from initial resistance to acceptance, and even celebration, also considering the impact the X Games has had on other mega-sports events, particularly the Olympic Games. In the second part of this chapter, we discuss the X Games politics of global expansion; the strategies and challenges experienced in seeking new audiences, and in producing X Games events in international contexts. We conclude by highlighting the ways in which the X Games as a mega-sports event differs from more traditional sporting mega-events.

Audiences: seeking/creating generation X

While the X Games have been a mainstay in the (particularly North American) action sports industry and culture for over two decades, it is important to recall that action sport participants were highly critical of the initial efforts by ESPN to capitalize on their self-generated and DIY activities and cultures (Beal and Wilson, 2004). The emergence of the first few X Games prompted vociferous debate among grass-roots practitioners who contested ESPN's co-option of their lifestyle into television-tailored "sports" (ibid.; Rinehart, 2008). Inevitably, incorporation, institutionalization and commodification continued regardless of action sport participants contrasting viewpoints. In so doing, action sport cultures increasingly became controlled and defined by transnational media corporations such as ESPN via the X Games, as well as others, including NBC via the Gravity Games that occurred from 1999 to 2006. According to professional US snowboarder Todd Richards:

> The X Games marked the end of one era but simultaneously gave birth to a whole new world of possibilities. It was sort of sad to say good-bye to being a bunch of misunderstood outcasts. A lot of joy was derived from the punk-rock spirit, and once the masses join your ranks … it's over. The image had already begun to change, but the X Games put the icing on the mainstream cake.
>
> (Richards with Blehm, 2003, p. 182)

Today, however, most action sport athletes recognize mass-mediated events such as the X Games as endemic to action sport in the twenty-first century, and are embracing the new opportunities for increased media exposure, sponsorship, and celebrity offered (Beal and Wilson, 2004). With the support of many action sport athletes and celebrities, the X Games have become an important forum for setting records and performing ever more technical and creative maneuvers for international audiences.

Blurring the boundaries between music festival and sporting event (Rinehart, 2008), the X Games have also been hugely successful in capturing the imagination of the lucrative youth market. In 1998, ESPN's different sport channels beamed the X Games to 198 countries in 21 languages (Rinehart, 2000). In contrast to the aging Olympic viewership, the medium age of these viewers was 20 years (Thorpe and Wheaton, 2011a, p. 833). In the first decade and a half since the first X Games, the event experienced exponential growth in terms of participants and television and online audiences. The 2012 Winter X Games were the most watched yet, with an estimated 35.4 million viewers in the United States tuning in to ESPN, and a digital media audience that was up 147 percent from the previous year (Hargrove, 2012). More recently, however, evidence suggests X Games viewer numbers in the US are declining (Paulsen, 2016). For example, domestic viewership of the 2016 US-based Winter X Games was down 11 percent from the previous year (Karp, 2016), which some are attributing to the decline of popularity of snowboarding – historically a mainstay of the Winter X Games (Higgins, 2016). Thus, in an increasingly competitive sport–media–culture context, the X Games continue to invest in ever-new strategies in their efforts to attract both action sport participants and mainstream viewers, and reach new audiences in the global market. In so doing, they are influencing the production and representation of other sporting mega-events also seeking younger (male) audiences.

The impact of the X Games: setting the stage for appealing to younger audiences

Roche (2000, p. 227) argues that sports mega-events are an important part of an "evolving global cultural economy". The X Games were instrumental in launching ESPN2 and helped spawn dozens of licensing deals including an IMAX movie, X Games skateparks, and X Games DVDs and toys. Today, the X Games continues to show innovation in mega-event management and media representation in their ongoing efforts to remain relevant to (relatively) younger (male-targeted) audiences. For example, the annual Summer and Winter Games events in Austin (Texas) and Aspen (Colorado), respectively, continue to celebrate a music festival environment, with the former attracting over 160,000 spectators throughout the four-day event held in 2014 (Mickle, 2014). The 2015 Summer X Games in Austin received extensive coverage with content distributed across multiple television and digital platforms. In the USA, ESPN and ABC televised a combined 20 hours of live competition with an additional 6.5 hours of live action exclusively on ESPN3 and supported across ESPN digital platforms, including XGames.com, the X Games Austin app, and through official X Games social platforms including Twitter, Facebook, Instagram, YouTube and Snapchat. Additionally, X Games Austin was televised and syndicated in more than 215 countries and territories to more than 439 million homes worldwide (Baron, 2015).

Over the past 5 years, the X Games have been particularly proactive in their development and use of social media, and have introduced specifically designed apps for iPhone, iPad, Android mobile and Android tablet that, for example, feature instant results, news, schedules, guest information (e.g., venues, parking), athlete bios, and live music from the events. The apps are highly interactive; for example one promoted the "Hypemeter", a "built-in game that lets you contribute to the overall excitement around X Games via tweets, Facebook posts or device inter-action (shaking your phone or tapping your tablet)" (Foss, 2014). They also continue to develop emergent technologies for more spectacular media coverage. For example, in 2015 drones were used for the first time to cover the skiing and snowboarding events from above (Alvarez, 2015; Thorpe, 2016). As a result of these ongoing developments in content, representation and an expanding array of media platforms, the average age of viewers of the Summer and Winter X Games – 33 and 34 years old respectively – remains younger than other mega-sporting events discussed in this book (Ourand and Karp, 2012). In comparison, the average age of Olympic viewers – 55 years and aging – is of great concern to the International Olympic Committee (Thorpe and Wheaton, 2011a, 2011b).

The diminishing numbers of young Olympic viewers prompted the IOC to pursue the incorporation of a range of youth-oriented action sports into both the summer (e.g. windsurfing, mountain biking, bicycle motocross) and winter (e.g. snowboarding, skier cross) programs. To further appeal to younger viewers, the IOC and some affiliated media conglomerates also began to draw heavily on the representational styles developed by the X Games. Action sport events at the 2010 Winter Olympics included youth-focused features such as live graffiti art displays, break-dancers performing in the stands, and DJs and bands during breaks in competition (Thorpe, field notes, February 2010). Commentators attributed the success of the Vancouver Olympics to the "jazzed-up formats" of some events (e.g., half-pipe and snowboard- and ski-cross) which, drawing on the "the razzmatazz and street credibility of the X Games", transformed the "sometimes stuffy Olympic arena" into a "party atmosphere" (Booth, 2010, paras 3, 11). These innovations appear to have been successful, with audience figures for the 2010 Winter Olympics claiming a 48 percent increase among 18 to 24-year-old viewers (Bauder, 2010). NBC coverage of the men's snowboard half-pipe final drew approximately 30 million viewers in the US alone (Dillman, 2010). Recognizing the success of the strategies employed during the Vancouver Olympic Games, a spokeswoman for the London Olympic Games explained: "the popularity of the ski and snow cross in Vancouver confirms that the way sports are staged can help capture the public imagination" (cited in Booth, 2010, para. 8). Continuing, she adds "we are drawing up detailed marketing and sport presentation plans for 2012 for each sport to ensure that they engage and inspire ... [and] connect young people to sport" (cited in Booth, 2010, para. 8).

The IOC continues to draw inspiration from the X Games and, in August 2016, announced that three new action sports – surfing, skateboarding and sport climbing – will be among the five new sports included in the Tokyo 2020 Summer Olympics (Wheaton and Thorpe, 2016). While the sporting cultures and industries of skateboarding, surfing and sport climbing were abuzz with this news, each sport also has factions arguing for and against inclusion, and competing agendas based on unique logistical and political issues (Thorpe and Wheaton, 2015). While the cultural politics within each action sport continues, for the IOC the motivation to include these activities is primarily to attract younger viewers, and, thus, sponsorship dollars. In so doing, however, the inclusion of more action sports will mean the introduction of new styles of participation and aesthetics in both performances and representations. We are also likely to see echoes of the X Games, particularly a music festival style atmosphere and increased use of social media for audience engagement and interaction.

(Re)producing the X Games: the politics of global expansion

According to Rowe (2003, p. 281), "The phenomenon of sport is consistently presented as a prime instance of the gathering force of globalization." This is certainly the case with the X Games (see Thorpe, 2014). Originally a US-based event, ESPN has been steadily expanding the X Games internationally in the pursuit of new markets and sponsors in local contexts. The first Asian X Games were held in 1998 in Phuket, Thailand, and have since been held in Kuala Lumpur, Seoul, and Shanghai. In March 2010, the first European Winter X Games were held in Tignes (France). The event was attended by more than 66,200 spectators, 150 athletes from around the world, and 370 international journalists over three days, and was broadcast to 166 countries (live and highlights) (OnBoard, 2010). The X Games has also organized smaller action sports events, qualifiers and demonstrations in Brazil, Canada, Japan, Korea, Malaysia, Mexico, Singapore, Spain, Taiwan, Philippines and UAE. In 2012, the Global X Games Series included six events, including the new locations of Barcelona (Spain), Munich (Germany) and Foz do Iguacu (Brazil). In this section we discuss the politics of producing the X Games in international contexts, focusing first on ESPN's attempts to expand into Asia and some of the cultural clashes that ensued, particularly between the Chinese government and the corporate-focused ESPN. We then examine their more recent attempts to produce the Global X Games Series, and the political, economic and cultural difficulties that they experienced in the process.

Producing the Asian X Games in China: cultural clashes

With governmental support and investment from both Western and Chinese corporate sponsors, China is increasingly hosting large international extreme sports events (e.g., Shanghai Showdown Gravity Games, Nanshan Snowboarding Open, the 720 China Surf Open). The Asian X Games – previously staged on Phuket Island, Thailand (1998–2001), Kuala Lumpur, Malaysia (2002–2004), and Seoul, South Korea (2005) – were held for the first time in the People's Republic of China in 2007. Shanghai hosted the three-day event, which attracted more than 200 of the world's top action sports athletes from more than 20 countries and from five continents. Between 2007 and 2012, the Kia X Games were sanctioned by ESPN, ESPN STAR Sports, and the Chinese Extreme Sports Association and hosted by Shanghai Sports Federation, Yang Pu District Government, and KIC Jiang Wan Stadium. Kia Motors, a secondary sponsor of the Asian X Games since 2005, renewed its support with a 3-year primary sponsorship to build the event in China as well as to gain valuable product exposure. Indeed, Kia Motors estimated that in 2005 alone, media exposure from the Asian X Games was worth approximately US$14 million to the company (Hyundai, 2005).

In 2011, however, a situation arose during the 2011 Asian X Games that highlights some of the complex politics and power relations occurring behind the scenes of the development of action sports in China (Thorpe, 2014). Unlike the Olympic Games and many other traditional sporting events, the X Games does not emphasize nationality (i.e., national anthems are not played for winners, athletes do not wear national uniforms) (Thorpe and Wheaton, 2011a). Adopting a nationalistic approach to the Asian X Games, however, the Chinese Extreme Sports Association (CESA) made the strategic decision to only allow "national athletes" to compete in the games. This caused difficulties for Shen Jian, one of China's top BMX riders, who had recently signed an exclusive endorsement deal with Vans. The CESA prohibited Jian from competing in the Games unless he wore a jersey emblazoned with the official Chinese sponsor's logo, which would have nullified his contract with Vans. Yet the CESA do not train or finance action sport athletes, and Jian was reliant upon his endorsement deal with Vans for his livelihood. Unwilling to compromise his relationship with Vans, he was banned from the competition. While Chinese athletes are rarely known for questioning authority, Jian was vocal in his frustrations: "CESA taught me nothing. I don't need to wear their clothing so they can make money and exploit me. We riders created this community, not CESA. The association's only power comes from the Communist Party" (cited in Levin, 2011, para. 36). While the American organizers of the Asian X Games followed the CESA's orders during the event, when the Vice President at ESPN's events management group was questioned about the incident he did not see this arrangement as consistent with the X Games philosophy of "always be[ing] an open playing field" with "qualifications done on ranking systems" (Harvey Davis, cited in David, 2011, part 2). It is difficult to know whether the conflict of interests between CESA and ESPN contributed to the decision not to host another Asian X Games after 2012. However, the lessons learned in working with local governmental groups and organizations in China certainly informed ESPN's approach to developing the Global X Games Series that was launched in 2013.

The Global X Games Series: the politics of production in local contexts

In May 2011, ESPN announced that the X Games were expanding globally to include six major events per year, including the Summer and Winter Games in the US, the European Winter X Games in Tignes, and three other annual events (determined via formal bidding processes). As revealed in the following comment from Scott Guglielmino, Senior Vice President of Programming and the X Games, ESPN recognizes the potential of action sports to expand into international markets:

> Action sports is a collection of activities that we think travels really well around the world. The reality of what we're doing here is we've created this huge stage for action-sport athletes, and we're taking that global now. We're providing an even larger platform for them to participate in and perform at, and grow themselves.
>
> *(Cited in O'Neil, 2012, para. 2)*

In contrast to other American-based sports such as baseball and American football, which have not been widely embraced by local audiences around the world, ESPN identifies action sports as integral "to our growth around the world ... driven by local relevance and in building a passionate connection between fans, our brand and our partners" (Russell Wolff, Executive President and Managing Director, ESPN International, cited in Supercross, 2012, para. 3). Integral to the Global X Games Series is not only the potential to reach new audiences, but also new sponsors. In the words of Eric Johnson, ESPN's Executive Vice President for Multimedia Sales, "Our goal is to get global sponsors involved in particular categories and create opportunities to sell locally based on whatever regions of the world we're in" (cited in Mickle, 2011, para. 13).

Somewhat ironically, the formal bidding process was modelled off the highly political (and often corrupt) approach employed by the International Olympic Committee (see, e.g., Bale and Krogh-Christensen, 2004) in which interested cities must first enter an initial bid, before being short-listed for a more intensive round of reviews as well as visits from the organizing committee. The X Games website touted the opportunity to become a host city, promoting the X Games as a global brand that host cities would do well to be connected with:

> It's all about youth, vitality and energy showcased on a world stage for millions to see. As host to the X Games, your venue, your community and your city become part of a dynamic brand – one that captures the unbridled passion and fearlessness of sport. ... As a host for the X Games, your city will become synonymous with the celebration of youth, lifestyle, creativity and community that is the X brand.
>
> *(Cited in Thorpe, 2014, p. 56)*

With more than 40 initial entries from 21 countries, ESPN was "thrilled with the response from cities around the world" (Wolff, cited in Supercross, 2012, para. 3). Nearly 20 of these entries then participated in a two-day workshop at the X Games in Los Angeles in August 2011, designed to "educate qualified applicants on the vision and long term strategy of the X Games" (Supercross, 2012, para. 2). Finally, in December 2011 the three new X Games host cities were selected from a group of nine finalists, namely Barcelona (Spain), Munich (Germany) and Foz do Iguacu (Brazil) with the understanding that they would host each year. "A lot of our decision on which cities to select was based on their [the host city and nation's] action sport culture and our point of view on how strong it was", said Guglielmino, adding that the new hosts will also introduce additional sports and cultural elements unique to their regions (cited in O'Neil, 2012, para. 4). ESPN was clear about the importance of glocalization in each of these locations: "one of the most exciting parts of this expansion" is, according to Wolff, the potential to "adopt [*sic*] the local flair of each host country" (cited in Thornton, 2011, para. 5).

However, not dissimilar from the bidding process for the Olympic Games, the decisions as to which cities would be awarded the X Games were deeply entrenched in broader social, political and economic power relations. In particular, ESPN was interested to enter new markets with strong action sports communities *and* the potential for significant growth. For example, it seems likely that the decision to reject Whistler (Canada) as a Winter X Games host was because ESPN did not feel that a Canadian X Games would offer a radically new market (Thorpe, 2014). The opportunity for market growth in Canada was considerably smaller than in Brazil, Germany and Spain.

In order to effectively record and distribute media coverage of the six annual events, ESPN devised a new "International Broadcast Centre" model. The competition coverage is produced at the events, before being integrated through a Digital Center control room at the ESPN Digital Center control room in Bristol (Connecticut, US). According to X Games Vice President, Tori Stevens, this has:

> created an unprecedented model in which we will be simultaneously creating a minimum of six unique telecast (sponsored world-feed, sponsor-free world feed, US customized feed, Spain customized feed, Brazil customized feed and a Germany customized feed). The sponsor-free world feed will allow us to reach numerous territories that have previously been unable to carry X Games live due to restrictions in many countries. We have made creative efforts to expand the distribution of this content both on and off of our networks around the world, and these feeds allow us to do that.
>
> *(Stevens, cited in Tobias, 2013, para. 6)*

It was anticipated that the six X Games events would produce a total of 130 hours of live TV coverage on ESPN networks in the US and around the world, and would be supplemented by coverage on digital platforms, including those of the host cities and a year-round action sports website hosted by ESPN.

Of course, image management is always of utmost concern to corporations such as ESPN and, thus, it was rare to find ESPN employees expressing doubts and difficulties with this mammoth undertaking. However, a leaked email from ESPN operations manager Severn Sandt to X Games staff revealed some of the financial and cultural concerns among upper management. In the email, Sandt wrote openly to staff involved in organizing the first of the new X Games events in Foz do Iguacu:

> I'm going to be completely honest with you: this global X Games series is far from a sure thing long-term. Financially, things are extremely difficult. I have personally banged my head against the budget wall for countless hours, especially on this event. Every negotiation has been exhausting, trying to wring every spare reais out of it.
>
> *(Cited in Koblin, 2013, para. 2)*

He encouraged staff to cut costs wherever possible at the event, before attempting to prepare the typically young American staff for the cultural differences they were likely to experience while working in Brazil. "Don't make fun of the people here or the way they do things", he warned, "You might find things you see here backward, ludicrous, even stupid. Hold your laughter till you get back home. We need these people to put the event on, so don't insult them" (cited in Koblin, 2013, para. 6). He also asked staff to "bring your patience" because "many people in Brazil do not operate at the same pace as most of us do". While the language used in this email shows little respect for cultural differences, it is possible that Sandt was writing for his audience of mostly young, male action sport enthusiasts and media and sports event workers familiar with producing events in the US, but with little awareness of, or concern for the cultural differences they are likely to experience while working abroad.

As Giulianotti and Brownell (2012, p. 206) explain, sport mega-events "provide a political space in which the transnationalization of local issues and the localization of transnational dynamics occur simultaneously". Indeed, while the local organizing committee in Foz do Iguacu were dealing with their own internal politics in preparation for hosting hundreds of international visiting officials, competitors, and media, and thousands of local spectators, the American-based X Games organizing committee were making plans based on balancing the broader economics of the X Games Global Series with local considerations. As outlined, these include accommodating cultural differences and sponsorship difficulties, and organizing staff in two locations to co-produce a sporting spectacle for a global audience. As this example illustrates, mega action sports events such as the X Games "act as transmitters of political processes between the domestic and international domains, facilitating reciprocal influences between the two levels" (Giulianotti and Brownell, 2012, p. 206).

Almost as soon as the three new international X Games host cities were announced, ESPN revealed that they were opening a new bidding process for US cities eager to host the 2014 Summer and Winter X Games. Thus, the X Games reaffirmed the US as the *hub* of this Global X Games spectacle, while also signaling the importance of both local (US) public and corporate support for the ongoing success and sustainability of such events. After 10 years in LA, the Summer X Games were moving due to contractual difficulties between the X Games and the Anschutz Entertainment Group (the Los Angeles entertainment giant behind Staples Center and several LA sports franchises). According to a study by the Los Angeles Sports and Entertainment Commission, hosting the games in 2010 had an economic impact of approximately $50 million, attracting as many as 58,000 additional visitor days in Los Angeles (cited in Gardner, 2013, para. 8). Four cities were shortlisted from more than 20 initial bids to host the US-based Summer X Games from 2014 to 2016, including Austin (Texas), Chicago (Illinois), Detroit (Michigan) and Charlotte (North Carolina). Austin, Texas, ultimately won the bid to host the annual US-based Summer X Games from 2014 to 2018.

The impetus behind the global expansion of the X Games was, according to Guglielmino, the realization that "action sports travel well. There aren't many sports that travel well" (cited in Thornton, 2011, para. 12). Action sports offer ESPN an opportunity to enter local markets that they have been unable to access with traditional American sports. Despite efforts to localize the events and capitalize upon the specific culture of each of the new host cities, the X Games is firmly controlled by the American-based media conglomerate ESPN. The global expansion of the X Games is clearly part of broader processes of Americanization. Yet, the lack of national symbolism associated with the events, and the already global media exposure of the games, have disguised an American media conglomerate for a global brand that has "become synonymous with the celebration of youth, lifestyle, creativity and community that is the X brand" (X Games, 2013).

While ESPN touts the Global X Games Series as empowering action sports athletes, providing them with "an even larger platform … to participate in and perform at, and grow themselves" (Guglelmino, cited in O'Neil, 2012, para. 2), the motives underpinning such developments were primarily economic: to attract new global *and* national sponsors, and to expand the reach of televisual and online media to previously inaccessible audiences. However, ESPN ultimately failed to fully imagine the cost and difficulties of such endeavors. Despite plans for a 3-year run in Brazil, Germany and Spain, the Global X Games initiative was cancelled after 2013, citing "the overall economics of these events do not provide a sustainable future path" (Chi, 2013, para. 1). Evidently, the sports media audience is not homogeneous, and the appetite for such events across different local, regional, national contexts is different, and needs careful consideration in assessing potential expansion.

Final thoughts: the X Games as sport mega-event with a difference

We conclude with some thoughts on the ways in which the X Games are similar and different to other sporting mega-events, with a focus on the role of sporting celebrities, corporations and the nation. According to Smart (2007), sport mega-events are "consumer cultural events", in which sports stars are:

> elevated to an iconic global celebrity status, represent[ing] local and/or national communities. The celebrities serve as role models, as objects of adulation and identification, but also increasingly as exemplars of consumer lifestyles to which spectators and television viewers alike are enticed to aspire.
>
> *(Smart, 2007, p. 130)*

Action sports stars competing at the X Games have certainly become internationally recognized celebrities who are overtly and covertly promoting consumer lifestyles. Like other sport celebrities they are also predominantly able-bodied, heterosexual young men, promoting and reaffirming the naturalness of the sporting realm as a masculine social space. Yet as Kusz (2004) has persuasively argued, it is also a mediated space that, in North America in particular, became a key cultural site in the construction of whiteness. While action/extreme sport spaces like the X Games are often represented as a "cultural space that is overwhelmingly white", it is "rarely ever imagined as a racially exclusive space" (ibid., p. 207). Despite the presence of female sporting celebrities and increasing ethnic and cultural diversity among competitors in many action sports, sport media still reproduce the gendered and racialized stereotypes, "associated with privileged forms of whiteness" (Comer, 2010, p. 21). In so doing, the X Games continue to reinforce the hegemonic position of the heroic Western (young) white male action sporting identity.

In contrast to most traditional sport "mega-events", which reproduce "sport's compulsive attachment to the production of national difference" (Rowe, 2003, p. 292), action sport athletes competing at the X Games are not representing the nation. Indeed, there are very few signs of nationalism or national identity at X Games events. While the athlete's nationality is sometimes declared during an event, spectators do not wave national flags, athletes do not wear national uniforms, and national anthems are not played as the athletes stand on the podiums. The X Games therefore seems better suited to the "carriage of the project of globalization" than most sport mega-events that are, as Rowe argues, so "deeply dependent on the production of difference that it repudiates the possibility of comprehensive globalization" (ibid., p. 282). Indeed, as the athletes receive their X Games medals they typically appear as "walking corporate billboards" for transnational corporations ranging from energy drinks to credit card companies (Messner, 2002); their equipment is covered in the stickers of their sponsors, and their bodies are branded with multiple logos on hats, T-shirts, jackets and pants. Some will even be seen holding or drinking from the bottles of their soft- or energy-drink sponsors as they receive their medals. In so doing, the athletes are representing national and global corporations rather than their nations. While many contemporary sports mega-events have increasingly become "ideal vehicles for corporate sponsors seeking to raise the global profile of their brands" (Smart, 2007, p. 127), the X Games and action sport athletes' relationships with commercial sponsors have always been integral to the production and consumption of these sporting spectacles. As illustrated in the case of the Asian X Games in China, the relationship between corporations and the state becomes particularly complicated and, indeed, political, as the X Games has attempted to expand into new territories with different governmental and sporting structures, and cultural value systems.

Our chapter has illustrated that, despite challenges, the X Games continues to play an integral role in redefining sports mega-events particularly in terms of styles and strategies for appealing to younger male viewers. We have also highlighted some important similarities and differences with mega-sport events focused on more traditional (often male) sports that deserve further scholarly attention. However, we cannot understand such cultural phenomena separate from developments in other mega-sporting events, and trends in the sporting media landscape more broadly. In particular, the impact of the X Games on the Olympic Games, in the format of events (i.e., more youth focused new sports), forms of representational style and embracing the different ways the media audience can engage, will be an interesting phase in the development of sport mega-events.

References

Alvarez, E. (2015). ESPN is bringing camera drones to the X Games. Retrieved from www.engadget.com/2015/01/21/espn-is-bringing-camera-drones-to-the-x-games (accessed 24 November 2016).

Bale, J. and Krogh-Christensen, M. (eds) (2004). *Post-Olympism? Questioning sport in the twenty-first century*. Oxford: Berg Publishers.

Baron, S. (2015). ESPN releases X Games Austin 2015 television schedule. Retrieved from http://tvbythenumbers.zap2it.com/2015/05/26/espn-releases-x-games-austin-2015-television-schedule (accessed 24 November 2016).

Bauder, D. (2010). Olympics prove popular with TV viewers. *Associated Press*, February 16. Retrieved from www.newsday.com/sports/olympics/olympics-prove-popular-with-tv-viewers-1.1764361 (accessed 6 January 2017).

Beal, B. (1995). Disqualifying the official: An exploration of social resistance through the subculture of skateboarding. *Sociology of Sport Journal, 12*(3), 252–267.

Beal, B. and Wilson, C. (2004). "Chicks dig scars: Commercialisation and the transformations of skate boarders identities". In B. Wheaton (ed.), *Understanding lifestyle sports: Consumption, identity and difference* (pp. 31–54). London: Routledge.

Booth, D. and Thorpe, H. (2007). The meaning of extreme. In D. Booth and H. Thorpe (eds), *The Berkshire encyclopedia of extreme sports* (pp. 181–197). Great Barrington, MA: Berkshire.

Booth, R. (2010). Formats jazzed-up to draw crowds at London 2012 Olympics. *The Guardian*, March 1. Retrieved from www.theguardian.com/uk/2010/mar/01/olympics-2012-bmx-shanaze-read (accessed 6 January 2017).

Chi, D. (2013). X Games Announcement. October 3. Retrieved from http://espnmedia zone.com/us/press-releases/2013/10/x-games-announcement (accessed 24 November 2016).

Comer, K. (2010). *Surfer girls and the new world order*. Durham, NC: Duke University Press.

David (2011). At 2011 X Games Asia, China's best talents were missing: Part 2. *China Sports Review*, May 13. Retrieved from www.chinasportsreview.com/2011/05/13/at-2011-x-games-asia-china's-best-talents-were-missing-pt22 (accessed 24 November 2016).

Dillman, L. (2010) Snowboarding's "X Games vibe" an unlikely but profitable fit with Olympics tradition. *LA Times*, February 21. Retrieved from www.cleveland.com/olympics/index.ssf/2010/02/snowboardings_x_games_vibe_an.html (accessed 24 November 2016).

Foss, J. (2014). New year-round X Games app launches. Retrieved from http://xgames.espn.go.com/xgames/article/8849915/new-mobile-apps-launch-x-games-2013 (accessed 24 November 2016).

Gardner, K. (2013). X Games names Chicago as host finalist. *DNAinfo Chicago*, April 30. Retrieved from www.dnainfo.com/chicago/20130430/chicago-citywide/x-games-names-chicago-as-host-finalist (accessed 24 November 2016).

Giulianotti, R. and Brownell, S. (2012). Olympic and world sport: Making transnational society? *The British Journal of Sociology*, *63*(2), 199–215.

Hargrove, K. (2012). X Games 2012 ratings soar. *Transworld Business*, 9 February. Retrieved from http://business.transworld.net/86566/news/x-games-2012-ratings-soar (accessed 24 November 2016).

Higgins, M. (2016). Snowboarding, once a high flying sport, crashes to earth. *The New York Times*, March 6. Retrieved from www.nytimes.com/2016/03/07/sports/snowboarding-once-a-high-flying-sport-crashes-to-earth.html?_r=0 (accessed 24 November 2016).

Humphreys, D. (1997). Shredheads go mainstream? Snowboarding an alternative youth. *International Review for the Sociology of Sport*, *32*(2), 147–160.

Hyundai (2005). Kia Motors bolsters brand image through Asian X Games 2005 sponsorship. Retrieved from www.hyundaimotorgroup.com/MediaCenter/News/Press-Releases/Press-release-0265-2005-0530.hub#.VtI794x94y4 (accessed 24 November 2016).

Karp, A. (2016). Audience analysis: UFC/Fox sees January decline; Winter X Games lowest since '04. *Street and Smith's Sports Business*, February 5. Retrieved from www.sportsbusinessdaily.com/Daily/Issues/2016/02/05/Media/Audience.aspx (accessed 24 November 2016).

Koblin, J. (2013). ESPN X Games memo asks staffers to work for free and not make fun of Brazilian people. Retrieved from http://deadspin.com/espn-x-games-memo-asks-staffers-to-work-for-free-and-no-471205365 (accessed 24 November 2016).

Kusz, K. (2004). "Extreme America": The cultural politics of extreme sports in 1990s America. In B. Wheaton (ed.), *Understanding lifestyle sports: Consumption, identity and difference* (pp. 197–213). London: Routledge.

Levin, D. (2011). Chinese athletes say no to the system. *The New York Times*, August 18. Retrieved from www.nytimes.com/2011/08/19/sports/chinese-athletes-begin-to-challenge-governments-tight-grip.html?pagewanted=all (accessed 24 November 2016).

Messner, M. (2002). *Taking the field*. Minneapolis, MN: University of Minnesota Press.

Mickle, T. (2011). Global expansion plans, Red Bull partnership boost X Games sponsorship revenue. *Smith and Smith's Sports Business Journal*, July 25. Retrieved from www.sportsbusinessdaily.com/Journal/Issues/2011/07/25/Marketing-and-Sponsorship/X-Games.aspx (accessed 24 November 2016).

Mickle, T. (2014). Austin delivers crowds to X Games; TV mixed. *Street & Smith's Sports Business*. Retrieved from www.sportsbusinessdaily.com/Journal/Issues/2014/06/16/Events-and-Attractions/X-Games-Austin.aspx (accessed 24 November 2016).

OnBoard (2010). Euro X Games 2011 dates released. *OnBoard Magazine*. Retrieved from https://onboardmag.com/news/euro-games-2011-dates-released.html#geSDOxgRJMk4atMj.97 (accessed 24 November 2016).

O'Neil, D. (2012). X Games expands globally. *ESPN*, Dec. 10. Retrieved from http://xgames. espn.go.com/xgames/cities/article/7862758/x-games-grow-three-six-events-2013 (accessed 24 November 2016).

Ourand, J. and Karp, A. (2012). Which sport can say: We are young. *Street and Smith's Sports Business*. Retrieved from www.sportsbusinessdaily.com/Journal/Issues/2012/03/19/ Media/Sports-demos.aspx (accessed 24 November 2016).

Paulsen (2016). Ratings roundup: Australian Open, College Hoops, Winter X Games. *Sports Media Watch*, February. Retrieved from www.sportsmediawatch.com/2016/02/sports-ratings-australian-open-serena-djokovic-viewership-college-hoops-cbs-overnights-x-games (accessed 24 November 2016).

Pickert, K. (2009). A brief history of the X Games. *Time*. Retrieved from http://content. time.com/time/nation/article/0,8599,1873166,00.html (accessed 24 November 2016).

Richards, T. with Blehm, E. (2003). *P3: Pipes, parks and powder*. New York: HarperCollins.

Rinehart, R. (2000). Emerging arriving sport: Alternatives to formal sport. In J. Coakley and E. Dunning (eds), *Handbook of sport studies*. London: Sage.

Rinehart, R. (2008). ESPN's X games, contests of opposition, resistance, co-option, and negotiation. In M. Atkinson and K. Young (eds), *Tribal play: Subcultural journeys through sport* (vol. IV "Research in the Sociology of Sport") (pp. 175–196). Bingley: Jai.

Roche, M. (2000). *Mega-events and modernity*. Routledge: London.

Rowe, D. (2003). Sport and the repudiation of the global. *International Review for Sociology of Sport*, 3(38), 81–94.

Smart, B. (2007). Not playing around: Global capitalism, modern sport and consumer culture. *Global Networks*, 7(2), 113–134.

Supercross (2012). Nine cities advance to final phase of X Games global expansion bid process. *Supercross*, January 26. Retrieved from http://supercross.com/nine-cities-advance-to-final-phase-of-x-games-global-expansion-bid-process (accessed 24 November 2016).

Thornton, P. (2011). Boosting the X factor in the X Games. *The New Zealand Herald*, May 28. Retrieved from www.nzherald.co.nz/sport/news/article.cfm?c_id=4&objectid=1 0728655 (accessed 24 November 2016).

Thorpe, H. (2011). *Snowboarding bodies in theory and practice*. Basingstoke: Palgrave Macmillan.

Thorpe, H. (2014). *Transnational mobilities in action sport cultures*. Basingstoke: Palgrave Macmillan.

Thorpe, H. (2016). Action sports, social media and new technologies: Towards a research agenda. *Communication and Sport*. doi:10.1177/2167479516638125

Thorpe, H. and Wheaton, B. (2011a). "Generation X Games", action sports and the Olympic Movement: Understanding the cultural politics of incorporation. *Sociology*, 45(5), 830–847.

Thorpe, H. and Wheaton, B. (2011b). The Olympic movement, action sports, and the search for generation Y. In J. Sugden and A. Tomlinson (eds), *Watching the Olympics: Politics, power and representation* (pp. 182–200). London: Routledge.

Thorpe, H. and Wheaton, B. (2013). Dissecting action sports studies: Past, present and beyond. In D. Andrews and B. Carrington (eds), *A companion to sport* (pp. 341–358). Oxford: Blackwell.

Thorpe, H. and Wheaton, B. (2015). Why are the Olympics in search of the X factor? *The Conversation*. Retrieved from https://theconversation.com/why-are-the-olympics-in-search-of-the-x-factor-48565 (accessed 24 November 2016).

Tobias, R. (2013). X Games VP Tori Stevens discusses global "X"pansion, challenges and successes. *ESPN Front Row*, March 21. Retrieved from www.espnfrontrow.com/ 2013/03/x-games-vp-tori-stevens-discusses-global-xpansion-challenges-and-successes (accessed 9 May 2013).

Wheaton, B. (2004). Mapping the lifestyle sport-scape. In B. Wheaton (ed.), *Understanding lifestyle sports: Consumption, identity and difference* (pp. 1–28). London: Routledge.

Wheaton, B. and Thorpe, H., 2016. *Youth perceptions of the Olympic Games: attitudes towards action sports at the YOG and Olympic Games.* Funded by an International Olympic Committee (IOC) Advanced Research Programme Grant. https://library.olympic.org/Default/doc/SYRACUSE/165853/youth-perceptions-of-the-olympic-games-attitudes-towards-action-sports-at-the-yog-and-olympic-games- (accessed 10 January 2017).

Wong, G. (2013). *The comprehensive guide to careers in sports* (2nd ed.). Burlington, MA: Jones & Bartlett Learning.

INDEX